More Praise for

THE GUARDED GATE

Winner of the
National Jewish Book Award for History

Named one of the *New York Times'*
100 Notable Books of the Year

"The story of this triumph of ignorance has been told before, but never more vividly than by Daniel Okrent. . . . A rigorously historical work."

—David Hollinger, *The Washington Post*

"[An] often surprising history . . . *The Guarded Gate* is reminiscent of Okrent's *Last Call: The Rise and Fall of Prohibition* in its elegant . . . prose and its focus on the unlikely alliances that converged to effect political change."

—*The Boston Globe*

"A vivid new book . . . jam-packed with appalling examples of anti-immigrant passions primarily targeted at Catholics and Jews."

—*The New York Times Book Review*

"If you think we have reached peak stupidity—that America's per capita quantity has never been higher—there is solace, of sorts, in Daniel Okrent's guided tour through the immigration debate that was heading toward a nasty legislative conclusion a century ago."

—George F. Will, *The Washington Post*

"Engrossing . . . It's a grim and sordid story, but Okrent is a companionable, witty, and judicious guide."

—*Commentary*

"A frighteningly timely book about a particularly ugly period in American history, a bigotry-riddled chapter many thought was closed but that shows recent signs of reopening . . . One of the narrative's great strengths is the author's inclusion of dozens of minibiographies illuminating the backgrounds of the racist politicians and the promoters of phony eugenics 'research.' . . . [A] revelatory and necessary historical account."

—*Kirkus Reviews*

"Deep and comprehensive . . . *The Guarded Gate* sharply reminds us that nativism has never been limited to its most savage enforcers like the Klan or neo-Nazis. It always has its 'civilized' voices, too, with lobbyists, funders, and advocates giving it respectable cover, domesticating it, putting it in *Good Housekeeping* rather than in *Der Stürmer.*"

—*The New York Review of Books*

"[A] sweeping history."

—*The New Yorker*

"Engrossing . . . this fascinating study vividly illuminates the many injustices that the pseudoscience of eugenics inflicted on so many would-be Americans."

—*Publishers Weekly*

"A sobering, valuable contribution to discussions about immigration."

—*Booklist*

"A steely-eyed look at America's eugenics movement."

—*Library Journal*

"[A] detailed, compulsively readable account . . . a must-read for anyone seeking a deeper understanding of the history of immigration in the United States—and how the past might be relevant to policy makers and citizens today."

—*BookPage*

"What's so unsettling about Daniel Okrent's spellbinding history of a previous immigration controversy is how it resonates with today's debate. Insightful, unsparing, and totally absorbing, this book frames the discussion against a compelling historical backdrop that describes the gap between the American ideal and the American reality."

—Lawrence Wright, Pulitzer Prize–winning author of *The Looming Tower* and *God Save Texas*

"In *The Guarded Gate*, Daniel Okrent has again taken a largely forgotten epoch in American history and brilliantly brought it back to life. Written with a grace that any novelist would envy, Okrent's book tells the story of the immigration battles of the early twentieth century in a way that's both fascinating on its own terms but also, alas, all-too-relevant to today's news."

—Jeffrey Toobin, CNN analyst and author of *American Heiress*

"Our two oceans have protected and insulated us, but they have also helped to incubate less attractive features. Daniel Okrent artfully and faithfully records our (earlier) dismal record on immigration and how those home-grown racist and xenophobic policies metastasized into exports with horrific worldwide consequences. This is a masterful, sobering, thoughtful, and necessary book."

—Ken Burns

"*The Guarded Gate* delivers a timely history of anti-immigrant fever centered in the elite eugenics movement a century ago. In this masterful narrative, sprinkled with wit, Daniel Okrent shows how the lesser angels of our heritage 'depopulated Ellis Island as if by epidemic,' leading to cycles of disgrace and reform."

—Taylor Branch, Pulitzer Prize–winning author of
Parting the Waters: America in the King Years, 1954–63

"Daniel Okrent is a gifted social historian. In this powerful, fast-paced, and highly relevant chronicle of bad science and fearful prejudice, Okrent helps us understand how and why our country lost its way about a century ago. Read it so that history does not find new ways of repeating itself."

—Evan Thomas, author of *The War Lovers*

INDIVIDUAL ANALYSIS CARD

NOTE:—1. These Cards are intended to accompany the *Pedigree Chart*—one card for each member of the family tree.
    2. If the study is to be of value, all statements—concerning both "good" and "bad" traits—must be frank and fair.
    3. In items numbers 19, 20, 21, 22, 32, 33, 39, 41, 43, 44, 46, 48, 51, 52, 56, 57, 58 and 59 grading by underscoring is called for. In these cases use the following system: *Underscore* with one, two or three lines according as the ability, the predilection, or the possession, as the case may be, is average, is somewhat above medium, or, is extremely high (such as is possessed by one person in 1,000); *Strike out* with one or two lines according to whether the grade for the special ability, the aversion, or the lack, as the case may be, is somewhat below medium, or is strikingly low. Absence of underscoring or striking out implies no consideration of the trait in the person.

FAMILY

1. Principal surnames on *Pedigree Charts*: Bucknell, Russell

INDIVIDUAL. A—HISTORY

2. Full name of individual (maiden name if a married woman) Lydia Eastlack Bucknell   ♀
4. Date of birth 4-20-1887   5. Location on the *Pedigree Chart*: Generation No. II ; Individual No. 14
(if chart is not plotted, relation to some central figure of the family tree)
6. Birthplace: Town East St. Louis County (or province) St Clair Co. State (or country) Illinois
7. Principal residences: East St Louis; Westtown, Pa.
8. If living, present address: Haddon Heights, N.J.
9. If married, to whom _____ Date. _____, No. of sons _____, No. of daughters _____
10. Education: Graduate Westtown School 1906; Oberlin college A.B. 1922
11. Church membership: Friends   12. Participation in church activities: Occasional committee work
13. Occupations—including a record of positions held and special achievements at successive ages:
School Secretary, Westtown, Pa 1908-1915; 1917-1920
14. Success in life—below, commensurate with, or above opportunities:
15. If dead, date of (or age at) death: _____ 16. Cause of death: _____
17. Additional biography: (Home life, early moral environment, opportunities, etc.) "Guarded religious education"
Parental care over choice of playmates and school companions
Home ideals high

B—TRAITS. I—PHYSICAL

18. Native country and racial stock of *each* of the *four* grand-parents.
(a) *Native country and province, state or town, regardless of blood or stock:*
FF Philadelphia USA. FM New Jersey USA MF Erie Co. Pennsylvania MM Philadelphia
(b) *Racial stock or blood, regardless of where born:*
FF English FM English MF English + Scotch Irish MM English (small part Spanish)
(e.g., English, Scotch, South Irish, German, French, Walloon, Jewish, South Italian, Jewish-Spanish, German-Dutch, English-Italian-Dutch, or the like).
19. Complexion (or skin color), (underscore): blond, intermediate, brunet. 20. Eye color (underscore): clear blue, blue with brown spots, yellow blue, brown, red brown, black.
21. Hair form (underscore): straight, wavy, curly, frizzy, wooly.
22. Hair color (before greying), (underscore): flaxen, yellow-brown, light brown, dark brown, black, auburn, clear red, red brown 23. Height (without shoes) 64 inches, at 35 years of age. 24. Weight at birth: 6½ pounds; weight 102 pounds (adult or present) of age. 25. History of change of weight during adult life: Max. wgt 117 Summer 1912
26. History (date or age) of falling hair (baldness) 27. Of turning grey occasional grey hair before 30. 28. Of failing or defective hearing 29. Of failing or defective vision Glasses 1916. Slight astigmatism 30. Of tooth decay One large filling age 18 31. Of failing strength 32. Eating: Amount (underscore)—too much, optimum, too little. Balance of rations (underscore) proper, poor. Mastication (underscore): thorough, medium, little, "bolts food" 33. Habitual exercise: Kind Walking, tennis Skating Amount (underscore): too much, optimum, too little. 34. Lesser diseases to which there has been liability: Tonsilitis, malarial fever, constipation Nosebleed
35. Grave acute illness: Appendicitis
36. Chronic diseases: Typhoid age 4.
37. Surgical operations (kind, age of patient, etc.) None.
38. Describe any natural defect, deformity, or birth-mark.
39. Condition of speech: Enunciation (underscore)—clear, lisping, stammering, stuttering. 40. Natural voice:
In speaking:—Strength medium Quality
In singing:—Strength Does not Quality sing Register
41. Use of hands (underscore): right-handed, left-handed, ambidextrous. 42. Ability to do (*not* habit of doing) manual labor: Kind best adapted to Sewing, drawing, clean How able therein: ability commensurate with effort.
43. Grade (underscoring) in: physical strength, physical energy, muscular coördination, physical endurance.
44. Natural walking gait (underscore): very brisk, moderate, leisurely, shuffling. 45. Describe any marked physical prowess or athletic ability 46. Sense of equilibrium (underscore): subject to sea-sickness, nausea from swinging, dizzy at height. 47. Sense of direction: How easily lost: Not easily lost 48. Grade, by underscoring, natural acuteness or dullness of the special senses:—
(a) sight, (b) hearing, (c) taste, (d) smell, (e) touch. 49. Other physical traits

II—MENTAL

in 1st 6th of class of 230 at Oberlin College

50. General mental ability—ease of learning at school, etc.. *7th 8th from top rank in class of Great Westtown School*

51. Grade by underscoring:—general memory, special memory (kind........................), apropos association, constructive imagination, poetic imagination, logicalness, concentration. 52. Special ability or its lack, *regardless of predilection or aversion*, (grade by underscoring) in ART:—singing, instrumental (kind.........), musical composition, sketching, painting, modeling, designing (kind.............), landscape work, architecture (kind............), handicraft *knitting* (kind *embroidery*), penmanship. CRAFTSMANSHIP:—carpentry, masonry, stonecutting, smithing (kind..........), pattern-making, founding, machinery, plumbing, glazing, plastering, painting, ... LETTERS:—spelling, composition, poetry, essay, fiction, history, satire, humor, drama, acting, public speaking, lexicography, learning languages. SCIENCE:—research (kind.........), mathematics (kind *Algebra*), physics, chemistry, natural history (kind *Birds*) medicine, surgery, invention, exploration, engineering. SOCIAL SERVICE:—teaching, preaching, law, social welfare, politics, leadership. BUSINESS:—salesmanship, buying, accounting, investing, organizing, operating. 53. Other mental (not temperamental) traits or accomplishments ......*Typewriting*...............

III—TEMPERAMENTAL

54. Prevailing mood ..*Cheerful, but not exuberant; serious, quiet*..

55. Periodicity in nervous behavior...*Depression often occurs at menstruation, not so frequently as formerly... Formerly, i.e. between ages of 18 and 28, very irritable at these times*

56. Characterize, by underscoring, in each of the following traits: regularity in habits; purpose and coördination in work; *Varies at different times* ability to profit from experience; lives at high, medium, or low nervous tension; hard or easy to get along with; predilection for companionship or for solitude; breadth or narrowness in views; interest in world's events or in neighborhood gossip; given to facts in hand or to day-dreaming; talks much or little; talks fast or slow. Reaction to success: *varies* —elation, conceit, "rests-on-oars." Reaction to adversity:—renewed energy, depression, gives up the struggle; *varies*

57. Evaluate, by underscoring:—common sense; industry; persistence; moral courage; physical courage; sensitivity to pain; moral discrimination; conscientiousness; self-control; self-respect; adaptability; unselfishness; courtesy; foresight; sincerity; modesty; honesty; frankness; punctuality; alertness; caution; curiosity; credulity; loyalty; ambition; self-assertiveness; bashfulness; will power; criticalness; ability to stand criticism; sense of humor; ability to take a joke; fondness for satire; pride; tenderness; sympathy; contentment; optimism; patriotism; care for the good opinion of others; leadership. 58. Nervous peculiarities (underscore):—excitability; fretfulness; cruelty; *In childhood* conceit; self-depreciation; holds-a-grudge; fainting spells; headaches; convulsions; walks in sleep; talks in sleep; *In youth* delusions (kind.........); talks to self; nightmare; seclusiveness; amnesia; wild imagination; propounds wild schemes; incoherent thought; other nervous traits ....; 59. Indicate by underscoring predilection for or aversion to:—study; reading (kind......................); literary production (kind *Essay*......); teaching (kind..............); foreign languages (which...........); statistics (kind............); music (kind............); art (kind.........); tinkering; invention; handicraft (kind *needlework*...); craftsmanship (kind.........); cooking; athletics (kind *Tennis, Hockey*); home life; rural or town life; travel; tramping; exploration; nature; gardening; amusement (kind..............); recreation (kind *Canoeing, camping* military life; sea life; eating; games of chance; use of tobacco; use of drugs (kind....); use of alcohol (kind................); money-making; saving; spending; being in the public eye; social position; dress; dancing; conversation; politics; philosophy; religion; charity; opposite sex; odd or weird things. 60. Other temperamental traits ....

PERSONAL APPEARANCE

.... the individual to this card—profile or full front views preferable. Label taking. Are such pictures attached? *Yes*...... How many? *One double headed*.

.cription of personal appearance—physiognomy, expression, carriage, etc.—should description is applicable.

Name of person filling out this ....*Lydia D. Bucknell*.. Address *Haddon Heights, N.J.*.. Date *July 1922*.
EUGENICS RECORD OFFICE, COLD SPRING HARBOR, LONG ISLAND, NEW YORK.
New Era Print 3-22 10M and Plate. Form No. 430

THE STRANGER AT OUR GATE.

EMIGRANT. -Can I come in?   UNCLE SAM.—I 'spose you can: there's no law to keep you out.

Above: Frank Beard cartoon, 1896. The political campaign against unrestricted immigration had just begun. *Previous spread*: Between 1910 and 1939, the Eugenics Record Office assembled intimate personal data on nearly a million individuals.

THE GUARDED GATE

Bigotry, Eugenics, and the Law That Kept
Two Generations of Jews, Italians, and Other
European Immigrants Out of America

Daniel Okrent

SCRIBNER
New York   London   Toronto   Sydney   New Delhi

Scribner

An Imprint of Simon & Schuster, Inc.

1230 Avenue of the Americas

New York, NY 10020

First Scribner trade paperback edition May 2020

SCRIBNER and design are registered trademarks of The Gale Group, Inc.,
used under license by Simon & Schuster, Inc., the publisher of this work.

For information about special discounts for bulk purchases,
please contact Simon & Schuster Special Sales at 1-866-506-1949
or business@simonandschuster.com.

The Simon & Schuster Speakers Bureau can bring authors to
your live event. For more information or to book an event,
contact the Simon & Schuster Speakers Bureau at 1-866-248-3049
or visit our website at www.simonspeakers.com.

Interior design by Kyle Kabel

Manufactured in the United States of America

3   5   7   9   10   8   6   4   2

The Library of Congress has cataloged the hardcover edition as follows:

Names: Okrent, Daniel, 1948– author.
Title: The guarded gate : bigotry, eugenics, and the law that kept two generations of Jews,
Italians, and other European immigrants out of America / Daniel Okrent.

Description: New York : Scribner, 2019. | Includes
bibliographical references and index.

Identifiers: LCCN 2019006830| ISBN 9781476798035 (hardcover) |
ISBN 9781476798059 (pbk.) | ISBN 9781476798080 (ebook)

Subjects: LCSH: Eugenics—Law and legislation—United States—History. | Sterilization (Birth
control)—Law and legislation—United States—History. | Discrimination in medical care—Law
and legislation—United States—History. | Human reproduction—Law and legislation—United
States—History. | Emigration and immigration law—United States—History.

Classification: LCC KF3832 .O37 2019 | DDC 344.74304/8—dc23

LC record available at https://lccn.loc.gov/2019006830

ISBN 978-1-4767-9803-5
ISBN 978-1-4767-9805-9 (pbk)
ISBN 978-1-4767-9808-0 (ebook)

For Bruce McCall
Best of readers, best of friends

and

For Oola
It's so nice to meet you!

When power is discovered, man always turns to it. The science of heredity will soon provide power on a stupendous scale; and in some country, at some time not, perhaps, far distant, that power will be applied to control the composition of a nation.

—William Bateson, geneticist, 1905

The day of the sociologist is passing, and the day of the biologist has come.

—Robert DeCourcy Ward, cofounder of
the Immigration Restriction League, 1913

AMERICA OF THE MELTING POT COMES TO END

—Headline, *New York Times*, 1924

By 1926, when this poster appeared at a Kansas fair, the merger
of eugenics and the anti-immigration movement was complete, and the
ethnic "ancestry of our children" was no longer up for grabs.

Contents

A Note from (and About)
the Author

I'll begin with my own beginnings. My father's family, shtetl Jews
from central Poland, arrived in the United States in 1910, when
the immigration gates were still wide open to all Europeans. My
mother's father, also Jewish, was a physician who emigrated from
Romania in 1922, under a temporary restrictive law that enabled
him to slip in before those gates clanged shut two years later. By
the time my mother and her mother arrived in 1930, my grandfather
had obtained citizenship, which enabled their entry.

I consequently can't claim spotless objectivity as I tell the fateful
story of how a perverse form of "science" gave respectability to the
drastic limits imposed on the number of Jews, Italians, Greeks, Poles,
and various other eastern and southern Europeans seeking to come
to America between 1924 and 1965. Neither do I wish to assert that
the sanctions imposed on these debarred millions were crueler than
those endured by Asians or Africans or other peoples who suffered
discrimination even crueler or of longer duration. *The Guarded Gate*
is not *the* story of the interplay between xenophobia and immigration
policy; it's one of several. That it happens to cut so close to my own
bone is inescapable but no more disqualifying than if earlier Okrents
had stood on the deck of the *Mayflower*. Save for those of us whose

antecedents were here before Columbus, every American has a stake in this story and presumably a predisposition of perspective.

About Language

As I was writing this book, the quotation marks I initially employed to surround the word "science" (as in the paragraph above) soon began to blemish the manuscript like some form of pox. I ended up deleting almost all of them. Their absence should not suggest my acceptance of forms of inquiry and assertion that were, in fact, not remotely scientific. Similarly, my uninflected use of "evidence"—and of "superior," "inferior," "inadequate," and comparably judgmental terms—connotes the context in which they were used and not my appraisal of what they were meant to describe. I also use "race" in the way it was employed in that distant time—not as a distinction of skin color but of ethnic background of any sort.

About the Publisher

Beginning on page 395, I acknowledge all the many individuals and institutions who helped me with my research and with various other aspects of this project. But I wish here to cite the special role of Scribner. Beginning in 1916 with the publication of Madison Grant's seminal *The Passing of the Great Race*, Charles Scribner's Sons (as the firm was then known) was effectively the official publisher of the scientific racism movement. Over the next decade and a half the company issued nearly a score of books that advanced the cause of immigration restriction by valorizing the racist principles on which it was based. The editors and their colleagues responsible for this publishing program are long dead; their successors of a century later could not have been more supportive of my effort to explore Scribner's unfortunate place in this story.

Ellis Island, 1925

Henry Curran, commissioner of immigration for the Port of New York, had been at his job long enough to know what to expect when a group of visitors came to Ellis Island in July 1925. He knew what they'd ask, and he knew how to answer.

A reform Republican in a city not quite suited either to reform or to Republicans, he had been badly beaten in New York's mayoral election in 1921, then rewarded for both his party loyalty and his skills as an administrator when he was placed in charge of the portal that welcomed 70 percent of the immigrants coming to the United States. Since its opening in 1892, the Ellis Island facility had grown to twenty-seven acres of inspection centers, detention areas, and hospitals. Built to process 5,000 people a day, at times it had to handle twice that number. Many of them exhausted and frightened, most of them impoverished, crowds of immigrants were funneled through a series of examination and processing stations. Those detained for further assessment were housed in dormitories—a series of enormous rooms divided into wire cages, frequently ridden with bedbugs, intended to accommodate 1,800 individuals but at times occupied by several hundred more. In one year the Public Health Service hospital on Ellis Island treated more than 10,000 immigrants hoping to traverse that final, single mile to a life in the

United States. Over the years more than 3,000 died in the hospital, their voyage incomplete.

On the base of the nearby Statue of Liberty, Emma Lazarus's famous poem invited the world to "give me your tired, your poor, your huddled masses yearning to breathe free." On July 1, 1925, when Henry Curran gave a tour for this particular set of visitors, many Americans still found a certain nobility, a confirmation of the nation's promise, in Lazarus's words and the images they evoked. By now, it was likely that even more citizens perceived evidence of menace, and threat, and inevitable national decline.

Among Curran's guests, those in the latter group couldn't help but be surprised by what they encountered on that fair summer Wednesday on the edge of New York's bustling harbor. "A visitor making a return trip to Ellis Island today after a lapse of several years would have difficulty in recognizing it," wrote an Associated Press reporter. Twenty ships discharged their passengers on the island on July 1 two years earlier; on this day only two steamed into port. In the main hall built to accommodate raucous thousands, fewer than six hundred newcomers stood in orderly lines. Where the visitors had expected filth, Curran presented scenes of what he called "spotless cleanliness" and an atmosphere of "fresh air untainted by odors." Where they might have expected a polyglot babel of Italian and Yiddish and Slavic tongues so foreign as not to be recognizable, or even imaginable, a serene quiet prevailed.

These newcomers, in fact, hardly seemed foreign at all. So when one of Curran's befuddled guests asked, "And who are all these people? Are they immigrants?" Curran offered the reply that he knew would surprise and delight his guests: "Today there is not one immigrant in a thousand who does not dress, walk, and generally look so much like an American that 'you will believe they are all really Americans.'"

In at least one way, they were. Since the passage of the Immigration Act of 1924, which had gone into effect exactly one year before Curran gave his tour, the incoming population had changed to conform to a very specific American image. Just four years earlier, 76 percent of all immigrants had come from the nations of southern and eastern Europe—from Italy and Greece, Poland and Russia, and the other nations jammed between the Baltic and Mediterranean Seas. Now the same countries accounted for a scant 11 percent of the newcomers.

Henry Curran was not by nature a bigot; serving later in his career as deputy mayor to the half-Italian, half-Jewish Fiorello La Guardia, he would celebrate "the ethnological crazy quilt" that had made New York "an electric, pulsing miniature of the world." But in 1925 Curran said that "the immigrants of today are of a better kind" than those who had come ashore on Ellis Island over the previous two decades. "They are better by reason of our new immigration law; the cause and effect are direct."

What he didn't say was what a major national figure had written four years earlier: "Biological laws tell us that certain divergent people will not mix or blend." He was not alone. The editors of the nation's most popular magazine had said continued immigration from southern and eastern Europe would compel America to "join the lowly ranks of the mongrel races." The leader of one of the nation's most esteemed scientific institutions had argued that "through science we have discovered" that neither education nor environment could alter the "profound and inborn racial differences" that rendered certain peoples inferior. The chairman of the congressional committee that drafted the new law was especially direct: the former argument for immigration restriction had been economic, he said, but now "the fundamental reason for it is biological."

It was an idea that had been gaining credence for years, supported by some of the nation's leading scientific institutions, amplified by political activists both reactionary and progressive, and soon embedded in the popular consciousness. Long-standing hatreds, and the moment's political exigencies, had assured that a version of the Immigration Act of 1924 would pass. But science—"biological laws"—imported from England and then popularized in the United States had made the arguments in support of it respectable and its consequences enduring. The newcomers who would arrive in years to come, said Henry Curran, "will be the kind we are glad to welcome."

PART I

Enough! Enough!
We Want No More!

Chapter One

The Future Betterment
of the Human Race

Charles Benedict Davenport left a vivid impression on one of his occasional collaborators during his period of greatest influence. Davenport "used to lift his eyes reverently," Margaret Sanger would recall, "and, with his hands upraised as though in supplication, quiver emotionally as he breathed, 'Protoplasm. We want more protoplasm.'" When she wasn't promoting the idea of birth control—and sometimes, tactically, when she thought it would help her cause—Sanger was one of dozens of prominent, if seemingly unlikely, Americans who waved the banner of eugenics in the first third of the twentieth century. The "protoplasm" that Davenport longed for was the genetic material that would create an improved human race—if the world followed the principles of planned breeding that embodied the eugenicist faith.

It's not hard to picture Davenport—tall, slim, his Vandyke always impeccable, his brow invariably creased and taut—in the state Sanger described. By his own description he was beset by a "nervous" temperament. A colleague said he "liv[ed] a life of his own in the midst of others . . . out of place in almost any crowd." When he wasn't carried away by the nearly ecstatic bouts of optimism that arose from one or another of his studies and experiments ("life is a succession of thrills," he exclaimed in midcareer), he was unconfident, defensive, even resentful. As a young biologist at Harvard in the 1890s, hunched over a microscope with an intensity of purpose that seemed to create its own force field, he provided a clear signal for those who didn't grasp his zeal intuitively by spelling it out for them in words he had inscribed on his eyeshade: "I am deaf dumb and blind."

That was a Davenportian way of saying, "Leave me alone; I have work to do." And he had plenty: in a career that stretched for nearly five decades, Davenport published 439 scientific papers, sat on the editorial boards of eight scholarly journals, maintained memberships in sixty-four scientific and social organizations, and trained generations of American geneticists (not to mention, along the way, a busload or two of charlatans). For four of those decades, operating out of a tidy scientific principality he established in the Long Island coastal village of Cold Spring Harbor, Davenport reigned as the nation's foremost advocate, investigator, and—there's really no other word for it—impresario of a science that altered the face of a nation.

The scientific colossus that eventually blossomed in Cold Spring Harbor, and that along the way would develop the intellectual arguments for limiting immigration to the United States by country of origin, began life in 1890 as the biological laboratory of the Brooklyn Institute of Arts and Sciences, a venerable civic institution that extended its reach thirty-five miles to the east on Long Island's north shore.* The thousands of men and women who worked in the Cold Spring Harbor laboratories over the decades to come would produce groundbreaking research in genetics, neuroscience, oncology, and other disciplines; eight of these people, including

---

* The acronym derived from the institute's name could be considered spookily premonitory, or merely unfortunate.

geneticist Barbara McClintock and James Watson, the codiscoverer of DNA, would win Nobel Prizes. Charles Davenport would never win a Nobel, but for a time his researches and his recommendations earned equivalent attention.

In 1898 the thirty-two-year-old Davenport was appointed director of the summer school of the biological laboratory. He was a Brooklyn boy of prominent family; another Davenport was treasurer of the Brooklyn Institute, and three more were among its donors. But anyone who might have suspected that he won his appointment through nepotism could not have been familiar with Davenport's work, or his personality. At the time, he had not yet located the path that would eventually lead him to his intense engagement with the study of human heredity, but his school-year labors at Harvard were productive and his range was prodigious: a paper on the effects of water on the growth of frogs, a book on statistical methods, another encompassing such topics as "chemotropism in the tentacles of insectivorous plants." He married Gertrude Crotty, a graduate student in zoology whose work he supervised, and so endeared himself to Harvard president Charles W. Eliot that Eliot invited the young couple to stay in his Cambridge house one summer while he was rusticating in Maine.

In later years Davenport would allow his ambitions to distort his work, eventually leading him dangerously past the edge of reason. But as a young man working at Harvard and beginning a family, he was a pure scientist. He was especially tantalized by an emerging field known as experimental evolution, an area of study for researchers seeking to unlock the Darwinian code in the controlled environment of the laboratory, thus abbreviating the millennia required to apprehend evolution in nature.

As attached to Harvard as he might have been—undergraduate degree, PhD, faculty appointment—Davenport did not find the university sufficiently accommodating for the work he wished to pursue. Each week, when the journal *Science* arrived in the Davenport household, Gertrude would scour the death notices, hoping to find news of an appropriate opening. In 1899 Charles accepted a full-time position at the University of Chicago but felt the strong pull of his seasonal appointment in Cold Spring Harbor. (Gertrude also held a faculty position at the summer school, teaching microscope technique.) For a natural scientist with interests as varied as Davenport's, the village and its surroundings were a version of paradise: seashore and estuary, ponds and streams, meadows and forests, every imaginable environment for gathering specimens. The train to New York from nearby Oyster Bay ran frequently enough to serve the wealthy families building their country palaces in the area (among them a young New York politician named Theodore Roosevelt), and its depot was close enough to town for an inveterate walker like Davenport. For the next four decades he could be seen striding purposefully down country roads, sometimes before dawn, to get to the station and then to the wide world beyond the principality he created in Cold Spring Harbor. He had a story to tell—a story rooted in the work of a singular British gentleman scientist, then translated by Davenport into a credo for America, and characterized by both men as nothing less than the basis for a new religion.

*   *   *

FRANCIS GALTON'S MOTTO, a colleague said, was "Whenever you can, count." He counted the number of dead worms that emerged from the ground near his London town house after a heavy rain (forty-five in a span of sixteen paces), and he counted the number of flea bites he suffered in 1845 while spending a night in the home of the Sheikh of Aden (ninety-seven, but even so he thought the sheikh was "a right good fellow"). Galton consumed numbers ravenously, then added them, divided them, shuffled and rearranged them so he could amaze himself with his own discoveries.

The extraordinary man who developed the theory that talent, intelligence, and even morality were bequeathed biologically believed that everything knowable could be expressed in numbers. Galton's major discoveries—among them the individuality of fingerprints, the movement of anticyclones, the statistical law of regression to the mean—elevated his obsessive collection of data from triviality to significance. But for every one of his substantial contributions to human understanding, he probably hit upon a dozen that were trivial. His meticulously constructed "Beauty Map" of Great Britain, he believed, established that Aberdeen was home to the nation's least attractive women. His essay "The Measure of Fidget," published in England's leading scientific journal, was an effort to "giv[e] numerical expression to the amount of boredom" in any audience by counting body movements per minute. Observation and enumeration convinced him that "well washed and combed domestic pets grow dull" because "they miss the stimulus of fleas." For good or ill, and often for purposes utterly irrelevant, this lavish reverence for numbers, his belief in their power, enabled Galton to live a life both intellectually distinctive and richly productive.

Having grown up surrounded by wealth and inheriting a good deal of it while still a young man didn't hurt. In a century (the nineteenth), a place (Victorian England), and his particular milieu (the cosseted world of wealthy amateurs), Galton was better armed than most for a life of inquiry and experimentation. His paternal grandfather, a gun manufacturer who grew rich supplying the British army with muskets, married one of the banking Barclays, whose family business was already more than a century old by the time Francis was born in 1822. A third grandparent was the daughter of a landowning Scottish nobleman descended from Richard Plantagenet, father of Richard III. These three compounded the fortune that Galton would inherit at age twenty-two, enabling him to live the life of a gentleman. His fourth grandparent may have provided the bloodlines (and Galton would come to care a great deal about bloodlines) that led him to the field of scientific inquiry. This progenitor was the obese, libidinous, polymathic physician and poet Erasmus Darwin, one of whose other grandsons would do fairly well in science himself.

We have it on the testimony of Lewis M. Terman, one of the pioneers of intelligence testing in America, that when Galton was a child, it was already clear that his IQ "was not far from 200." Among the thousands of children Terman had personally tested by the time he announced this impressive assessment, it was true that he had yet to encounter an IQ greater than 170. It is also true that Terman arrived at his conclusion six years after Galton's death at eighty-eight, and had never met him, much less tested him. And it's conclusively true that Terman had a horse in this particular race: much of his career was predicated on principles first elucidated and techniques first developed by Galton himself.

Still, Terman had a point. Francis Galton was precocious to roughly the same degree that an ocean is large. He could read at two, mastered Latin at four (around the time he wrote to his sister to inform her that "I read French a little" as well), quoted freely and at length from Sir Walter Scott at five, was intimate with the *Iliad* by six. The spirited self-confidence that would for the next eight decades mark his prose, his speech, and virtually every delighted leap of his lush and expressive eyebrows had received an early familial boost when his father had sent seven-year-old Francis, alone, on a journey by pony from their estate in England's West Midlands, with instructions to stay at a particular inn along the way. The boy managed without difficulty—and without ever becoming aware of the servant following a careful two miles behind.

Tall and thin, his face framed by spectacular muttonchops that seemed to provide architectural support for what an admirer called "a forehead like the dome of St. Paul's," Galton possessed an emotional buoyancy as well. He floated blithely from one endeavor to the next, ever productive, ever sanguine. When he wrote about his "rather unusual power of enduring physical fatigue without harmful results," he wasn't boasting. More than twenty books and two hundred journal articles spilled from his pen, the last of them published in his eighty-ninth year.

By all accounts Galton was an amiable person and a charming host, but he was also a thoroughgoing snob. He never saw reason to challenge the class system that produced him, nor did he ever miss a chance to take advantage of its benefits. And though the Galtons (like the Darwins) were ardent abolitionists, Francis didn't doubt the inferiority of black people. This was hardly a rare attitude in Victorian England, but one would think that a man of science would seek firm evidence to support his beliefs, especially a man as data crazed as Galton. But no: "It is seldom that we hear of a white traveler [in Africa] meeting with a black chief whom he feels to be the better man," he wrote in 1869.

The case can be made that Galton came to his belief in the heritability of talent partly because it was self-affirming—an implicit endorsement of the familial process that reached its apotheosis in his own genius. It certainly didn't arise from his earlier work. "Until the phenomena of any branch of Knowledge have been submitted to measurement and number," Galton declared late in life, "it cannot assume the status and dignity of a science." But before he reached his forties, Galton's science was neither meaningfully scientific nor particularly dignified. As a medical student—a program of study he never completed—he decided to sample every drug in the basic pharmacopoeia; working alphabetically, he never made it past croton oil, a powerful purgative that produced violent bouts of diarrhea. He did attain membership in the Royal Geographical Society after conducting a self-financed two-year expedition to southwest Africa, accompanied by nine "white or whitish people,"* ten "natives," eighty-six oxen, thirty small cattle, and two wagons. The titles of some of the journal articles he published between 1855 and 1865 probably indicate the best way to define Galton's nature at this point in his life: "Signals Available to Men Who Are Adrift on Wrecks at Sea," "On a New Principle for the Protection of Riflemen," "First Steps Towards the Domestication of Animals." He never got around to publishing his findings from a three-month investigation into the proper temperature for brewing tea.

Charles Darwin and Francis Galton barely knew each other when young, which was partly because of their age difference (Darwin the elder by thirteen years), but more likely because grandfather Erasmus was as profligate as he was prolific: his children—twelve legitimate and (at least) two not—produced grandchildren almost too numerous to list, much less to know one another. The first substantive communication between the two cousins didn't take place until 1853, when Darwin was forty-four and Galton thirty-one; the older man wanted to compliment the younger on his first book, *The Narrative of an Explorer in South Africa*.

But without Darwin's influence, Galton would likely never have begun his explorations into the nature of heredity. In this regard, he was no different from virtually everyone else who had been exploring the boundaries of biology in the British scientific world of the 1850s. Natural scientists were clamoring for data on "tides, the analysis of life insurance tables, bills of mortality, population censuses," wrote Janet Browne in her magnificent biography of Darwin. "Raw information flooded in from every corner of the world, piling up in London's learned societies and in government corridors." At the same

* Galton used "whitish" to describe two black men who "have lived with Whites all their lives."

time, philosophers were contemplating the perfectibility of society and trying to discern the meaning of the individual. The protean thinker Herbert Spencer drew on biology, anthropology, sociology, and other disciplines to build a unified theory of the structure of human society (among its tenets: all forms of public charity or welfare are interruptions in the natural order of the universe). Then, in 1859, Darwin published *On the Origin of Species* and imposed his revolutionary views on a new model of science—a universe liberated from the intangible and unverifiable homilies of religion, supposition, and superstition.

Darwin's book, Galton would recall half a century later, "made a marked epoch in my own mental development as it did in that of human thought generally. Its effect was to demolish a multitude of dogmatic barriers by a single stroke." The theory of natural selection was, to Galton, a call to revolution, an assault on "all ancient authorities whose positive and unauthenticated statements were contradicted by modern science." If the development of species was not guided by a divine hand, he reasoned, neither were the minds of men. As physical qualities were provably heritable, so must be "the peculiarities of character." Darwin had defined the principles of natural selection in the animal world; now Galton dared to adapt them to the lives of humans. In the words of Galton's protégé, disciple, and biographer Karl Pearson, "the inheritance of mental and moral characters in man [became] the fundamental concept in Galton's life and work."

Galton first set out to prove it in two articles that arose from his research—if one must call it that—in the peculiar pages of a book called *A Million of Facts*. Advertised as "a useful reference on all subjects of research and curiosity, collected from the most respectable modern authorities," the book was a weird compendium of random information compiled by a schoolteacher/publisher/hosiery manufacturer named Richard Phillips, whose singular beliefs included the conviction that the law of gravity was in error. But the volume did contain within its five hundred–plus pages a long section, headed "Biography," that provided Galton with the raw information he would use to establish that men are born, not made.

Galton counted 605 "notabilities" who lived in the four centuries between 1453 and 1853 and concluded that fully one in six was related to someone else on the list. Never mind that Phillips included such "notabilities" as "Aikin, Dr., a tasteful writer, died 1815." (This was the entire entry.) Or that the complete "biography" of a somewhat better-known figure, the French novelist Alain-René Lesage, read, "the author of *Gil Blas* was very deaf; he wrote for profit, and got fame also." Thomas à Becket was (again, complete entry) "a factious and arrogant churchman, who was killed in 1170, at Canterbury."

From this dubious source (whose author, incidentally, Galton misidentified as Sir *Thomas* Phillips), he moved on to a gumbo of others. Galton examined page proofs of a yet-to-be-published listing of nineteen thousand prominent men (he got that author's name wrong, too), and then a cross section of *Men of the Time*, a sort of *Who's Who* of contemporary figures in which fully two out of seven had relatives in the volume as well. Thrilled by this gratifying discovery, he moved from the generic to the specific, counting his way through a dictionary of painters, a directory of prominent musicians (in French), lists of scientists, lists of lawyers, lists of writers. He finally concluded that one out of eight men of great accomplishment had a father, son, or brother of similar attainments.

Proving . . . what, exactly? Looked at today, Galton's research and his conclusions seem risible. His sources were at best problematic; his measures of eminence were arbitrary (they were in many cases measures of fame, not accomplishment). He failed to see that the sons of "eminent" men were likely to enjoy careers that benefitted from their fathers' privileged positions. Heredity certainly played a large role in determining an individual's makeup, but to discount the influence of wealth, and educational opportunity, and social connections, and access to resources—this was preposterous.

The articles that arose from Galton's studies were published in 1865. To amplify his research, he offered a series of eccentric extrapolations. "Most notabilities have been great eaters and excellent digesters," he asserted, "on literally the same principle that the furnace which can raise more steam than is usual for one its size must burn more freely and well than is common."* He also offered prescriptive counsel for the good of the nation, notably a series of incentives to encourage the inherently superior to marry each other in a mass wedding at Westminster Abbey, where Queen Victoria "will give away the brides." Wedding presents? Five thousand pounds per couple, so they needn't worry about earning a living and could get right down to their assigned business: fulfilling their patriotic responsibilities by making superior babies for the benefit of Britain.

In 1869 Galton expanded these articles into *Hereditary Genius: An Inquiry into Its Laws and Consequences.* The supportive data that made up the bulk of the book mostly demonstrated his mania for counting and list making, the pages filled with enumeration and analysis of poets, military commanders, clergymen, even "very excellent oarsmen." In historical digressions, Galton cited genealogies from the Roman Empire to show the durability of heredity (all those Scipios) and employed some extremely acrobatic math to calculate that precisely 1 in 3,214 ancient Athenians who reached the age of fifty was "illustrious." The narrative chapters that begin and end the book are chiefly used to make the case that would provide ballast for the entire mode of thought that arose from Galton's work on heredity: that selective breeding could be employed to improve the species, much as it had with dogs and horses. And in the book's conclusions, he added a sentence that was an augury of hereditarian arguments yet to come. "Let us do what we can," he wrote, "to encourage the

---

* Galton revisited this idea in an 1884 paper, "The Weights of British Noblemen During the Last Three Generations."

[Private, for Consideration.]

EUGENICS CERTIFICATES

The time seems to have arrived when the question should ~~ought~~

to be seriously discussed, whether it be practicable &
~~advisable~~

advisable to issue Eugenic Certificates, that would &

ought to be, accepted as trustworthy, & that would be inexpensive

& yet self supporting.

The subject is full of difficulties but I think, they can all of them

can ~~I think~~ be met if certain restrictions &

requirements be ~~acceded to~~ permitted, of which the following

are the chief —

1. The purport of the certificate to be that in the

opinion of the Judges, the achievements of the holder

& those of his near Kinsmen prove ~~show~~ him to be

distinctly superior in Eugenic Gifts to the majority

of ~~his class~~· those of a similar social position.

2 That certificates be granted, at first only to men, between

the ages of 23 to 30 inclusive, & belonging who belong to the educated
classes.

Galton's proposal for granting official certificates to those
"distinctly superior in eugenic gifts."

multiplication of the races best suited to invent and conform to a high and generous civilization."

According to Louisa Galton, who kept a meticulous diary of her husband's professional life, the initial edition of *Hereditary Genius* was generally "not well received." An especially savage commentary, in the *Saturday Review*, declared Galton's lists of "disjointed facts" to be "inert and lifeless . . . logically worth nothing." But praise from one particular quarter provided balm for whatever wounds Galton's ego might have suffered. Charles Darwin, his travels and energies constrained by illness, had been homebound in Kent, listening to his wife read aloud from Galton's book. They were not fifty pages into it when he felt compelled to write to his cousin. His excitement was so intense, he said, that he felt the need to "exhale myself, else something will go wrong in my inside. I do not think I ever in all my life read anything more interesting and original."

Some Darwin scholars have argued that the great man's enthusiasm should not be taken as an endorsement; it could simply have been an expression of cousinly generosity, a diplomatic response to Galton's worshipful regard for him. Additionally, in subsequent years Darwin took specific exception to certain interpretations and recommendations Galton put forth. Still, barely a year after his breathless letter, Darwin was willing to openly declare his faith in Galton's work, in the first edition of *The Descent of Man*: "We now know, through the labours of Mr. Galton, that genius . . . tends to be inherited," and it is also "certain that insanity and deteriorated mental powers run likewise in families." This seemed, and seems, reasonable enough. But where Darwin saw tendencies, his cousin veered toward absolute conviction. And unlike Galton, Darwin did not propose that a radical reordering of society through the manipulation of marriage and child-rearing should be erected on so frail a foundation.

By the time *Descent* was published, in 1869, the Darwinian modes of thought that had already spread through the world of natural science had invaded distant fields of inquiry. The new journal *Nature* effectively became the house organ of the scientific modernism that Darwin had initiated. The mathematician W. K. Clifford declared that "all new reasoning in the sciences, biology to sociology, must [now] rely on the scientific law of evolution." In 1864 Herbert Spencer had coined "survival of the fittest," an epithet that mutated into a flag permanently affixed to Darwinian thinking.* Henry Adams, who had come to London to serve as secretary to his father, the American ambassador, saw "evolution . . . rag[ing] like an epidemic."

Galton's scientific reputation advanced in the wake of this intellectual tidal wave, accelerated by the potent fusion of his boundless energies and a concomitant gift for publicity. His astonishing productivity continued unabated, and he found new and attention-getting ways to express it. He offered £500 in prize money (and publication of their names in a forthcoming book) to people who sent him the most detailed family records, covering everything from height to "artistic faculty." At the mobile "Anthropometric Laboratory" he set up at the International Health Exhibition in South Kensington in 1884, more than 9,300 people lined up to pay three pence apiece to be measured not just by scale or yardstick but also by a phalanx of machines largely invented by Galton himself. This array of rods, pulleys, lights, and weights could evaluate with Galtonian precision such (presumably hereditary) variables as keenness of sight, "swiftness of blow," sensitivity to pain, and "the delicacy" of the senses. Londoners unwilling to be measured but eager to watch could stand outside the lab and gape through an open lattice constructed to

---

* Darwin himself didn't use the term until the fifth edition of *Origin of Species*, published ten years after the original. The term "social Darwinism" did not gain wide currency until it was used by the American historian Richard Hofstadter in the title of his *Social Darwinism in American Thought*, published in 1944.

accommodate their curiosity. Over the next several years Galton set up his lab in Dublin, Oxford, Cambridge, and other cities, each installation extending the reach of his renown and the public's grasp of his theories.

One other skill proved invaluable: his fecund gift for language. In an 1874 volume titled *English Men of Science*, he came up with "a convenient jingle of words," repurposed from Shakespeare, that have endured far longer than Galton's renown: "nature and nurture."* Nine years later, in *Inquiries into Human Faculty and Its Development*, he finally attached a name and a definition to the entire field of study he had initiated, promoted, and made his own: "eugenics," extracted from the Greek *eugenes*, meaning "good in stock."

[Like the idea of state-planned marriages, equating the breeding of humans to plant and animal hybridization was a trope as old as Plato's suggestion that humans should be selectively mated in the same fashion as sporting dogs.]William Penn used it when he said that "men are more careful of the breed of their horses and dogs than of their children," and early investigators into the nature of heredity could barely avoid it. The modern revival of the trope was best articulated by Galton himself, when he declared that just "as a new race can be obtained in animals and plants . . . with moderate care in preventing the more faulty members of the flock from breeding, so a race of gifted men might be obtained, under exactly similar conditions." Darwin raised the same notion two years later in *The Descent of Man*, and as the doctrine of eugenics leapt the Atlantic and began to spread, so did easy extrapolations from man's experiments with lower species. In 1883, addressing the National Academy of Sciences, Alexander Graham Bell suggested that just as

---

* From *The Tempest*, Act IV: Prospero describes Caliban as "A devil, a born devil, on whose nature / Nurture can never stick."

it was possible to "modify . . . our domestic animals" through selective breeding, "we could also produce modifications or varieties of men."

Table II. Combinations of Temper in marriage (per cents)										
Tempers of Husbands	Observed pairs. Tempers of Wives					Haphazard pairs. Tempers of Wives				
	good		bad tempers			good		bad tempers		
	1	2	3	4	5	1	2	3	4	5
good 1	6	10	9	6	2	13	5	10	3	2
good 2	4	2	5	2	—	5	2	4	1	1
bad 3	14	4	9	3	2	11	5	8	2	2
bad 4	7	3	3	2	1	6	2	5	1	1
bad 5	3	—	2	—	1	4	2	3	1	1
good	22		24			25		21		
bad	31		23			30		24		

For his study of "Good and Bad Temper in English Families," Galton gathered, analyzed, cross-referenced, and sorted appraisals of 1,981 individuals.

[But "selective breeding" also implies that the process of selection would cull certain individuals from any planned breeding program, and just as ancient as Plato was the notion that undesirable "varieties" of humans could be eliminated through proscriptions on their reproduction.] In 1875, on a speaking tour in upstate New York, the American suffragist Victoria Woodhull asserted that "the criminal and vicious classes were made so by their mothers during gestation." Several years later, she declared that reproduction among the hereditarily deficient—in her view, a group that included drunkards, criminals, and carriers of "hereditary sensuality and vice"—should be considered "a crime against the nation." The line tying Galton's optimistic "positive eugenics" to Woodhull's "negative eugenics" was direct; Galton himself recognized the connection, advocating the denial of "the liberty of propagating children which is now allowed to the undesirable classes."

Inevitably, negative eugenics would address not only people afflicted with the sort of undesirable traits identified by Woodhull (as well as blindness, deafness, and other purely physical deficiencies), but races and ethnic groupings as well. In his earliest days as a eugenicist, Galton had employed his usual mathematical skills (diluted by his usual set of presuppositions) to rank the "ability" of the ancient Greek as "two grades higher" than the Victorian Era Briton, who was in turn perched two grades above the African, who was superior to the aboriginal Australian. But it was a little-noted speech he gave in August 1891 that contained the germ of a movement that was on the brink of being born. When Galton rose to speak in the theater at the Royal School of Mines, just off Piccadilly, it was to address the Seventh International Congress of Hygiene and Demography, which had brought together Europe's and America's leading experts in the field that would later be known as public health. This particular event was strictly for the Division of Demography.

Galton didn't consider himself a demographer. The term itself was only fourteen years old, and his polymathic tendencies were too capacious to be summarized in a single word. But his election as president of the organization confirmed the importance of his statistical methods to the nascent field of population studies, and many of the papers delivered at this congress were dependent on them. One was devoted entirely to the data gathered from the several thousand university students who had been measured over the past several years at the Anthropometric Laboratory he had set up at Cambridge. The author of that paper—logician John Venn, inventor of the so-named diagram*—had analyzed the massive collection of

---

* Venn was not the only eponym at the congress; other attendees included John Langdon Down, who first identified the genetic syndrome that bears his name, and Joseph Lister, whose advances in sterilization were later commemorated in the names of a pathogenic bacterium. And a mouthwash.

measurements with Galtonian exactitude and concluded that the most brilliant students were physically . . . well, pretty much like all the others.

Galton's presidential address was not so predictable. It did not address techniques of measurement or computation, nor did it contain references to his various studies of eminence in families. The topic, he declared at the beginning, was "the future betterment of the human race," but tucked subtly into it was concern for an issue that had hardly been addressed in Britain up to that point yet was the logical extension of much of Galton's work and thought. He encouraged the demographers to study the effects of legislation on national populations, and specifically to determine whether the laws would have been different "if the question of race" had been considered.

Galton was sixty-nine. The beetling eyebrows, apparently untamable, formed an unruly shelf above his eyes; the luxuriant sideburns that framed his face had thinned and grown gray. He had many years of public life ahead of him—he lived to nearly ninety, and worked until the end—but two sentences in his speech to the demographers could have been plucked from his text, shipped across the Atlantic, and made the credo of an American immigration restriction movement just beginning to declare itself. [Much more care is taken to select appropriate varieties of plants and animals for plantation in foreign settlements than to select appropriate types of men," he told the demographers. "Discrimination and foresight are shown in the one case, an indifference born of ignorance is shown in the other." It was an idea waiting for a crusade.]

* * *

CHARLES DAVENPORT'S SEARCH for the world-changing protoplasm that he so desired could be said to have begun in January 1902, in the Diplomatic Room of the U.S. State Department. Theodore Roosevelt, president for just four months, found himself in control of the territories the United States had acquired during the Spanish-American War and was already planning to extend the nation's reach to the slender waist of Central America, where he intended to build a canal connecting the oceans. Roosevelt's closest associates were nonetheless able to step away, at least for a moment, from the administration of empire. The host for the meeting in the Diplomatic Room was Secretary of State John Hay, and Secretary of War Elihu Root was among his guests. But for the day's particular purposes, the most important figure present was the industrialist Andrew Carnegie, who had convened the founding trustees of the Carnegie Institution of Washington for their first meeting.*

"Gentlemen, your work now begins," Carnegie told the group. "Your aims are high, you seek to expand known forces, to discover and utilize unknown forces for the benefit of man. Than this there can scarcely be a greater work." The tone and cadence of Carnegie's comments could have been accompanied by trumpets. But they came with something even better: $10 million in U.S. Steel bonds.

At the time, this initial endowment was greater than the sum that all of America's universities—combined—had at hand to finance basic research. To Davenport the Carnegie money, which the industrialist had specifically earmarked for that purpose, gleamed like El Dorado. Tapping into it could provide not only a ticket to year-round residence in Cold Spring Harbor but could also build the facilities and house the staff he needed for a dream he had begun to nurture: a permanent laboratory devoted to the study of evolution. Shortly after the Carnegie Institution's founding, he told the trustees that his proposed Biological Experiment Station required "a plot of ground

---

* The CIW should not be confused with the better-known Carnegie Corporation (also known as the Carnegie Foundation) or the Carnegie Endowment for International Peace. After Andrew Carnegie retired from business to devote the remainder of his life to philanthropy, he endowed twenty-three separate organizations bearing his name. In 2007 the CIW rebranded itself the Carnegie Institution for Science.

in the country, near the sea, presenting a great variety of conditions, not too distant from a scientific center and its libraries." And, he added, he just happened to have in mind a place that fit all those requirements. He could provide another necessary element himself: the time that evolution studies required. "My age is 36," he said. "The chances are that I shall have 25 years" to dedicate to the laboratory. "I propose to give the rest of my life unreservedly to this work."

The earnestness of the intention, the grandiosity of its expression: this was essential Davenport. Equally characteristic was the unrelenting campaign he waged to win the trustees' support. Rejected on his first attempt, Davenport kept returning to the group with a ceaseless gush of appeals, each one modified in a significant way: He needed less money. He could persuade the Brooklyn Institute to provide the land. He wasn't sure he was willing to give up tenure at Chicago, then he was. He flooded individual trustees and the members of the board's zoological advisory committee with special appeals. At one point nobility, humility, or sheer desperation prompted him to assume an entirely new posture. "If it appears to the committee that a better director is available" to run the Biological Experiment Station, he wrote, he hoped the CIW would fund it nonetheless. Not that Davenport believed this: a few weeks later, in a letter to a trustee, he said he was "embarrassed to speak freely" about his qualifications. He then took three full pages to make them irrefutably clear.

When Charles Davenport first encountered eugenics, questions of race or ethnicity could not have been further from his mind. Human biology itself was beyond the broad scope of his interests. He was still teaching zoology at Harvard when he sent reprints of some of his scientific papers to Galton, in 1897. Davenport was particularly interested in the statistical techniques Galton had developed, and his enthusiasm brought genial acknowledgment. "What gratifies me most," Galton told the young scientist, "is that you perceive a unity in my work although there is much variety in the subjects." What gratified the chronically excitable Davenport was the photograph of Galton enclosed in the same letter, a prize he had requested.

Like Galton, Davenport came from a wealthy family with a powerful connection to its own past. His father had written a genealogical history that traced his roots back to Orme de Davenport, "born in the 20th year of William the Conqueror, 1086," and paused to note with button-busting italics that Orme's Pilgrim descendants, who settled New Haven, Connecticut, were "*the constructors of society.*" Also like Galton, Davenport was a counter. As a boy in 1870s Brooklyn, he kept a ledger of every penny that he earned or spent. He recorded weather statistics daily, and by his midteens was providing meteorological data directly to the federal Weather Bureau. Bird migrations, astronomical phenomena, the habits of insects—the abundance and variety of the natural world captured him as a child and kept him enraptured through a lifetime of inquiry and experimentation. Over the course of his career, Charles Davenport studied snails, mice, mosses, canaries, sheep, poultry, mollusks, and various other species. Few contemporaries achieved his stature as an animal geneticist. But the work that would make his wider reputation, and eventually stain it irredeemably, was the study of man.

But that came later. In 1902, when Davenport visited Galton in London on his way home from a European bivalve-hunting expedition, he was preoccupied with his effort to win the Carnegie Institution's backing for his proposed Biological Experiment Station in Cold Spring Harbor. The two men shared a quiet dinner, and the thirty-six-year-old supplicant left with the seventy-nine-year-old master's promise of support. Back home, Davenport kept hammering the Carnegie trustees, the advisory committee, and anyone else he could enlist in the cause. Finally, the trustees granted him $34,250 (the 2019 equivalent of slightly more than a million dollars) to create the Station for Experimental Evolution, plus an additional annual appropriation enabling it "to continue indefinitely, or for a long time." When his appointment to the directorship was confirmed a month later, Davenport commemorated the event with his usual unwieldy combination of self-effacement and rapturous zeal. "Yours unworthily," he wrote at the bottom of the letter he sent to Gertrude that day, reporting the good news. But in the privacy of his diary he all but shouted: "THIS IS A RED LETTER DAY!"

Dynamite exploded on Cold Spring Harbor's western shoreline in the winter of 1904; it was the only way to penetrate the frozen ground before pouring the foundations for the buildings Davenport and his staff would require. The reverberations also marked the beginning of a historic change at the Brooklyn Institute's biological laboratory.

Until then, the warm months in Cold Spring Harbor had belonged to the student biologists at the summer school, who spent their days rambling through the fields and marshes with nets and pails and Mason jars, gathering specimens for laboratory study. "Biology is a science which permits more or less running wild on the part of its devotees," wrote a recent Smith College graduate attending the 1902 summer session. Evenings were given over to what she called "a social atmosphere for relaxation"—campfires, good fellowship, singalongs. The best-loved song was "The Sad Fate of a Youthful Sponge," a zoological rhyme devised by a Smith professor, who set his words to the melody of "The Battle Hymn of the Republic."* These were biology students, after all.

The dedication ceremony for Davenport's new venture was more sober in tone. Among the fifty dignitaries who traveled to Cold Spring Harbor via special rail car on a pleasant June day in 1904 was the featured speaker, Hugo de Vries, director of the botanic

---

* Opening stanza: "There was a little blastula no bigger than a germ / Who performed invagination from his mother's mesoderm. / And soon his nascent cilia with joy began to squirm / In ecstasy supreme."

garden at the University of Amsterdam. De Vries's topic was "The Aims of Experimental Evolution," and his speech was as complex as it was very, very long. Yet his presence at the event, particularly in so prominent a role, was an acknowledgment of a recent discovery that had rewritten the rules of heredity and that, misinterpreted in Cold Spring Harbor, would have a profound effect on the American eugenics movement. Four years earlier, de Vries had been one of three investigators who all but simultaneously rediscovered Gregor Mendel's lost 1866 paper, "Experiments in Hybridization."

The story of Gregor Mendel and his pea plants has been told numberless times: how the humble monk, over the course of seven unnoticed years in the garden of an Augustinian monastery in the Moravian city of Brno, light-years distant from the Royal Societies and International Congresses and the other hubs of British scientific research, crossed and recrossed more than 10,000 pea plants, counted and classified some 300,000 peas, and in the process made one of the most celebrated scientific discoveries in history. But the idea of a recessive trait that could be passed along unnoticed through the generations before suddenly announcing itself in a pair of blue eyes, in great height, or (the early eugenicists would soon believe) in uncommon intelligence, remained unknown to the other scientific explorers of the age, including Galton and Darwin, until 1900, sixteen years after Mendel's death.*

De Vries in fact had already arrived at the same basic insights that Mendel had extracted from his pea plants. By conducting cross-breeding trials with a variety of evening primrose, he established that certain factors of inheritance (soon to become known as genes) were expressions of a specific characteristic (in Mendel's studies, for instance, the color of the flowers on his pea plants); that some of these factors are dominant and others recessive; that a dominant

---

* Eighteen months before he died, Darwin received a copy of a treatise on plant hybrids by the German botanist W. O. Focke. After Darwin's death the book was found in his library, the three pages that mention Mendel's experiments still uncut.

gene would always manifest itself in combination with a recessive gene; and that the recessive gene would nonetheless be passed along to the next generation, expressing itself only if paired with another recessive gene.

Mendel's flowers didn't modulate into pink or mauve or any other in-between hue; they declared themselves either entirely purple (dominant) or entirely white (recessive), which made their color a "unit character"—a specific trait determined by a single pairing of genes. The best example of a unit character in humans is blue eye color, a recessive trait that has a one-in-four chance of expressing itself in a child whose parents both carry the gene that manages it. As would soon be discovered, such binary, on-off determinants were far more common in lower species than in humans.

Human genetics was not a subject of inquiry at the Station for Experimental Evolution at the time of its founding, but the selection of de Vries to inaugurate the work of Davenport's lab was certainly an affirmation of the Mendelian revolution. Although at first resistant, Davenport soon grasped Mendel's importance, partly through the persuasive efforts of British biologist William Bateson, one of the codiscoverers of Mendel's lost paper, who coined the term "genetics." Davenport understood recessive genes. Crucially, though, he got unit characters wrong—a misapprehension that would lead him and his followers down a path strewn with danger and, in time, disaster.

In the station's early years, most of the other experimenters who came to work there were drawn by the alluring combination of Mendel's science, Davenport's missionary zeal, and Carnegie's money. Ten acres adjoining the lab were soon populated by breeding menageries of sheep, cats, finches, snails, moths, and carloads of other species, along with a long line of scientists who were queued up to study them. Marine biologists set up their tanks on the first floor of the main laboratory building, ornithologists and entomologists encamped on the second, and the local people Davenport described as "interesting and intelligent neighbors" made their land available for experiments both botanical and zoological.

Davenport did everything. He prowled pet shops and animal shows to acquire breeding stock, buttonholed those interesting (and in many cases wealthy) neighbors for additional funds, and recruited "corresponding members" working in distant labs (Francis Galton accepted, but only on the condition that the appointment was strictly honorary). He also conducted his own notable studies of chickens and canaries, and began a years-long correspondence with Alexander Graham Bell about the sheep experiments Bell was conducting in Nova Scotia. "I have recently killed off all my four-nippled rams," Bell wrote to Davenport in 1904, "retaining only rams that have six nipples" for breeding. When four-nippled culls inevitably popped up in future generations, he added, Davenport would be welcome to them.

It was the express wish of the U.S. Department of Agriculture to see animal and plant breeders working together that led to the founding of the American Breeders Association; it was the Mendelian revolution that imbued their collaboration with greater meaning. At the ABA's first meeting, in December 1903, attendees heard papers on soybeans, sheep, corn, and teaching "thremmatology"—a recent (and blessedly short-lived) coinage denoting "the science of breeding." At its second meeting, topics included the improvement of cigar-wrapper tobacco and the breeding of mildew-resistant sand cherries. Then, at the 1906 annual conference in Lincoln, Nebraska, eugenics finally made its public debut and the *Washington Post* memorialized the moment. Even in a newspapering era that held little regard for accuracy and less for subtlety, the article bore a headline guaranteed to catch the eye: SCIENCE TO MAKE MEN AND WOMEN BETTER.

The story itself wasn't quite so sanguine about the power of science. It reported that the American Breeders Association had appointed "a committee on eugenics, the science of the breeding of man." The committee didn't have any answers yet, but speaking for the group, Assistant Secretary of Agriculture Willet M. Hays explained that such progress had already been made in "modifying the heredity" of plants and animals through careful crossbreeding that "the question is naturally suggested as to how heredity in man may be improved."

By adding human breeding to its remit, the ABA began the first American effort to elevate Galtonian theory into something both programmatic and, at least as conceived, scientific. The very membership of the committee suggested heft. The chairman was naturalist David Starr Jordan, president of Stanford University. Members included Bell, as celebrated a scientist (even if his science was far removed from biology) as there was in America; Luther Burbank, the "Wizard of Horticulture" who might have been Bell's closest rival in public esteem; the University of Chicago sociologist Charles R. Henderson; and Charles Benedict Davenport of Cold Spring Harbor, New York, who more than anyone else would bring eugenics into wide public consciousness, introduce it into the nation's political debate, and elevate it into the realm of scientific respectability.

Chapter Two

Thrifty, Capable Yankee Blood

When Oliver Wendell Holmes Sr. first called his Boston peers "the Brahmin caste of New England," he defined them gently. For "generation after generation," Holmes wrote in 1860, this breed of "distinct organization and physiognomy" had composed a "harmless, inoffensive, untitled aristocracy."

It's even possible that Dr. Holmes believed that. But if the members of the deeply inbred Boston aristocracy who gathered around Beacon Hill and the Back Bay were truly harmless and inoffensive, it was partly because they perceived no wider world where harm might be inflicted or offense taken. Theirs was an intimacy of both blood and choice. They attended the same schools; they belonged to the same clubs. As children, dressed in velveteen, they all learned the quadrille at Signor Papanti's dancing academy; as adults, traveling, they all stayed at the same hotels. "When the individuals of one group find a complete peace and happiness and fulfillment in the association with one another," asked the narrator of John P. Marquand's novel of Brahmin emotional austerity, *The Late George Apley*, "why should they look farther?" Henry Adams disagreed. Years after he permanently relocated to Washington, DC, in what could only be considered a vain attempt to flee his past, Adams identified a chronic ailment he called Bostonitis. It was, Adams wrote, an inflammation that arose from a sufferer "knowing too much of his neighbors, and thinking too much of himself."

Grandson and great-grandson of presidents, a man whose pedigree on his father's side was equaled in heft by the wealth that came down through his mother, Adams, in fact, approved of very little, himself included. His erudition was matched only by his cynicism, his eloquence by a sort of aesthetic dyspepsia that made him shrink into the past. Born in 1838, he nonetheless considered himself a child of the eighteenth century. By the time the twentieth century arrived and he had written the rumination on medieval Europe he called *Mont Saint-Michel and Chartres*, he had decided he belonged, instead, in the twelfth. But in the famous second sentence of *The Education of Henry Adams*, writing in the third person, Adams reached back yet further to locate himself. "Had he been born in Jerusalem under the shadow of the Temple and circumcised in the Synagogue by his uncle the high priest under the name of Israel Cohen," he wrote, "he would scarcely have been more distinctly branded . . ." than he had been by the Boston he could never truly escape.

It was a telling image for the opening of the book that would forever define him. By the time he wrote *The Education*, which was published privately in 1907, Adams had succumbed to a convulsive anti-Semitism. In Paris during the treason trial of the falsely accused Alfred Dreyfus, he characterized the defendant as "a howling Jew." A trip to Spain and Morocco led him to say he had "seen enough of Jews" and had come to the conclusion that the Spanish Inquisition was "noble." Adams's dear friend the statesman and diplomat John Hay, himself no ally of the new immigrants arriving on American shores, said that when Adams "saw Vesuvius reddening the midnight air he searched the horizon for a Jew stoking the fire."

In *The Education*, Adams was marginally more careful with his animus. But his presentation of one particular Boston recollection might have made concrete what many of his fellow Brahmins perceived. If you try to put yourself in Adams's place—taking into consideration his lineage, his wealth, the era in which he lived—you might be able to understand what he encountered, perhaps while crossing Boston Common. A man in his—what: twenties? thirties? fifties? It was impossible to tell. He wore a long black frock coat of cheap gabardine. His untamed beard spilled down the length of his chest, flakes of dandruff and lint and crumbs marking its path. His face, possibly pockmarked or otherwise scoured and turned ashen by malnutrition, was framed by side curls that fell to his collar. He probably smelled; a bathtub or washbasin was likely unavailable more than once a week to such a man. What Adams saw, he wrote, was "a Polish Jew fresh from Warsaw or Cracow . . . a furtive Yacoob or Ysaac still reeking of the Ghetto, snarling a weird Yiddish." His Yacoob or Ysaac might as readily have been a Giuseppe from the parched farmland of Sicily, or perhaps a Zoltan from the crowded streets of Budapest, and they, too, might have provoked Adams's reaction to the Polish Jew: the stranger's presence in America, he wrote, made Adams identify with "the Indians or the buffalo who had been ejected from their heritage." He wasn't alone.

If Henry Cabot Lodge knew Francis Galton, the evidence is lost in the boundless and scattered correspondence of the latter and in the somewhat bowdlerized letters of the former. But Lodge—politician, scholar, memoirist, xenophobe—certainly knew Galton's work; for one thing, they both published articles in the same journal. More to the point, though: in 1891, just months before Lodge first rose in Congress to urge limits on immigration, he used Galton-like analysis to prove the superiority of his own racial heritage. Taking inspiration from a British article that had sorted "intellect" by geography,* Lodge

---

* No article in *The Nineteenth Century* (the publication Lodge cited) bore the title he mentioned, but he was obviously referring to "On the Geographic Distribution of British Intellect," by a young Hampshire-based physician who later abandoned medicine for a literary career: Arthur Conan Doyle.

sifted through fifteen thousand names in a six-volume encyclopedia of American biography, sorted them by ethnicity and location, and concluded that men of English heritage from Massachusetts occupied the pinnacle of American "ability." Conveniently, there was probably no one more English in heritage nor more firmly planted in the Massachusetts soil than Lodge himself.

There wasn't a box on the Brahmin checklist he didn't tick: Colonial ancestry. Cousined marriage. Generations of engagement, root and branch, with Harvard. A web of familial connections to everyone else who mattered in Boston (including Elizabeth Higginson Cabot, "the common grandmother," as one of her descendants had it, of "Cabots, Jacksons, Lees, Storrows, Paines and other Boston families"). A family seafaring fortune derived in part from trade in opium and slaves wasn't uncommon in Brahmin Boston, either. The subject of Lodge's first book was his great-grandfather George Cabot, who made his name as a Federalist politician, acquired his wealth as a privateer, and forged his politics from a deep loathing for both the French Revolution and the democratic ideas of Thomas Jefferson. Thomas B. Reed, a Mainer who was Speaker of the House for six years, acknowledged that his friend Lodge arose from "thin soil, highly cultivated." Elected to Congress in 1886, Lodge in 1892 entered the Senate, where he would serve six terms. Few politicians stood taller than Henry Cabot Lodge in the politics of late-nineteenth- and earlier-twentieth-century New England, and no one was more certain of his inborn claim to his eminence.

The most memorable accomplishment of Lodge's career was undoubtedly his relentless and successful campaign to shatter Woodrow Wilson's post–World War I dream by keeping the United States out of the League of Nations. But historian George E. Mowry's precise assessment of Lodge could have applied at any point in his decades as a public figure: he was "one of the best informed statesmen of his time . . . an excellent parliamentarian [with] a mind that was at once razor sharp and devoid of much of the moral cant typical of the age." Mowry's appraisal of Lodge's personality was equally acute: "He was opportunistic, selfish, jealous, condescending, supercilious. . . . Most of his colleagues of both parties disliked him, and many distrusted him." When he was defeated for reelection to the Harvard Board of Overseers in 1890—probably as unkind a cut as someone like Lodge could suffer—a commentator said, "The fact is Mr. Lodge's best friends . . . have been disgusted" by his dedication to his own self-interest.

Assessing his patrician bearing, another contemporary said one could "throw a cloak over Lodge's left shoulder and he would step into a Velázquez group in the Prado and be authentic." But reality can eclipse imagination. The superb three-quarter-length portrait of the forty-year-old Lodge that John Singer Sargent painted in 1890, eventually a prized possession of the Smithsonian's National Portrait Gallery, captures him at the very moment he began his Galton-like search for the correlation between ethnicity and talent in that six-volume biographical dictionary. In his vested suit, the fingers of his right hand engaged with his gold watch fob, Lodge emanates a glacial hauteur, his lips tight and severe, his eyes cast with imperious disregard toward some distant point off the canvas. Studying it, you could reasonably feel that you are despoiling him by your very presence. And if the faraway look suggests that he's contemplating the inevitable decline of aristocratic privilege, that would be appropriate as well.

The faint rosiness that Sargent applied to his cheeks provides the only clue that there might be a different Lodge—the one so loyal to his mother, to whom he wrote weekly whenever they were in different cities; so beloved by his much admired wife, Nannie (more formally: Anna Cabot Mills Davis Lodge); and so treasured by his best friend, the gregarious and companionable Theodore Roosevelt. To the public he was Mr. Lodge; to his Brahmin friends he was "Cabot." His intimates, though, called him "Pinky," indicating that somewhere, encased deep within this icy enclosure, there resided at least the potential for human feeling.

As much as Lodge was a creature of Boston, even more was he swaddled in the fabric of an extreme form of Anglo-Saxonism. Early Anglo-Saxon law had been the subject of his doctoral dissertation (his was one of the first PhDs in political science granted by Harvard). He divined that his own ancestry went back to the Norman invaders led by William the Conqueror in 1066. To Lodge's mind they were unquestionably "the most remarkable of all people who poured out of the Germanic forests."

Though his racial views came to him naturally, at least one association helped intensify them: in 1873 the editor of the *North American Review*, who had been his teacher at Harvard, invited Lodge to join him as assistant editor. The *North American* was virtually the private journal of the Brahmin intelligentsia, its circulation minuscule, its contents an expression of the worldviews of the learned Bostonians who had been its editors, among them Edward Everett, Charles Eliot Norton, and James Russell Lowell. Next in this starry line of succession was the man who offered the job to Lodge: Henry Adams, who may have seen his protégé as a potential successor. Adams valued his energy, admired his intellect, and perhaps thought Lodge could alleviate what Adams described as his own "terror": that the *North American* would "die on my hands or go to some Jew."

In the event, the *North American* went to a Mayflower descendant who transplanted it immediately to New York. Adams left Boston permanently for Washington, and Lodge devoted the rest of his life to politics and writing. In the late 1880s, around the same time that Francis Galton first published in the *North American*, Lodge returned to the magazine as an occasional contributor—most notably in an 1891 article that proclaimed it was time to "guard our civilization against an infusion which seems to threaten deterioration." The article's title signified what soon became Lodge's preeminent cause: "The Restriction of Immigration."

Henry Cabot Lodge was the perfect specimen of that class of Brahmins afflicted by Adams's Bostonitis. Joe Lee, equally wellborn, was in most ways his opposite. They were related, of course (it was Lee who had characterized Elizabeth Higginson Cabot as their breed's "common grandmother"), and they both laid claim to Beacon Hill, Harvard, and great wealth. ("Cabots without money are a queer species," Lee once said.) But where Lodge was imperious, Lee had a common touch that made him the most beloved of Bostonians. The fact that Lodge, like most of his class, was a lifelong Republican and Lee an eternal Democrat barely hinted at their differences. Lee—always Joe, never Joseph—battled the era's plutocrats, kept a copy of Marx's *Das Kapital* in his bedroom, and devoted his entire adult life to the support, financial and otherwise, of the principles he believed in.

In Lee's handsome brick house on Beacon Hill, said a friend, "not a day passed without some good deed being done it." Among Lee's many beneficences was the Massachusetts Civic League, which he served, said an admirer, as "founder, official head, leading spirit and generous and constant supporter" (his support included the gift of a nearby bowfront federal-era row house to serve as league headquarters). His role with the Associated Charities of Boston, Lee once said, was "Chairman of the Committee on Difficult Problems," a description he relished. Nationally, he was known as the "Father of the American Playground," the result of his lifelong commitment to children's activities. He poured large sums into such organizations as Community Service of Boston and into the Kowaliga School, a training academy run by and for blacks in central Alabama, and small sums into projects as varied as the English Folk Dance Society and the Women's International League for Peace and Freedom. He forswore his interest in the family's magnificent estate in Beverly Farms, on Boston's North Shore, and spent summers instead in a small beach house on the South Shore, in Cohasset. His idea of entertainment was reading Emerson out loud to his children. On at least one occasion this so excited him that he felt compelled to take a walk to ease the stimulation of the experience. The first important article Lee ever published (and he published nearly as frequently as he breathed) was entitled "Expensive Living—The Blight on America." Once, after he sent a $25,000 donation to Harvard, Lee asked a friend the next day whether it made sense for him to spend $6.50 on a mooring stone for his boat.

Boston adored him. Newspapers extolled his "helpful, sympathetic spirit," his "brotherly smile." He was "whimsical and unusual," a lifelong friend recalled, "extremely original in his personality—he was just Joe, there was no one like him." Tall and thin, bright of eye and quick to smile, he "was the life of the party without telling jokes or stories or making any effort on his part to be jolly. He was just plain pleasure to have around and lent something intangible to any occasion."

One chronicler of New England life called Lee "Boston's most distinguished private citizen." This was the sort of comment that had always made him squirm and that he would usually deflect with droll self-deprecation. At one testimonial dinner, as speaker after speaker offered arias of praise, Lee turned to a companion and whispered, "They are trying to make me out a personage."

The only elective office Joe Lee ever held was a seat on the Boston School Committee, where he could sidestep the dismal factional politics of the day to effect radical change. Soon the city's school-children had annual dental examinations and periodic physicals. Single-handedly, Lee "put the law governing the Extended Use of Schools on the books," said his fellow committee member Judge Michael H. Sullivan. The Extended Use law effectively turned the city's schools, previously a tumultuous clatter of Italians, Irish, Russian Jews, and innumerable other nationalities, into a shared cultural, civic, and recreational asset for all Bostonians. Debates and lectures, dance and music presentations, athletic events and other programs: Could there have been a better way of bringing together polyglot Boston, where 74 percent of the population in 1910 were either immigrants or children of immigrants?

Probably not. But if Joe Lee had truly had a choice, he would have wished the polyglot crowds out of existence, or at least out of Boston. For the one political cause to which this friend of the common man devoted the most time, money, and sheer fervor for more than twenty years was the movement to restrict immigration. When a measure was introduced in the Massachusetts legislature to provide working immigrants with evening sessions for citizenship proceedings, he called it "a vicious naturalization bill." He feared that "all Europe" might soon be "drained of Jews—to its benefit no doubt but not to ours." And in a letter to one of his closest associates he declared that "the Catholic Church is a great evil"; revealed his fear that the United States might "become a Dago nation"; and needed only six words to explain the necessary preventive strategy: "I believe in exclusion by race."

*   *   *

THE ANTI-IMMIGRANT FIRE that began to consume the energies of both Lodge and Lee in the 1890s was hardly confined to Beacon Hill, nor was it new; the country's uncomfortable engagement with immigrants had deep roots. The Europeans flocking to America, a well-known editor wrote in 1753, "are generally the most stupid sort of their own nation," and unless they are turned away they "will soon so outnumber us" that the English language would be imperiled. Those immigrants were German; the offended writer was Benjamin Franklin.

American xenophobia was off to a good start. For decades to come, attitudes toward immigrants formed a perfect sine wave, periods of welcoming inclusiveness alternating with years of scowling antipathy. Early on, though, nascent bias lurked behind a seemingly open door. At the Constitutional Convention in 1787, James Madison made the case for immigration as an engine of national growth and prosperity. Yet at the same time schoolchildren were learning from the ubiquitous *New-England Primer* to "abhor that arrant Whore of Rome," the Catholic Church.* In the 1830s Samuel F. B. Morse, already a well-known painter but not yet celebrated as the inventor of the telegraph, published a rant titled *Foreign Conspiracy Against the Liberties of the United States*, assaulting the "body of foreigners . . . held completely under control of a foreign power" that had sent them here to create a Catholic theocracy. But even then, the young nation continued to absorb without evident pain the relative trickle of immigrants—by most measures barely a million, all told, in the five decades following ratification of the Constitution.

But when the *Phytophthora infestans* fungus devoured the Irish potato crop in the 1840s, hundreds of thousands beset by famine fled to America. Not long after, emigration from Germany accelerated in the wake of the failed revolutions of 1848. Total immigration between 1851 and 1860 alone spiked to more than 2.5 million. The response was so intense and swift that a political party devoted to an extreme form of nativism was able to elect five U.S. senators, forty-three House members, and seven governors within six years of its founding. Originally organized as the secret Order of the Star Spangled Banner, then officially known as the American Party, its more familiar name arose after members were instructed, when asked about the group, to say "I know nothing." But the Know Nothings did not hide their goals. In Massachusetts, a Know Nothing governor was elected to three terms beginning in 1854 and led an eagerly compliant legislature to enact a law denying the vote to those who could not read and write in English—even if they had already been naturalized as citizens. To twenty-first-century eyes, any overlap

---

* Among the *Primer*'s rather more useful contributions to the American character: the quatrain that begins, "Now I lay me down to sleep / I pray the Lord my soul to keep."

between New England's nineteenth-century abolitionists and its immigration restrictionists might appear to be counterintuitive. But among the antislavery campaigners it was not at all unlikely: many agreed with Frederick Douglass, who in 1855 condemned a system that allowed "the colored people [to be] elbowed out of employment" by European immigrants.

Labor surpluses were at the very heart of much of the restrictionism that continued to seethe throughout the rest of the nineteenth century (and would recur periodically well into the twenty-first). But when the labor market was tight, principles were loosened. During the Civil War, when the Union's need for both the instruments of war and the men who would wage it turned surpluses into severe shortages, Abraham Lincoln asked Congress to find a way to *increase* immigration. The nation, he said, could tap into the "tens of thousands of persons, destitute of remunerative occupations" who were "thronging our foreign consulates and offering to emigrate to the United States." Congress quickly obliged, passing "an act to encourage immigration" in 1864.

Operating under this authorization, the American Emigrant Company sent its agents abroad, largely to England and the Scandinavian countries, to recruit laborers on behalf of mining companies and other businesses suffering manpower shortages. Employers were obliged to pay the AEC for the immigrants' passage across the Atlantic (a voyage conducted, the advertisements promised, "with the most careful regard to comfort and safety"), and the immigrants were obliged in turn to repay their employers from their wages. One of the founders of this venture in "contract labor"—a rather more benign term than the equally accurate "indentured servitude"—was a former senator from Connecticut; its supporters included several exemplary abolitionists who did not share Frederick Douglass's concerns, among them Charles Sumner and Henry Ward Beecher.

Until the brief life of the 1864 act (postwar recession led to its revocation in 1868), the federal government had kept its hands off immigration policy. But by the early 1880s, two factors compelled Congress to seize control of the issue. The first—the patchwork of state laws and regulations, particularly involving per capita "head taxes" that were meant to cover the cost of newly necessary social services—was largely procedural.* The second was driven by—there's no other word for it—race hatred.

The Chinese Exclusion Act of 1882, which halted immigration of all "skilled and unskilled [Chinese] laborers," arose from the boiling resentment toward Chinese immigrants that dated back to their initial arrival in large numbers in the wake of the 1849 gold rush, numbers soon amplified by the railroad companies' ravening hunger for cheap labor. ("Why should I pay a fireman six dollars a day for work that a Chinaman would do for fifty cents?" asked James J. Hill of the Northern Pacific.) As early as 1854 it was unlawful in California for a Chinese person to testify in court against a white. In 1878 the U.S. Supreme Court barred Chinese and other Asian immigrants from citizenship. The Fifteenth Amendment, enacted just eight years earlier, had eliminated race as a criterion for denying citizens the right to vote—but it said nothing about the right to citizenship itself.

Americans of the era, especially in the western states, harbored what one newspaperman called an "instinctive hatred of the Chinese," and the 1882 law—extended in 1892, made permanent in 1902, and anchored in legislative and judicial cement until 1943—institutionalized it. It also provided implicit sanction for immigration opponents to base their arguments not solely on the labor issues that underpinned the statute but on notions of racial inferiority. American Federation of Labor president Samuel Gompers, who would hold his anti-immigration stance unflinchingly for decades (though himself an immigrant Jew from England), could say that

---

* The western states in particular were incensed that New York, for instance, collected a head tax from a newly arrived laborer, but if he found his way west and into a poorhouse or a jail, he became a financial burden to the state that housed him.

THROWING DOWN THE LADDER BY WHICH THEY ROSE.

Thomas Nast cartoon, 1870.

the Chinese "have no standard of morals." The editor of the *Fresno Republican* could call the Chinese "biped domestic animals in the white man's service." When sociologist Edward Alsworth Ross, a prominent progressive academic who would become one of the leading intellectual patrons of the immigration restriction movement, made the case for excluding Chinese laborers, he did not flinch from invoking racial characteristics: "the yellow man" is a threat to the white man, he wrote, "because he can better endure spoiled food, poor clothing, foul air, noise, heat, dirt, discomfort, and microbes. Reilly can [outwork] Ah-San, but Ah-San can underlive Reilly."

The rising numbers of Chinese immigrants might have posed a problem in the western states, but to most New Englanders they might as well have been populating the moon (Henry Cabot Lodge's idea of the West, said a political associate, was Pittsfield, Massachusetts). Boston's eyes were cast east, toward the polyglot jumble of Austria-Hungary, the vast reaches of the Russian Empire, the impoverished villages of southern Italy. In 1882 fewer than 15 percent of European immigrants came from the regions east of Germany and south of present-day Austria. Then everything changed.

Factors both general and specific initiated the explosion in immigration that would accelerate so powerfully for the next forty years. The relative infrequency of war in the post-Napoleonic era, a decline in the infant death rate, and in some countries the gradual spread of sanitary practices had more than doubled the population of Europe in less than a century. The weblike spread of railroads across the continent had made ocean ports accessible, and the age of steam had increased the speed of transatlantic passage and the capacity of the ships making the voyage.

Those were by and large salutary changes. Others, however, were cruel. In 1881 the assassination of Czar Alexander II became the ostensible justification for an unchecked wave of pogroms inflicted on Jews in the Russian Empire, compounding the already straitened circumstances that had long circumscribed their lives. The anti-Semitic May Laws of 1882 placed restrictions on the right of Jews to settle in certain areas and on their freedom to conduct business. By one estimate, total Russian Jewish immigration to the United States in the 1880s leapt to 140,000, a sevenfold increase from the previous decade. In southern Italy, desperate poverty and the remnants of medieval vassalage were made combustible by a cholera epidemic that killed more than 50,000 and provoked widespread panic and flight. In 1877 only 3,600 Italians immigrated to the United States; by 1887 the annual number had increased more than twelvefold. In the same period, Polish immigration multiplied by fifteen times, Hungarian by twenty-six. Greeks, Serbs, Slovaks, Ukrainians, Albanians, Ruthenians—it was as if all of eastern Europe were emptying out. In 1888 the American Economic Association, taking note, announced a prize contest: $150 for the best essay on "The Evil Effects of Unrestricted Immigration."

It was around this same time that patrician Bostonians took note of the changing nature of immigration and realized that this new wave was different from the earlier one they had experienced—and they had hardly tolerated that one. The first refugees from the Irish potato famine had begun to arrive in Boston Harbor in 1845. Ten years later, the city was 20 percent Irish. In the eyes of the Unitarian abolitionist Theodore Parker—he was one of the so-called Secret Six who financed John Brown's raid on Harpers Ferry—the "American Athens" was becoming the "American Dublin." Charles Francis Adams Jr., Henry's older brother, railed against universal suffrage, predicting a "government of ignorance and vice [dominated by] a European, and especially Celtic, proletariat on the Atlantic Coast."* Charles Eliot Norton—a man of unchallenged cultivation and worldliness, friend to Charles Darwin, committed reformer, admired scholar—wistfully invoked the "higher and pleasanter level" of New England "before the invasion of the Irish." But in 1884 Boston elected its first Irish mayor, and only those afflicted by a willful social blindness could not see the city's political future.

Still, as conscious of (and even as repelled by) the Irish as the Brahmins were, they *knew* them, or at least believed that the

---

* Adams didn't stop on his side of the Alleghenies. He also foresaw, with equal distaste, government in the hands of "an African proletariat on the shores of the Gulf, and a Chinese proletariat in the Pacific." And lest the third Adams brother be left out of this collection of family incantations, it's worth quoting Brooks, the youngest, writing in the aftermath of the Panic of 1893: "Rome was a blessed garden of paradise beside the rotten, unsexed, swindling, lying Jews, represented by J. P. Morgan and the gang who have been manipulating our country for the last four years."

relationship between an employer and his servants yielded meaningful knowledge. That both groups spoke the same language was not an uncomplicated truth; on the other side of the Atlantic, their respective forebears had been locked in the uneasy embrace of colonizer and colonized since the time of Henry VIII. But when one insulted the other, which they did with equal passion, translation was unnecessary.

Then came Adams's furtive, reeking, snarling Yacoob and Ysaac. And Giuseppe and Luigi and Mario, Janos and Miloslav and Leszek. The so-called new immigration from eastern and southern Europe that began to gather momentum in the early 1880s would change Boston nearly as much as the Irish immigration had. By 1900 more than 400,000 Bostonians, out of a population of 560,000, had at least one foreign-born parent. The city's North and West Ends became swarming hives of strange sounds, strange smells, strange people. African Americans had lived in the West End for decades, and though abolitionist ardor rarely extended to any commitment to social equality, the city's black population was at least familiar. The newcomers were an invasive species. "No sound of English, in a single instance, escaped their lips," an astonished Henry James wrote after visiting Boston for the first time in twenty years. The recent Italian immigrants James encountered on Boston Common were "gross little aliens." Sociologist Frederick A. Bushee was horrified: "There are actually streets in the West End, while Jews are moving in, negro housewives are gathering up their skirts and seeking a more spotless environment."

The poverty that had compelled the immigrants to leave their homelands and endure a transatlantic crossing in steerage was nearly unimaginable. In his futurist novel *Looking Backward*, published in 1888, Edward Bellamy describes his time traveler, Julian West, encountering "pale babies gasping out their lives amid sultry stenches, of hopeless faced women deformed by hardship." When Julian tries to bring this "festering mass of human wretchedness" to the attention of a group of wealthy Bostonians gathered at an elegant dinner party in a Commonwealth Avenue mansion, barely a mile away from "streets and alleys that reeked with the effluvia of a slave ship's between-decks," they are indifferent. "Do none of you know what sights the sun and stars look down on in this city," he cries, "that you can think and talk of anything else? Do you not know that close to your doors a great multitude of men and women, flesh of your flesh, live lives that are one agony from birth to death?"

They did not. Dr. Richard Clarke Cabot—another cousin of both Lodge and Lee—was a staff physician at Massachusetts General Hospital (and taught social ethics at Harvard on the side). MGH was perched at the edge of the West End, and a typical day would bring thirty patients through his office. On one such day, Cabot experienced a sort of Brahmin epiphany. "Abraham Cohen, of Salem Street, approaches, and sits down to tell me the tale of his sufferings," Cabot wrote. "The chances are ten to one that I shall look out of my eyes and see, *not* Abraham Cohen, but a *Jew*; not the sharp clear outlines of this unique sufferer, but the vague, misty composite photograph of all the hundreds of Jews who in the past ten years have shuffled up to me with bent back and deprecating eyes. I see a Jew,—a nervous, complaining, whimpering Jew,—with his beard upon his chest and the inevitable dirty black frock-coat flapping about his knees. I do not see *this* man at all. I merge him in the hazy background of the average Jew."

Cabot's sudden awakening was profound in its effect. He would soon bring the first Jewish doctors onto MGH's staff (when the hospital was already 101 years old, he noted dyspeptically), and also served as head of the medical staff at the city's first Jewish hospital. But his encounter with Mr. Cohen of Salem Street illustrated the relationship between the old Boston and the new. To wellborn Bostonians of the 1880s and 1890s, the immigrants in their midst were simultaneously invisible and in plain sight. "The trouble with Boston," Charles Francis Adams Jr. insisted, "is that there is no current of outside life everlastingly flowing in and passing out." The presence of the immigrants was palpable, but their substance was not.

*   *   *

"THE DUDE OF NAHANT"*—that's what Henry Cabot Lodge was called early in his public life, after both his manner and the narrow finger of land north of Boston that he considered his "ancestral acres." Other epithets quickly adhered to him as he began to climb the political ladder, first as a member of the Massachusetts legislature, then in his campaigns for Congress in the 1880s: "Lah-de-Dah" Lodge, "the Silver Spoon Young Man." But it would be unfair to suggest that Lodge was nothing more than a pampered aristocrat who wore his narrow racism as securely as he did the eight-button vest in Sargent's portrait. The same sort of reform instincts that inspired Joe Lee harmonized with something deep within the Brahmin soul and resonated with Lodge as well. Seeming contradictions occupied the same mind comfortably. Celebrant of inherited privilege, Lodge was also Congress's most fervent advocate for the meritocracy of the civil service. "Although rich by any standard," a biographer wrote, "he had an aristocratic disdain for what were called in that day 'robber barons.'" Assailant of the immigrant "other," Lodge's advocacy of black voting rights was unshakable.

Still, the posture Lodge assumed when, in 1891, he began his campaign for the mandatory use of a literacy test to screen out unworthy immigrants was a peculiar one. The idea of a literacy test was initially put forward by Edward W. Bemis, a socialist economist and labor union advocate, in an obscure Massachusetts theological journal. Bemis was not above a little Anglo-Saxon chest-thumping ("vigorous New England stock . . . hardy yeomanry . . . best elements of English life") but his argument was in both its general thrust and its particulars almost exclusively economic: the immigration of unskilled workers lowered American wages. A literacy test requiring the immigrant to prove he could read in his native language was the surest way to weed out those unfit for anything but manual labor.

---

* Some sources say "Duke," not "Dude"—but they're wrong. See Notes, page 407.

That apparently sounded useful to the well-tuned ears of an adept politician. The overriding reason for such a law, Lodge wrote in the *North American Review,* was to serve "as a protection and a help to our workingmen, who are more directly interested in this great question than any one else can possibly be." When he introduced federal legislation mandating a literacy test for immigrants in February 1891, he asked the *Congressional Record* to append the article to his remarks from the House floor. It contained a litany of phrases that might have come from an American Federation of Labor brochure: "unskilled labor . . . flood of low-class labor . . . absolutely destroy good rates of wages . . . tendency toward a decline in wages . . . pulling down the wages of the working people . . . reducing the rates of wages . . . maintain the rate of American wages . . ." The Lah-de-Dah Dude of Nahant was now Henry Cabot Lodge, Friend of Labor.

THE INEVITABLE RESULT TO THE AMERICAN WORKINGMAN OF INDISCRIMINATE IMMIGRATION.

A typical characterization of an Italian immigrant, from 1892.

[Unlike Edward Bemis, though, Lodge was not content to let economics alone bear the burden of his desires. He knew that literacy rates in the impoverished regions of southern Italy and parts of the Jewish Pale of Settlement in western Russia and adjacent lands were exceedingly low, and thus exceedingly useful.] "The immigration of people of those races which contributed to the settlement and development of the United States," he said from the well of the House, "is declining in comparison with that of races far removed in thought and speech and blood from the men who have made this country what it is." He wanted to "sift the chaff from the wheat." [America's problems, he said, were "race problems."] If he'd had a copy of his recently published history of Boston at hand, he could have shared with his colleagues a sentiment he expressed in its pages with startling frankness: "Race pride or race prejudice, or whatever it may be called . . . has long since ceased to be harmful." And, he added with a complacent flourish, "it has had other effects which have been of very real value."

The comprehensive immigration bill Congress passed that session did not contain Lodge's literacy test. Even so, the 1891 law was a landmark as imposing as the expanded immigration center on Ellis Island scheduled to open at the end of the year. The law formally placed all immigration policy and enforcement under federal control; ordered deportation of aliens who entered the country illegally; and provided for the rejection of "idiots, insane persons . . . persons suffering from a loathsome or a dangerous disease," and various other undesirables, including polygamists. These were added to the list of those barred under previous laws, mainly convicts, paupers, and the equally despised Chinese.

To Lodge and others like him, the 1891 act was insufficient. But the debate did provide respectable cover for the expansion of anti-immigrant sentiment. Fearful of a multiplying "foreign vote," the editors of *The Nation* warned that stricter tests needed to be applied either at the port of departure or the port of arrival, for if the

immigrant "is once let loose, all precautions about him are idle." The
New York Times reported darkly on a violent "secret Polish society"
in the Shenandoah Valley. A mob in New Orleans lynched eleven
Italian immigrants, reputedly members of the Mafia, who had been
accused—and then acquitted—of the murder of the city's police chief.
(Lodge shook an admonitory finger at the rioters but insisted that
"such acts as the killing of these eleven Italians do not spring from
nothing without reason or provocation" —namely "the utter care-
lessness with which we treat immigration in this country.") Months
later, when a few young Russian Jews were hired at a New Jersey
glass factory, its workers embarked on three days of xenophobic riots.

THE AMERICAN RIVER GANGES.

Thomas Nast cartoon, 1871: Catholic prelates perceived as amphibious beasts.

The financial panic that gripped the country that same year
enabled the anti-Catholic American Protective Association to attain
a membership approaching a million. The organization had been

founded in Iowa in 1887 by a small-town lawyer convinced that Jesuits were "winding their fingers long and bony around the throat of this nation." When a crowd of restrictionists was elected to Congress in 1894, the APA could claim plausible credit. For the literacy test—and for Lodge—the winds could not have been more favorable.

* * *

ON MAY 31, 1894, the day the Immigration Restriction League was born in a law office in downtown Boston, more than two thousand Italian immigrants gathered just a hundred yards away in historic Faneuil Hall, the "Cradle of Liberty," to address a number of the problems they faced in their new country. Seven different immigrant organizations were represented. The main address in English was delivered by the secretary of the Massachusetts Society for Promoting Good Citizenship, who said, "As an American I desire to call attention of the city of Boston to the many abuses which these poor people have to suffer."

The young men who met that same afternoon in the nearby law office on State Street thought such attention misplaced. This proved to be especially so for three of them, who would play instrumental roles in the organization created that day. All three had been classmates not only at Harvard (Class of '89) but before that at G. W. C. Noble's Classical School for Boys on Beacon Hill. All three were situated culturally, socially, and economically at the interlocked, self-contained, and impermeable center of the Boston patriciate. The meeting had been initiated by Robert DeCourcy Ward, whose ancestors had arrived in Boston with John Winthrop in 1630. Prescott Farnsworth Hall was part of what his wife described as one of "the old-time families [who] spent the winters in Boston and summers in Brookline"—which is to say that they would pack off for the country each June . . . and travel four miles west. But that signified wealth, not lineage, and Hall felt the need to establish his "old-time" credibility by invoking his direct descent from Charlemagne. The third cofounder, Charles Warren, needed only to trace his ancestry back to at least three passengers on the *Mayflower*.

As young as they were, Ward, Warren, and Hall were not without other distinctions. Ward, Harvard's first professor of climatology, joined the faculty in 1891, at twenty-four. Later in life Warren would win the Pulitzer Prize for *The Supreme Court in United States History*. Hall never attained his classmates' level of eminence, but this was not for want of effort; he engaged in several of the reform movements of the day and wrote books on landlord-tenant law. Apart from the restriction cause, Hall's other passions included Wagnerian opera, Rosicrucianism, miraculous healing, and what he called "psychical research." A lifelong depressive and insomniac raised by his invalid mother "like a hothouse plant" (said Hall's wife), he was socially awkward, detached, unworldly. But of the three, he would make the greatest commitment to immigration restriction. One of his colleagues said "he did the work of ten men" to advance the cause.

Judging by Warren's brief minutes of the first few meetings, one could explain the formation of the IRL with an adage common to the era: "no two Bostonians could have an idea in common without forming a club around it." The league's founders, none older than twenty-seven, might puff their chests with pride in their philosophical commitment (as the IRL constitution phrased it) to "the further judicious restriction or stricter regulation of immigration." But if anything material was to come of it, they would have to reach beyond their own youthful circle.

At this, the men of the IRL were superb. To invoke another Boston aphorism, this one contrived by Oliver Wendell Holmes Jr., "No generalization is wholly true, not even this one"—but to say that the Brahmins and their close associates were receptive to the IRL's argument was about as wholly true as a generalization could be. They recruited the widely admired historian and lecturer John Fiske to serve, at least nominally, as the league's president. Boston's leading philanthropist, Robert Treat Paine, signed on as a vice president, as did Henry Lee, Joe Lee's father. Vice presidencies of organizations like the IRL were largely honorific, even if more so for the organization than for the individual: a group like the IRL could acquire an affirming aura from the shiny names on its letterhead.

One who chose to support the IRL financially, but on the condition that his name was *not* used, was John Murray Forbes. Possibly Boston's wealthiest man, Forbes built his fortune in the Chinese opium trade, multiplied it in the railroad industry, then put it to use to support abolitionists and to finance publication of *The Nation*, which was founded in 1865 with his backing.

Forbes was in his eighties when Charles Warren asked him to join the IRL. Writing from Naushon Island, a seven-and-a-half-square-mile paradise off Cape Cod that Forbes had purchased in 1842 (and where his descendants continue to spend their summers 177 years later), Forbes prefaced his letter with an emphatically underscored "Strictly private." In elegant longhand reaching down the page from a letterhead adorned with an engraving of a handsome yawl, five sails flying, Forbes promised financial support. He couldn't have been clearer about the reason. "The great struggle . . . ," Forbes told Warren, "centers on keeping our voting power and our reserves of public lands out of the reach . . . of the horde of half-educated and wholly unreliable foreigners now bribed to migrate here, who under our present system can be dumped down on us annually."

True to Brahmin form, Forbes concluded his letter by asking Warren if he was "the son of our [customs] collector Winslow Warren, and thus closely connected with many of my intimate family friends of years past." The Boston aristocracy was one family, and with very few exceptions the family was lined up against the tide of immigration.

Joe Lee had not been present at the founding meeting of the IRL, but his association with the organization was inevitable. He had tiptoed into charity work in his late twenties but still had not found the single driving passion he so earnestly sought; at twenty-seven he'd even traveled to Russia to seek advice from Leo Tolstoy, whom he found a "mere old crank" on philosophical questions (though he did enjoy their conversation about Beethoven). To Lee, there was no contradiction in his determination to improve the lot of Boston's immigrant poor and his simultaneous wish to bar, or at least narrow, the door they entered through. Uneducated, unpropertied, and unwashed they might be, but the alien crowds bursting the bounds of Boston's slums in the early 1890s were an intractable Fact, and they could not be expected to adapt without assistance. Charitable aid could be offered out of a sense of openhearted generosity, or it could emanate from a very different impulse: the conviction that whatever pestilence the immigrants brought—disease, crime, dependency, anarchy—was a contagion that, unchecked, would infect the entire city. Extending assistance to the immigrants in order to protect the privileges of the wealthy was hardly a paradox; it was simple self-preservation. For a classic progressive like Lee, helping the masses who were already here was just, and it was judicious. To keep more from arriving was at least the latter.

Lee was thirty-two and on a nine-month tour of Europe in 1894 when the immigration problem began to nag at him; he even wrote to an official at the Massachusetts State Board of Lunacy and Charity, requesting copies of the U.S. immigration laws. That same summer John F. Moors—one more cousin, who managed the family money and was probably Lee's closest friend—wrote to tell Lee what the young men of the IRL were up to.

Lee had spent three weeks in St. Moritz to indulge in the essential Grand Tour luxury of "taking the baths," a pause before traveling to London to indulge in a characteristic Joe Lee endeavor: discussing socialism and trade unions with various Englishmen. He wrote to

Margaret Copley Cabot—yet another cousin, but in this instance soon to become his wife—and repeated Moors's news: "There is a society started in Boston to do the work I thought of." Less than a year later Prescott Hall, seeking funds, sent Lee a recent league publication that Hall considered the IRL "bible." Its title was "Study These Figures and Draw Your Own Conclusions." The figures indicated that the percentage of immigrants coming from northwestern Europe had dropped from 74 percent in 1869 to 48 percent in 1894, while the percentage coming from eastern Europe and Italy over the same period had soared from 1 percent to 42 percent.

If any readers of the IRL pamphlet had difficulty coming to the conclusion Hall desired, he might have directed them to a letter he sent to the *Boston Herald* in June 1894: "Shall we permit these inferior races to dilute the thrifty, capable Yankee blood . . . of the earlier immigrants?" This may have been the first public expression of the undergirding of the restriction movement: that the impoverished steerage passengers disgorged daily at the Long Wharf immigration station—and at Ellis Island down the coast in New York, and in Baltimore and Philadelphia and other port cities—were not merely different. They were biologically inferior.

Joe Lee didn't sign on immediately, but this first direct contact with the IRL augured what was soon to come: a four-decade engagement with the league as its primary financial underwriter, its leading strategist, its personal emissary to four U.S. presidents. The Immigration Restriction League could not have existed without him.

*   *   *

ELEVATED TO THE SENATE IN 1892, Henry Cabot Lodge soon began his effort to reintroduce the literacy test, drawing support from the constituency he valued most: in a general sense, the people Oliver Wendell Holmes Sr. had called Boston's "sifted few." Boston's best had begun to declare themselves for restriction around the time that

Phillips Brooks, the Episcopal bishop of Massachusetts who served as a sort of Brahmin moral conscience, joined the Sons of the American Revolution. It was an act, he said, meant to signify his belief that "our dear land at least used to be American."* Then along came the passionate young founders of the Immigration Restriction League and the name-brand officers they had recruited among the Boston elite. The IRL aligned itself with Lodge in what was effectively its first public action, the release of a fourteen-page pamphlet calling for an "educational test" to weed out the unwanted.

But it was someone Lodge had known and been allied with politically for two decades whose public support for restriction went far beyond decorating the stationery of the IRL with his name. Francis Amasa Walker's array of credentials conferred an authority that Lodge, despite his political eminence and his writerly achievements, could not hope to attain: Civil War hero (wounded at Chancellorsville, retired as brigadier general), economist ("the favorite and obvious choice" to be first president of the American Economic Association), public servant (commissioner of Indian Affairs, director of the U.S. Census), and educator (third president of the Massachusetts Institute of Technology).

Lodge may have previously referenced the "race problem," but once clad in his help-the-workingman disguise he was required to make his racial points obliquely. Walker was as direct as a bullet. In an article in the *Yale Review*, he described the new immigrants as "vast masses of filth" who came from "every foul and stagnant pool of population in Europe." Arguing for a $100 entry fee for all new immigrants—the 2019 equivalent of nearly $3,000—he made the case that such an amount "would not prevent tens of thousands of thrifty Swedes, Norwegians, Germans" and the like from entering,

* To this day the bishop's legacy is commemorated in the Phillips Brooks House Association, a 117-year-old Harvard student organization that "strives for social justice" and counts diversity and community building among its primary goals. He is somewhat less well known as the lyricist of "O Little Town of Bethlehem."

but would debar the impoverished multitudes of eastern and southern Europe. He drew on Jacob Riis's compassionate account of life in the ghettoes of New York, *How the Other Half Lives*, not to evoke sympathy but to inspire loathing: the people Riis met were["living like swine." They engaged in "systematic beggary at the doors of the rich" and "picking over the garbage barrels in our alleys."]In a footnote that was essentially an exasperated aside, Walker paused in his peroration to ask, "Will the reader trouble himself to remember by what sort of men and women this country was first settled?"

Surely not the people he later described with the five words that would be invoked repeatedly over the next quarter century by those who judged immigrants not by their worth as individuals but by the presumed deficiencies embedded in their ancestry. The immigrants filling the halls of Ellis Island, standing in queues on Long Wharf, and waiting expectantly at every other immigration portal, wrote this former head of the Census Bureau (who presumably ought to know), were "beaten men from beaten races."

"Where Mrs. Lodge summoned, one followed with gratitude," wrote Henry Adams, "and so it chanced that in August [1895] one found one's self for the first time at Caen, Coutances, and Mont-Saint-Michel in Normandy."

It was on this five-month voyage in the grand style (it also took in London and Spain) that Adams, traveling with the Lodges, discovered the mystical connection to the twelfth century he evoked in *Mont-Saint-Michel and Chartres*. Lodge, in turn, found lavish evidence of the Norman brilliance he considered his inheritance— the cathedral at Amiens, the Bayeux Tapestries, Mont-Saint-Michel itself. On the other side of the racial ledger, he came up with his own version of Francis Walker's epithet: traveling in Spain, Lodge determined that the "repellent" Spaniards were "a beaten & broken race." He also discovered a recent book by the sociologist Gustave

LeBon, *Les Lois Psychologiques de l'Évolution des Peuples* (published subsequently in English as *The Psychology of Peoples*). As Walker's work would help free Lodge to express his xenophobic contempt without trimming his language, LeBon's gave his arguments the illusion of scholarly gravity.

Gustave LeBon was a physician, anthropologist, and pathbreaking sociologist whose most enduring concept (praised by Freud, adapted by Hitler) was the mind—or, perhaps more accurately, the mindlessness—of "the crowd." He also despised democracy, trembled at the thought of socialism, considered women biologically inferior, and believed the history of race explained the history of the world. Adams and the Lodges returned to the United States from their European journey in November 1895. Four months later, when Lodge rose to address the Senate about the need for a literacy test for all immigrants, he had internalized LeBon's racial arguments so thoroughly one might have suspected a form of transatlantic ventriloquism.

Referring to the Frenchman as "a distinguished writer of the highest scientific training and attainments," Lodge offered a hymn to "the qualities of the American people, whom [LeBon], as a man of science looking below the surface, rightly describes as homogeneous." To make his case, he first treated his Senate colleagues to a capsule history of the Western world ("capsule" is actually the wrong word; it went on for paragraph after lengthy paragraph) that began with the Roman conquest, arched through the migrations of the Celtic and Germanic tribes, and then alit upon the Norsemen, ancestors of his own Norman forebears. "They came upon Europe in their long, low ships," Lodge intoned, sounding more like a 1930s-era newsreel narrator than a Gilded Age politician, "a set of fighting pirates and buccaneers, and yet these same pirates brought with them out of the darkness and cold of the north a remarkable literature," as well as "the marvels of Gothic architecture." And, most important, "these people"—along with their British descendants, and the French Huguenots, and the Dutch and Swedes, and even the Irish*—were "welded together and [then] made a new speech and a new race."

[There was no avoiding it: no longer making the slightest attempt to hedge his language or suppress his prejudices, Lodge told the Senate that a literacy test "will bear most heavily upon the Italians, Russians, Poles, Hungarians, and Asiatics, and very lightly, or not at all, upon English-speaking emigrants." And, he argued, why should it be otherwise? "The races most affected by the illiteracy test† are those . . . with which the English-speaking people have never hitherto assimilated, and are alien to the great body of the people of the United States."]This was the crux of the campaign for the literacy test that would focus the immigration debate for nearly a quarter of a century, with Lodge as its primary champion, evangelist, and propagandist: the test was a simple device that could be used to keep out precisely those nationalities that Lodge wanted to keep out.

Lodge's speeches were singular; no one else could possibly have delivered them. His voice, once likened to "the tearing of a bed sheet," was reedy and metallic. His literary allusions—taken from Carlyle, Macaulay, Matthew Arnold—were recondite. He had the irksome habit of presenting his arguments like a demagogue engaging with followers hungry for confirmation, not evidence:["*No one*" desires the new immigrants; "*everybody* now admits" the wisdom of Chinese exclusion; "*history teaches us*" that "if a lower race mixes with a higher in sufficient numbers . . . the lower race will prevail."]

Now, as he approached the end of his speech, he cast aside allusion, stepped away from stipulation, and landed at the heart of his

---

* The Irish had long been an affront to Lodge, but after he embarked on his political career, he had to temper his tempers. The people he had once characterized as "hard-drinking, idle, quarrelsome, and disorderly" now carried a terser designation—"Massachusetts voters"—and were consequently spared his invective.

† Lodge and his allies always favored the term "illiteracy test," but in later iterations (as in this book) "literacy test" became the more broadly used terminology.

argument: keeping the nation open to the new immigrants posed the "single danger" that could devastate the "mental and moral qualities which make what we call our race." He did not hold back: "The danger," he declared, "has begun."

But even then, Lodge wasn't through. It was a reflection of the times, and also of Lodge's literary inclinations, that he hoped to inspire the anti-immigration forces with a poem. Thirteen years earlier it was poetry that had, in a way, first set the terms of the immigration debate. Emma Lazarus had only recently awakened to the persecution of Jews in the Russian Empire when she was asked in 1883 to help raise money for the construction of the Statue of Liberty's pedestal. By then, this nonobservant Jew (of purest Sephardic origin) had already been celebrated by Boston's best. Ralph Waldo Emerson had invited the young poet to visit him in Concord. Henry James, living now in France, engaged her in friendly correspondence. And just two weeks after Lazarus first gave a public reading of the poem that would soon decorate the statue's base—and that still expresses the statue's essence—James Russell Lowell wrote to declare his admiration. To Lowell, whose anti-Semitic impulses were just as instinctive (if not quite as grotesque) as Henry Adams's, Lazarus's passionate invitation to "the huddled masses / yearning to breathe free" was nonetheless "just the right word to be said." It gave the statue, he wrote, "a *raison d'être*."

But it was the music of a very different immigration poem that heralded Henry Cabot Lodge's *raison* on the Senate floor on March 16, 1896. Its author, Thomas Bailey Aldrich, was the worst sort of Boston snob, which is to say a late convert to the conventions of Beacon Hill and the Back Bay. Born in New Hampshire to a family of modest means, he'd made his early reputation in New York before settling into a five-story mansion (plus cupola) on Mount Vernon Street, just down the block from Joe Lee's house. Like Lowell he served as editor of the *Atlantic Monthly*, and like Lowell he was venerated by Lodge as a paragon of Bostonian virtue.

Aldrich was also a poet and novelist of facile but evident gifts, and as Lodge seized leadership of the anti-immigration movement in Congress, Aldrich became its de facto laureate. His anthemic text, obviously a response to Lazarus, was called "Unguarded Gates." No one described it more accurately than Aldrich himself, who said his poem was a "misanthropic" work expressing his "protest against America becoming a cesspool of Europe." Following nineteen stirring lines proclaiming America an "enchanted land / . . . A later Eden planted in the wilds," Aldrich gets to his point:

> Wide open and unguarded stand our gates,
> And through them presses a wild motley throng . . .
> Flying the Old World's poverty and scorn . . .
> Accents of menace alien to our air . . .
> O Liberty, white Goddess! Is it well
> To leave the gates unguarded? . . .

Just as Lazarus's "Give me your tired, your poor . . ." would come to serve and to inspire immigration advocates over the years, so would Lodge's invocation of Aldrich's unguarded gates still be invoked in the halls of Congress as those gates slammed shut nearly three decades later.

Lodge could not have asked for a better reception to his speech. His friend Theodore Roosevelt, the thirty-seven-year-old New York City police commissioner, wrote to tell him it was "an A-1 speech," and that he had even written to France for copies of LeBon's works. (Roosevelt was yet another cousin of Joe Lee's, although in this case only by marriage.) Newspaper support in Boston was hearty (the *Advertiser* said the speech was "among the most scholarly and logical discussions [of immigration] in recent times"), and papers across the country picked up an item that likely would have delighted Lodge had he learned about it: members of the "Russian-Nihilistic Club" of Chicago burned him in effigy. He had even been able to keep out of his bill a measure introduced by his Massachusetts colleague Senator George F. Hoar that would have provided an exemption for refugees from war or political oppression.

The test Lodge's bill proposed was really very simple: immigrants sixteen and older would have to prove their eligibility for entry into the country by reading five lines of the U.S. Constitution, translated into their own language [A provision exempting women from the test had been added in the House specifically to ensure the continued supply of maids, cooks, and other domestic servants] The House version of the bill also contained a clause, eventually deleted, requiring immigrants to "read and write the English language or the language of their native or resident country." The Senate bill required only English "or some other language," which didn't please Herman J. Schultheis, a former member of a commission appointed to investigate immigration issues. "Any one may be able to read and write 'some other language,'" he complained. "A Sicilian chimpanzee would be able to pass that, but would not be able to read and write in his native Italian."

Lorenzo Danford of Ohio, the chairman of the House Immigration Committee, saw a similar problem involving a different immigrant group. He altered the bill's wording specifically to keep out "a class of people who have been thrown on our shores . . . known as the Russian Jews"; neither Yiddish nor Hebrew being the language "of their native or resident country," knowledge of neither one would have allowed admittance. Another House member, Stanyarne Wilson of South Carolina, made a cleverly winking argument for the bill when he described the "very races" the test would exclude: "We can not mention them by name, by statute, on grounds of public policy and of comity between nations, but . . . this act will accomplish the same purpose." Unconstrained by concerns of comity or, really, anything else, lame duck representative Elijah A. Morse of Massachusetts, concluding his three terms in the House, was forthright:

the new immigrants from "southern Europe, from Russia, from Italy, and from Greece [are] entirely a different class of immigrants, with a civilization, with wants and necessities, far below the American standard. And the purpose of this bill is to exclude that undesirable immigration." How undesirable? Some of them, Morse added for the apparent benefit of the unconvinced, come to the United States with "little else than an alimentary canal and an appetite."

But neither coy euphemism nor outright racial invective—nor a lopsided 217–36 vote in the House—could carry the day. On March 3, 1897, the very last day of his presidency, Grover Cleveland vetoed Lodge's bill, and there were not enough votes in the Senate to override. The president (whose ancestors had been in the United States since the 1640s) had spoken sympathetically about immigrants as far back as the first of his annual messages to Congress in 1885, when he condemned mob action against Chinese workers in Wyoming. [More recently, Cleveland had praised the new immigrants as "a hardy laboring class, accustomed and able" to earn a living. Now, in his veto message, he declared that the Lodge bill would mark "a radical departure from national policy." To date, he continued, "We have encouraged those coming from foreign countries to cast their lot with us and join in the development of our vast domain, securing in return a share in the blessings of American citizenship." On one point Lodge would have had to acknowledge, at least privately, that the president was right. The literacy test, said Cleveland, was merely "the pretext for exclusion."]

As Lodge prepared for the bill's rebirth in the next session of Congress, he was certain the new president would support it. He had privately opposed William McKinley's nomination for the presidency (and years later carefully deleted references to this opposition from his published correspondence) but drew confidence from McKinley's inaugural address. Hatless on the steps of the Capitol, his pince-nez firmly in place, the new president read from a text that warned of the risks inherent in "a citizenship too ignorant to understand or too vicious to appreciate" American institutions. Editorialists assured readers that congressional action followed by McKinley's speedy signature would soon put the literacy test into the statute books.

But political exigencies—a recovering economy, the rising ethnic vote, the efforts of some new opponents—intervened and were then compounded by legislative inertia. Some suspected McKinley himself of quietly working to kill the bill. Desperate in Boston, Prescott Hall managed to get on the president's appointment calendar, and subsequently reported that McKinley might be using some of the league's own language in his annual message to Congress. But when the document emerged two weeks later, not one of its twenty thousand words addressed immigration. Given a free pass by the popular new president, Congress exhaled and failed to act. Henry Cabot Lodge turned most of his attention to the war against Spain and other imperial adventures. The literacy test was dead. Shortly thereafter, it appeared, so was the Immigration Restriction League, which in 1899 voted to forgo an annual meeting, disbanded its executive committee, and donated its papers and records to the Boston Public Library.

Apart from Lodge and Thomas Bailey Aldrich himself, no one employed the image of gates unguarded more fervently than Prescott Hall, who over time would probably devote more hours, more effort, and more complete conviction to stopping immigration than any other individual. But the cofounder of the IRL could rarely enhance his passion with public action. Chronically neurasthenic, inherently private, beset by unabating insomnia and a morbid stew of other, vaguer ailments, Hall would turn inward in moments of crisis. And in at least one despairing moment, when it appeared that the literacy test or any other effective restriction legislation would be doomed by politics, he turned to poetry.

Unlike Lazarus, who extended her arms to welcome huddled masses, and unlike Aldrich, who sought to post sentries at the gates to keep those masses out, Hall didn't bother with metaphor or imagery—or, for that matter, with euphemisms, or distinctions between the lettered and the illiterate, or anything else but the certitude of his own beliefs. He wrote:

> Enough! Enough! We want no more
> Of ye immigrant from a foreign shore
> Already is our land o'er run
> With toiler, beggar, thief and scum.

It was an argument of sorts, but on its own not a convincing one. The anti-immigration movement needed something more than slogans and poems and the loathing that inspired them.

Chapter Three

The Warfare of the Cradle

Emma Lazarus's huddled masses, Thomas Bailey Aldrich's wild motley throng, and Prescott Hall's beggar, thief, and scum generally entered the United States in the same fashion: from deep within the bellies of the transatlantic ships that steamed into American harbors. Steerage travel was perfected by Albert Ballin, a lower-middle-class Jew from Hamburg who eventually rose to become the chief executive of the mammoth Hamburg-American Line. At one point Ballin had 175 ships at his command—a fleet larger than the merchant marine of any European power except Germany itself. Hamburg-American vessels had been coming to America to ferry timber and other products eastward to Europe. Contemplating the empty, wasted space on the westbound leg, Ballin conjured a commodity that could fill it, a commodity far more valuable than timber: immigrants. As it happened, filling a vessel's hold with hundreds of passengers had a subsidiary benefit: the added ballast made the ship easier to steer.

Ballin's vision became phenomenally lucrative for his company and all the other shipowners in Hamburg and Bremen and Rotterdam, in Liverpool and Antwerp and Naples, virtually wherever there was a European port accessible to people wishing to travel across the Atlantic. One reliable estimate, calculated in 1901, found that the cost of bringing a passenger to an American port in the cramped, dark, and unsanitary steerage compartment of an oceangoing ship cost the steamship line $1.70 (2019 equivalent: roughly $55), at a time when the average fare was $22.50 (slightly more than $700). At an allotted one hundred cubic feet per person (equivalent to a space measuring five feet by four feet by five feet), operators of the larger ships could cram two thousand immigrants into steerage, feed them a rudimentary diet of bread and herring for the ten-to-twelve-day crossing, and pull in profits previously unimagined.

To feed this bountiful money machine, steamship companies maintained networks of recruiting agents throughout the poorest parts of Europe. Priests, rabbis, schoolteachers, postmasters—anyone with a wide range of acquaintances who was also literate enough to fill out the requisite forms—could collect the equivalent of a couple of dollars' worth of commission per traveler, payable in advance as a deposit against the price of a ticket. Francis Walker of MIT claimed that a rural notary in Hungary could earn an entire month's income by persuading a family of five to make the transatlantic voyage. In southern Italy, the steamship companies employed more than 150 dedicated agents, who collectively ran a network of some four thousand subagents scattered through the city slums and across the impoverished countryside. One Italian-American scholar liked to tell the story of the mayor of a provincial Italian town greeting a visiting dignitary: "I welcome you in the name of five thousand inhabitants of this town, three thousand of whom are in America—and the other two thousand preparing to go."

In eastern Europe, agents would also arrange their customers' overland travel to the embarkation ports on the North Sea. Across the decades, tens of thousands of them passed through a bustling Polish rail junction that would prove similarly convenient for another purpose half a century later: Oświęçim, also known as Auschwitz.

The power of the steamship companies was one of three impediments that Henry Cabot Lodge had to contend with throughout his long career battling the immigrants and their advocates. Naifs like Prescott Hall of the IRL may have proceeded from the assumption that the facts were so plain, the dangers so evident, that reasonable men could not possibly disagree with him. But Lodge knew better. In addition to the steamship companies, formidable political opposition came from the massed influence of the large American manufacturing and natural resources companies avid for cheap labor, and from a third foe that Lodge was unwilling to define publicly. Weeks before Grover Cleveland stamped his veto on the literacy test, Lodge had told associates to expect it, hinting darkly that certain unnameable and "insidious" elements were likely to turn the president against them.

Lodge and his allies handled the manufacturers with relative ease, even insouciance. Samuel Gompers of the American Federation of Labor considered unrestricted immigration "this pressing evil" and formed an unholy alliance with Lodge—blue collar joins Brahmin— in support of the literacy test. (The test, Gompers would write in his memoirs more than a quarter century later, was "the only issue upon which I have ever found myself in accord with Senator Lodge.") By adding the support of labor to the measure's purely xenophobic appeal, Lodge had been able to outmaneuver the corporations. "We knew their strength and had beaten them," he told an IRL official after his bill had made it through the House and Senate.

Lodge had been much more concerned about the steamship lobby, whose financial incentives for defeating the test were enormous. ["I do not know when I have been [made] more indignant than by this active interference accompanied by threats to members of Congress on the part of foreign corporations," Lodge fumed] Price wars between German and British shipowners had cut into their profits somewhat, but when Albert Ballin of the Hamburg-American Line decided to make common cause with his competitors, a lavishly funded army of opponents rallied to the antirestriction cause.

Lobbyists swarmed the Capitol Building. Some members of Congress lined up for postretirement employment with the steamship companies while others, still in office, solicited direct payments. The North German Lloyd line alone enlisted more than two hundred affiliated representatives in the western states to wire their congressmen—at NGL expense—and persuade them of the abundant economic benefits that derived from open immigration. They might have turned a few minds in Congress when they suggested an alternative even scarier than an influx of illiterate Europeans. Chicago-based George W. Claussenius, who organized the effort on behalf of North German Lloyd, told reporters that the Lodge bill "discriminates against white Europeans" in favor of "negroes and half-breeds, who, while they may have our sincere sympathy, are of no use in improving western farms."

Lodge had taken that argument and simply chosen a different line of demarcation—not the one that separated Europeans from African Americans but the one that sliced Europe in half, the northern and western countries on the protected side, the southern and eastern lands debarred. It was precisely this divide that provoked the third and most potent of Lodge's opponents, the bloc that Lodge had labeled "insidious" and was so reluctant to discuss, at least in writing. "Influences [on Cleveland] were used yesterday which I will explain to you when we meet and which were very hard to overcome," he told his protégé Curtis Guild Jr., a future governor of Massachusetts. To Robert Ward, the Harvard climatologist who was one of the Immigration Restriction League's three founders, Lodge said these other forces represented neither corporations nor political factions. As he did with Guild, he declined to identify them until he could tell Ward about them in person.

Lodge seemed to derive his greatest gratification from the plenitude and power of his enemies; one contemporary said he "considers himself so far superior to the ordinary run of people that the mere addition of another enemy to his long string means nothing to him one way or the other." But in this instance, constraining himself from describing his enemies even in private correspondence, his circumspection was more than uncharacteristic. It suggested that these enemies were not only ominous but that the mere utterance of their names in so negative a context was potentially explosive. Lodge's unnamed and "insidious" opponents in the immigration wars were almost certainly members of America's moneyed and influential German Jewish community.

For a quarter of a century, beginning with the moment when Jacob Schiff, the eminent Kuhn, Loeb banker, made a personal plea to Grover Cleveland to veto the literacy test, Lodge, the IRL, and their allies would have to contend with an array of influential organizations dominated by wealthy German Jews.* The first of these groups, choosing a name that explicitly acknowledged the influence of the Immigration Restriction League, called itself the Immigration Protective League. It was followed by the Committee on Civil and Religious Rights of the Union of American Hebrew Congregations, the National Liberal Immigration League, the American Jewish Committee, the Friends of Russian Freedom, and many others of similar provenance. Collectively, they composed a formidable and enduring opposition—even though by many measures the bankers, merchants, and other civic leaders who led these groups had more in common with the restrictionists they opposed than with the immigrants they worked so hard to defend. The emergence in the 1890s of organized, wealthy, and well-connected Jews working on behalf of the immigrants presented Lodge and his colleagues with an opposition that few Boston Brahmins had encountered.

Boston had never been particularly unwelcoming to Jews in the

---

* Many were not specifically from Germany, but came from Austria, Bohemia, and other parts of central Europe. The useful modifier "German" is less descriptive of their disparate nationalities than of their shared language and culture. The eastern Europeans, of course, spoke Yiddish.

years before the new immigration began to accelerate. Credentials seemed to trump origins. When the future Supreme Court justice Louis D. Brandeis, Kentucky born, emerged from Harvard Law School in the late 1870s, he was almost immediately accepted into the city's legal and social aristocracy. Prescott Hall not only worked with Brandeis on municipal reform efforts (as did Joe Lee) but at one point shared a two-man law practice with a Jewish partner, Edward Adler. The writer and Unitarian minister Edward Everett Hale, a sort of father figure to the liberal branch of Brahmin Boston, expressed credible shock when he encountered mentions of anti-Semitism in the 1880s; it had been utterly unfamiliar to him while growing up in the 1830s.

In New York as in Boston, as well as in a number of other metropolitan centers, the integration of well-educated Jews of central European (and sometimes Sephardic) extraction into elite social and business circles had been routinely accepted for years. In New York, Emma Lazarus's father was one of the founders of the Knickerbocker Club, which was created in 1871 specifically because the city's elite considered the membership criteria of the nearby Union Club egregiously lax. Banker Jesse Seligman was a member of the similarly patrician Union League Club for twenty years and one of its officers for fourteen.

But in the early 1890s this tradition of openness was snapped as if by violent reflex. In 1893, while Seligman still served as the Union League's vice president, his son Theodore was blackballed from membership. "To speak frankly," said one member, "a majority of the men who frequent the club habitually are opposed to the admission of Hebrews." The Seligmans had not changed; Theodore, a lawyer, was as well regarded as his father. But two miles downtown, on the swarming pavements of the Lower East Side (soon more densely populated than Bombay) and in the West End of Boston, in South Philadelphia, along Maxwell Street in Chicago, and anywhere else the newcomers from eastern Europe settled, the change in the city's

Jewish population was evident. It was accelerating, and to the members of the Union League and others like them, it was appalling.

The Jews of the Seligmans' world were guilty not by association with these impoverished aliens—they hardly associated at all with the eastern Europeans—but simply by a common ethnic origin that might have been centuries distant. In Boston even Brandeis began to find himself on the outside of circles that had previously welcomed, or at least tolerated, him. When his law partner was married in 1891, the bride's family would not allow Brandeis to attend the wedding. Edward Everett Hale's "amazement," as he called it, at the sudden appearance in Boston of an anti-Semitism he had not known in his youth did not take into account the demographic kindling that stoked it. When Hale was eighteen, in 1840, there were some one hundred Jews in the city; by 1890 the number had increased two hundredfold.

This seemingly new anti-Semitism among the Protestant upper classes wasn't entirely a product of the 1890s as much as it was the newly overt expression of an attitude both normative and persistent. A few club memberships and business relationships did not obscure the fact that a finely bred young woman who came of age toward the end of the nineteenth century could refer to a Harvard law professor as "an interesting little man, but very Jew," or declare that she'd "rather be hung" than attend another "Jew party," where she had been "appall[ed]" by all the talk of "money, jewels . . . and sables." In the world of such a young woman, these comments were unremarkable, even unnoticed. But the source of these particular expressions might indicate the ubiquity and persistence of this seemingly inherent anti-Semitism: Eleanor Roosevelt, at the age of thirty-three.

Her biographer, Blanche Wiesen Cook, explains how a paragon of tolerance like Roosevelt could hold such views: her instinctive anti-Semitism, which would evaporate as her life experience deepened, was "a frayed raiment of her generation, class and culture."

Frayed it may have been, but for men and women of her background, that was partly because it was worn so often.*

The irony was that the aristocratic German Jews who offended Roosevelt were comparably offended by the newcomers. Most of the Germans had arrived in the United States before the Civil War and in a couple of generations were well established in their new country. They were educated, cultivated, prosperous—in a formulation offered a century later by novelist Philip Roth in a somewhat different context, they were more accurately described as Jewish Europeans, not European Jews. Many practiced a version of their religion (if they practiced at all) that was light in ritual, modern in outlook; its very name, Reform Judaism, proclaimed an affirmative separation from its ancient roots. The eastern European newcomers were unlettered, unworldly, and by the westernized standards of the German Jews altogether unacceptable. It was as if a royal family suddenly discovered a lost line of unwashed, uncouth kin who embarrassed them by announcing their connection—then horrified them by moving into the palace.

The German Jews were overwhelmed—in numbers, yes, but even more threateningly, in the perception of gentiles. As early as 1884, Cyrus L. Sulzberger (whose son, grandson, great-grandson, and great-great-grandson would all serve as publisher of the *New York Times*) attributed some of "the prejudice against us in Christian hearts" to "ill-manners" and other forms of disreputable public behavior among the new immigrants. One example offered by the easily bruised Sulzberger: when an immigrant Jew speaks loudly

---

* The Eleanor Roosevelt more familiar to modern readers was expressed in her work in a Lower East Side settlement house in the early 1900s and her resistance to a cousin's entreaty to leave her job and come to Newport lest she contract "an immigrant's disease." The "very Jew" professor was Felix Frankfurter, twenty years before Eleanor's husband appointed him to the Supreme Court.

to a restaurant waiter, "he becomes a proper topic for public criticism." A leading German-language Jewish newspaper referred to the eastern European Jews as "uncouth Asiatics." Rabbi Isaac Mayer Wise, founder of Hebrew Union College (Reform Judaism's first American seminary), said, "We are Americans and they are not. We are Israelites of the nineteenth century in a free country, and they gnaw the bones of past centuries." The derogatory term "kike" was itself favored by German Jews (some etymologists believe the term originated with them), who used it as a label to distinguish the lowly newcomers from their own, established elite.

The functional definition of "Jew" was mutating right before the eyes of the German Jews, spiraling further away from their own self-image with every steamship that deposited the contents of its steerage compartment on Ellis Island. The cultivated, modern burgher was being supplanted by a strange creature speaking a guttural, alien language, practicing a medieval religion, and beset by "ignorance and depravity," according to an article in the *American Israelite*, a leading Reform publication. "Therefore," the writer concluded, it was "no wonder that a well-defined demand is arising for discrimination in immigration." The anti-Semitism that kept the younger Seligman out of the Union League was exactly what the German Jews feared, proof that their perceived position of acceptance, even privilege, was imperiled by the swarming "kikes."

At times the established Jews looked for a safety valve to relieve the pressure. In the early 1880s, in the wake of the czar's assassination and the resulting pogroms, the first mass inflow of Russian Jews induced a self-protective reaction. The Hebrew Emigrant Aid Society (not to be confused with the very different and somewhat later Hebrew Immigrant Aid Society) was formed to assist the newcomers by sending as many as possible away from New York as quickly as possible. This effort to "receive [and] disperse" led to the creation of small colonies of Russian Jews in the somewhat plausible southern New Jersey town of Vineland, and in such unlikely locales as the metropolis of Cotopaxi, a hamlet 150 miles south of Denver in central Colorado. In all, HEAS and its affiliates dispatched Yiddish-speaking Jews to sixteen different settlements scattered across the vast country, the most distant one, in Oregon, bearing the wishful name (if you had been driven from Ukraine) New Odessa.

The federal government provided army tents for the Vineland settlers and gave each of the seventeen families shipped to Cotopaxi the 160 acres customarily allotted to homesteaders. HEAS, for its part, gave them assistance in New York, train fare west, some seed money for the colonies, and good riddance. As Augustus A. Levey, the secretary of HEAS, saw it, there was little choice. "The ineffaceable marks of permanent pauperism" scarred the new immigrants, Levey wrote. The inevitable crimes that would be committed by "these wretches," he continued, "will throw obloquy over our race." The best place for them, in a word, was elsewhere.

Levey and his colleagues in New York were not outliers. Jewish leaders in Cleveland and Milwaukee announced that they would not tolerate the importation of additional eastern European Jews to their cities. In Boston, wish became action: the *Hebrew Observer* reported that the local branch of HEAS met 415 Russian Jews at the docks and "promptly [shipped] them back to New York as soon as they arrived." An additional 75, suffering in penury through the brutal winter of 1882–3, declared that they preferred to return to Russia. When offers to pick up the tab for their repatriation came from the Boston Provident Association and the Board of Charities—de facto subsidiaries of Boston's native-born elite—the established German Jews of Boston finally realized the hollowness of their own deeply held belief that they were different from the easterners. What mattered was not what they believed, but what the gentiles believed. And a growing portion of the most influential gentiles thought there was very little difference at all.

The conscious resettlement of Jewish immigrants away from the

East Coast would continue throughout the period of greatest immigration. United Hebrew Charities, the most firmly established of the German Jewish philanthropies, led the effort, shooing many of the refugees westward—and over a period of years sending more than 7,500 of them (mostly the unemployed and their families) back to Russia. As late as 1905 the influential rabbi Jacob Voorsanger of Temple Emanu-El in San Francisco thundered that neither "sympathy nor sentiment of affection generated by kinship . . . should prevent us from appreciating the justice of cutting off Jewish immigration." Jacob Schiff continued to support the immigration of the Russian Jews but in 1907 he subsidized a program that redirected German ships to the port of Galveston. Over the next seven years some 10,000 eastern European Jews found themselves first touching American soil in Texas. Once there, they were distributed throughout the West and Midwest, their final destinations usually determined by a specific community's need: if Kansas City lacked a kosher butcher, for instance, Schiff's allies in Galveston would send the next one off the boat to Kansas City. This didn't always work out to everyone's satisfaction. In his *Galveston: Ellis Island of the West*, historian Bernard Marinbach relates the story of an immigrant who was dispatched to Sioux City, Iowa. Not long after he arrived he wrote to his wife in Russia, begging her to sell everything they owned and send him train fare to New York.

Eventually the organized German Jewish communities in New York and other large American cities assumed a new position regarding their eastern European relations. They really had no choice. To the wealthy gentiles of the period, the distance separating the German Jews and the eastern newcomers grew disappearingly small, and as the language of the anti-immigrationist campaign became increasingly and explosively racialized, the German Jews were wounded by the shrapnel. Most were compelled to become advocates for those they had previously scorned. Mount Sinai Hospital, which the German

immigrants had established in New York in the middle of the nineteenth century (and formally named, at first, Jews' Hospital), finally
agreed to serve kosher meals. In New York and Philadelphia, German
Jews initiated the kehillah movement, a conscious effort to bring
together the two distinct Jewish communities. Political alliances
between uptown and downtown began to sprout as well. Cyrus
Sulzberger, who had earlier attributed anti-Jewish prejudice to the
crude manners of the immigrants, would in time tell a congressional
committee, "Large numbers of Jewish immigrants have arrived in
this country since 1880. [Instead of] pulling down our standards of
living, they have done the reverse."

*　　*　　*

IN SEPTEMBER 1901, two years after the defeated and disheartened
Immigration Restriction League shut down its operations, it was
brought back to life by a bullet. The man who shot William McKinley
at the Pan-American Exposition in Buffalo, Leon Czolgosz, was
more than a murderer: he was a declared anarchist, and by his very
name (if you thought about such things) patently un-American.
Never mind that Czolgosz was a natural-born citizen who first drew
breath in Alpena, Michigan, in 1873. Two weeks after the president
died, four men of the IRL felt the urge to gather in Prescott Hall's
office to resume the efforts they had suspended after Congress's
failure to enact Henry Cabot Lodge's literacy test during McKinley's presidency.

They had reason to be hopeful. Hadn't Theodore Roosevelt, the
new president, once told Lodge that the net effect of Cleveland's
veto of the literacy test was "to injure the country as much as he
possibly could"? Before the year was out, Roosevelt would open
his annual message to Congress with a eulogy to McKinley, follow
that with an attack on Czolgosz and other anarchists, and ask the
House and Senate to enact "a careful and not merely perfunctory

THE UNRESTRICTED DUMPING-GROUND.

Two years after the assassination of William McKinley (upper left),
Judge cartoonist Louis Dalrymple portrayed the new immigrants as
verminous, murderous, and (by implication) complicit.

educational test" to keep out immigrants who did not possess "some
intelligent capacity to appreciate American institutions and act sanely
as American citizens."

He sounded like his best friend, Lodge.

Throughout much of his public life, Theodore Roosevelt beat the
drum for what was essentially a eugenic view of American progress.
Because few men of the era beat a drum with quite the vigor or
virtuosity that Roosevelt brought to the task, he made a substantial
contribution to the growing acceptance of Galtonian thinking in the
United States even if he may not have fully recognized its potential
as a weapon in the immigration wars.

Like his niece Eleanor, Roosevelt generally wore his racial views as if they were a suit of clothes inherited from an older sibling: they had grown threadbare with time, they fit him loosely, and he rarely appeared in them in public. But whatever biases he had inhaled in his privileged New York childhood were amplified from the moment he arrived at Harvard as a seventeen-year-old in 1876. He met Henry Cabot Lodge in the very thin atmosphere of the inalterably Protestant Porcellian Club, a Harvard institution so undisturbed in its exclusiveness that a man like Lodge, who had graduated four years before Roosevelt, could remain comfortable there the rest of his life. Through Lodge, Roosevelt was befriended by Thomas Bailey Aldrich, who had sung of the "Unguarded Gates." Among the teachers who most influenced him was Nathaniel Shaler, a widely admired Harvard professor of geology (and nominal officer of the Immigration Restriction League). Based on his experience as "an observant foot traveler" in Europe, Shaler believed that just as it would take "some centuries of sore trial" for the typical American to revert to the living standards of an eastern European peasant, it was likely true that it would take equivalent centuries for the latter to rise to the status of the former. Also like niece Eleanor, Uncle Theodore recoiled from the "Jew bankers" he encountered at a party, whom he considered "gold-ridden" and who threatened the onset of a "usurer-mastered future."

But when Roosevelt made Oscar Straus of New York the nation's first Jewish cabinet member in 1906, Straus would recall, the president told him he had put him in the job (secretary of commerce and labor) "to show Russia and some other countries what we think of Jews in this country." Early in his presidency Roosevelt visited Ellis Island, engaged with several of the new arrivals, and showed genuine concern for their welfare (he was particularly upset that doctors examining immigrants for trachoma did not wash their hands thoroughly). In the opening paragraph of his autobiography he referred with a sort of mischievous glee to the first Roosevelt in the New World, who arrived in New Amsterdam in 1644, as "a 'settler'—the euphemistic name," he wrote, "for an immigrant who came over in the steerage of a sailing ship in the seventeenth century, instead of the steerage of a steamer in the nineteenth century."

Still, the Roosevelt who threw himself delightedly into the bubbling stew that was America at the turn of the last century—who as New York police commissioner had given a notoriously anti-Semitic German politician visiting the city an all-Jewish detachment of bodyguards, and who invited Booker T. Washington to dinner at the White House—was, inescapably, a prisoner of his own class. "Mr. Roosevelt is always talking about his policies but he is discreetly silent about his principles," Mark Twain said, and some of those unarticulated principles lay unseen in a psychic fortress of class and race supremacy that could never be fully breached.

In the private life of the Roosevelt family, this class isolation was expressed most clearly in his wife's attitudes. Edith required her sons to research the family origins of any new friends; shunned anyone who was not, she said, "*de notre monde*"; and with breathtaking cruelty said of her servants, "If they had our brains, they'd have our place." Her husband was far more open-minded but was equally persuaded that people like him, his friends, and his family were innately superior. From a world of such sequestered self-regard came a nativist attitude that Roosevelt considered patriotic. Despite all of his demotic (if not exactly democratic) impulses, he was determined to preserve the position of the Anglo-Saxon aristocracy, which he considered essential to the nation's success, even its survival. Several years before he became president he expressed the belief that the preservation of his class would come only from its members' commitment to large families (he was himself a father of six). It was a worldwide problem; he fretted about the southern Italians, whom he called "the most fecund and the least desirable population of Europe," and came to fear that the Hawaii planters' importation of Asian laborers would lead to "the extinguishment of [the planters'] blood." If "native

Americans"* of the northeastern states were to maintain their position, it was essential that they reproduce more rapidly than the proliferating immigrants and thus emerge triumphant from what Roosevelt memorably called "the warfare of the cradle."

Roosevelt was not a hater, steeped in the toxic prejudice that drenched so many around him. He would in time become an enthusiastic fan of Israel Zangwill's play *The Melting Pot*, which bequeathed that resonant phrase and the concept it represented to the American consciousness. But as president he was fearful. The declining birthrate panicked him, and he spoke of it repeatedly. Married couples who engaged in "willful sterility"—that is, who chose not to have children—deserved "the severest of all condemnations." In a speech to the National Congress of Mothers in 1905 he attributed a couple's decision not to have children to "viciousness, coldness, shallow-heartedness, self-indulgence," and other similarly repugnant qualities. Even after he left the White House, Roosevelt would not let go of what he truly believed to be a question of existential consequence. It was those who did their patriotic duty by having four or more children upon whom "the whole future of the Nation, the whole future of civilization rests."

Throughout his public years of pounding lecterns, tabletops, and the ears of his listeners, Roosevelt was usually careful not to distinguish between segments of the population while he searched desperately for those who would save the world. "I, for one, would heartily throw in my fate with the men of alien stock who [were having families of sufficient size and] were true to the old American principles," he wrote at one point, "rather than with the men of the old American stock" who were not doing their reproductive duty.

---

* Long before it was used to describe people descended from North America's aboriginal, pre-Columbus peoples, "native American" was a term adopted by the restriction movement to describe purebred Protestants of their own lineage. Much of Brahmin Boston considered what the twenty-first century knows as "native American" rather less positively: Oliver Wendell Holmes Sr. called them "a half-filled outline of humanity . . . [a] sketch in red crayons of a rudimental manhood."

Yet Roosevelt hinted at something different when he was more certain of his audience. He may have moved beyond the idea he'd expressed to his pal Henry Cabot Lodge in 1896—"I'd like to see a white man now and then," he'd told Lodge, whose company he missed.* But in 1908, as his presidency neared its end, his position was nonetheless clear. To Stanford president David Starr Jordan—who just happened to be chairman of the eugenics committee of the American Breeders Association—Roosevelt confessed that he was "melancholy," because "the best men" were "content that the citizens of the future come from the loins of others."

If novelist Owen Wister, his friend of four decades, can be believed, Roosevelt did not hedge at all in private conversation. A decade after Roosevelt's death, Wister recalled a comment he had once made about the birthrate. "It's simply a question of the multiplication table," Roosevelt had said, in Wister's recollection. "If all our nice friends in Beacon Street, and Newport, and Fifth Avenue, and Philadelphia, have one child, or no child at all, while all the Finnegans, Hooligans, Antonios, Mandelbaums and Rabinskis have eight, or nine, or ten—it's simply a question of the multiplication table. How are you going to get away from it?"

"It" could have been defined by a term Roosevelt began using in 1902 and that soon entered the national vocabulary in the debate over immigration. As vivid and as potent a phrase as his "warfare of the cradle" might have been, it paled in comparison to this one: "race suicide."

But what, exactly, did Roosevelt mean by "race"?

"Of all vulgar modes of escaping from the consideration of the effects of social influences on the human mind," John Stuart Mill wrote in

* Written during Roosevelt's tenure as New York City police commissioner, this was one of the many not-quite-suitable-for-public-consumption sentences Lodge excised from the two-volume edition of the Roosevelt–Lodge letters published in 1925.

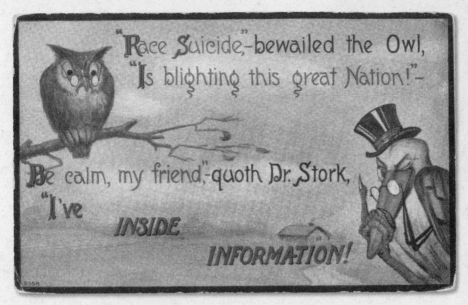

"Race Suicide,"-bewailed the Owl,
"Is blighting this great Nation!"-
Be calm, my friend,"-quoth Dr. Stork,
"I've INSIDE INFORMATION!

Why the stork on this popular postcard saw reason to be calm is
unclear, but his imaginings no doubt coincided with Roosevelt's fondest
dreams, which W. A. Rogers illustrated in a 1905 cartoon (facing page).

1848, "the most vulgar is that attributing the diversities of conduct and
character to inherent natural influences." Vulgar it may have been, but
to the race theorists of the nineteenth and early twentieth centuries it
was irresistible: if a person could attribute his virtues to his pedigree,
he was beyond challenge. The obverse was an even more powerful
notion, for without the proper pedigree a man was ipso facto inferior.

In the same year that Mill wrote, the revolutions that rocked
Europe dislodged an idea from the frozen set of prejudices that
encased the life of Count Arthur de Gobineau. A French nobleman,
royalist, novelist, diplomat, and—proudly—racist, Gobineau was
gripped by two unshakable convictions: that the world had started
to come apart with the French Revolution, and that "race" was mankind's defining issue. In 1855 he bequeathed to generations of racists
to come his four-volume *Essay on the Inequality of Human Races*, the

foundational text of what would become known as scientific racism. Gobineau's supporting evidence was scientifically negligible, his logic broken-backed. But his narrative talent was vigorous, and for those eager to be persuaded, it was a gift. One of his earliest fans was Richard Wagner, whose wife wrote to Gobineau to say that "my husband is quite at your service, always reading *The Inequality of Human Races* when he is not at work" on his operas. And a few decades later one of Wagner's own enthusiasts, stuck in a Bavarian prison, embraced Gobineau with comparable enthusiasm: *Mein Kampf* is awash with Gobineau's ideas.

In his early thirties Gobineau was for a brief time secretary to Alexis de Tocqueville. In 1843 that great student of democracy told Gobineau that "one is fascinated both by what you could be and by what one fears you may become." Ten years later, having read the *Essay*, Tocqueville's fears were realized: he told Gobineau that his ideas were not only erroneous but "very pernicious." The *Essay* delineated in excruciating detail (and with highly suspect authority) a world of three races made virtuous only by the white: ["Everywhere the white races have taken the initiative, everywhere they have *brought* civilization to the others," he insisted. Without the white, the black and yellow bordered on the worthless. Only by segregating itself from the black and yellow could the white remain pure.] (Interestingly, this belief led him to a certain ambivalence regarding slavery: the proximity of white and black inevitably led to miscegenation.) He did acknowledge that a certain amount of race mixing was necessary, or at least it had been long ago—without a little bit of black stirred in, he wrote, whites would never have been able to achieve "artistic genius." But, like the peril faced by a chemist brewing an explosive concoction in his lab, the quantity had to be just so much and not a droplet more. It was this sort of mixing, Gobineau believed, that allowed Greece to thrive and Rome to fall. It also created the various subraces (which would later be called ethnic groups or perhaps nationalities) that Gobineau and his followers would begin to sort, classify, and rank as if they were tomatoes entered in an agricultural fair.

Nearly a century after Gobineau (and for scientific racism it was quite a century), modern genetics inflicted fatal wounds on race theory, and by the time the Human Genome was sequenced in the 1990s, long-held concepts of race were all but demolished. Of the roughly twenty thousand protein-coding genes allocated to each human, it turned out that a relative handful manifest themselves in what are today generally considered the signifiers of race—skin color, hair texture, nose shape, and so on. We can accurately identify people by color, or language, or nationality. Yet as genetic signifiers for what lies beneath the visible surface, these characteristics are essentially meaningless. As Thomas F. Gossett made clear in his invaluable *Race: The History of an Idea in America*, attempts to sort Europeans by race are "anthropologically unintelligible."

But in the nineteenth century, for those who wished to examine the world through a racial microscope, the product of their efforts soon became dogma, independent of Gobineau's convulsive hatred. "Racial" distinctions were parsed with robust enthusiasm and exquisite (if widely varying) precision. Gossett notes that Charles Darwin's great ally Thomas Huxley identified four races, the influential German biologist Ernst Haeckel (who coined "ontogeny recapitulates phylogeny") counted thirty-six, and the French anthropologist Joseph Deniker enumerated seventeen races that could be subdivided into thirty distinct types[Like so much assertion, speculation, and theory issued forth in the last decades of the nineteenth century, to some degree this ferment of racial analysis was a direct, if almost certainly unintended, product of the Darwinian revolution. Once you establish that not everyone is descended from Adam and Eve—and thus not genetically related to one another—anything goes: racial differences, racial hierarchies, racial hatred.]

The century's discussion of race culminated in two books published in 1899, both of which would play major roles in the race controversies of the century ahead. The first, Houston Stewart Chamberlain's *Foundations of the Nineteenth Century*, would become, like Gobineau's *Essay* (which it cites repeatedly), an essential text of Nazi ideology. Chamberlain was a well-off Englishman (though not related to the political Chamberlain family) who moved to Germany at age thirty, drawn by his passion for the music and, even more, the racial ideology of Richard Wagner. Chamberlain may not have written at Gobineau's length (*Foundations* was a mere two volumes), but he outdid the Frenchman in his attachment to Wagner: not only did Chamberlain write his biography, he eventually married the composer's daughter and settled in the Bavarian city of Bayreuth, the beating heart of all things Wagnerian.

No wonder: in its loopy mythologizing of Teutonic virtue, *Foundations* is nearly as complex and as opaque as the Ring Cycle. Anti-Semitic, anti-Catholic, fanatically pro-Aryan (a term summoned into its modern usage by Gobineau), it also became a text so endearing to Adolf Hitler that in 1927 he and Joseph Goebbels paid homage to Chamberlain by visiting him on his deathbed, and Hitler returned for the funeral. For present purposes, let one of its sentences serve as a summary of its main argument: "Physically and mentally the Aryans are pre-eminent among all peoples; for that reason they are by right . . . the lords of the world."* If any great historical figure was not Teutonic, Chamberlain found a way to make him one: "That Dante is Germanic [is] so clear from his personality and his work that proof of it is absolutely superfluous." (Marco Polo, Francis of Assisi, and Galileo all made the cut as well.) The book was a huge bestseller in its original German (Chamberlain adopted the language as his own, with the same enthusiasm he brought to his alliance with the *Volk*), and when translated into English it carried an approving introduction by Lord Redesdale, grandfather of the famous Mitford sisters. Its other British fans included George Bernard Shaw (who called it "a masterpiece of really scientific history") and, Redesdale told Chamberlain, Winston Churchill. When it was finally published in the United States in 1910, Theodore Roosevelt, by then ex-president, savaged it. But it did find a particularly enthusiastic supporter in Prescott Hall, who recommended it to Joe Lee as "the most delightful summer

---

* And let these sentences summarize Chamberlain's view of certain non-Aryans: "And here a fact occurs to me which I have received from various sources, viz., that very small children, especially girls, frequently have quite a marked instinct for race. It frequently happens that children who have no conception of what 'Jew' means, or that there is any such thing in the world, begin to cry as soon as a genuine Jew or Jewess comes near them! The learned can frequently not tell a Jew from a non-Jew; the child that scarcely knows how to speak notices the difference. Is not that something?" Chamberlain doesn't comment on the reaction of tots to approaching Catholics but does point out that the Church of Rome reigns over "chaotic mongreldom."

reading." On receiving Hall's letter, Lee lifted his pen to scrawl one word across its top: "Get."

But as provocative as *Foundations* was, and as comforting to those looking for historical justifications (however fanciful) for their preconceptions, beyond the most intensely xenophobic circles, in the United States it was not as influential as the other signal book on race that came out in 1899. That was William Z. Ripley's *The Races of Europe*, which by its very title helped firm up the notion that "white" was not a race, but merely a convenient rubric for a collection of *distinct* races. Unlike Gobineau and Chamberlain, Ripley was a genuine scholar (even if his scholarship was somewhat diluted by his range of subjects: an economist by training, he at various times taught sociology, anthropology, and physical geography at MIT, Columbia, and Harvard). He also was not (or, perhaps, not especially) an anti-Semite, a racist, or a crank; Gobineau appears nowhere in his book's six hundred–plus pages. Although much of his work doesn't hold up under twenty-first-century standards, Ripley was careful. He dismantled the existence of an Aryan race in seven well-informed, tightly argued pages. On the very first page of the book he warned readers not to think of race as a factor entirely independent of "social contact," indicating that he believed nature and nurture were irretrievably intertwined. Near the book's end he explained that most "social phenomena" we associate with one particular race—in this case the "Alpines"—arise "not [from] racial proclivities" but from "geographical and social isolation."

Still, Ripley did find the Alpines distinct—one of three separate European races, along with the Teutonic and the Mediterranean; he excluded Jews entirely from his European triumvirate and placed them in a separate category. The Teutonics were tall, blond, and blue-eyed; the Alpines shorter and somewhat darker; the Mediterraneans slim and darker still. He didn't rank them qualitatively. He recognized the extent of European cross-fertilization and its consequent effects on any effort to identify "pure" members of each race. Like

John Stuart Mill, [Ripley considered the attribution of specific "social, political, or economic virtues or ills" to any specific race "vulgar."] But by seeming to establish the very concept of different European races, Ripley effectively sanctioned the central arguments of two groups that would later draw on his work for both sustenance and justification: the eugenicists and the immigration restrictionists.

But that was still a decade into the future. In 1902 "race" was used as convenient shorthand. In the American context, when people like Theodore Roosevelt spoke of the future of "the race" or "our race," they were almost always speaking of white Americans of native birth and parentage.

"William does not leave as many children as 'Tonio," wrote Edward A. Ross in 1914, "because he will not huddle his family into one room, eat macaroni off a bare board, work his wife barefoot in the field, and keep his children weeding onions instead of at school." It's no surprise that the man who first introduced the phrase "race suicide" into public discussion in 1901 would later be the author of this remarkable statement. By the time Ross thus reduced the more than two million Italians who had immigrated to the United States in the preceding decade to macaroni-eating exploiters of wives and children, he had been peddling his ideas of racial inferiority for far longer than a decade. This was the same Ross who, writing of Chinese laborers just a few years before he trained his focus on William and 'Tonio, had asserted that "Reilly can outdo Ah-San, but Ah-San can underlive Reilly." Originality was not a trait he particularly valued.

But provocation was. Ross was a scholar, an ideologue, a publicist, an aphorist, and something of an agitator. A solid six feet six inches tall, his strong cheekbones framing a substantial mustache, he stood out in any crowd not just because of his singular appearance but because of a booming self-confidence that was always insuperable, often insufferable, and that somehow managed to both emphasize his imposing stature and amplify his thunderous voice. The product of a midwestern farm boyhood that had been wrenched out of shape by the death of his parents before he turned ten, Ross emerged from the guardianship of three different families to pursue an academic life, receiving his PhD at Johns Hopkins (where Woodrow Wilson was one of his teachers) at twenty-four. In an autobiography published when he was seventy, he wrote that "there may come a time in the career of every sociologist when it is his solemn duty to raise hell," and in his own case he had found that time ten years into his career, when he was teaching at Stanford. Addressing an audience of labor leaders, he condemned the Central Pacific Railroad for hiring Chinese workers. The fact that his salary effectively originated with the Central Pacific—it was the source of the fortune that founded Stanford—did not deter Ross; given his brassy self-assurance and his appetite for attention, it could have been the impetus that drove him to speak out. Jane Lathrop Stanford, widow of the university's benefactor and by 1900 its sole trustee, demanded Ross's firing.* When university officials capitulated, thus confirming what Ross called the "hollowness" at the center of the relationship of scholar and patron, he was delighted. His case provoked the sympathetic resignations of several other Stanford faculty members. And in time he could take justifiable pride in his role in the advent of the American system of academic tenure and the formation of the American Association of University Professors, which adopted the defense of academic freedom as its primary mandate.

Ross's dismissal also put him firmly on the national stage. From Stanford he went to the University of Nebraska and then to the University of Wisconsin, where he happily took on the role of prairie radical, allied with the archprogressive governor Robert M. La Follette. He advocated for labor unions, opposed "the ruthless

---

* Years later Ross dismissed the Leland Stanford family and its storied partners in the Central Pacific—Charles Crocker, Collis Huntington, and Mark Hopkins—as "Sacramento hardware merchants."

practices of business men," supported the socialist presidential candidacy of Eugene V. Debs, and at seventy-four would achieve the pinnacle of his public life when he was elected national chairman of the American Civil Liberties Union. Ross's books sold hundreds of thousands of copies, and he agreeably (if a little too smugly) made one of them, *Capsules of Social Wisdom*, "available in attractively bound reprints, numbered and paged suitable for a gift." The "capsules" consisted of a lifetime's gathering of some six hundred maxims, folk dicta, and self-evidencies along the uninspired lines of "A few scorn riches, but *no one* scorns good repute!"

Such chestnuts didn't have quite the heft of "race suicide," which Ross first unveiled in a 1901 speech. "There is no bloodshed, no violence, no assault of the race that waxes upon the race that wanes," Ross told the annual meeting of the American Academy of Political and Social Science. "The higher race quietly and unmurmuringly eliminates itself rather than endure individually the bitter competition it has failed to ward off from itself by collective action." Like many progressives of the day—like, for instance, Joe Lee—Ross had no difficulty reconciling his ethnic intolerance with his quasi-socialist views on the role and responsibilities of government; the latter did not click into place until the ferry bound for the Manhattan piers departed Ellis Island. Once immigrants were admitted, Ross and Lee believed, government and charitable institutions had the obligation to "Americanize" them. As historian Mike Wallace has written, "'Progressive' was a fuzzy term for an ambivalent politics."

But for Ross, there was a gap between the wish and the act: he was not convinced that Americanization was possible. After establishing his eminence in both the academic world and the political sphere, Ross won greater fame with a series of articles and books expressing his belief that many of the immigrants coming into the United States early in the twentieth century were members of "the lower races"—in truth, barely human. Even when immigrants were "washed and combed" in their Sunday best, he wrote, the observer could not help but be repelled by the "hirsute, low-browed, big-faced persons of obviously low mentality." These "oxlike" people, he insisted, "clearly belong in skins, in wattled huts at the close of the Great Ice Age." What the phrase "race suicide" may have meant to Theodore Roosevelt, who popularized it, was somewhat vague, at least to those not in his immediate circle. To Ross, who first brought it to Roosevelt's attention, there could be no doubt what it meant. "A people that has no more respect for its ancestors and no more pride of race than this," he concluded, "deserves the extinction that surely awaits it."*

The idea of the reproductively deficient American of northwestern European origin—the everyman "William" who couldn't keep up with progeny-producing, macaroni-eating "'Tonio"—descended directly from Francis Walker, the MIT president who had famously deprecated the southeastern Europeans as "beaten men of beaten races." Walker said that the reason for the tumbling birthrate among native-born Americans was obvious: Why would the previously dominant "races" bring children into a world degraded by immigrants who were "unfit to be members of any decent community"? It was a practical choice as well: How could the children of the native-born possibly hope to compete with men willing to work for pennies and to live like animals?

But for all his dismissive, vituperative, even hate-filled assaults on the southern and eastern European immigrants ("vast masses of filth . . . living like swine"), Walker never suggested that the "beaten races" were *biologically* different; they had been "brutalized," he argued, by social, political, and historical circumstances that had rendered

* The year before Ross defined "race suicide" in his speech to the political scientists, a small New York publisher issued "A Yellow World," a pamphlet purporting to consist of a group of letters by the son of a Chinese nobleman, addressed to the Viceroy. Whoever actually wrote it had a somewhat different definition of Ross's ostensible coinage but an equally vigorous style: "Nothing proves the incapacity and childishly barbaric smallness of the Caucasian brain than the bombastic policy of race suicide pursued by that nation of pudgy braggarts known as Great Britain."

them inferior. He even acknowledged that the "great majority" of the immigrants were unobjectionable. His was more an economic argument than a racial one.

Ross drew no such distinctions. "The superiority of a race cannot be preserved," he declared in 1904, "without *pride of blood*." If his bellowing italics failed to make the point, he spelled out what he felt was required: "an uncompromising attitude toward the lower races."

According to Owen Wister, Ross's notion of "race suicide" was associated with Roosevelt just as much as "Speak softly and carry a big stick," and its implicit call to action was echoed in the popular press. No less a figure than the black scholar and activist W. E. B. Du Bois would adapt it for his own use, invoking the term to criticize the reproductive efforts of "educated and careful" families who were having "few or no children" (he also argued that black people needed to "train and breed for brains, for efficiency, for beauty"). Race suicide also became a subject of academic papers produced, inevitably, by those who had the most to lose. One such study, in the *Yale Alumni Weekly*, rolled out an armamentarium of tables, graphs, and pie charts to demonstrate that the average married graduate in the Yale classes of 1867–1886 had but 2.02 children. Once their unmarried classmates were factored in, added a Boston commentator gravely, it was obvious that they "had failed to reproduce themselves."

The apotheosis of this sort of thinking would wait until 1916, when a series of articles on race suicide would provoke a wealthy Harvard-trained physician named John C. Phillips to explore the crisis at his alma mater (Phillips also happened to be an avowed eugenicist, a devoted member of the Immigration Restriction League, and a few years later, Joe Lee's neighbor on Mount Vernon Street). Phillips's study revealed the discouraging news that the situation was not much better in Cambridge than in New Haven; between 1850 and 1890, average family size among Harvard alumni had dropped 30 percent. It also indicated that the women of Wellesley College were having only 0.86 children per graduate, which Phillips considered "pathetic." And, in the most brutal of these statistical blows to Brahmin preeminence, one calculation indicated that the continuing failure to reproduce in robust numbers would mean that 1,000 Harvard graduates in the class of 1916 would have but 50 living descendants in 2116. Lewis Terman, whose influential *The Measurement of Intelligence* was published the same year as Phillips's study, invoked those fate-freighted numbers several years later, and delivered this equally unsubstantiated clincher: at current rates of reproduction, while the number of Harvard progeny will have dropped from 1,000 to 50, "1,000 South Italians will have multiplied to 100,000."

Joe Lee would make use of the concept of race suicide with a question directed to the Boston ladies bountiful who were active in social services: "When you are helping the dear Roumanian lady who has fifteen children and the dear Italian ditto who has 25," asked Lee, "what is becoming of your children you are not having?"

*   *   *

THE "DEAR ITALIAN DITTO," fear of "a Dago nation," "wop"—the terms tossed about in the correspondence of the anti-immigrationists or freely invoked in congressional debate were mere hints of a reality too rarely acknowledged in memoirs of the period: that the eastern European Jews were not the largest immigrant group—nor, at first, the people most despised by the nativists. Both distinctions belonged to the Italians, who had begun to arrive in large numbers in the 1880s. In 1850, the year Henry Cabot Lodge was born, 431 Italians left their homeland for the United States. By 1887, the year Lodge entered Congress, the annual number had rocketed to 47,622. It inched up to 59,431 ten years later, when the literacy test was murdered by Grover Cleveland's pen. And a decade after that, fully 285,731 Italians entered the States in a single year. Overall, in the first decade of the twentieth century, more than two million Italians arrived on American shores, most of them from Sicily and the south, most of them desperately poor, and by one estimate 68 percent of them illiterate.

To the American-born patriciate of Boston, New York, and other cities, the Italians were, unlike the Jews, completely incomprehensible. In his 1880 novel, *Democracy*, written before he was fully seized by his deranged anti-Semitism, Henry Adams created the wealthy German Jewish Schneidekoupon family. Adams saw them as largely unexceptionable members of Washington's highest social realms, intimates of the book's admirable heroine.* Prescott Hall, whose anti-Semitism would become the primary engine of his encompassing xenophobia, did not let it deter him from forging his partnership with Edward Adler. Joe Lee admired Louis Brandeis greatly, had productive relationships on public matters of mutual interest with both Brandeis and Felix Frankfurter, and when he ran for a seat on the Boston School Committee, his running mate was a Jewish lawyer named Moses H. Lourie, whom he considered "a thoroughly straight and high-minded and very intelligent man." The fact that a few Jews were acceptable (at least until they were not) demonstrated to many of the most ardent restrictionists that, as a people, they were somewhat responsive to the civilizing effects of education, culture, and material success. They could be cultivated; they could be well-spoken; they were capable of learning which fork to use.

But for all practical purposes, the only Italians the patricians encountered on even a semiregular basis were fruit peddlers and bootblacks. Secretary of State Elihu Root, who had staunchly supported Theodore Seligman's application to join the Union League Club, compared recent immigration from southern Europe to "barbarian invasions." David Starr Jordan said that "there is not one in a thousand

---

* It's true that Adams did have some sneering fun at the Schneidekoupons' expense: their name, in German, means "coupon clipper."

from Naples or Sicily that is not a burden on America." At one point retired Supreme Court justice Henry Billings Brown, writing from his eighteen-room Flemish Renaissance mansion near Washington's Dupont Circle, called for a complete ban on immigration from Sicily and Calabria. In 1906 a *Washington Post* editorial writer stooped to acknowledge that "there is no better agricultural laboring class in the whole world than the real Latin peasantry." But, he continued, 90 percent of the Italians coming to the United States were "the degenerate spawn of the Asiatic hordes which, long centuries ago, overran the shores of the Mediterranean." They were coming to America "to cut throats, throw dynamite, and conduct labor riots and assassination."* Even those who managed through talent and hard work to penetrate the redoubts of the privileged were ridiculed. In a novel published in 1902 (one year after his enormous success with *The Virginian*), Owen Wister described the "shiny little eyes . . . furtive and antagonistic" of an Italian student at Harvard. "I don't think Oscar owns a bath," one of his classmates says with a smirk.

Inevitably, as the downtown Jews struggled to rise, some of them sought to consign other groups, including the Italians, to lower rungs of the ladder. The anti-immigration movement, said the Russian-born physician, economist, and social reformer I. M. Rubinow, was not anti-Jewish; it was anti-Irish, anti-Polish, anti-Italian. "The Americans may be right," wrote Rubinow; those other groups, he insisted, "are culturally inferior." In sectors of the labor movement Italians who weren't despised as strikebreakers were nonetheless seen as directly responsible for low wages. This was particularly so in the case of the so-called birds of passage— laborers who would come for several months, then return home with their savings. In the period

---

* The *Post* editorial was read on the floor of the Senate two weeks later during a debate on another iteration of the literacy test by Furnifold M. Simmons of North Carolina, whose dramatics were as flamboyant as his name. Consider this, from 1928: "I would rather die, I would rather have my right arm cut off, I would rather have my tongue cleave to the roof of my mouth, than to vote for" a Catholic for president.

of greatest immigration, for every ten Italian immigrants who came to the United States there were seven returning to their homeland. When Jacob Riis wrote with a discomfiting condescension that the Italian immigrant in New York was content to "live in a pig-sty," he may have been describing circumstances tolerable only to men intent on saving every conceivable penny to take back home to their desperately poor families. But even at his most sympathetic, Riis slapped with one hand while he embraced with the other: "With all his conspicuous faults, the swarthy Italian immigrant has his redeeming traits. He is as honest as he is hot-headed." Joe Lee dismissed an assertion that the "inborn suavity" of the Italians would improve the nation's manners. Because "this inborn suavity takes the form of sticking a stiletto into your friends and enemies and acquaintances," he wrote, "it seems to me that it is an undesirable substitute" for American etiquette. This wasn't a private communication. It was the heart of a letter to the editor published in a Boston daily.

The Italian immigrants were not without their advocates. But their fellow countrymen hadn't nearly the political or financial might of the German Jews, many of whom had arrived in the United States endowed with both money and education, and most of whom had been in the country for decades. The Italian-born and Naples-trained physician Antonio Stella—older brother of the futurist painter Joseph Stella—was instrumental in a number of efforts to help the newcomers, engaging in issues related to public health (he was particularly active in the battle against tuberculosis, which was often endemic in the slums) and public perception (notably with his proudly pro-immigrant book, *Some Aspects of Italian Immigration*). Enrico Caruso—as it happens, Stella was the great tenor's personal physician—was among prominent figures who supported the Society for Italian Immigrants. Sympathetic assistance came from such surprising groups as the Connecticut chapter of the Daughters of the American Revolution, who were supporting a principle not dissimilar from some of Joe Lee's charitable efforts: whatever one's attitudes toward the foreigners, once they were here, it was necessary to educate them. Toward this end, the DAR commissioned immigration advocate John Foster Carr to write a series of how-to-be-American books directed at Italians, Jews, and Poles. *Guida degli Stati Uniti per L'Immigrante Italiano* provided some basic American history and geography along with useful explanations of tasks as relatively complex as opening a bank account and as basic as personal hygiene ("Bathe the whole body once every day," Carr shouted in boldface type*). Carr's book also included the encouragement to get out of town: "Do not be deceived by the good wages that are often paid in large cities," read an official translation. "Thousands of Italians have made extraordinary successes here in farming and gardening."

A more thoroughly empathetic version of Americanization, as the civilizing process became known, was rooted in the settlement house movement. These all-purpose educational-recreational-social-cultural-job-training-and-sometimes-medical agencies were usually funded by prosperous citizens who recognized the need to provide services to the new immigrants crowding their cities. One such was the Civic Service House in Boston, founded by Pauline Agassiz Shaw, whose husband was an Adams and whose father was the famous (and immovably anti-Darwinian) Harvard naturalist Louis Agassiz. Jane Addams used an inheritance from her wealthy father to open her famous Hull House in Chicago in 1889, and six years later Jacob Schiff financed the Henry Street Settlement on Manhattan's Lower East Side, where Lillian Wald started the Visiting Nurse movement. Across the East

---

* A few years earlier, in a magazine article defending the Italians, the generally sympathetic Carr provided earnest, if discouraging, context: "Like all their immigrant predecessors," he wrote, "Italians profess no special cult of soap and water." But, he added with what he must have considered reassuring affirmation, "here too are differences, for some Italians are cleaner than others."

River, the Italian Settlement opened its doors in 1901 in a building directly beneath the vaulting span of the Brooklyn Bridge.

The Italian Settlement dedicated itself to the area's teeming crowds of Neapolitans, Sicilians, and Calabrians. The founding director remained in his job for forty-two years, so devoted to the neighborhood's immigrants that in 1908 he traveled to Sicily in the wake of the merciless Messina earthquake that killed some 25,000 people. He carried with him a list of 160 people to look for—relatives of his clients in Brooklyn—but in the tumult of the ruinous disaster he could locate only 67 of them. To those he gave aid; for the rest, he could only mourn. But, he recalled afterward, "our experience with south Italians in this time of crisis . . . deepened our sense of their good natural qualities and their promise of their value as citizens among us."*

The Italian Settlement's director was necessarily engaged with the immigration politics of the era. He opposed the literacy test and any increase in the head tax charged each arriving immigrant. The nation's "duty to the immigrant," he believed, was absolute. But at one point, the director did suffer a bout of despair. "We have neglected the immigrant," he wrote to his brother. "We have put upon him burdens he was unable to bear and responsibilities which he never carried out in his own land, and when the result of our negligence and indifference and infidelity comes home to us, we do not decry our own deficiency, but put all the blame on him instead of sharing our part of it."

The director of the Italian Settlement was William E. Davenport, the Connecticut-born son of a prominent Brooklyn family. His brother Charles ran a biological laboratory on Long Island.

---

* One such was a Calabrian teenager named Angelo Siciliano, who on a field trip to the Brooklyn Museum became entranced by the classical sculptures, particularly the *Discus Thrower*, the *Dying Gladiator*, and other imposing physical specimens. The boy asked Davenport if he could develop a similar body. Decades later, Siciliano—by then known as the bodybuilder Charles Atlas—recalled Davenport's life-altering reply: "If you were willing to work hard enough you could."

Chapter Four

The Kindled Fire

The relationship between the celebrated Henry Cabot Lodge and the virtually anonymous Prescott Hall endured through a quarter century of shared restrictionist effort. But even after Grover Cleveland vetoed the literacy test and William McKinley snubbed it, they did not march arm in arm. Both men may have arisen from the same Brahmin thicket of schools and clubs and dancing classes, but their differences created a distance that their shared xenophobia could not compress. While the worldly Lodge enjoyed a social life that had him out for dinner nearly every night, the chronically neurasthenic Hall was private and remote. Lodge traveled widely, while Hall's voyaging largely took place along the four-mile stretch between his office in the city and his "country" place on High Street in Brookline, a house he built next door to his father's Greek Revival mansion. Lodge's ruddy vigor kept him active in public life well into his seventies; Hall—thin to the point of emaciation and perpetually ailing—was effectively an invalid by his late forties.

More crucially, Lodge was engaged by a wide range of issues, as one would expect of a U.S. senator—in his case, enthusiasm for protective tariffs and a belligerent foreign policy, and resistance to such liberalizing reforms as the direct election of senators. Hall had his avocational interests—music, nature study, his "psychical" communication with the dead—but over the years, as he took on more and more of the Immigration Restriction League's work, and as this effort replaced nearly everything else in his life, his law practice would shrink to the point of disappearance. In time he found himself accepting a small salary from the league as well as a contribution to his office expenses. He was, said one colleague, "the mainspring, the backbone" of the IRL, a zealot consumed by an inner fire.

But as much as Hall was convinced that his feverish production and dissemination of research and propaganda would carry the day, and as much as Lodge believed that his power in the Senate and his intimate friendship with the president would bring his campaign to success, neither man was able to get meaningful restriction enacted into law. After Cleveland's veto of the Lodge bill and its subsequent failure to get through the next Congress, the literacy test scarcely had a pulse. Despite Roosevelt's endorsement it hadn't passed in 1902, had been dropped entirely from the Immigration Act of 1903, and in 1904 Lodge himself was compelled to delete it from the Republican platform. Once again the IRL suspended activity, its prospects discouraging, its treasury bare. Then, the next year, Joe Lee hired Kansas-born James H. Patten to lobby Congress on behalf of immigration restriction.

Patten was only twenty-eight when Lee put him on his personal payroll, but he had in hand his freshly issued diploma from Harvard Law School (and, Lee was pleased to tell Lodge, Harvard bachelor's and master's degrees as well). He also brought with him a young man's enthusiasm and energy, which he would retain with scant diminution over a four-decade career devoted to keeping unwanted immigrants away from American shores. After moving east from Kansas in 1896 to study in Cambridge, Patten told a friend many years later, "I then found in Boston . . . a few patriots with vision and a deep sense of public service." As long as there was an Immigration Restriction

League, Patten represented it in Washington, always at Joe Lee's personal expense; they became so close that at Lee's funeral in 1937, Patten was one of the very few non-Bostonians among the small crowd of Brahmins the Lee family enlisted as honorary pallbearers. Patten occasionally lobbied for a few other organizations, but their names suggest that there was little conflict with his primary client. They included the Sons of America, the Patriotic Civic American Alliance, the American Purity Federation, the American Citizenship Foundation, and the General Board of Patriotic Societies. Patten's last appearance before a congressional committee, in 1939, was devoted to testifying in support of a bill providing for the deportation of aliens "who advocate the making of any changes in the American form of government."

Describing the IRL's work to a friend after Patten had been on the payroll for several years, Joe Lee said it "consisted primarily in keeping in Washington the ablest lobbyist in the United States." Patten was more than the league's buttonholer/arm twister/cajoler of senators and congressmen. He was also its legislative draftsman, its primary agent in election campaigns against pro-immigration candidates, its liaison with labor unions, farmers' groups, and other regiments in the restrictionist army. When legislative action was at its highest pitch, he was in touch with Lee almost daily. Often he displayed a grammatical tic that seemingly caused no concern among his anti-immigration compatriots: untroubled by the conflation of nouns and adjectives, Patten would speak of the "Jew congressional district" or "the Jew argument" or "another jew meeting." He was nothing if not ecumenical, though: his reports also included references to "Chink legislation" and "the latest Chink move."

Within a year of Patten's hiring, the IRL was back in action as yet another version of the literacy test came into view in Congress. Reporting to Lee in March 1906, Patten said popular opinion was with them: "fully one-third" of the incoming congressional mail addressed immigration restriction. "Never has there been a time," he told Lee, "when Congressmen and Senators have been so over-whelmed with personal correspondence urging legislation."

There is of course no reliable way to measure public opinion ret-roactively. Still, there's no question that anti-immigrant sentiment was on the rise in many parts of the country in the first several years of the twentieth century. This was not the case only in large cities, where the peculiar alliance of native-born plutocrats and labor union members continued, but as has often been the case throughout U.S. history, perhaps more so in those areas populated with the fewest immigrants. But action provokes reaction, and as the literacy test once again rose to the fore, so did the increasingly potent opposition.

In Boston, even among the most Brahmin of the Brahmins, strong voices gave comfort to those who would keep the gates open. One such was Thomas Wentworth Higginson—Unitarian minister, abolitionist, devoted mentor to Emily Dickinson, and a member of one of the most firmly established Brahmin families. When the literacy test was first under consideration, Higginson publicly wel-comed even the most impoverished eastern and southern Europeans. He wrote, "If the patricians of those races will not come—and why should they, since they have more exclusive privileges at home?—we must accept the plebeians, in the knowledge that they may provide us with patricians in their grandchildren a century hence."

But Higginson was well known as a radical, ready to disrupt the social structures that kept his brethren aloft on Beacon Hill and the newcomers consigned to their ghettos. More surprising opposition to the IRL came from someone whose credentials were nonpareil: "In general," wrote Charles W. Eliot in 1905, some thirty-six years into his institution-defining tenure as president of Harvard, "the attitude of the Immigration Restriction League has struck me as vicious, economically, politically, and sentimentally." The United

States had been built on immigration since 1607, he concluded, "and never faster or better than in the last fifty years."

Eliot's stature in Boston and Cambridge was Olympian. A decade later, when Louis Brandeis's nomination as the first Jewish justice of the Supreme Court was hanging in the balance, Eliot wrote a letter of support. "Next to a letter from God," said one of Brandeis's supporters, "we have got the best." (Eliot's Harvard successor, the restrictionist A. Lawrence Lowell, gathered fifty-five signatures on a petition *opposing* Brandeis.) To some in the IRL, Eliot's opposition to immigration restriction was considered heresy. Richards M. Bradley, a rising figure in the IRL who was soon to become one of its key officials, tried to persuade Eliot that the antirestrictionists who publicly applauded his position "have no interest in common with you." In other words: they are not our kind.

That did not deter Eliot, even though he himself was hardly a model of incorruptible tolerance. He was on the record opposing intermarriage between different nationalities (a position that won him quite a lot of support among some Jewish organizations). He insisted that blacks and Asians could never be assimilated. In 1924, when he was ninety, Eliot would ask Joe Lee, whom he had known forever, if Lee could suggest a Democratic candidate for president who was "Anglo-American by race"—namely, someone other than the Irish Catholic Al Smith. But Eliot never gave an inch on the question of immigration. He told an Italian American group that "the more Italian immigrants that come to the United States the better," and he would even oppose the so-called Gentlemen's Agreement that Theodore Roosevelt negotiated with the Japanese government in 1908, cutting off the flow of Japanese immigrants to Hawaii and other parts of the United States.* In a 1914 letter to his old friend

---

* This agreement ensured that Japan would no longer issue passports to laborers; in exchange, the United States would permit entry to the wives of Japanese men already in the country and would compel the city of San Francisco, in the grip of anti-Asian fever, to allow Japanese children into its public schools, from which they had been barred.

Charles Francis Adams, Eliot wrote, "You and I are about the same age and began life with much the same set of ideas about freedom and democracy. But you have seen reason to abandon the principles and doctrines of your youth, and I have not."

Richards Bradley had been right: such a man was of great use to the opponents of immigration restriction. Eliot knew it, too, and he was happy to enhance the stature of the most prominent pro-immigration organization, the National Liberal Immigration League; he lent his name to the Liberal League even before it held its first general meeting and maintained his association with it for years. The most well-financed and well-organized group opposing immigration restriction, the Liberal League, largely composed of prosperous German Jews, was formed specifically to oppose the literacy test when Lodge and his allies resuscitated it in 1906. It also happened to take the most radical (by restrictionist standards) position on immigration, opposing any restrictions at all beyond those involving criminality or health-related issues.

The Jews who organized the Liberal League drew allies from other national groups, including the Italians, the Poles, and the Irish (one of the NLIL's most devoted political supporters was Congressman James Michael Curley of Boston, whose detestation of the Brahmins was perhaps even greater than their loathing for him). As useful as their support was, it was nothing compared to the benefits that came from an alliance of both convenience and logic with men whose names could have been on the manifest of the *Mayflower*. When the Liberal League published its first book, *The Immigrant Jew in America*, featured authors bore the surnames James, Paulding, and Patton. Charles W. Eliot was joined on the league's letterhead by the wealthy merchant Cornelius N. Bliss, Episcopal bishop Henry Codman Potter of New York, the crusading Presbyterian cleric Charles H. Parkhurst, and Eliot's fellow college president Woodrow Wilson of Princeton. At the time, Wilson was halfway through his transition from anti-immigration bigot (who considered southern

Italians "sordid and hapless") to pro-immigration statesman (who praised "the great people of Italy")—which is to say, he was halfway along the path that led from the cloistered academy to the avid vote-chasing tumult of a national political campaign.

Even more valuable than a roster of starched white names was the support of the American industrial establishment. Here, too, Eliot was a bellwether. An enlightened and liberal man for the era, he nonetheless detested trade unions and welcomed their opposition. "The more letters Mr. Gompers writes about the restriction of immigration the better," he told the Liberal League's first president, Edward Lauterbach. More statements from the AFL president, he continued, "will persuade people that the serious support of restriction measures comes chiefly from trade-unionists. The selfishness of their efforts is perfectly plain." At one point Eliot complained bitterly to a staff member that the league letterhead bore a union label, a fact he found "extraordinary and repulsive." The label soon disappeared from league stationery.

That was an easy call, given the support the Liberal League won from capitalist America, eternally thirsty for low-paid labor. Andrew Carnegie—himself an immigrant, even if from unthreatening Scotland—backed the league. The National Association of Manufacturers, whose president believed that labor union gains would result in "despotism, tyranny, and slavery," signed on as well. Additional support came from such figures as Senator LeRoy Percy of Mississippi, one of the league's founding members, whose interest in immigration was intimately connected to his eleven-thousand-acre plantation in the Mississippi Delta, where more than 150 Italian farmworkers labored under a grim form of peonage.*

Inevitably, as big business moved increasingly toward the pro-immigration position, exerting its considerable influence in Congress

---

* Percy's son was the poet and memoirist William Alexander Percy; his great-nephew, whom W. A. Percy raised, was the novelist Walker Percy.

and elsewhere, labor's antipathy toward imported workers grew yet more intense. The United Order of American Mechanics issued a statement asserting that 80 percent of immigrants "were the most illiterate and vicious types of the European underworld," and business responded with an argument best expressed by George W. Wickersham, the corporate lawyer who served as William Howard Taft's attorney general. "If the manual laborer is shut out," he told a friend, "we will soon be in a condition where we will have nobody to dig our ditches!" But for all the encouragement and backing and even political clout bestowed upon it by its Protestant supporters and corporate sponsors, there was no denying the Liberal League's lineage. "Hebrew money is behind the National Liberal Immigration League," Edward A. Ross insisted. The race suicide theorist was oddly admiring. The league's publications, he believed, "emanated from subtle Hebrew brains." To Ross, the NLIL's continued fight against the literacy test underscored an exasperating irony: "The brightest of the Semites," he wrote, "are keeping our doors open to the dullest of the Aryans!"

Prescott Hall, however, was no ironist. His response to the rise of the Liberal League was governed by two separate aspects of his makeup. The first was his gentlemanly deportment. Hall carried on an exquisitely calibrated bow-and-curtsy correspondence with league officials, each side sending the other organizational information, correcting each others' facts with overstated politesse, thanking one another "for the interesting criticism." Liberal League official Nissim Behar was so engaged by Hall's manners that he was moved to write, "I look on you and other restrictionists as men whom we must respect and even love. When the Bible says 'Love Thy Neighbor,' it makes no exception against restrictionists."

The second aspect of Hall's reaction to the Liberal League was less decorous. Confiding in a prominent blue-blooded New Yorker who was thinking of supporting the new organization, Hall told him that despite the glittering Anglo-Saxon names in the NLIL camp, "the real people actively interested are a group of Jews, who would like to weaken the existing laws in every way for the benefit of their co-religionists in Europe." At one point he discussed trying to turn an NLIL worker into a spy for the IRL. Several years later, after his polite exchanges with his NLIL counterparts had ceased, Hall engaged with a colleague in New York in an effort to gather some information about the organization's inner workings. Hall's confederate had a solution: "It is impossible to get any information in the Liberal Leagues [*sic*] Headquarters if you look too refined, but I can probably get some Jew to go in for me."

*　　*　　*

THE REINTRODUCTION OF literacy test legislation in 1906 provoked the most intense battle over immigration since Lodge's bill first demarcated the front lines of the immigration debate. Lodge turned over the honor of introducing this latest version to Representative Augustus Gardner, but that was probably less a matter of strategy than an expression of Brahmin pride: Gardner was Lodge's son-in-law.

The IRL, which had been reinvigorated by James Patten's energies and had begun a much more active engagement with Washington, agreed to a number of modifications in the measure. The new legislation no longer stipulated that the literacy test material had to be a quotation from the U.S. Constitution. It also raised the age at which an immigrant had to prove literacy from fourteen to sixteen, and helpfully agreed to exempt blind immigrants from the law's provisions. More tellingly, the initial restriction bill Gardner introduced in early 1906 also called for an increase in the head tax charged each immigrant, from $2 (not quite $60 in 2019 dollars) to $5 (nearly $150), and further required each immigrant family to have $25 (more than $730) in its possession upon arrival. Proponents could argue that this did not discriminate against specific nationalities, as it was applied equally to all nationalities. In truth, it was no less discriminatory than a measure that would have barred entry to anyone who couldn't recite the Episcopalian doxology: cash, like knowledge of Protestant ritual, was in short supply in eastern and southern Europe.

The restrictionists' effort to find anodyne proxies for measures clearly aimed at the Italians, Jews, and other unwanted groups was significant. The growing ethnic vote led anti-immigration figures in both parties to tiptoe around the issue of nationality and to find other ways to achieve their aims. In congressional debate, restrictionists could attempt to avoid charges of bias by finding ways to praise immigrants from groups they found questionable while still making restrictionist distinctions—for instance, one senator's assertion that "the few who came during the [pre-1880] period from eastern and southern Europe were representatives of the best elements of their nationalities," unlike the newcomers. In other words, it wasn't the nationality that offended, only these recent, distasteful elements of the nationality. Yet more imaginative was a purportedly humanitarian measure that won the favor of both Lodge and Lee, calling for an increase in the air space required for each passenger on an inbound ship from 110 to 200 cubic feet. And while Lee could say that it would make passage "more comfortable and more decent" for immigrants, he did not fail to point out that it would also reduce steerage capacity, which in turn would cut the steamship companies' profitability. And that, he explained, would have to increase "the amount charged to the immigrant."

The bill that made its way to the House floor in 1906 had bipartisan managers, broad public support, an absence of blatantly biased language—and, as a chastening reminder to the undecided, the cold reality of nearly 900,000 immigrants arriving at Ellis Island alone, more than in any previous year. The outnumbered congressional opposition came largely from representatives from urban ethnic districts, such as Republican Richard Bartholdt of St. Louis and

Democrats Jacob Ruppert Jr. of New York and Adolph Sabath of Chicago. Bartholdt, born in Germany, was an internationalist who wanted Esperanto taught in American schools (during World War I, Joe Lee told Lodge he thought Bartholdt was a German agent). Ruppert, a wealthy German American brewer, was in his last term in Congress, on his way to becoming principal owner of the New York Yankees. Sabath, in his first term, was a Bohemian Jew who had come to the United States alone at fifteen. He could be both an outspoken advocate for the antirestriction position and, in the eyes of those who wanted to shut the gates, a symbol of what they wished to keep out: "uncouth" and "ill-mannered" (said James Patten), his deportment tending toward the confrontational, his syntax garbled and his pronunciation unsteady (he continued to say "wote" for "vote" throughout the forty-five years he spent in the House). Sabath was unmistakably "foreign."

But the member of Congress who put his indelible imprint on the 1906 incarnation of the literacy test was the body's leading Republican—the North Carolina–born, Indiana-bred, Ohio-educated, rural Illinois–based Speaker of the House, Joseph G. "Uncle Joe" Cannon, than whom no politician could have been less avuncular. After Lodge inserted his test into a comprehensive immigration reform bill with little Senate resistance, it was the House's turn to act on Augustus Gardner's amended version. The bill passed comfortably. Then Cannon launched what the *New York Times* called "one of the most extraordinary spectacles ever seen on the floor of the House."

First he maneuvered a revote. Then Uncle Joe demonstrated the aptness of his other nickname—"Czar Cannon"—by stepping down from the Speaker's chair into the well of the House and joining his lieutenants as they buttonholed, browbeat, and otherwise bullied straying members who had voted against his wishes. Cannon roamed the House floor, manhandling some of the insubordinates and shaking them by the lapels. His tyrannical control of the House's procedures would lead a few years later to an unprecedented revolt, but in 1906 Cannon remained all-powerful, and enough members changed their votes to defeat the literacy test by a narrow margin.

Cannon might have needed muscle to line up the Republican regulars against the party's xenophobes and the progressives who, supported by organized labor and various urban reformers, generally backed immigration restriction. (The Democrats were similarly divided.) But for his own motivation, Cannon, who led his party's conservative wing, needed only an understanding of demographics. The previous decade's steerage passengers were fast becoming this decade's voting citizens. The National Liberal Immigration League had recruited the mayors of Detroit, Chicago, Cleveland, and Syracuse to rally against restriction. The Catholic Church intensified its support for open immigration; Cardinal James Gibbons of Baltimore, the nation's senior Catholic prelate, met with Theodore Roosevelt to make the antirestriction case. And despite his long-standing commitment to the literacy test and his promise to Gardner that he would sign it if it was enacted by Congress, Roosevelt chose not to press the matter. When Lodge implored his best friend to try to revive his bill in a political statement he was preparing to issue, Roosevelt refused. If he were trying to influence Congress, the president said, it would be different. However, the particular message he was working on was aimed at voters, and a push for immigration restriction, he told Lodge, would be "a disadvantage politically." Roosevelt (and Cannon) could count: the portion of the U.S. population that was either foreign-born or had at least one foreign-born parent was about to hit 50 percent. A large portion were still children, and many had not yet attained citizenship. But Roosevelt—the leading exponent of the theory of race suicide—was compelled to acknowledge that the immigrants were winning "the warfare of the cradle."

From the restrictionist standpoint, the immigration bill that finally emerged from the House-Senate conference committee in

1907 and was signed into law by Roosevelt was a near-total failure. Cannon had appointed Ruppert and another pro-immigration New Yorker, William Bennet, to the committee and ordered them to brook no compromise relating to the Senate-approved literacy test. Only slight modifications in existing law made it through, including a minor increase in the head tax from $2 to $4, but in nearly all other respects Lodge, Gardner, and their confederates had been rendered impotent. Cruel insult was piled on top of crippling injury in a provision that granted the secretary of commerce and labor the ability to overrule the rejection of specific immigrants—and in 1907 the secretary happened to be Oscar Straus, the Jewish cabinet member and immigration advocate who was already regarded suspiciously by the IRL. In the end, the final bill mandated an idea floated by the Liberal League and its allies that guaranteed further delay and inaction: the appointment of a study commission.

In Washington, Representative Bennet wrote to his Liberal League associates to congratulate them. Had it not been for their influence and actions, there "would have been an educational test upon the statute books today," and two hundred thousand "deserving immigrants" would have been barred from the United States each year.

In Boston, Joe Lee wrote to "My Dear Cousin Lodge": Could Cabot possibly arrange an appointment to the commission for the IRL's James Patten? It was a feeble squeak from a man who usually displayed a hearty appetite for meaningful action. The Immigration Restriction League, it appeared, was once again out of ammunition.

*   *   *

"THE OLD CHARM OF MOUNT VERNON STREET," wrote Henry James after his 1904 visit to Boston, provided "the happiest street-scene this country could show." To James, happiness resided not in display but in tranquility: the twin columns of elms, the stately march of redbrick row houses stretching west from the golden dome of the Massachusetts statehouse down the slope of Beacon Hill, "the felicity of scale" that promised solidity and serenity. On the pleasant early-spring evening in 1908 when the members of the executive committee of the Immigration Restriction League made their way to Joe Lee's home at 96 Mount Vernon, the elms were about to bud. Speaker Cannon's demolition of the previous year's immigration legislation had sent the league into another one of its somnolent and silent periods, but now, like the elms, the IRL was preparing to show signs of vigorous life.

It had been just six weeks since the league's semiweekly executive committee meetings had been moved from Prescott Hall's downtown law office to Lee's noble Greek Revival home. The IRL's decisions no longer emerged from the somewhat ludicrous exercise that had Hall and Robert Ward meeting in Hall's office, just the two of them, with Ward delivering the chairman's report while Hall listened and took notes, then Hall delivering to Ward the treasurer's and the secretary's reports. Starting in January 1908, meetings held at Lee's house guaranteed one essential ingredient: the presence of Lee himself. He had avoided executive committee meetings in the fourteen years since the league's formation, but now he was no longer content to reach into his wallet and otherwise remain in the shadows. Nor did his wallet close up: in February alone, drawing on his personal funds, he wrote eleven checks for league expenses as substantial as James Patten's salary and as trivial as postage stamps.

On this March day many of the IRL's supporters in Greater Boston would be preparing for the next day's Republican Party district meetings, where the process of choosing a presidential candidate was about to begin (not Lee, though: he remained a Democrat, supporting the archpopulist William Jennings Bryan, whom he once said "embodies the democratic idea of government as opposed to the plutocratic idea").* The *Boston Globe* reported that a lethal bomb had detonated in New York's Union Square, killing one and leading to the immediate arrest of six immigrants; in its headline the *Globe* added the man-bites-dog news hook: ONE AMERICAN AMONG SUSPECTS. In Boston Harbor a White Star liner discharged several hundred Italians and Portuguese from its steerage deck.

That evening, gathered beneath the soaring ceiling of Lee's mahogany-trimmed front parlor, its windows fronting the quiet calm of Mount Vernon Street and a substantial fireplace (one of ten in the four-story house) anchoring the west wall, the men of the IRL got down to business. Hall and Ward gave their reports and then Lee offered his, largely a summary of recent immigration developments. Most were discouraging, including the news from London that the steamship companies had persuaded British authorities to allow them to reduce the required amount of air space per passenger. It's impossible to know from the distance of more than a century exactly how the conversation proceeded or the range of subjects it covered. But the minutes reveal at least one of the evening's topics. Before adjourning, the committee passed judgment on three resolutions. The first two were inconsequential, but the last was not: "VOTED," the minutes read, "that we enlist on our side those who favor eugenics."

The next day Prescott Hall wrote to Alexander Graham Bell and asked to be introduced to America's leading eugenicists. Within weeks Joe Lee had in hand a reading list he had requested, featuring articles by Francis Galton, Galton's apostle Karl Pearson, and one by the young American biologist Raymond Pearl titled "Breeding Better Men: The New Science of Eugenics Which Would Elevate the Race by Producing Higher Types." By year's end Hall produced

---

* He'd also declared, in the same statement, his opposition to the 1900 Republican ticket. Because William O. McKinley was "not immortal," wrote Lee, he was concerned about a vice president "who believes in war simply as an educational institution, because it is good for people's nerves and strengthens the muscles of the back and legs"—an imaginative and not wholly inaccurate characterization of McKinley's running mate, Theodore Roosevelt.

IRL Publication No. 51, *Eugenics, Ethics & Immigration*, which made a classic progressive case: just as compulsory education and pure food laws were designed to "protect people from harm and raise them to a higher type," so would a eugenic approach to immigration. Effective laws or regulations were necessary, he noted, because "wars and pestilences no longer eliminate the unfit as formerly."

* * *

AS ORIGINALLY CONCEIVED and then developed, Charles Davenport's Station for Experimental Evolution in Cold Spring Harbor was not congenial to the study of humans. The laboratories and breeding aquaria, the 8.2 acres of experimental gardens and the livestock shed, the multiplying strains of fruit flies developed by a staff entomologist (who shared some of his flies with Thomas Hunt Morgan, who would win a Nobel Prize for his groundbreaking work with their descendants)—none of this pertained to human beings. Evolutionary development in fruit flies could be discerned within months; humans required millennia. A young researcher named Roswell Hill Johnson, later the coauthor of the leading textbook on eugenics, had not yet called for laws to "prevent the outbreeding of superiors by inferiors," as he would in the pages of Margaret Sanger's *Birth Control Review* in 1922; working for Davenport in 1907, he was thoroughly engaged by a huge mass of hibernating beetles that had been unearthed on a hilltop in eastern Washington State and transported to Cold Spring Harbor.

Davenport's own work ranged from the study of heredity in poultry (he recorded and enumerated virtually every possible variation in poultry genetics: pigmentation, tail length, even changes from generation to generation in "nostril height") to "color-pattern of the lady beetles." This earnest assortment of biological inquiries may have reached a pinnacle (at least in terms of labor required) in a study of "vegetable teratology," or the science of physical malformation in plants; that one had required the dissection of 125,000 different specimens of passion fruit.

But buried in a report on experiments in natural science that he submitted to the Carnegie trustees in 1910, Davenport also provided a brief description of a pamphlet about "better breeding" that has "awakened interest in the improvement of mankind." Advancing the cause, he wrote, had called for "the establishment of a eugenic record office" at Cold Spring Harbor in connection with the American Breeders Association. Its work would be supported by "an outside source." And what a source it was: by the description of the *New York Times*, "the richest woman in the world."

Immigration, race, direct engagement in political debate—none of this was on Charles Davenport's mind when he established a branch of his Cold Spring Harbor domain dedicated to the study of the eugenic aspects of heredity. He was interested in "how [a] characteristic will be distributed among the children" of a human mating. After he and his wife concluded a series of studies of Mendelian inheritance of eye and hair color, he began to think that genetic characteristics that would produce "effective, socially fit men and women" might similarly be passed along from parent to child. So, too, might epilepsy, imbecility, and certain forms of insanity. Positive eugenics, negative eugenics—however ominous the latter might sound to modern ears, Davenport was comfortable investigating whether "weak and vicious stock" could be eliminated by proscribing certain marriages; it was an idea, he suggested to one potential donor, that was merely "preventive medicine." But driven as always by the need for data, he wanted to move beyond speculation to evidence. This was to be the mission of the Eugenics Record Office (named after the similar institution Francis Galton had established in London)—the collection and analysis of data that would hasten the advent of eugenic practices in America.

Davenport had begun to prepare the foundation for the ERO in the summer of 1906. Among the young people who came to Cold Spring Harbor to study at the Biological Laboratory that summer was twenty-four-year-old Mary Harriman, the daughter of E. H. Harriman, monarch of the Union Pacific and Southern Pacific Railroads. She had already displayed an inclination toward philanthropy and service while a nineteen-year-old undergraduate at Barnard College when she founded the Junior League for the Promotion of Settlement Movements. "We were just a group of girls anxious to do something in the city we loved," recalled her friend and fellow Junior League officer Eleanor Roosevelt.

The organization she started in New York would grow into a national institution, for more than a century providing young socialites an opportunity to do good works—and, critics could say, not incidentally providing a status credential that would ensure their continued recognition as socialites. But a young woman of Mary Harriman's wealth needed no such credential, and no one could ever challenge the bone-deep sincerity of her commitment. Her engagement with the causes she espoused was so boundless that at times she could be seen driving her carriage uptown to Barnard's campus on Morningside Heights, dictating a torrent of memos and letters to a secretary in the seat next to her. She was so entranced by one enthusiasm that it led classmates to give Mary Harriman a new nickname: "Eugenia."

Harriman had discovered the wonders of eugenics in her biology classes at Barnard; one of her teachers was H. Fairfield Osborn, the paleontologist who would in time become the most prominent scientific advocate for eugenic restrictions on immigration. In 1906 Davenport gave Harriman the opportunity to pursue her studies as one of the students and recent graduates who came to work with him in Cold Spring Harbor each summer. This in turn gave Davenport the opportunity to meet Mary's fabulously wealthy father when he sailed into the harbor to visit his daughter and tied up at the Biological Lab's wharf. For someone who was beginning to think of sources of financial support for his dreamed-of eugenics institute, it was a fortuitous connection. One colleague remembered that Davenport began his fundraising effort by methodically paging through *Who's Who* to compile a list of rich Long Islanders. Engaging with the Harriman family was a far more efficient tactic, and Davenport began devising a plan with Mary to elicit the family's support. "Things will probably move 'slowly,'" she told him in February 1909, "but then most 'surely.'"

When E. H. Harriman died later that year, Davenport's planning was unsettled. Now the Harriman whom Davenport needed to know was Mary's mother, also named Mary. She herself was a railroad heiress (her father had given E. H. his start in the industry), a breeder of horses and cattle, a committed social activist, and now the sole beneficiary of her husband's vast estate. In a will just three sentences long, her husband's fortune of $70 million (2019 equivalent: nearly $2 billion) was placed in her firm, capable, and extremely disciplined hands.

This enormous sum, and Mrs. Harriman's wish to give much of it away—her husband's bequest gave her "a great opportunity," she said—also brought to her door six thousand supplicants seeking, in total, some $267 million in benefactions. She thereupon commissioned a study of the six thousand requests, financed publication of a book of more than four hundred pages devoted to an analysis of philanthropic activity, and along the way began dispensing gifts to causes she supported. One of her goals, she said, was "to help the unfortunate ones." Another was "to insure the equal opportunity for all to become efficient." And a third was to prevent "the decay of the American race."

Tall and slim, as reserved in manner as her daughter was expansive and vigorous, this Mary Harriman* was distinctive in her era for the forward role she played in large-scale philanthropy—partly because she was virtually the only woman of her time who did so, but also because she took a far more active role in distributing her money than the male Rockefellers and Carnegies or any of the other families who had amassed Gilded Age fortunes and then turned their attentions from accumulation to patronage. There was no Harriman foundation, no board of advisors or staff of program officers. She made the decisions, and she wrote the checks.

By the time Charles Davenport traveled into New York from Cold Spring Harbor to meet with Mrs. Harriman in February 1910, the object of his interest was well settled in to her position as head of the family and custodian of its fortune. She was waiting for Auguste Rodin to complete the marble bust of her husband that their daughter had commissioned in the last months of E. H.'s life, and she was still using black-edged stationery for her correspondence. But Mary Harriman's energies were prodigious, and the value she placed on efficiency afforded little space for reflection. She was fifty-eight years old, the mother of six, and she ran her many households, their staffs, and various associated ventures with the polite hauteur of an aristocrat, sharpened by the precision of . . . well, of an especially rigorous railroad conductor. In fact, she had long been involved in her husband's business affairs: an officer of the Union Pacific said she had "a knowledge of railroads equal to that of any man I have ever come in contact with."

It may give a sense of the contours of Mrs. Harriman's wealth in 1910 to know that she owned a mansion in Manhattan; a 10,000-acre ranch in Idaho; a fox-hunting haven in the rolling grasslands of

---

* Her full name was Mary Williamson Averell Harriman, her daughter's merely Mary Williamson Harriman. The Averells—her father's family—were commemorated in the middle name of her second son, the future diplomat and New York governor W. Averell Harriman.

Fauquier County, Virginia; a 186-foot oceangoing steam yacht called the *Sultana* (staffed by a crew of sixty-five); and a country home called Arden on the west bank of the Hudson River fifty miles north of New York. Calling Arden a "country home" is comparable to calling the Hudson a creek. Arden's main house, designed by the architects of the New York Public Library, contained 100,000 square feet of living space. Situated on a 50-acre plateau that had been carved by dynamite from the granite of the surrounding hills, overlooking lakes and mountains and forests stretching to limitless horizons, it was served by a private railway that approached it through 45,000 acres of Harriman land—more than enough land to accommodate the island of Manhattan three times over.

But it was to Mrs. Harriman's Fifth Avenue palazzo that Charles Davenport came to press his suit. Young Mary had invited him to lunch with her mother.

Davenport's plans were not small, nor was the sum required to execute them: he believed he needed an endowment of roughly $12.5 million (2019 equivalent: $350 million). This sum would support a staff of nearly two hundred centered in Cold Spring Harbor, with branch offices in nine American cities and foreign offices in London, Berlin, Naples, and Bucharest. Fieldworkers supervised by each of these offices would be charged with compiling pedigrees for tens of thousands of people of both "the sub-normal as well as the normal classes," and tracing their various physical, mental, and even emotional characteristics from generation to generation. Subjected to Mendelian analysis, the data would, he believed, lead to "one of the most important pieces of work that could be undertaken in this country": the identification of "fit matings." Such a fund, he had told the younger Mary Harriman, "would meet with universal commendation as the wisest sort of a monument to the memory of Mr. Harriman that could be thought of."

As was so often the case with Davenport, his enthusiasms tended to overwhelm a more prudent approach. Recognizing this in himself, his confidence sank in the days before the Harriman luncheon. Developing the elaborate six-page plan he had given to the younger Mary, the dispirited Davenport confessed in his diary, was "probably time lost." As he traveled into the city for the meeting, he may have already begun thinking of alternative sources, among them John D. Rockefeller and Jacob Schiff, both of whom he would also approach. (Schiff's reply, delivered by his secretary: "I am instructed to say Mr. Schiff regrets that he cannot see his way to interest himself in the Eugenics movement.")

Mrs. Harriman demanded absolute punctuality—railroad habits again—and Davenport no doubt arrived at her home on time. If Mary had prepared him for her mother's austere formality, it could only have heightened his apprehension as he approached the imposing brownstone edifice at the corner of Fifth Avenue and East Sixty-Ninth Street. Judging by his recent discouragement, Davenport was probably ill-prepared to lift what a close associate called Mrs. Harriman's "cloak of formality and preciseness." By the time he emerged from his lunch with the Harriman women, however, Davenport was ecstatic. His report to his diary featured the same descriptor he had used six years earlier, when the Carnegie Institution had agreed to fund his lab: "A Red Letter Day for humanity!"

Mrs. Harriman initiated her involvement with Davenport's proposed Eugenics Record Office by underwriting the purchase of seventy-five upland acres and a large frame house adjacent to the Biological Laboratory in Cold Spring Harbor. (Whether there would be more to follow was at first unclear, a circumstance that led him to solicit Rockefeller and Schiff.) As he tried to pry open Mrs. Harriman's checkbook that much farther, Davenport enlisted Stanford president David Starr Jordan, the prominent ichthyologist (thirty-one species of fish bore his name) and Darwinian absolutist (he professed to believe that unrestricted immigration would retard evolutionary progress) who chaired the eugenics committee of the American Breeders Association—the group that the *Washington Post* had introduced in 1906 with the headline SCIENCE TO MAKE MEN AND WOMEN BETTER. (Jordan was also the man who had fired Edward A. Ross from his Stanford job ten years earlier.) Davenport told Jordan that Mrs. Harriman was "feeling around for opinion" on the value of studying bloodlines, and hoped that Jordan might help her find her way.

Later that summer Jordan made what he called a "little visit" to Arden. Mrs. Harriman had an interest in the work of the Sierra Club (founder John Muir once spent six weeks in her city home), and Jordan was one of its first directors. On this trip, though, his stated purpose was to learn more about E. H. Harriman, whose work and life he had mentioned a few weeks earlier in a speech at the Stanford commencement ceremonies. Jordan may have been the son of farmers from northwestern New York state, but railroad millionaires were nothing new to him: the university he had headed since its birth seventeen years before had been founded and thereafter funded by a fortune built on the rails of Leland Stanford's mighty Central Pacific. Jordan knew how to live among the rich and how to talk to them. After his "little visit" to Arden and its 150 rooms, its paintings and tapestries, its gardens and fountains and sculptures, he wrote to thank his hostess for providing "my glimpse into a sound and wholesome home life."

Before he left, deploying the practiced skills of a university president experienced in separating donors from their dollars, Jordan contrived to turn a sound and wholesome evening in the mountains with both Mary Harrimans toward a discussion of Davenport's project. He later confessed to Davenport that he wasn't sure he had made much progress, despite young Mary's support. Yes, he believed Mrs. Harriman would put up operating funds for the project's first year and possibly additional sums after that, "but she doesn't want to build an institution."

Jordan misjudged. Mrs. Harriman's engagement with Charles Davenport's dream of a eugenic future was pure, and it was complete. From the beginning she took an interest in nearly every aspect of the ERO. She sailed into the harbor aboard the *Sultana* to visit its offices, she played a role in designing accommodations for its fieldworkers, she attended meetings of the ERO's scientific board in Washington. She even sent four of her prize Holsteins to graze on the adjacent land. Davenport took care to acknowledge her contributions to the process of "uplifting our country by improving the blood of our nation." But he engaged as well in the deferential foot shuffling of a courtier, at one point going so far as to describe that process as "those broad plans of yours, in which I am permitted to have a part."

Such plans they were, and such a part he played! Over the course of the next seven years, Mary Williamson Averell Harriman would provide more than 95 percent of the total cost of creating and operating the institution that made eugenics part of the national vocabulary under the passionate, headlong, and in the long run imprudent leadership of Charles Davenport.

*   *   *

HARRY H. LAUGHLIN'S momentous engagement with Charles Davenport and his work began in 1907. That was three years before Laughlin arrived in Cold Spring Harbor to direct the day-to-day operations of the new Eugenics Record Office, fourteen years before his appointment as an advisor to the congressional committee rewriting the nation's immigration laws, and not quite three decades before he was honored in Nazi Germany as "the farseeing representative of racial policy in America." This astonishing and frightening career began in a henhouse. Laughlin needed some information about chicken breeding, and Davenport had done important work as a poultry geneticist. At the time, Laughlin was a twenty-seven-year-old instructor at his alma mater, the North Missouri Normal School (among his courses: "Nature Study and Agriculture"), in his hometown of Kirksville. His request for information led to an invitation to visit Cold Spring Harbor the next summer, which in turn led Laughlin to tell Davenport the following winter, "I consider the six weeks spent under your instruction to be the most profitable six weeks that I have ever spent." The cliché is unavoidable: Little did he know.

When Laughlin learned that Davenport and his wife would be traveling to Columbia, Missouri, early in 1909 to attend an American Breeders Association meeting, he invited them to stop over in Kirksville. By the summer of 1910, as Davenport prepared to hire a superintendent to head the Eugenics Record Office's inaugural staff—still responsible for the entire Carnegie Institution operation in Cold Spring Harbor, Davenport needed to delegate day-to-day responsibility for the ERO—the mentor-protégé relationship had ripened. Laughlin had "youth and energy and an excellent disposition on his side," Davenport wrote to Mrs. Harriman, "as well as special interest and some training in the work" the ERO would be conducting.

Laughlin's only post-baccalaureate training had consisted of a few semesters' work at Iowa State College of Agriculture and Mechanical Arts (he did not earn a graduate degree). His "special interest" had been displayed in what Davenport called "one or two very clear little papers on the principles of human heredity," plus his single summer's work in Cold Spring Harbor and the fact that he had been gathering family histories from his students and sending them along to Davenport. But Laughlin's outlook was sunny, his energy was prodigious, and his future would prove boundless. Although he would become best known as America's foremost advocate of the involuntary sterilization of "defectives," Laughlin's role in the use of eugenics to stanch unwanted immigration would be as close to determinative as that of any other individual.

Some thirty-eight years after Harry Laughlin took over responsibility for the ERO, after his death and Davenport's, after the eugenics creed had been thoroughly discredited and the ERO had closed down for good, its repository of index cards containing the painstakingly gathered data recording the "traits" of more than three-quarters of a million individuals was acquired by the Dight Institute for Human Genetics at the University of Minnesota. Sheldon C. Reed, the institute's director at the time, came to a clear conclusion after familiarizing himself with the ERO material. Most of it, he told an interviewer, was "worthless."

But if you had wanted to use that data to influence public policy in 1910 and the two decades to follow, the ERO files were valuable beyond price. A few months after the ERO opened its doors, Davenport received a small donation from John D. Rockefeller—evidence, Davenport believed, that what he and his colleagues were doing was truly significant. Reporting the gift to Mrs. Harriman, he underscored his conviction with words that were almost too prophetic. "You see what a fire you have kindled!" he told her, his unbounded ardor nearly igniting the page. "It is going to be a purifying conflagration some day!"

The ERO officially opened for business on October 1, 1910, in the handsome old house Mrs. Harriman had bought for Davenport. He marked the opening in a letter he sent her, once again rolling out his favorite exclamation: "This is a Red Letter day!" Having thus acknowledged his patron, Davenport paused a few weeks later to address his inspiration. Francis Galton, now by the grace of King Edward VII recognized as Sir Francis, was eighty-eight and in the last months of his life. He had already willed his fortune to the benefit of the eugenics laboratory he had established at University College in London and to the maintenance of an endowed chair in his name. In recent months he had been writing a utopian novel based on his eugenic principles, a perfervid and in the end unpublishable work called, both obviously and improbably, *Kantsaywhere*. The book imagined a world of men who were "well built, practiced both in military drills and athletics, very courteous, but with a resolute look that suggests fighting qualities of a high order." Such paragons would be born to couples who had been allowed to reproduce only because they scored high enough on a series of complicated tests measuring appearance, intelligence, and other qualities. The higher the score, the more children they were allowed to beget. *Kantsaywhere* was largely unconcerned with immigrants, except from the other side of the usual equation: in Galton's imagined utopia, the eugenically inferior were encouraged to emigrate.

In the real world of Cold Spring Harbor, Davenport told Galton, "the seed sown by you" was sprouting in the eighty acres of ERO land, in the fireproof vault built to accommodate the anticipated mountain of pedigrees and genetic histories, in the staff of nine he had already brought on board, and in the "very cordial relations" he had established "with institutions for imbeciles, epileptics, insane and criminals," all of them vital to his ambitious project. He acknowledged that he was pursuing a form of negative eugenics, but believed that it would result in "positive advice" for the genetically disadvantaged. "We cannot urge all persons with a defect not to marry," he explained, "for that would imply *most* people, I imagine." But, he added, "we hope to be able to say, 'despite your defect you can have sound offspring if you will marry thus and so.'" As this new world came into being, Davenport told his hero, "humanity will more and more appreciate its debt to you."

A visitor to Cold Spring Harbor in the fall of 1910 would have found an institution off to a sprinting start. Almost from the moment Mrs. Harriman wrote her first checks, Davenport had begun redirecting not only his own efforts but also those of the biology students he recruited for summer work. The bugs and plants and fishes they had studied in previous sessions were forgotten. Now all was eugenics.

He had created "a well-assembled machine," he told Mrs. Harriman. "We have already determined in a preliminary way two things that were not known before: namely that the children of two tall parents are tall and that the children of two slender parents are usually (or always?) slender." It took just four more days for him to leap from this seemingly self-evident declaration to a rather more problematical assumption, conveyed to Mrs. Harriman with ecstatic emphasis: "the children of two parents who are both artists, or singers, or both have high mechanical skill will *all* have the same capacity!" Any provisos, caveats, or other hedges were washed away by his cascading passion. From 1910 forward for the next quarter century, hundreds of papers bearing Davenport's name appeared in academic journals, science magazines, and occasionally the popular press, their subjects a virtual inventory of human variety: Skin pigment. Epilepsy. "Postnatal Growth of the Human Nose." Too often the passion of a believer overcame the caution of a scholar. In one particularly egregious example, he determined that thalassophilia—love of the sea—was a sex-linked characteristic, essentially because all admirals were men. "Seamen know that their cravings for the sea are racial," he added. It wasn't that they went to sea because they lived near water, Davenport argued; their ancestors had moved to the shore because genetic impulses drew them there.

Much of Davenport's study of human inheritance was predicated on one gigantic scientific error: his belief that characteristics as complex and as unmeasurable as memory, loyalty, and "shiftlessness" were determined by a single unit character—in other words, that the origin of each was, genetically speaking, no more complicated than the color of the flowers on one of Gregor Mendel's pea plants. A stunning assumption for such a well-trained scientist, it was less so for a man consumed by a near-messianic fervor. This unquestioning belief made it possible for Davenport to propose—with even more certainty than Galton had ever claimed—that the human species could be altered through the encouragement of matings that were propitious and the suppression of those that were not.

The year before the ERO opened for business, Davenport had addressed an audience of physicians on what he had learned about human inheritance concerning eye color and the like. Then he veered into a brief detour toward the subject of what was then known as "imbecility"—specifically, how it was passed from generation to generation. Within his conclusively grave statement on the subject (in effect, an endorsement of involuntary sterilization for the mentally deficient) lay the kernel of the argument that would in a few years rescue the anti-immigration campaign from more than a decade of torpid ineffectuality. "Where the life of the state is threatened," Davenport told the doctors, "extreme measures may and must be taken." Even after other investigators conclusively determined that most human traits are the product of the interaction of many, many genes, Davenport continued to believe that a single gene, independent of environment or any other factors, could compel a man to go to sea. Even after R. C. Punnett, a British geneticist of unimpeachable authority, determined that it would take 250 generations—roughly 8,000 years—of selective breeding before feeblemindedness* could be effectively eliminated in the United States, Davenport remained convinced that the application of eugenic policy could save the nation from genetic doom. He still wasn't talking about race or ethnicity. But if Davenport had any doubts about the other policy implications of eugenics, he managed to suppress them.

The evidence that kept Davenport's faith aloft—the data that was the reason for the ERO's very existence—was as flimsy as it was

---

* The formal designation used at the time for what became known as "mental retardation" and later as "intellectual disability."

expansive. From the finest eastern colleges he recruited the troops he needed to gather the information that would support the eugenic argument. Before he sent them out on their assignments, the students, almost all of them women, went through six weeks of training—or, as some critics would have it, indoctrination. In the summer months classes were often conducted on the grassy expanse in front of the ERO's main building. Arrayed in lawn chairs on a pleasant July afternoon in their long white skirts and frilly, high-collared blouses, the young women of the ERO could have been gathered for afternoon tea. Only the presence of an ERO staff member, standing beside a blackboard that had been moved out to the lawn, betrayed the real purpose of this pastoral tableau: teaching them how to conduct the interviews that were their core responsibility and inculcating in them Davenport's warped version of Mendelian theory.

Much of the ERO's work would be conducted with the cooperation of scores of mental hospitals, poorhouses, prisons, and other public institutions throughout the country whose managers were interested in eugenic inquiry. If the institutions would provide the fieldworkers' travel, housing, and living expenses, Davenport would pay their salaries, provide necessary supplies, and share the data they gathered. He also sent interviewers to places where they would largely have to function on their own: A forgotten corner of the New Jersey Pine Barrens that had fostered generations of inbreeding. A pocket of central Connecticut where they studied the effect of the replacement of "old stock" by recent immigrants. Ellis Island.

The Rosetta Stone for this massive collection of presumably genetic information was a system Davenport and Laughlin created and codified in *The Trait Book*, a periodically revised document that eventually listed 3,500 human attributes and defects. Each one was assigned a numerical value so the interviewer could fully describe an individual on a single index card. Some traits the fieldworkers were asked to identify were obviously genetic: hair color, skin color, hair texture. Less obvious, perhaps, but potentially pertinent: disease

flaxen hair 1463
flexible boned 204
flexibilitas cerea ... 31623
florists 0912
flower makers, arti-
  ficial 09791
flow of words 45544
flowers, breeding of. 0912
fœtus, mummified.. 9623
fondness 494252
fondness of children 49013
fondness of children
  of opposite sex... 49014
food preparers 0975
foolhardiness 4432
foot-ball 45958
foot, clubbed 21054
foot, deformed 2105
foot, flat 21051
foot, general form
  of 2103
forceps application. 9642
forehead 14828
forehead 228
forehead, bumps on. 2284
forehead, depression
  in 2283
forehead, high 2281
forehead, low 2286
forehead, protruding 2282
forehead, peculiar
  hairiness of...... 14811
forehead, receding.. 2287
forehead, wens on.. 2285
foresight 479
forestry—foresters. 09171
forgery 3545
forgetting, periodic. 41522
forgetting, specific.. 41521
forgivingness 4848
form, love of...... 42112
form, (art) taste in. 4234
form of hair 142
fornication 3514
forwardness 4735
France 9744
frankness 4835
fraud 3544

freckling 127
Friedreich's ataxia. 3311
Friedreich's disease. 333
friends, capacity for
  making 49011
frigidness .. 42612, 4942
frivolousness .4627, 4644
frowns 272
fugues 31852
funnel-breasted 2451
fussiness 46161

Galicia 97461
gall bladder and
  ducts 67
gall stones 676
galloping consump-
  tion 98312
gamblers, profes-
  sional 09290
gambling 4243
game laws 35285
games, love of..... 424903
gangrene 195
gardeners 0912
gardening 423991
gastralgia 6531
gastritis 653
gatophobia 42231
genealogists 09267
general diseases ... 08
generalization 4212
general paralysis .. 3167
general traits 0
generosity 4852
geniality 4913
gentleness 4621
geology, ability in.. 3167
geology, teacher of. 0938
German measles ... 08194
Germany 9743
German-English 97 42 × 43
German-So. African
              97 43 × 68
gigantism 022
gillslits, open 722
girdle 24
glanders 0821

This page from the Eugenics Record Office's all-encompassing *Trait Book* indicates the range of detail Davenport and Laughlin asked their fieldworkers to extract from their interviews and other research.

history, harelip, speech impediment. Then the coding went off the rails. Interviewers were expected to determine subjects' ability to retain urine, whether they were "excited then depressed by alcohol" (or just one or the other), if they were "easily offended." Did the subject suffer from "backwardness" or "mythomania" or "wanderlust"? Did he have "philosophical tendencies"? Was he "rattle-brained"? Did he have a "taste" for "sentimental drama" or natural history or cartoon-making? Was he open or was he secretive? Trustful or suspicious? Whining? Overdevoted? Melancholic? Did he display special ability for penmanship? Chess? Maybe paleontology? Did he violate game laws?

The assumption that anyone on earth (much less a recent college graduate with but a summer's worth of training) could determine and classify each of these "traits" based on an interview was absurd. Worse, the fieldworkers were expected to make these determinations not only for the person interviewed but for as many relatives as possible, going as far back as four generations—often relying for this information on recollection and hearsay and neighborhood gossip (which the ERO euphemized as "community reactions"). From one fieldworker's report in 1916 on a man who had died fifty years earlier: "He is remembered by a few of the oldest settlers of the locality as a peculiar, silly old fellow who drank a good deal, stole sheep and household valuables from his neighbors, and did not seem to be very intelligent." Another: "Her wedding outfit was ready when she suddenly became enamoured of the good looks of a worthless sojourner in town and ran away with him. . . . She seems to have had little moral stamina."

From this gigantic miasma of "data"—in just the first seven years of ERO operations, more than half a million index cards went into the vault—would presumably come the investigator's ability to draw genetic inferences, which could become conclusions, which in turn might eventually be applied to a eugenic program of "selective breeding." And selective breeding would fulfill Davenport's most overheated dreams: as he told an audience of young women in Minnesota, it would "determine the standing of the nation sixty years hence."

He did put some effort into assembling pedigrees for families and individuals he considered "prominent." Almost every issue of the *Eugenical News*, which the ERO would begin publishing in 1916, contained a brief biography of some notable figure ("Traits of Buffalo Bill") built on suspect sources (in this case his widow's memoir) and laden with ostensibly meaningful indicators of eugenic quality (his "love of excitement and danger" would be "useful in securing the desired mate against rivals and for purposes of self-defense"). But Davenport grew ever more concerned with those he termed "defectives," a catchall for those he enumerated in a letter to Mrs. Harriman: "insane, feeble-minded, epileptic, criminal, incorrigible, and blind individuals." It was true that these pathologies were relatively easy to trace across generations; a criminal record was a lot more accessible than, say, measurements of artistic ability. Yet it was also true that environmental influences—in Galton's terms, nurture rather than nature—did not figure in the ERO's calculations and determinations. The primary subjects for study were wards of the state living in public institutions, and by that very fact wildly unrepresentative of the population at large. Additionally, in the Pine Barrens and other remote corners of the map, Davenport's "tactful field workers," eliciting their information from the least sophisticated of subjects, were likelier to arrive at conclusions without the paper trail of evidence—birth certificates, church and school records, and so forth—one might find among more privileged subjects. Thus, owing to the skewed process employed to locate and select its interview subjects, the work of the ERO veered ever further from the positive eugenics of improvement and ever closer to the negative eugenics of prevention. One prominent British scientist who was predisposed to approve of the study of heredity in a eugenic context dismissed the ERO's work out of hand. Its flaws, he said, were nothing less than "careless presentation of data, inaccurate methods of analysis, [and] irresponsible expression of conclusions."

*   *   *

IN ITS OWN RATHER DIFFERENT (but even more ludicrous) way, the Immigration Restriction League was interested in data as well. The league didn't send investigators into the field; instead, it relied on a series of questionnaires about immigration policy that periodically emanated from Prescott Hall's office. Hall directed the IRL surveys to groups no more representative of the population than the league's membership itself: men listed in *Who's Who*, "all living graduates of Harvard Medical School," prominent white southerners, labor union officials. Under the guise of gathering "facts" that rarely approached even the suburbs of valid evidence, the IRL was reaching out to what it believed to be its own audience through what a subsequent century would know as push polls. Claiming to solicit meaningful opinions but actually advancing its own arguments and assertions, the league was in fact trying to recruit new supporters and rally the recruited to its cause. A particularly risible survey question asked participants to rank "classes of persons . . . which are desired," limiting the choices to these categories: "native born; persons from northern Europe; skilled persons; families with some money, intending to settle in the country; British; Scandinavians; Germans." The following question, asking which groups were *not* desired, gave only these options: "foreign born; southern and eastern Europeans; Asiatics; illiterates; those settling in the city and averse to country life; immigrants distributed from eastern cities."

Even Joe Lee, who generally preferred to operate in the background, stepped forward with his own poll. His other engagements at the time were, characteristically, both local and progressive. They included an effort to create a Boston Juvenile Court (his primary ally in that campaign was the Boston Council of Jewish Women) and an array of donations to the city's Family Welfare Society, its Legal Aid Society, and the Industrial School for Deformed and Crippled Children, as well as a $70,000 check (2019 value: $2 million) he wrote for the Massachusetts Civic League's new headquarters building. Lee's personal poll, however, displayed a different aspect of his engagement with public issues. The questions sought only yes or no answers, but not without making a few unsubtle points along the way. Read one, "Would you exclude persons who, whether or not inferior to the present American race, are not adapted by their ideals and traditions to combine with us in building up a better national life and ideal?" Another may have been simpler in its phrasing ("Do you believe in putting the less desirable citizens who now collect in the slums on the farms?"), but it was rather elaborate in the explanation that Lee appended to it: "An objection is [this] accentuates the evils of immigration as a method of selection by putting the least desirable where they will have the largest families, driving the American from the only place where he is otherwise likely to survive, and, by leaving room in the slums, perpetuating the demand for immigration of the worst sort."

When Samuel J. Barrows, a former congressman from Massachusetts who had moved on to prison reform efforts in New York, challenged the questionnaire's core assumptions, Lee was quick to respond: "I agree with you that the Jews and the Italians are excellent people," he acknowledged. "The question is, are they better than the native American?"

To Prescott Hall, the answer was self-evident. He wasn't the only one who knew that the immigrants were inferior and should be stopped at the American door; the near unanimity among the IRL's survey respondents convinced him that the nation overwhelmingly supported his view. At one point, when the House of Representatives Committee on Immigration tabled a literacy test bill, its report made a point of citing the testimony of those witnesses who had spoken out against the measure. Hall was dumbfounded. "This gives the impression that public opinion is largely opposed to the proper regulation of immigration," the disbelieving Hall told a supporter. "We know from our recent canvass that such is not the case, the replies being over 25 to 1 in favor of further selective tests." Could Hall possibly have believed that one could gauge "public opinion" from a series of questionnaires directed only to propertied men of high social standing, almost all of whom happened to bear Anglo-Saxon surnames?

He could, and he did: Hall's world was hermetically sealed, and the responses to some of the questionnaires must have thrilled him. Some were specific in their condemnations: "The immigrant is a brutal destroyer," wrote Charles Barker Bradford, a celebrated sportsman. "He spoils every bit of nature in his own country, then comes to new fields in our country to destroy them." Others had more general objections, to "filthy, lousy, and diseased" children, "scum of the earth," the "off-scourings of European nations" (this last coinage came from Hudson Maxim, the inventor of smokeless gunpowder). E. Mead Wilcox, a professor at the University of Nebraska, urged a measure tougher (and potentially far more effective) than anything the IRL dared to recommend: raising the immigration head tax from $4 dollars to $4,000.

The survey enterprise brought in some more supporters, and along with the pamphlets and articles Prescott Hall and Robert Ward continued to turn out, it enabled the IRL's leaders to persuade themselves that they were keeping the restriction crusade simmering, if not nearly boiling, in the years immediately after Uncle Joe Cannon strangled the literacy test. Cannon had of course compounded the crime when he used the tepid Immigration Act of 1907 to establish a study commission; any possible congressional action was on formal hold, subject to what turned out to be four years of investigations and deliberations. In the interim, the men of the IRL used some of their energies to follow up on the eugenic arguments they had begun to study in 1908, when Hall wrote to Alexander Graham Bell and Joe Lee began his deep reading on the subject. Soon Hall and Ward, trying to formulate the proper language for making the case against "racial intermixture," sought help from William Z. Ripley, who had made the distinction between Teutonic, Alpine, and Mediterranean in *The Races of Europe*. Ripley advised them not to use race as a criterion for immigration restriction because "the data are so unreliable," and to rely instead on "the economic argument."

That was no deterrent. Ward and Hall were too enamored of their own theories to be distracted by contrary beliefs. Citing Ripley's work (improperly) as well as Galton's (somewhat irrelevantly), Ward published an article insisting that immigration was "a racial [question], perhaps even more than an economic one." It was the first full, public declaration by the IRL that it was entire nationalities, and not only illiterates, that were tainted and had to be kept out. The United States "was founded by picked men and women," and it was imperative to stop the immigration of inferior people. Lee assured an associate that "the general tendency to talk eugenics is going to help us."

Yet Lee had not realized just how useful that talk was soon to become. "General tendency" began to evolve into intentional design in 1911, when Hall sent a query to a fellow member of the Harvard Class of 1889. Hall's letter began, "Dear Sir, I write to ask if your laboratory has published any material on eugenics." It ended with a friendly P.S.: "Perhaps I ought not to address a classmate so formally, but we regard you as a famous man now."

Charles B. Davenport replied the very next day.

Chapter Five

Short, Sober, Musical Rapists

In the decade that opened the twentieth century, the entire field of hereditary science that had been ripped apart by the discovery in 1900 of Mendel's famous paper experienced a radical remaking. So did much of American life. Theodore Roosevelt declared the nation's arrival as a world power by dispatching the U.S. Navy's "Great White Fleet" on a two-year, globe-circling display of American might. In the South, segregation—and subjugation—based on race hardened into place. With the birth of the mass-produced Model T, the novelty of the automobile was supplanted by its rising ubiquity. For imperialists, southern racists, and prophets of the rising industrial state, the new century was filled with nothing but promise. For the anti-immigration movement, it had brought nothing but despair.

Not once had the restrictionists achieved a meaningful victory. Worse, from their point of view, the problem that had motivated both their anxieties and their actions—namely the preservation of the nation's Anglo-Saxon character and composition—had spiraled into a crisis. Back in 1896, when Henry Cabot Lodge told the Senate that "the danger has begun," even he may not have anticipated what lay ahead. Ships of a single transatlantic service, the Cunard Line, made thirty-five trips in 1901 just from Liverpool to Boston. Deepening poverty in Naples, Sicily, and neighboring areas sent more than 220,000 emigrants from Italian ports in a single year. The 1903 massacre that began on Easter Sunday in Kishinev, in present-day Moldova, initiated a savage new wave of pogroms that left several thousand Jews dead and sent tens of thousands more fleeing imperial Russia. Poles, Greeks, Hungarians, Slovaks—a freshening torrent rushed westward from the entire continent. All told, between 1900 and 1910, the 3.7 million European immigrants who had arrived in the 1890s were joined by an additional 7.6 million. And to those who would argue that the immigrants were a positive addition to the national welfare, restrictionists could cite a report issued by the immigrant-friendly United Hebrew Charities. The report warned that New York City alone was home to nearly 100,000 Jews who were "unable to supply themselves with the necessaries of life."

American nativists were not isolated in their fear of this surging wave. In the United Kingdom, the prominent socialist Sidney Webb warned that the falling birthrate among the British would soon lead to "national deterioration" while their country "gradually [fell] to the Irish and the Jews"—and this was *after* Parliament's adoption of the Aliens Act of 1905, which had already cut the number of Jewish immigrants allowed into the UK by more than two-thirds. New Zealand, the Cape Colony in southern Africa, and Australia all imposed literacy tests, the last of these an expression of what became popularly known as the "white Australia" policy. Canada tightened its immigration laws in 1906 and again in 1910. In 1906, writing about what he learned in a visit to America, H. G. Wells told his British compatriots that the immigration of that era was comparable to the slave trade (even if "different in spirit") because it created "a practically illiterate industrial proletariat."*

American politicians in both parties avoided committing the nation to new immigration policies similar to those imposed on

---

* Wells was also confirmed in his faith in negative eugenics. It was "exceedingly abominable," he wrote, "to make life convenient for the breeding [of the] feeble, ugly, inefficient" and others "born of unrestrained lusts."

the Chinese in 1882—that is, bans that were race-based or absolute. They instead whittled a complex series of restrictions based entirely on individual distinctions, each successive immigration bill enacted immediately before and during Theodore Roosevelt's presidency establishing new subcategories of the inadmissible. Anarchists, epileptics, polygamists, "lunatics," people with "poor physique," people beset by diseases contagious (trachoma, tuberculosis) or "loathsome" (syphilis, gonorrhea, leprosy), people deemed so incompetent and so impoverished they were "likely to become a public charge" (such individuals were inevitably referred to as "LPCs")—all these were now excluded. But despite these and other similar disqualifications, between 1880 and the onset of World War I only a tiny number— fewer than 1 percent—of European immigrants were debarred from entry. And for the restrictionists, that wouldn't do.

In the spring of 1911 Prescott Hall's ingenuous letter requesting printed material on eugenics must have seemed inconsequential to Charles Davenport. His attention was fastened at the time on accelerating the development of his new eugenics operation in Cold Spring Harbor and also preparing for the publication of his first book on the subject, *Heredity in Relation to Eugenics*. Both efforts were consonant with his belief that selective breeding could improve a population—selective breeding plus, as he had said in 1909, "extreme measures" that might include involuntary sterilization. The book is spattered with racial stereotyping, but Davenport did not believe that ethnicity was an especially meaningful factor in any eugenic program. "The fact is," he wrote, "no race per se, whether Slovak, Ruthenian, Turk or Chinese, is dangerous and none undesirable." What mattered, he maintained, was the genetic makeup—the "germ plasm," as he called it—of the individual (which, half a century before the discovery of DNA, was unknowable with any precision). He even made the point that there was likely no such thing as a "pure"

European of any sort, given the importation of slaves from Africa in the first millennium, and he endorsed the argument that even New England's finest would meet "a pathetic and unedifying end" without the infusion of new, foreign blood. His engagement with some of the darkest eugenic ideas was soon to become a passionate romance, but he was not—or at least not yet—a racist.

Consequently, in those early days Davenport's epistolary conversation with his old classmate was somewhat chilly, if polite. "Would you not agree," he wrote to Hall, "that there might be good Greeks or Servians [sic] and undesirable Norwegians and English? Would you not agree also that there might be illiterates who would add desirable hereditary traits to the germ plasm of our country, and on the other hand there would be educated criminals?"

No, Hall did not agree, and he charged right through Davenport's demurral. He did acknowledge that it might seem "ungracious" for the leaders of the Immigration Restriction League to believe that people who shared their ethnic background were superior to those of less favored parentage. But he did not tiptoe around the implications embedded in the preference. "I know the men who have worked with me for many years, giving a great deal of time with no compensation," he said, "and I know that while they may be prejudiced, they are sincere."

Sincere? If sincerity were adequate justification for bigotry, Hall deserved a medal for it. He had long been ready to apply eugenic principles to the immigration issue. At age twenty-five, less than a month after Hall and his two friends first discussed the formation of the IRL back in 1894, he wrote a letter to the *Boston Herald* that revealed the nature of his sincerity: the blunt assertion that southern and eastern Europeans were "physically different races . . . from those already here." He went on to catalog "the dirt, the lowered standards of living, the ignorance and the race deterioration" among the immigrants, and began clipping articles about eugenics as early as 1897, when the word was barely known in the United States. At one point he wanted to bless the organization he had cofounded with a new name: the Eugenic Immigration League.

It's hardly surprising that Hall and his comrades were readier than Davenport to accept the racial implications of eugenic theory. Davenport had discovered Galton only fourteen years earlier; the families of Hall, Lee, and most of the other members of the IRL had been calibrating, curating, and celebrating their bloodlines for centuries. Most of the men of the IRL were comfortable relying not on the claims of science but on what they knew intuitively. Lee, who as the perfect model of the progressive rationalist probably had more faith in science than most of his colleagues, felt no need to invoke it when discussing immigration. Phrases like "the comparative capacity of different races," "race selection," and "fitness of different races . . . for taking part in democracy" invaded his usually casual prose, as if they were contractual boilerplate, though supported neither by logic nor evidence—only by decades, even generations, of unchallenged use.

Davenport, though, was a scientist, and the eminence he had achieved was built on the foundation of data he relentlessly gathered in his research. If immigration was a eugenic issue in the first decade of the century, it was only so at the periphery of his consciousness. The human phenomena he was beginning to explore in the early days of the Eugenics Record Office were specific and focused: hereditary albinism, the causes of imbecility, the consequences of inbreeding among the Pennsylvania Amish. Only with data, he believed, could science leap the chasm separating mystery from knowledge. At one point he told Hall, who persisted in trying to push Davenport toward activism on the immigration issue, "As ever, I am pressed less by the need of more legislation than by the need of more facts."

*   *   *

IT WAS IN 1911 that Charles Davenport began his blinkered transit from eugenic investigator to race partisan. In the same letter in which he had tried to persuade Prescott Hall that every nationality was composed of good and bad individuals, he proposed that the eugenics committee of the American Breeders Association form a subcommittee to analyze the family traits of recent immigrants. There is no evidence to suggest that at the time he felt the study would identify congenital deficiencies particular to any ethnic group. To Davenport and the ERO, the ABA's work would simply provide yet more data for their swelling files. To Hall and the IRL, though, the immigration subcommittee would be far more fruitful: it would provide them with keys to the eugenic kingdom.

The year before, Hall's IRL colleague Robert Ward, the Harvard climatologist whose scientific credentials were so useful to the organization he had helped found, had published an article extolling the "picked men and women" who had settled the American colonies. Appearing in the *North American Review*—where else?—and titled "National Eugenics in Relation to Immigration," it mentioned Galton, invoked Darwin, and offered what in time would essentially become the credo of the joined forces of immigration restriction and eugenic progress. America had "a remarkably favorable opportunity for practicing eugenic principles in the selection of the fathers and mothers of future American children," wrote Ward, "through our power to regulate alien immigration."

Yet while Ward believed that "there are certain parts of Europe from which it would be better for the American race if no aliens at all were permitted," Davenport was not yet ready to make such distinctions as he had demonstrated in *Heredity in Relation to Eugenics*, which was published the same year as Ward's article. It was Davenport's first venture aimed at the general public, and it forcefully—and repeatedly—expressed his belief that every ethnic or national group harbored both desirable and undesirable immigrants. For instance: when one judges the mass of immigrants as a group, he argued, "One is apt to lose sight of the potential importance to this nation of the individual."

One couldn't be clearer than that. But if the book represents Davenport's relative broad-mindedness in the early days of the ERO, it even more reveals the sloppiness of his thinking on the specifics of human genetics, the field he had only recently plunged into with his singularly Davenportian zeal. He constructed his various arguments (mostly about mating in general; only one chapter out of nine concerns immigration) from a mix of scrupulous evidence, reasonable intuition, less reasonable guesswork, old wives' tales, and outright class bias. Typical of his seemingly willful suspension of disbelief was the flabbergasting clause (which begs for the italics Davenport didn't supply) that punctures this sentence: "The oft repeated story that Abraham Lincoln was descended on his mother's side from Chief Justice John Marshall of Virginia, *whether it has any basis or not*, illustrates the possibility of the origin of great traits through two obscure parents." On the contrary, the statement only illustrates how his increasing enthusiasm for his eugenic mission led him to breach even the most forgiving scientific standards. Concerning immigration, the passage where he indulges most egregiously in stereotyping is particularly revealing: "Unless conditions change of themselves or are radically changed, the population of the United States will, on account of the great influx of blood from South-eastern Europe, rapidly become darker in pigmentation, smaller in stature, more mercurial, more attached to music and art, more given to crimes of larceny, kidnapping, assault, murder, rape and sex-immorality and less given to burglary, drunkenness and vagrancy than were the original English settlers." The horror! Battalions of short, sober, musical rapists were poised on the American doorstep! But with proper evaluation and selection of individual immigrants, he calmly explained, "we may expect to see our population not harmed but improved by this mixture with a more mercurial people."

Typical of his half-digested reasoning (and of his normative, caste-based prejudices) as this analysis might have been, Davenport's notions about gathering the necessary information for the eugenic future were even more cockeyed. He closed the book with a plea for the collection and analysis of the pedigrees and traits of all twenty-four million American schoolchildren and their millions of parents, conducted by the nation's 630,000 schoolteachers "through a series of visits on Saturday afternoon or during vacations," and intended to produce "advice" for families "as to how their children should marry." Even if such an unlikely undertaking—untrained investigators collecting unverifiable data about unquantifiable characteristics—were to ensue, the focus was on what could be learned about the individual, not the group.

It may have been inevitable that Davenport's views on immigration would eventually converge with Hall's and Ward's when he appointed them—utter amateurs in genetic matters—to the Breeders Association's immigration subcommittee. He also capitulated quickly when Hall argued that another member Davenport was planning to appoint, pro-immigration journalist Herbert F. Sherwood of the *New-York Tribune*, was "a paid agent" of the National Liberal Immigration League. But the scientist in Davenport made him dig in his heels in defense of another of his nominees, anthropologist Franz Boas of Columbia University.

Hall objected to Boas, heatedly. He said he was related to Emil Boas, the general manager of the Hamburg-American Line (he was not). He also insisted that he'd been given a "fat job" on the immigration commission Congress had created in 1907 "to please the steamship companies" (in fact, Boas's work for the commission resulted in one of the most important anthropological studies of the early twentieth century). But Davenport valued him for his scholarly attainments. He also believed the committee's work could be enhanced by someone who favored open immigration laws; scientific method almost demanded it.

Thomas F. Gossett once wrote that Franz Boas possibly "did more to combat race prejudice than any other person in history." "My ideas have developed because I am what I am," Boas wrote late in his life, "and have lived where I have lived." This statement, in tone and substance, was a concise reflection of both his personality and his philosophy. The personality—rigid, formal, austerely certain— allowed not an inch for doubt. The philosophy defined a potent counterforce to any racial interpretation of genetics: the individual was an independent organism shaped by his life circumstances. Genetic makeup ("I am what I am") was a canvas; environmental influences ("I have lived where I have lived") were the brush and the paint that gave the canvas life.

As a fifteen-year-old boy in northern Germany, Boas told his sister that "If I do not become really famous, I do not know what I will do. It would be terrible if I had to spend my life unknown and unregarded." His ambitions were fully requited. Boas's stature in his field was—and more than a century after he did his most famous work, remains—unmatched. At his death in 1942, his students— among them Robert Lowie, Margaret Mead, Ruth Benedict, and Melville Herskovits—were the outstanding figures in American anthropology.* To journalist Joseph Mitchell, writing in 1937, Boas was "unquestionably the greatest anthropologist in the world." Boas himself was slightly more circumspect. "Actually," he said in 1902, "it is very easy to be one of the first among anthropologists" in the United States.

Early in his career Boas made no effort to cloak his disregard for the prevailing race theories promoted by his American-born counterparts. In 1894, around the time the president of the American Association for the Advancement of Science, anthropologist Daniel G. Brinton, was busying himself comparing the cranial capacities of European whites, African blacks, and orangutans, Boas delivered

---

* Another prize Boas student eventually gave up anthropology for other pursuits: novelist Zora Neale Hurston.

a speech that shredded the underpinnings of race-based arguments. Uncharacteristically eloquent (Boas's prose was usually as stiff and unapproachable as his person), the speech conclusively demonstrated that environmental factors played an enormous role in the development of individual talents and other characteristics, irrespective of race. Conclusively, that is, unless you chose not to listen, and it was not insignificant that Brinton (and others like him) were particularly deaf to Boas's argument: a year later, Brinton insisted that anthropology could provide "a positive basis for legislation, politics, and education as applied to a given ethnic group." In one way, at least, Brinton was right—politicians and pressure groups would use a perversion of anthropology for those purposes for the next three decades.

Boas was argumentative by nature. Throughout the early stages of his career he would repeatedly resign from prominent positions over matters of principle and loudly proceed to make those principles known. His face bore notable scars that he usually attributed to a clawing by a polar bear while doing fieldwork in the Arctic—but to family members and a few others, he insisted that the scars, including a particularly disfiguring one carved into the left side of his face from mouth to ear, came from duels he had initiated in response to anti-Semitic slurs as a university student in Germany. "Apocryphal or not," wrote his protégé A. L. Kroeber, "the tale absolutely fits the character of the man as we later knew him in America."

By the time Charles Davenport approached Boas about joining the Breeders Association immigration subcommittee, the two men had known each other for slightly more than a decade. Boas was interested enough in Davenport's work to have traveled to Cold Spring Harbor with his daughter to visit with him. Davenport knew Boas's work because it was impossible for someone tiptoeing into even the shallowest pools of anthropological study not to know what this revolutionary thinker and scholar had accomplished, particularly in the field of ethnology. His time among the Eskimos in the Arctic reaches of Baffin Island had established Boas in scientific circles; a period of intense and fruitful study of the Kwakiutl and other indigenous peoples in British Columbia, where Boas and colleagues confirmed the linkage between aboriginal groups in Asia and North America, would make him preeminent among anthropologists. Photographs of Boas posing as an aboriginal for the makers of dioramas at the American Museum of Natural History might suggest a playful nature; in fact, they only demonstrate his passionate quest for precision and truth.

Like Davenport—and Francis Galton—Boas was in thrall to data. The same obsessiveness applied in his private life as well. He worked seven days a week, usually including a stretch of four or five hours after dinner each night. His daughter remembered that his attention to his bank accounts was so meticulous that if his numbers were off by so much as a single cent, he could spend hours hunting for the missing penny. Hard and humorless, Boas did not suffer fools, unprepared students, journalists, or critics gladly, or even politely. He had no use for psychoanalysis, believing that each individual's problems were his own to solve. His fundamental conservatism could be discerned from the title of one his doctoral theses: "That Contemporary Operetta Is Equally to Be Condemned on Grounds of Art and Morality." One could infer from the frequency with which Boas exclaimed them that his favorite words were "Nonsense!" and "Preposterous!" His motto, one of his students said, was "icy enthusiasm." Robert Lowie recalled how he dreaded encountering Boas on the Columbia campus, and Margaret Mead considered him "somewhat frightening." Still, Lowie, Mead, and his other protégés cherished the demanding way Boas challenged them. If he sought acolytes, they would only be those he could harden in the crucible of his rigor.

At times, Boas's professional investigations betrayed a tone deafness that left him open to criticism, both unfair and fair. A version of the former occurred shortly after he became a U.S. citizen in 1891, when he embarked on a study of schoolchildren in Worcester, Massachusetts, to determine growth rates among members of the city's various ethnic groups. Even though Boas hired women to measure the girls, he was naive about the possible reactions to his work. The *Worcester Daily Telegram* let him know right away, declaring itself determined that he "would never lay a slimy finger on a single Worcester schoolchild." (Despite the paper's insistence that Boas's project would leave "innocent youngsters . . . at the mercy of a perverted old lecher who would paw their tender bodies at will," the school board approved his plans.) Six years later, when he asked Arctic explorer Robert E. Peary "to bring us a middle-aged Eskimo to stay [at the American Museum of Natural History] over the winter" because it would enable him to collect information of "the greatest scientific importance," Boas's fevered quest for data and evidence ended in tragedy. Peary brought back not one Eskimo but six and put them on display on his ship when it docked in New York Harbor (enticing more than twenty thousand people to pay twenty-five cents each for the chance to see them). Eight months after their relocation to the museum building on Central Park West, four of them were dead from pneumonia. Determined to continue his studies, Boas had the flesh stripped from their bones, which soon became part of the museum's collection.

But the same monomania that Boas brought to the Worcester experiment and the Eskimo misadventure also defined his commitment to the one great cause of his life: the destruction of the "presumed hierarchy of racial types," as historian George Stocking called it. By his own account, Boas was raised without religion, and thus, he said, "spared the struggle against religious dogma that besets the lives of so many young people." Still, he was Jewish by inheritance and culture. His consciousness of anti-Semitism, both in Germany and the United States, certainly heightened his sensitivities, and his dedication to the rights of black Americans was thorough and persistent. Some critics have said that his studies of racial similarity and difference originated in an ideological opposition to any claim of ethnic superiority. This opposition, they argued, set him off on a search for the evidence he needed to discredit his adversaries' opinions. The countervailing view maintains that it was not Boas's ideology at all, but simply his intense observation and measurement of so many different peoples that first led him to a hypothesis—which, scholar that he was, he then insisted on confirming in the field. One such effort started in 1908, when he began a mammoth inquiry among New York immigrant children that produced evidence he believed would put an end to the idea that race was a definable and unchangeable reality.

The United States Immigration Commission that emerged from the ashes of the 1907 iteration of the literacy test bill, and under whose auspices Boas would conduct his investigation, was born of unlikely parentage. Uncle Joe Cannon, who had single-handedly demolished the literacy test's chances, was the leader of the conservative Republican majority in the House of Representatives. In the Senate, few were as conservative as Henry Cabot Lodge, who had already invested sixteen years in the effort to enact the literacy test. Yet the commission, chaired by Senator William P. Dillingham of Vermont—who, it was said, "wore the label 'reactionary' without protest"—turned out to be almost the very model of a Progressive Era inquiry. It spent more than three years gathering evidence, another year preparing its report. It employed a lengthy roster of recognized scientists and other experts. Its members traveled to Europe to conduct on-site inspections of potential immigrants, even visiting the impoverished towns and villages of southern Italy, where hundreds of thousands had begun their journey across the Atlantic. Historian Jill Lepore once wrote that the progressives of that era "could make a science out of licking envelopes if they set their mind to it." This particular venture sought to prove its scientific validity by presenting its findings in a staggering forty-two volumes of testimony, statistics, research reports, and, finally, recommendations.

Two documents of enduring significance emerged from what

Lodge hailed as "the most exhaustive inquiry into the subject [of immigration] which has ever been made." One was the *Dictionary of Races and Peoples* compiled by Daniel Folkmar, an anthropologist of negligible stature and minuscule accomplishment. The book's sources included Daniel Brinton (the anthropologist who had placed the African "midway between the orangutang [*sic*] and the European white"), the French eugenicist Georges Vacher de Lapouge (author of *The Aryan and His Social Role*, he believed in two white races, one "superior" and the other "inferior"), and Prescott Hall. Starting from a premise that stressed the stability of racial differences across the centuries, Folkmar somehow identified six hundred distinct racial and ethnic strains. His *Dictionary* presented its "findings" with a brief bibliography, not a single citation for any of its presumably factual content, virtually no supporting data—and, nonetheless, a straight face.

The other document that stood out was the commission's Volume 38, *Changes in Bodily Form of Descendants of Immigrants*, by Franz Boas. Over a two-year period Boas and a team of thirteen assistants had taken exquisitely detailed physical measurements of 17,821 Jewish, Italian, Bohemian, and Scottish immigrants and their U.S.-born children. They focused on head shape—specifically, the so-called cephalic index, which expressed the shape of an individual skull as the ratio of its width to its length, and which most anthropologists considered, in Boas's words, "one of the most stable and permanent characteristics of human races." A number above 80—that is, head width at least 80 percent of head length—denoted round-headedness (the term of art was "brachycephalic"), while a number under 75 indicated long-headedness ("dolichocephalic"). Since the 1840s, craniometry—skull measurement—had been a central element of biological and anthropological research. (And at times an extreme element: one prominent European researcher, anthropologist Aurel von Török, somehow managed to make five thousand separate measurements on a single skull.) Before he entered the academic world, Boas had supported himself partly by selling skulls he had gathered in his fieldwork to other researchers.

Scientists as distinguished as Thomas Huxley had measured skulls in their search for markers of evolutionary development, and philosopher Bertrand Russell considered it an "obvious fact" that "one can generally tell whether a man is a clever man or a fool by the shape of his head." Craniometry inevitably seduced the leading eugenicists, starting with Galton, and most of the race theorists, notably William Z. Ripley, who had used it as a primary indicator of the distinctions between his three races of Europe.

Boas could hardly have picked a more potent weapon. European race supremacists like Vacher de Lapouge had based their arguments all but entirely on the presumed immutability of the cephalic index. And so did Boas—by disproving it. His analysis of those 17,821 skulls revealed that the longer a family had been in the United States, the more likely it was that the heads of their children would move toward the American mean. The characteristically round-headed eastern European Jews saw their children become ever more long-headed. Similarly, southern Italians generally had long heads, but the heads of their children born in the United States were measurably rounder. The impact of environmental influences (particularly nutrition) had negated the presumed dominance of inheritance. Nurture had triumphed over nature. Boas concluded that "there can be no stability in mental traits of the races, as is often assumed." If even skull shape was mutable across generations, he maintained, so were *all* physical and mental traits. Those who sought to establish that physical characteristics of nationalities and ethnic groups were unchangeable were now obliged, he said, to bear the burden of proof. *

Boas was swamped with requests for copies of his report to the commissioners. He pleaded with Senator Dillingham to have the

---

* More than a century later, Boas's findings faced a serious challenge. A detailed account of the controversy can be found on the website www.livinganthropologically.com, in Jason Antrosio's article "Human Skulls: Anthropology on Head Shape Variation and Plasticity" (2011). The comments attached to Antrosio's paper vividly illustrate the continuing contention over Boas's work.

Government Printing Office go back to press. He said he was compelled to pay "exorbitant prices" to acquire copies from sellers of
secondhand books. One he sent to Jacob Schiff. The banker had
long been interested in Boas's work and at times had supported it
financially. When Schiff wrote to Boas to thank him for the book, he
clearly hadn't looked at it yet; he told Boas he was taking it with him
on a trip to Alaska, "where I shall have time to carefully read it and no
doubt shall get pleasure and instruction therefrom." Had Schiff cracked
the cover of *Changes in Bodily Form of Descendants of Immigrants*,
he would have immediately seen that instruction was unlikely and
pleasure unimaginable. Boas had produced 575 mind-numbing pages
consisting almost entirely of columns of numbers. His "unrelenting
empiricism," as one anthropologist called it, compelled him to present
his evidence in all its deadening and repetitive detail. He believed
he was providing proof, and he believed proof could not be ignored.

But then it was, at least by the Dillingham Commission. In their
final report, the commissioners greeted Boas's work with a barely
suppressed yawn. Yes, his findings were "entirely unexpected" and
possibly even "of great importance," and maybe it would be a good
idea for others to pursue the subject, but there really was nothing
else to say about it. Not a word in the commission's formal recommendations to Congress reflected anything that had emerged from
Boas's work. Folkmar's *Dictionary*, on the other hand, had brought
together what the commission called "reliable" data that was "useful
in promoting a better understanding of the many different racial
elements that are being added to the population of the United States
through immigration." With the enactment of the primary recommendation arising from its extensive labors, the commissioners
believed, Folkmar's "different racial elements" might be sorted out.
Their recommended filtering mechanism, naturally, was the perfect
proxy for ethnic discrimination: the literacy test.

The fact that the American Breeders Association's committee on immigration was a subgroup of the organization's eugenics wing was telling. Implicit in the committee's very creation was the conviction that immigration would have an effect on any national eugenic program. When he invited Franz Boas to join the committee, Davenport knew that Boas's exhaustive head-shape study had challenged this linkage. Having seen his findings ignored by the Dillingham Commission, Boas would reasonably have thought that he might instead be able to use his participation on this new committee to influence the nature-nurture debate. The Dillingham Commission, organized by politicians, had sought confirmation; this new committee, organized by a scientist of Davenport's stature, would presumably seek evidence.

But apart from his advocacy for Boas's inclusion, Davenport's contribution to the committee he appointed bordered on the negligent. The men who commandeered the five-member committee virtually upon its creation—Robert Ward and Prescott Hall, who took it up as a nearly full-time endeavor—brought to its work scientific credentials that were alarmingly thin. Ward's most recent book was a study of climate (based, he wrote, on "lecture notes which have been accumulating for the past ten years"). He had no credentials at all in genetics, biology, anthropology, sociology, or any other discipline that intersected with the committee's brief. Hall's "scientific" work consisted of credulous essays on séances, telepathy, and "astral projection." Appalled by the shoddiness of their approach, Boas declined to attend their meetings or take part in drafting their eventual report.

For Ward and Hall, nothing could have pleased them more than Boas's recusal. Their decision to hitch the Immigration Restriction League to the rising eugenics movement, prefigured four years earlier in Joe Lee's living room on Mount Vernon Street, had now paid off. Davenport, the nation's leading eugenicist, stood on the sidelines while the men of the IRL became the de facto spokesmen on immigration issues for the Breeders Association, the nation's leading genetic organization (which in fact would soon change its name to the American Genetic Association). Shortly after Davenport proposed the creation of an immigration committee, Ward published an article defining, with Davenport's approval, the committee's stated goal: "securing laws which will [bring] only normal and superior heredity to our country." The next month, Hall weighed in with "The Future of American Ideals," an article that began by quoting the progenitor of scientific racism, Arthur de Gobineau, and drew shamelessly on Houston Stewart Chamberlain's blatantly racist view on "race mixture." Hall's article explained that Jews—his preferred usage was "Hebrews"—were "an Asiatic race," and that southern Italians were actually African because of the "negroid migration from Carthage." He also likened unwanted immigrants to the gypsy moth and the sparrow, both of which "were not considered dangerous when first imported."

Four months after the committee was formally convened, in the spring of 1912, Ward and Hall produced a draft report with little or no input from its three other members. James A. Field, an economist from the University of Chicago, was happy to endorse it, and the fourth member, Alexander E. Cance of Massachusetts Agricultural College, whose specialty was the promotion of farmers' co-operatives, agreed to sign it even though he had never attended a committee meeting—nor, he admitted, had he given the report more than a cursory look.

The fifth member refused to sign. Boas was categorical. Hall was offended, if unsurprised ("very few Jews have any manners," he'd told Field after Boas had failed to attend some early meetings). With four names attached and Boas's dissent noted, the published report argued that even more dangerous than insane or feebleminded immigrants was "the much larger class of aliens" consisting of those whose heredity just didn't measure up. Their admission to the United States, the report concluded, could only be to the "detriment of the public health and the eugenic future of the race."

*   *   *

IN THE EARLY YEARS of the Eugenics Record Office, Charles Davenport stayed away from active involvement in applied science. "We scientists don't perform any experiments in eugenics," he said in January 1913. "The human race does plenty of that!" He and his wife were chatting with a reporter from the *New York Times*—amiably and with occasional drollery—about the work they were doing in Cold Spring Harbor. All the marrying and reproducing that had been going on for millennia, Davenport said, had produced many different human variants, but they likely shared a lot in common. "The fact remains," he told his visitor, "that practically every Anglo-American could prove his descent from William the Conqueror." Pause for effect. "And also from his jester."

For the staff and the trainees, it was a marvelous time to be at the ERO. Its early strides brought out Davenport's confident and generous aspect, sidelining (at least for a while) the dyspeptic and anxious side of his nature. From down the road in Oyster Bay, the retired Theodore Roosevelt sent Davenport an endorsement: "Some day we will realize that the prime duty, the inescapable duty of the good citizen of the right type is to leave his or her blood behind him in the world, and that we have no business to permit the perpetuation of citizens of the wrong type." Visits from such dignitaries as former cabinet member and current senator Elihu Root, accompanied by the incumbent secretary of war, Henry L. Stimson, confirmed Davenport in his conviction that the ERO's work was important. Davenport's domain was well funded, well equipped, and increasingly well known. "To Cold Spring Harbor," the *Times* would say, "all America's streams of eugenic interest flow." Davenport traveled frequently, delivering speeches, meeting with colleagues, spreading the word. When he was away, his wife was in charge. Strong and capable, she was respected in the field they both worked in, and at times was listed as the senior author of their jointly written academic papers. Three children brightened the Davenport home, and an eager staff mined the mountain of evidence that would someday give life to the Davenport dream. As Gertrude Davenport put it, there was nothing suspicious, scary, or even worth questioning about the eugenic quest: "A eugenist"—the term in use at the time—"is simply a sane, well-balanced person, who works, sanely, for the betterment of the race."

Occasional diversions lightened the mood at the ERO, including presentations by the extracurricular Record Office Dramatic Club. The content of the club's productions was not idly chosen. The main character of *Acquired or Inherited?*, directed by Harry Laughlin and cowritten by his wife, Pansy, was a widower "interested in Eugenics" whose niece was being courted by both an "indolent and wealthy" suitor and "an ambitious electrician"; another character was named "Hare Lip Peggy." As "The Sad Fate of a Youthful Sponge" ("There was a little blastula no bigger than a germ . . .") had been the theme song for the era of zoological inquiry in Cold Spring Harbor, a new ditty provided a soundtrack for the fieldworkers in the era of eugenics: "We are Eugenists so gay / And we have no time for play, / Serious we have to be / Working for posterity." A further verse was somewhat less buoyant: "Trips we have in Plenty too / Where no merriment is due. / We inspect with might and main, / Habitats of the insane." The lyrics didn't really scan but they made their point: by studying "defectives" the ERO could secure the American future.

The defectives studied at the ERO were not defined by their ethnic origins. In the narrow universe occupied by Davenport and his followers, how could they have been? "There were no Negroes. There were no immigrants," E. L. Doctorow wrote decades later on the opening page of his novel *Ragtime*, set in early-twentieth-century New York; neither group occupied even a corner of the comfortable mindset of the comfortable upper-middle-class family at the novel's heart. That same psychic blindness prevailed in Davenport's world on Long Island's North Shore, where there were no Others of any kind. The industrialists and merchants and railroad princes—Dodges and Winthrops, Lovetts and Cravaths—amassing outsized country estates in Glen Cove and Oyster Bay were of course Anglo-American.* So were the burghers in the nearby villages and the farmers in the outlying areas, and so were the staff in the Cold Spring Harbor labs and their young colleagues, fresh from Smith and Bryn Mawr and Radcliffe, who were training to be fieldworkers. Servants and laborers who came from different stock were present, including the occasional Italian gardener that Davenport's brother William had sent out from his settlement house in Brooklyn. But servants and laborers were defined by their functionality, not their personhood.

Davenport may have watched the ABA immigration committee's deliberations (such as they were) from a relative distance, but he could not help but be influenced by his deepening engagement with Hall and Ward. Despite his eccentric characterizations of various nationalities in *Heredity in Relation to Eugenics*, Davenport contended that America need only be concerned about *individuals* with questionable traits. He even argued that the assimilation of Italians, for instance, "will add many desirable elements to the American complex." Yet in 1912, as the ABA committee was completing its report, Davenport told Hall that "modern studies of heredity have rendered the old idea of the melting pot, particularly the idea that traits will blend and disappear, quite untenable." At Hall's urging, Davenport also removed Boas from the future deliberations of the immigration committee and replaced him with the economist Irving Fisher. Fisher was arguably the most important economist in the United States, but his vociferous public commitment to immigration

---

* The most notable exception was banker Otto Kahn—born Jewish in Germany but so deracinated (his children were christened in the Episcopal Church) that sociologist Dixon Wecter called him "the flyleaf between the Old and the New Testaments." Kahn's house in Cold Spring Harbor had 127 rooms, 50 baths, and a dining room that seated 200.

restriction was inversely proportional to his comprehension of basic genetics, which was nil. Shortly thereafter, Davenport declined to help Boas round up the relatively minimal funding he needed to finish the physical studies he had begun for the Dillingham Commission. He presented a much more congenial face to his new allies, at one point telling the *New York Times* that "the great families of Boston in the early part of the nineteenth century . . . constituted nearly pure strains of scholarship and social leadership respectively. And the characteristics of these strains are inheritable."

Others in the eugenics camp similarly turned their attention to the immigration question. Willet M. Hays, the assistant agriculture secretary in the Roosevelt administration who had founded the American Breeders Association, declared that it was time for American consulates abroad to start determining the "genetic fitness" of immigrants in order to keep "defective blood" out of the country. Stanford president David Starr Jordan, who had been so instrumental in helping Davenport persuade Mary Harriman to underwrite the ERO, now lent his name to the IRL's letterhead as a member of its National Committee and appeared on a list of college presidents declaring themselves in favor of "further restriction of immigration." Jordan believed that the "steady influx of people of other breeds" was the "main cause for the deterioration" of American government. Harry Laughlin of the ERO, a fledgling just beginning to spread his wings, prepared a report for another ABA body that needed no more explanation than was apparent in its name: the Committee to Study and to Report on the Best Practical Means of Cutting Off the Defective Germ-Plasm in the American Population.

Davenport himself revealed his evolving attitudes, perhaps unintentionally, in a 1914 letter to his social-worker brother. William Davenport had asked if Charles might find room for a laborer he knew from the Italian Settlement. Charles had always been polite when William made such requests, but now he exploded, in a four-page letter that veered from regret to rage and then settled in to something close to despair. "I am very blue, anyway, about the future of this country," he told William. "I sometimes feel that the only thing is to leave the United States and go to a country like New Zealand or Australia which appreciate the importance of good blood. . . . Excuse me, my dear brother, this rambling letter. You see that the point is that, with very great regret on my part, it will be out of the question" to hire the young Italian. He seemed to be saying that enough—about William's earnest good works, about immigration, about what he believed to be the dilution of the American gene pool—was more than enough.

Robert Ward could not have been surprised by Charles Davenport's enlistment in the restrictionist cause. Saluting America's leading eugenicist in an essay titled "The Crisis in Our Immigration Policy," Ward was succinct: "The day of the sociologist is passing," he wrote, "and the day of the biologist has come." Not quite as succinct but far more ominous, and equally prescient, was something William Bateson had said back in 1905: "When power is discovered, man always turns to it. The science of heredity will soon provide power on a stupendous scale; and in some country, at some time not, perhaps, far distant, that power will be applied to control the composition of a nation."

Chapter Six

To Hell with Jews, Jesuits, and Steamships!

"To play Providence to a race of men is a rather big undertaking," *The Times* of London observed in 1912. Its editorialists also wondered "whether any of us are really wise enough to know how a human society ought to be constituted," a concern largely ignored at the event that had prompted the article.

This signal moment in the legitimization of eugenic thinking took place at various London venues for six July days not a year after Francis Galton's death. Galton may have missed the spectacular inaugural ball for the field he invented, but he was nonetheless ubiquitous in both spirit and likeness: every one of the four hundred delegates to the First International Eugenics Congress wore a badge bearing the Congress's logo, a portrait of the great man himself. The new holy trinity of human inheritance—Darwin, Mendel, and Galton—was honored by what conference planners billed as a display of their "relics" in the exhibition hall; especially ghoulish (or perhaps devout) delegates must have been disappointed to find only a display of photographs and a few letters. At the opening banquet in the grand ballroom of the immense Hotel Cecil on the Victoria Embankment, where former prime minister Arthur Balfour gave the introductory address; at the party hosted by the American ambassador and his wife at Dorchester House; at the Duchess of Marlborough's elegant soiree in her Mayfair palace; and at all the various late-afternoon and evening teas, receptions, and outings arranged by the host committee, delegates from twelve nations celebrated their "baby science" (as the congress's chairman called it) and the man who had given it birth.

At the panels and plenary sessions at the University of London that occupied the rest of the six days, the physicians, biologists, anthropologists, and other scientists among those who had gathered for the congress put their scholarly imprimatur on Galton's conception by their presence. Charles Davenport, of course, was there. So was William Bateson, who would soon become extremely skeptical about eugenics. So was Alfred Ploetz, founder of the German Society for Racial Hygiene, who would not.

Thirty years earlier, on the death of Charles Darwin, it was Galton who had initiated the effort that led to the improbable entombment of Britain's most famous freethinker within the Anglican walls of Westminster Abbey. Now Galton was memorialized at an event presided over by Darwin's son Leonard, who welcomed the delegates by reminding them that "the end we have in view, an improvement in the racial qualities of future generations, is noble enough to give us courage for the fight." Major Leonard Darwin was a military engineer who, unlike three of his brothers, had declined to pursue a profession in the sciences because, wrote Janet Browne, "he thought himself the stupidest" member of the Darwin family.

Still, by virtue of his patrimony Major Darwin lent a whiff of scientific authority to the congress's British sponsor and host, the Eugenics Education Society, which he served as chairman and then honorary president for thirty-two years. Medical historian Kenneth Ludmerer has described the EES as "a miscellaneous group of zealots and cranks," a characterization that is both concise and generous. The organization's founder was distinguished only by the fact that he lived next door to Galton and by the delicious singularity of his name: Montague Crackanthorpe. Like many of the society's eager members,

Crackanthorpe had absolutely no expertise in any scientific field. A barrister by training, his greatest scholarly accomplishment may have been an article on a fishery dispute in the Bering Sea that he wrote for the *Encyclopaedia Britannica.* Other members of the First International Congress's organizing committee had somewhat oblique qualifications as well: literary hostess and arts patron Ottoline Morrell; suffragist and temperance worker Lady Henry Somerset; Havelock Ellis, the radical sexologist (whose interest in eugenics led him to introduce Margaret Sanger to the subject); the Russian anarchist nobleman Prince Peter Kropotkin. And, from the American eugenics community, climatologist (and Immigration Restriction League cofounder) Robert Ward.

Ward, however, was not the head of the congress's American delegation. That role fell to another amateur, Bleecker Van Wagenen, representing the eugenics committee of the American Breeders Association. A book publisher of aristocratic birth and philanthropic inclination, Van Wagenen brought greetings from "the brotherhood of Eugenists of the United States," who "hoped through the Congress to obtain wider scientific facts, which were especially needed in America." Van Wagenen's address to the congress forthrightly addressed "sterilization and other means for eliminating defective strains from the human population."

With this audience it was not necessary to mince words, and Van Wagenen did not: "Defective inheritance," "inferior blood," "eliminated from the human stock"—his language was as sharp as a surgeon's knife. In Britain as well as in the United States, enthusiasm for negative eugenics had eclipsed the positive version. Galton's dreamy notion of social improvement through eugenically wholesome matings had given way to a far darker idea, social improvement through the sterilization of "defectives" (in more decorous eugenic circles they were referred to as "socially inadequate"). By 1912, seven American states had followed Indiana's example and enacted laws providing for the involuntary sterilization of certain wards of the state, particularly habitual criminals, and especially those convicted of sex crimes. In some states those condemned to involuntary surgery included "imbeciles" and even epileptics confined to state institutions.

Immigration barely made it onto the congress's agenda. An Italian anthropologist challenged Franz Boas's findings on the mutability of head shape, and a statistician employed by the Prudential Insurance Company offered intimations of race suicide: his analysis of the fecundity of various ethnic groups in Rhode Island demonstrated that "the native-born of native stock" were not reproducing as rapidly as the immigrants. This state of affairs, he said, was "bound to have a lasting and injurious effect on national life and character."

By the standards of most participants, the First International Eugenics Congress was a success, the audience rising at its conclusion to offer Leonard Darwin what the official proceedings described as "a storm of applause." But the event was not without its skeptics. One was Prince Kropotkin, whose pedigree was as thoroughgoing as his radicalism. His father was a member of the family that produced the four czars named Ivan (including both "the Great" and "the Terrible"), his mother the daughter of a Cossack general who had been a hero in Russia's defeat of Napoleon. He grew up in a Moscow home with fifty servants and at a country estate with seventy-five more, and he emerged with an abiding distaste for the privileges of wealth and the presumptions of nobility. Arrested for revolutionary activity when he was thirty-two, Kropotkin proceeded to spend forty years in exile, eventually settling in London and joining the circle of radicals and iconoclasts, among them George Bernard Shaw, who were nurturing a utopian interest in eugenics. Shaw said Kropotkin "was amiable to the point of saintliness."

At the congress, though, when the discussion got around to sterilization, either voluntary or not, Kropotkin expressed his doubts about the possibility of a eugenic paradise with a stinging rebuke. Whom did its advocates propose to sterilize? he asked. "Those who produced degenerates in slums, or those who produced them in palaces?"

But Kropotkin was an amateur. Samuel G. Smith, a liberal Methodist clergyman who was also founder of the department of anthropology and sociology at the University of Minnesota, brought more substantial credentials to the discussion. Granted a slot on the official program on the congress's third day, when the announced topic was "Education and Eugenics," Smith used his moment for broader purposes, striking right at the heart of the entire eugenic idea. "Genius was the surprise of history," he said. Lincoln, Michelangelo, Luther, and so many others arose from ordinary families that to attribute the disproportionate accomplishments of the wellborn to genetic superiority was to devalue the importance of education and upbringing. "Shakespeare could have done nothing among the Hottentots," Smith said, "or Beethoven among the Alaskans." He declared that the world "suffered more from the vices of the rich than from those of the poor," and he lacerated the assumption that criminality—or any other character trait—was genetically inherited.

Smith underscored this last point with a simple history lesson that finally brought the immigration question to the fore. "As to the criminally born," he told the delegates, "England knew what to do with them: she sent them to America to found the first families of New York or Virginia."

*   *   *

EULOGIZING SMITH FOLLOWING HIS DEATH in 1916, a friend recalled how he "pierced below the superficial and grasped the heart of a question." Judging by the rapidly growing interest in eugenics in the United States in the second decade of the twentieth century, Smith was in the minority. As eugenic doctrine rose toward wide acceptance throughout the country, its popularization was both extensive and superficial. The *Woman's Home Companion* created a Better Babies Bureau that examined more than 150,000 infants during the 1913 agricultural fair season. When the sponsors of a Better Babies competition in Iowa turned to Charles Davenport for counsel, he soberly advised them to "score 50% for heredity before you begin to examine a

baby," as the parents' genetic bequest was every bit as important as the
infant's visible charms. Willet Hays of the American Breeders Association suggested that men and women be given a unique eleven-digit
"number name" indicating their genetic lineage, so that "mating with
those of equal genetic excellence" could be guaranteed. The governor of
Connecticut called for clergymen to refuse to officiate at marriages for
the genetically unfit, and several states passed laws declaring marriages
involving a feebleminded person voidable. At Princeton University,
the Triangle Club's annual musical show in 1914 featured a song called
"Love or Eugenics." The lyricist, a seventeen-year-old freshman from
Minnesota named F. Scott Fitzgerald, asked wellborn Archie Chol-
mondeley to choose between "Kisses that set your heart aflame / Or
love with a prophylactic dame." In New York, Broadway impresario
David Belasco explained that he chose actors for one of his productions "by taking thought of all the laws of heredity and eugenics, and
by applying them to every man and woman in the numerous cast."

By the mid-1910s, the eugenic idea had penetrated
popular culture, as on this novelty postcard.

Even as eugenic ideas were embraced by the untrained, the unserious, and the unbaked, the readiness of substantial, credentialed institutions and investigators to accept the early claims of the eugenicists made a certain amount of sense. Science knows only what it knew yesterday, as altered by what it learns today; tomorrow's discoveries are suspended in fog. In the early 1910s, the sun shone so brightly over the eugenics movement that even the U.S. Public Health Service signed on to it, offering official certification to individuals who wished to prove their eugenic suitability for marriage. Its first certificate was granted to architect Homer B. Terrill of Washington, after the Surgeon General's office put him through "the most approved line of investigation known to the science of eugenics and pronounced him fit." In Colorado, an employee of the state legislature advertising for a "eugenic wife" had candidates submit their bona fides, which were then evaluated by a physician who was a member of the state's board of health.

Scholars and educators also rushed toward a eugenic future with enthusiasm. Harvard, Columbia, Wisconsin, Northwestern, and other universities added eugenics to their curricula. Booker T. Washington, who harbored the belief that self-improvement could be passed along genetically, invited Davenport to speak at the Tuskegee Institute. And in 1914 George Hunter, head of the biology department at DeWitt Clinton High School in New York City, wrote a textbook that was destined to become one of the most famous ever published in America. Drawing heavily on Davenport's work and extolling eugenics as "the science of being well born," *A Civic Biology* went through several editions and was used by teachers across the country—among them John T. Scopes of the quiet little town of Dayton, Tennessee, which would owe its clamorous 1925 "Monkey Trial" to the book's discussion of evolution.

Which is not to suggest that eugenics belonged strictly to the secular modernists. Around the same time that Scopes was spreading Hunter's adaptations of Davenport's theories, the popular lecturer

Albert E. Wiggam declared, "Had Jesus been among us, he would have been president of the First Eugenics Congress." The eugenics bandwagon had room for everybody.

"This is a book that should be studied by every adult who is interested in eugenics," Dr. A. C. Rogers wrote in 1912, "and who is not?" Rogers was editor in chief of the era's leading journal on feeblemindedness. The book was *The Kallikak Family*, by Henry H. Goddard, which filtered the abstractions of Mendelian theory through a Galtonian screen and rendered them vivid by trying to apply them to human characteristics. It was, Rogers concluded, "epoch-making," and he was very nearly right.

Goddard had begun his academic life at the University of Southern California in 1887, teaching Latin, history, and botany, and serving as USC's first football coach. As coach, he retired undefeated (career record: 2-0); as academician, he converted to the study of psychology and eventually established himself as director of research at one of the nation's first facilities devoted to the scholarly exploration of mental deficiency, the Vineland Training School in southern New Jersey.

When *The Kallikak Family* was published in 1912, it made Goddard famous. His message was compelling. Goddard and his associates had spent two years studying families who could trace their origins back six generations to a Revolutionary War militiaman named John Woolverton, scion of "a family of good English blood." One line descended from the "respectable girl" he married after the revolution, yielding 496 entirely normal descendants across six generations, many of whom inherited the extensive real estate holdings Woolverton amassed during his lifetime. The other arose from "an unguarded moment" in a tavern when Woolverton "step[ped] aside from the paths of rectitude and with the help of a feeble-minded girl, start[ed] a line of mental defectives that is truly appalling." By Goddard's calculations, the 480 descendants of Woolverton's unfortunate dalli-

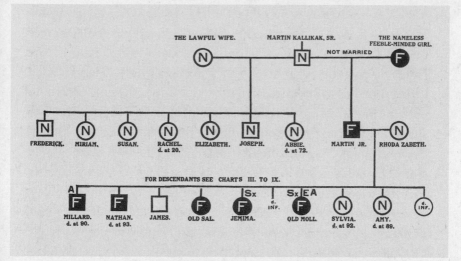

The first generation of Martin Kallikak's family, plus the next generation sired by "Old Horror," Martin Jr. "F" denotes feeblemindedness, "A" stands for alcoholic, and "Sx" for sexually immoral. Similar codes were employed for various other debilities showing up in further generations, including insane, syphilitic, criminalistic, deaf, and tuberculous. Normal individuals were blessed with an "N."

ance (according to Goddard, the son begot on that fateful night was widely known in late life as "Old Horror") included 143 feebleminded prostitutes, drunks, criminals, and otherwise blighted souls.

To spare any of the Woolvertons the ignominy that might attach itself to such a tale, Goddard renamed the family's progenitor Martin Kallikak, the surname a portmanteau taken from the Greek. *Kallos* is generally defined as "beauty." *Kakos* is more versatile in its meaning: one dictionary's garland of definitions includes "bad," "worthless," "ugly," "wretched," "vile." For Goddard's purposes, any one of them would have sufficed. But Goddard's purposes themselves were dubious. Elizabeth S. Kite, the fieldworker who found, judged, and classified all those Kallikaks, was even sloppier than Davenport's trait gatherers, and no better trained. When assessing the "bad" Kallikaks of the present generation, she made judgments of feeblemindedness based on appearance (one subject's deficiencies were proven by his "drooping jaws," another was categorized as "a repulsive, vulgar creature") or living conditions ("sights of misery and degradation," "the hideous picture that presented itself"). Seeing poverty, Kite attributed it to genetic flaws inherited from the girl in the tavern. Unable to witness, much less interview, "bad" Kallikaks of earlier generations, she relied instead on gossip, rumor, and folktales that had filtered down through the generations. The fact that "good" Kallikaks were almost certainly raised in better conditions and with more resources than their unfortunate cousins was deemed insignificant—at least in comparison to the invisible power of presumably deficient genes, as manifest in nothing more than the visible presence of poverty.

Still, to a reading public excited by the book's avid critical reception ("a remarkable study," "a remarkable human document," "an impressive lesson of the far-reaching and never-ending injury done to society by a single sin"), *The Kallikak Family* proved that human virtue (or its absence) was hereditary. The photographs of Old Horror's descendants and their dilapidated, ramshackle dwellings rather luridly demonstrated that a lesser, degenerate breed of humans was a social danger.* In all, *The Kallikak Family* played a part in the popularization of eugenics that approached the role that *The Birth of a Nation* assumed in the sanctification of southern Reconstruction mythology.

But it was Goddard's other major accomplishment that would have the most enduring impact on the eugenics movement, the immigration restriction campaign, and many other aspects of American life. By translating the Binet-Simon intelligence test into English in 1908 and revising it for American use, he established IQ testing in the national consciousness. When the French psychologist Alfred

---

* Goddard even found a moral lesson in assessing what he called Martin Kallikak's "thoughtless act" in the tavern: "Now that the facts are known, let the lesson be learned; let the sermons be preached; let it be impressed upon our young men of good family that they dare not step aside for even a moment."

Binet and his associate Théodore Simon developed the test, they explicitly eschewed any suggestion that intelligence was innate, believing their scale of measurement useful only to compare children of similar educational and cultural backgrounds. "Of one thing Binet was sure," wrote Stephen Jay Gould. "Whatever the cause of poor performance in school, the aim of his scale was to identify in order to help and improve, not to label in order to limit."

And that was the one thing that Henry Goddard chose to ignore. Employing a numerical scale to distinguish degrees of feeblemindedness, he affixed to each segment a label of hideous and enduring potency. A person with a "mental age" of two or less was an "idiot." Someone with a mental age of three to seven was labeled an "imbecile." And for those whom Goddard judged to have a mental age of eight to twelve, he coined the word "moron," adapted from the Greek word for "stupid" or "dull." In common usage the word entered the language as comfortably as if there had been a seat reserved for it. In the immigration debate, it was all but enthroned.

*　　*　　*

UNTIL HENRY CABOT LODGE pulled the ever-ripe literacy test out of his drawer in 1912 and offered it to the Senate for the first time in six years, Joe Lee and his colleagues in the Immigration Restriction League hadn't understood the long game Lodge had been playing. While the Dillingham Commission was conducting its protracted inquiry, the IRL's leadership even came to doubt Lodge's commitment. In 1910 Lee had told the league's man in Washington, James Patten, that "we have our eye on" Lodge, who has "a tendency to wobble" on the literacy test. Restriction legislation, mused an increasingly grumpy Lee, "is on the White Queen's plan of jam every other day—that is, jam yesterday and jam to-morrow, but never jam today." More gravely, he suggested that the IRL prepare to attack Lodge if his support for the test continued to weaken. Lee and Prescott Hall both felt the need to persuade Harvard president A. Lawrence Lowell—unlike his predecessor C. W. Eliot, he was a longtime IRL supporter—to lean on Lodge because, Hall said, Lowell was "an expert on nation-building Brahminism." He proved his expertise, after a fashion, in his appeal to Lodge: "My own studies," Lowell told the senator, "have led me to feel more and more strongly the absolute necessity of homogeneity for the success of popular government."

But persuading Lodge of such a need was about as necessary as persuading Captain Ahab of the existence of whales. Ever since he'd first introduced literacy test legislation in 1895, it had been a goal just inches out of reach, but now he had the implement that would help the restrictionists grab the brass ring: the Dillingham Commission report. The test was no longer only Lodge's pet project; with the commission's endorsement, it had been anointed. Joe Lee and his IRL colleagues picked up the banner. Lee's primary public concern in 1912 was opening the Boston schools in the evenings to better serve the city's immigrants. Privately, Lee had a different goal: he told his cousin Harry Cabot that he was prepared that year to spend $10,000 (2019 equivalent: roughly $265,000) on behalf of the literacy test "if I have to pawn my socks."

The most striking difference between the campaign for the 1912 version and Lodge's original drive for the literacy test lay not in its substance but in the language he and his allies employed to present it: the calumny previously directed at specific nationalities was superseded by benign terminology suggesting ethnic neutrality. Gone were the specific references to "Italians, Russians, Poles, Hungarians, and Asiatics"—Lodge's 1896 roster of those who were "alien to the great body of the people of the United States." At no point in the new debate did he refer, as he had sixteen years earlier, to a "lower race." He further advanced his cause by handing over most of the floor debate to William Dillingham, whose chairmanship of the commission had endowed him with the credibility implicit in its forty-two lumbering volumes of official findings.

Courtly almost to the point of unctuousness, as different in style from Lodge as alkaline is from acid, Dillingham was careful not to defame specific ethnic groups. At one point he even went out of his way to assert that the majority of the insane confined in American mental institutions came from "the very nations from whom we would like to secure" new immigrants: the nations of northern and western Europe. The literacy test, Dillingham explained earnestly if disingenuously, had nothing at all to do with the innate qualities—mental, emotional, or otherwise—of the members of any particular ethnicity; it was merely a device that would repel the illiterate laborers who were lusting after American jobs. Elihu Root had been secretary of war and secretary of state; by now he was U.S. senator from New York, effectively established as the regent of the nation's ruling class (his law clients included Morgans, Belmonts, Whitneys, the Standard Oil Trust, and the Sugar Trust). In the Senate debate Root declared, "I do not wish to be understood as saying a word that in any degree implies an assertion of our superiority to the peoples of southeastern Europe." He only wished, he said, to bar "a continual stream of men whose minds are closed to the principles and the sentiments of our American institutions and our American civilization."

Root's comment was a wink directed at those of his colleagues who were gripped by a loathing for immigrant radicals—most of whom happened to be from Italy or eastern Europe. Senator William Borah of Idaho had an archetype in mind: "the immigrant who lands here with a half-intelligible curse upon his lips for the Government to whose shelter he has fled." As far back as the debate over Lodge's 1896 bill, pro-immigration politicians had been pointing out that socialists and anarchists, who as often as not inhaled their ideology directly from the complex writings of Karl Marx and the Russian radical Mikhail Bakunin, were more likely to be literate than the apolitical immigrant. Grover Cleveland had underscored this argument in his 1897 veto message when he said he'd take in "a hundred thousand" illiterates who want to work hard rather than admit "unruly agitators." The latter, he said, can read, write, and use "inflammatory speech" to "arouse . . . the illiterate and peaceably inclined."

But this was an argument that Root, Borah, and their restrictionist colleagues had no difficulty ignoring. The searing fear of radicalism had infused a powerful and generalized strain of xenophobia into the nation's politics. How could it not, when the leader of 1912's massive Lawrence, Massachusetts, textile strike was Arturo Giovanitti (of Ripabottoni, Italy), the most prominent socialist in New York was Morris Hillquit (born Hillkowitz, in Riga, Latvia), and the best-known anarchist in the nation was Emma Goldman (from Kovno, Lithuania)? Businessmen who had relished unrestricted immigration as a bountiful source of cheap labor now had reason to shrink from the same source as it grew increasingly organized, unionized, and radicalized.

Southern senators, who also liked their labor cheap and had long seen its importation as another way to keep the black man down, had opposed the 1896 literacy test by a vote of 15–3; now, in 1912, they backed it 16–1. They probably hadn't been persuaded to their position by the anti-immigrant stance of Booker T. Washington, who insisted that "the Negro [is] more like the southern white man, more willing and able to observe the ideas of the culture of the white man [than] any other race which is now coming into the country." But they might have been moved by a letter from the IRL, sent only to southerners in Congress, arguing that the unwanted immigrants "have not the same objections to interbreeding with the negroes that northern races have," and thus might yield "an increase of negro half breeds."

Generally speaking, many of the immigration restrictionists—and almost all of the scientific racists—were far more concerned with the possibility of black-white "interbreeding" than they were with the status of blacks themselves; the inferiority of African Americans, they believed, was a settled question, but their potential multiplication through miscegenation was not. Chief Justice Roger Taney, in 1857's *Dred Scott* decision, wrote that Negroes were "a subordinate and inferior class of beings." In the same era the influential Harvard naturalist Louis Agassiz and his followers considered whites and blacks separate species. Theodore Roosevelt may have invited Booker T. Washington to dinner at the White House, but he told a friend that blacks were "altogether inferior to whites." By the mid-1910s, when the Jim Crow laws in the South had hardened into permanence and Woodrow Wilson was imposing rigid segregation on the federal workforce, a scientist of Charles Davenport's training and expertise felt no need to cite evidence to support his belief that blacks were, relative to whites, congenitally feebleminded. By the mid-1920s, one scientific racist who wondered whether blacks and whites were biologically related could declare that the status of "the Negro . . . at the present moment is not a live issue."

However, to congressional southerners in 1912, the live issue was what effect further immigration would have on the rigid system of segregation they had hammered into place. John Lawson Burnett, an ecstatic restrictionist from Alabama who had served on the Dillingham Commission with Lodge, sponsored the literacy test in the House and led the southern delegation as if on a holy crusade. From the eight westernmost states, where anti-Japanese fever had burst into an epidemic of restrictionist action, congressional support was unanimous. An outspoken opponent of the literacy test, Representative Adolph Sabath of Chicago (originally from Zabori, Bohemia), tried to demonstrate his loyalty to certain racist ideas by saying he supported "Asiatic and Mongolian" restriction, but stopping Europeans—white people!—was a bridge too far. But the congressional march toward a literacy test could not be stopped. In April 1912, the Senate voted 57–8 to include the test in the pending immigration legislation. Mindful, though, of the growing importance of the ethnic vote, Burnett held back the House version until after that fall's presidential election, when all the chamber's members would be on the ballot.

The imminent enactment of a literacy test led the doubters in the IRL to recalibrate their wavering feelings about the man who had been steering the bill's course for nearly a quarter of a century. "Hurray . . . for Lodge," James Patten wrote to Robert Ward during the 1912 congressional debates. "No man could be of more service or use to us than he is and has been." The IRL had also begun to mimic the ethnically neutral language Lodge had adopted. Joe Lee was especially tactical about this. Not only were the occasional derogations of Italians and Jews that dotted his private correspondence absent from his public statements, but when debate over restriction legislation began to heat up, he now avoided not only insult, but any hint of ethnic characterization. The literacy test bill, he admitted privately to Lawrence Lowell, "keeps out the southern and eastern Europeans." But, he explained, this was an "argument we are going easy on. I am myself doubtful whether it pays to use it" (even though, he admitted, "it is my favorite"). Drafting a letter to the editor of the *Boston Post*, Lee took an editing pencil to the typescript he had prepared, crossed out "the illiterate races," and replaced it with the dispassionate "illiterates."

And later, at a critical moment in the literacy test's march toward enactment, Lee warned associates not to use any arguments "that will suggest racial prejudice" in a letter-writing campaign he was asking them to join. The intended recipient of those letters was the one individual whose final assent would be necessary for the literacy test to become law, William Howard Taft.

It was not easy being Taft, at least when he was president. As imposing as he was physically (estimates range from 250 to 350 pounds, with most tipping toward the latter figure), he was less than commanding either personally or politically during his four years in the White House. Selected by Theodore Roosevelt to be his successor, Taft never felt truly comfortable with his benefactor's gift. "When someone addressed him as 'Mr. President,'" wrote historian Thomas A. Bailey, "he would instinctively turn around to see where Roosevelt was."

As its backers prepared to place the 1912 Immigration Act and its literacy test in Taft's ample lap, they believed they had slight cause to worry. Roosevelt would certainly have signed it in 1906 had Joseph Cannon not derailed it in the House, and Taft—the amiable, Yale-educated descendant of Tafts and Howards who had emigrated from England in the seventeenth century—was considered unlikely to strike out in a different direction. Henry Cabot Lodge told Prescott Hall that he found it unimaginable that Taft would veto the test "in order to oblige some very small sections of our population."

Lodge characteristically underestimated the "small sections" Taft might wish to please—the recent immigrants generally, and perhaps the well-established German Jews specifically, given their active and continuing engagement in the immigration wars. In 1910, recognizing the changing nature of the electorate, Lodge told Lawrence Lowell that "certain elements which have grown largely in the last few years resist any restriction," and—one can almost hear his dismay in his concluding thought—"those who are here have votes." Yet even Lodge did not perceive the cross-cultural connections among various immigrant groups that had been forming in the slums and factories of New England. In the Lawrence textile strike alone, workers of Irish, Italian, French Canadian, Polish, Russian, and Syrian origin locked arms in common cause.

Lodge must have noticed the appeals to ethnic voters that permeated the 1912 presidential race. All three candidates—Republican Taft, Democrat Woodrow Wilson, and an angry Theodore Roosevelt, who had broken with his protégé and returned to the arena as the candidate of the Progressive Party—chased the growing ethnic vote. Addressing a group of roughly one hundred foreign-language newspaper editors in September, Wilson insisted he and they were equally American and came out forthrightly against the literacy test. In an emphatic speech delivered late in the campaign, Taft said, "I am proud of our country that we have had its doors swinging easily open for the industrious peoples of other countries." And even Roosevelt ran on a platform that pledged its dedication to protecting immigrants—including noncitizens—from "indifference and neglect."

In the end, Lodge and his Immigration Restriction League allies saw that voters from the ethnic groups they sought to block would make no difference in the presidential race; the split in the Republican Party virtually guaranteed Wilson's electoral college victory. On December 18, having evaded the judgment of the electorate through its well-considered delay, the House approved the literacy test by a vote of 178–52. Fifteen long years had elapsed since Cleveland's veto, and on its periodic reappearance seven successive Congresses had failed to approve the test. With the Senate's 57–8 vote already in hand, its legislative journey was complete.

The pro-literacy test margins in both houses were sufficient to withstand the unlikely possibility of another presidential veto, but the antirestriction forces, led by the National Liberal Immigration League, nonetheless did their best to persuade Taft. Always hypersensitive to allegations that it was a Jewish organization, the National Liberal Immigration League drew clear benefit from the visible presence of an Irish American—James Michael Curley, who served simultaneously as congressman from Massachusetts and the league's Washington lobbyist—representing its interests in the Capitol. The Liberal League also intensified its other public efforts at institutional deracination. One of the league's anti–literacy test brochures in 1912 included the endorsements of fifty-four "prominent persons who have signified their opposition to any restrictive legislation": one social activist (Jane Addams), one famous educator (C. W. Eliot), twenty-four Catholic bishops, two cardinals, the Supreme Knight of the Knights of Columbus, and the bearers of twenty-five other decidedly non-Jewish names.

On Thursday morning, February 6, 1913, the Liberal League and Curley took their case to the lame-duck president, who would relinquish his office to Woodrow Wilson in just four weeks. Taft had decided to predicate his decision on a formal debate of his own devising. It was quite a scene. The East Room of the White House had been set up like a courtroom, albeit a courtroom hung with gold velvet drapes and trimmed in red Tunisian marble. More than two hundred witnesses and their supporters filled gilded chairs adorned with yellow ribbons. From a large armchair flanked by several members of the White House staff, a gavel in his hand, Taft presided as representatives of organizations for and against the bill competed for his signature or his veto. The entire immigration act contained thirty-eight separate sections running to thousands of words, but for three hours veto supporters (and most of their opponents) focused almost entirely on the content of a single paragraph in Section 3: the literacy test. Advocates for the bill included a vice president of the AFL, the head of a national farmers' group, the president of Johns Hopkins University, and Representative Caleb Powers, who represented a portion of Kentucky said to have fewer citizens of foreign birth than any other congressional district in the nation. Curley and the Liberal League had brought in witnesses representing organizations of Italian Americans, Finnish Americans, Polish Americans, and many other nationality groups, as well as such luminaries as the philanthropist Julius Rosenwald and the celebrated Serbian American physicist Michael (born Mihajlo) Pupin. Curley concluded his presentation by handing Taft a pro-veto petition purportedly signed by half a million people.

Eight days later Taft released his veto message. He thought the immigration bill, overall, was quite good. He was rejecting it "with great reluctance." This was especially difficult, he added, because it had been approved by such large numbers in both houses of Congress and had been "recommended by an able commission that had conducted an extensive investigation." Nonetheless, he concluded, he simply could not agree to the literacy test.

In Boston, Prescott Hall's response was both convulsive and specific: "To hell with Jews, Jesuits, and Steamships!" In Washington, more practical men immediately began the override process. They needed two-thirds majorities in both the House and the Senate. The original bill had drawn support from 74 percent of those voting in the lower chamber, 88 percent in the upper. Taft could do little to win support; only two weeks away from his involuntary retirement to private life, his influence was negligible. Senators and congressmen knew the issue well and knew how they felt about it. The debate was as dependent on amusing tricks of rhetoric and allusive coyness than on anything substantive. In the House, when Lodge's son-in-law, Representative Augustus Gardner, offered statistics detailing the supposed criminal inclinations of illiterate immigrants, Curley trapped him in his own logic: "How many illiterates," Curley asked, "have been arrested for forgery?" On the other side of the Capitol, Senator John Sharp Williams of Mississippi, in favor of the bill, declared—perhaps obtusely, probably knowingly —that he had "no sort of prejudice against foreigners. I am, upon the contrary, of the absolute conviction that a German or a Frenchman is as good as I am." Of other ethnicities, he said nothing.

Lodge had little new to add. How could he have? Clutching a copy of his first congressional speech on the subject, delivered in 1891, he repeated its arguments nearly verbatim. Clearly frustrated by Taft's unexpected veto, Lodge ended his tactical retreat into ethnically neutral language and reverted to the unconcealed bigotry that had motivated him all along. "This country was settled and built up by the people from Great Britain and Ireland, from Scandinavia, from Holland, from Germany, and from France," he said. But now, in

1913, as had been the case for more than two maddening, frustrating decades, the immigrants "coming into this country from eastern and southeastern Europe" were "offspring of a different civilization." He even pulled Thomas Bailey Aldrich's poem out of his files ("Wide open and unguarded stand our gates / And through them presses a wild motley throng . . ."). The measure designed to close those gates, which Lodge had conceived so many years before, had twice gotten overwhelming support from both houses. How could it be denied? How could *he* be denied?

The Senate stood with Lodge, voting 72–18 to override. But the House sustained Taft's veto by the narrowest of margins. A change in just five votes would have made the bill law. Instead it crashed, said the *New York Times*, "on the rock of the literacy test." It was as if the antirestriction forces had been inspired by the words of their own unlikely bard, an insurance man from Philadelphia named Louis S. Amonson, whose seven-stanza response to Aldrich's poem was read into the *Congressional Record*. It began:

> We've dug your million ditches.
> We've built your endless roads.
> We've fetched your wood and water,
> And bent beneath the loads.
> We've done the lowly labor
> Despised by your own breed.
> And now you won't admit us
> Because we can not read!

*　　*　　*

BASED ON THEIR BACKGROUNDS, one would think Woodrow Wilson and Henry Cabot Lodge might have gotten along. Both were well educated (Wilson received his PhD from Johns Hopkins ten years after Lodge earned his at Harvard). Neither could be accused of having the common touch (Wilson once said of himself, "I am a vague, conjectural personality, more made up of opinions and academic prepossessions than of human traits and red corpuscles"). Both, of course, traced their ancestry back to Great Britain.

More crucially, Wilson was forthrightly (even if, during his 1912 election campaign, embarrassingly) on the record about certain European immigrants. In his five-volume *A History of the American People*, published shortly after he was named president of Princeton in 1902, Wilson had warned readers with phrases that might have come from Lodge himself: the "sturdy stocks of the north of Europe" were now imperiled by "multitudes of men of the lowest class from the South of Italy and men of the meaner sort out of Hungary and Poland, men out of the ranks where there was neither skill nor energy nor any initiative of quick intelligence." Elsewhere he wrote of the "corruption of foreign blood," and "ever-deteriorating" genetic materials. But during his 1912 campaign Wilson had danced his way out of responsibility for his 1902 opinions with surprising deftness for an academic-turned-politician (the *Boston Transcript* called it a "somersault"), and he had won the full-throated support of immigrant groups. Lodge, however, told allies he would make no compromise in yet another effort, sometime during Wilson's first term in office, to engrave the literacy test into law.

Taft's veto had inflamed anti-immigrant feeling, and Lodge's reversion to his race-based vocabulary seemed to sanction a concomitant loosening of restraints in public debate. At the same time, however, Lodge was beginning to warm to the more contemporary vocabulary of restriction. "The waves of democracy have submerged the old and narrow lines within which the few sat apart, and definition of a man's birth and ancestry has become more necessary," he wrote on the very first page of a memoir published not long after Taft's veto. He then appended a coda that, coming from him, all but certified the new path the restrictionists were exploring: "Darwin and Galton have lived and written, Mendel has been discovered and revived, and the modern biologists have supervened." Like Prescott Hall, Robert Ward, and Joe Lee, Lodge had become acutely aware of the potential power of the eugenic interpretation of immigration.

Word was spreading. At the First International Conference on Race Betterment in Battle Creek, Michigan, 1,500 activists discussed immigration legislation specifically designed "to keep the blood of the race pure." In an article published in a leading peer-reviewed medical journal, a professor of anatomy at Tulane University warned readers that the distinctive shape of the Jewish nose arose from habitual use of the quadratus muscle, which he defined as "the muscle of disgust, contempt, and disdain, which lead to scorn, acknowledging guilt." But no one in a position of prominence seized the opportunity to racialize the immigration discussion more adroitly than Edward A. Ross, the father of race suicide theory.

By 1913, this outspoken ally of progressive politicians and reformers was teaching at the University of Wisconsin and was about to ascend to the pinnacle of his profession as president of the American Sociological Society. His interest in immigration and its effects on "the race" had not diminished. Taft's veto of the literacy test appalled him. Writing to Prescott Hall, he said he considered the veto "a dreadful thing," and uttered the sort of condemnation that today may seem almost comically pale but that would likely have impressed a man as formal and particular as Hall. "I feel so strongly about it that I doubt if I would care to meet [Taft] at dinner, if I were invited to do so," Ross said. He soon embarked on a writing project that would express the strength of his feeling far more forcefully.

The venue for his project was *The Century*, a monthly magazine both prestigious and popular. In the late 1800s it had published Mark Twain and Henry James; in the years ahead, contributors would include Bertrand Russell and W. E. B. Du Bois. Over the course of twelve monthly issues beginning in November 1913, the magazine published H. G. Wells, Jacob Riis, and Rudyard Kipling, among many others. Nothing they wrote had the impact of Edward

A. Ross's "Examination into Immigration." The magazine's editors said it was a project that "cannot fail to stir every American deeply." One of those stirred, Prescott Hall, described Ross's series more specifically: "He is tackling especially the 'humanitarians,'" Hall told Charles Davenport, enabling him "to knock down some of the fool arguments for the melting pot."

The series and the book that memorialized it were both called *The Old World in the New*. Supporters of immigration restriction hailed it: "so keen an insight, so sound a judgment" (*Louisville Courier-Journal*), "most illuminating" (*Rochester Democrat and Chronicle*). Opponents of restriction attacked it, but even they acknowledged *Old World*'s power. A reviewer for the *New York Times* assailed Ross for "a prejudice amounting almost to a bitterness," and then ruefully acknowledged Ross's ability to conceal that prejudice with his "brilliant and readable style."

Month by month, chapter by chapter, Ross unspooled his evaluation of each of the major immigrant groups that had come to America since the arrival of the Puritans. Scholar though he was, he offered nothing at all in the way of data or any other kind of factual support. He relied instead on generalities, hearsay, and imagination, moving effortlessly from the general to the ethnically specific and back again, rarely citing sources but ever definitive in his limitless judgments. "That the Mediterranean people are morally below the races of northern Europe," he proclaimed with the absolute authority he arrogated to himself, "is as certain as any social fact." Immigrants from throughout southern Italy "lack the conveniences for thinking." Neapolitans were "a degenerate class" that was "infected with spiritual hookworm," and displayed "a distressing frequency of low foreheads, open mouths, weak chins, poor features . . . and backless heads." Jews demonstrated "a monstrous and repulsive love of gain." Poles were "uncleanly, intemperate, quarrelsome, ignorant, priest-ridden and hard on women and children." Ross's apparently authoritative sources for this last judgment, he said with his usual blithe inattention to anything resembling proof, were certain unnamed "farmers."

He did not stop with mere characterization. Ross brought his series to its climax with arguments saturated in the cruel, distorted, and scientifically problematic doctrine of negative eugenics. "It is fair to say that the blood now being injected into the veins of our people is 'sub-common,'" he declared. He established this, he reported, one afternoon while watching 386 people, mostly garment workers, as they passed through New York's Union Square on the way home from work. Fewer than 10 percent "had the type of face one would find at a county fair in the west or south." They were not, in other words, Us. They threatened the nation not simply by their economic threat (itself made urgent when "low-standard men undercut high-standard men"), but by what was stored in their genes. "To one accustomed to the aspect of the normal American population," he wrote, "the Caliban type shows up with a frequency that is startling." The "crooked faces, coarse mouths, bad noses, heavy jaws, and low foreheads" of the immigrants posed what Ross called an "unthinkable" future: a mingled, degraded America.

In Ross's lurid telling, the two vectors that had been moving inexorably toward each other for a full decade, eugenics and xenophobia, were seamlessly merged. He also engaged actively with the Immigration Restriction League and offered to travel to Washington to make his case for the literacy test to his old graduate school teacher President Wilson. But to the degree that Ross was anticipating the next turn in the immigration restriction movement, his most important—and most revealing—utterance may have been embedded in what was nearly a throwaway line in his lengthy accounting of the genetic and social deficiencies of the eastern and southern Europeans. Slavs, he had written, "are immune to certain kinds of dirt. They can stand what would kill a white man."

The distinction had nothing to do with Slavs per se. The point was this: all these people elbowing their way onto Ellis Island and from there into this threatened nation, all these invaders with "lips thick, mouth coarse, upper lip too long, cheekbones too high, chin poorly formed"—not only were they not American, they weren't even white.

Lodge, Burnett, and their congressional allies resumed the final stages of their campaign for a literacy test not long after Ross published his prophesy about "the extinction that surely awaits" a nation that lacked "pride of race." Once more House and Senate passed the bill by what appeared to be veto-proof margins. Once more a president—this time, Wilson—invited advocates (Edward A. Ross among them) and foes into the East Room for a debate. Once more, just as James Patten had visited Taft to make his case for the literacy test in person, the IRL tried to win a president's favor by sending an emissary —this time its leading Democrat, Joe Lee—to the White House. And once more a president killed the measure with his veto power. The object of the literacy test, Wilson said, "is restriction, not selection"; it represented a bigotry designed to exclude. The president's corrosive antipathy toward black Americans was well established by then. His feelings about Asians were similar; during the 1912 campaign he had said that "Oriental coolieism will give us another race-problem to solve and surely we have had our lesson." But the eastern and southern Europeans posed no race problem to Wilson. They had votes. They were white enough.

On February 4, 1915, when twelve Democratic members of the House withdrew their support for the bill, Wilson's veto was sustained by a bare four votes. Prescott Hall had believed the bill was "the greatest chance that native Americans have had since Cleveland vetoed the bill which would have kept Jews out." He had also believed that Wilson would sign it. James Patten, who had been lobbying Congress for a decade, told an associate that the failure of this last attempt was "our Waterloo."

But the executive committee of the Immigration Restriction League may have been cheered by an oddly buoyant letter from a supporter in New York. He said he was much encouraged by the work in this Congress, and it was only a question of time to get the bill through. This was not the last thing that Madison Grant would have to say on the subject of immigration.

PART II

The Perfect Weapons
of Science

Chapter Seven

Heaven-Sent Madison Grant

O f all the clubs and societies that formed a wreath both glittery and gentlemanly around the Manhattan life of Madison Grant, none suited him better than the Half Moon. He enjoyed his rich social life and his many friendships at the Union Club, the Knickerbocker, the University, the Tuxedo, and the Turf & Field. The Society of Colonial Wars, which he had cofounded (its membership closed to those who could not trace their American roots back to 1775 or before), enabled him to confirm his exalted genealogy. His raffish side found him in the company of artists, writers, and fellow-traveling aristocrats at the Century Association, and he could attend to his political passions at meetings of the American Defense Society, whose chairman believed "a widespread conspiracy of revolutionary forces," led by Republican senator Robert La Follette of Wisconsin, was plotting to seize control of the federal government. Grant's interest in environmental issues found a productive outlet among the ninety members of the Boone and Crockett Club, founded by Grant's fellow club officer Theodore Roosevelt to "promote manly sport with a rifle"; at the American Museum of Natural History, where he served for many years on the executive committee alongside his closest friend, museum president H. Fairfield Osborn; and most especially at the Bronx Zoo—of which Grant was founder, funder, and for decades its guiding spirit.

But the Half Moon Club, named for the ship Henry Hudson sailed into New York Harbor in 1609, was prepotent: it was social, it was exclusive, it was scientific, and it came to be decidedly political. Conceived by Grant and Osborn in 1906, its membership was confined to twenty-four men. Other charter members included J. P. Morgan Jr. (Osborn's cousin) and architect Charles F. McKim. Over the next several years they were joined by sculptor Daniel Chester French, who created the Lincoln Memorial; illustrator Charles Dana Gibson, whose "Gibson Girl" became the Gilded Age's paradigm of beauty; Nicholas Murray Butler, for forty-six years the president, and the personification, of Columbia University; and others made clubbable by their eminence, their congeniality, and their nearly pure Anglo-Saxon heritage. (The one exception was Serbian American physicist Michael Pupin, who had become well known and wealthy for inventing the device that made long-distance telephony possible.) By the time the Half Moon concluded its final "voyage" (as Grant called their meetings) in 1934, nearly every major figure in the American eugenics movement, and many in the anti-immigration movement, had signed up for the trip.

Grant rode the "voyage" metaphor as far as it could take him. The calligraphed invitations he sent out two or three times a year announced the club's next "cruise"—in fact a dinner, most often convened at the University Club's neo-Renaissance palazzo on Fifth Avenue. Members and invited guests were asked to "reserve a cabin" for each cruise, which "set sail" at 7:00 p.m. As host, Grant called himself the "Master Mariner"; the evening's speaker was the "pilot." Members—"the crew of the Half Moon"—signed each evening's program under the heading "adventurers." Unable to extend the seagoing imagery any further, he came up with no better name for the invited guests than "associate adventurers." But he did attach a nautical tag to the menus: an evening's meal that (for one example) ran from beluga caviar through Filet of Flounder Bercy and Squab au Cresson bore the label "Rations."

Kitted out for each voyage in white tie and tails, the men of the Half Moon and their guests treasured their renown, their exclusivity, and an impressive roster of "pilots." Sir Ernest Shackleton recounted his adventures in the Antarctic. Prince Albert of Monaco spoke about deep-sea exploration. Hiram Bingham, the explorer who found Machu Picchu, called his talk "To the Lost City of Peru." But even in the early years, the subject would occasionally veer away from exploration and adventure. In 1908, William Z. Ripley, author of *The Races of Europe*, came down from Harvard to speak about "The Migration of Races." And in the spring of 1914, Edwin G. Conklin, a prominent Princeton biologist, gave a talk titled "Through the Channels of Heredity." Given the topic, Fairfield Osborn asked Grant to invite Charles Davenport to join Conklin's voyage; Davenport, Osborn said, was "an eminent leader in the eugenics movement in this country." Overgilding the lily, Osborn also told Grant that Davenport was "Director of the Carnegie Foundation," which was not remotely correct. His need to explain Davenport's qualifications suggests that Grant wasn't yet fully aware of Davenport's signal importance in the advancement and popularization of eugenic ideas.

Not everyone present that April evening was a eugenicist, nor were they all sworn foes of immigration. One of the invited associate adventurers was the great geneticist Thomas Hunt Morgan (he and Conklin had been graduate students together), who would soon declare that he considered much of eugenic science—perhaps even some aspects discussed that night—"reckless" and "unreliable." Another was Simon Flexner, the son of Jewish immigrants (from Bohemia and Germany) who could trace his own remarkable journey through the melting pot from sixth-grade dropout to his appointment as director of the Rockefeller Institute for Medical Research, a position he would hold for three decades. As it happened, the Rockefeller family and its foundation both made occasional contributions to Davenport's work in Cold Spring Harbor, until Flexner alerted them to scientific holes in the eugenic argument.

Still, the Half Moon event had great potential. Consider: Conklin, the evening's speaker, was about to publish *Heredity and Environment in the Development of Man*, in which he cited Davenport's work extensively and warned of the dire "biological consequences" that made "the problem of immigration so serious." Osborn—Master Mariner for this particular voyage—would for the next two decades steer the engines of science and myth that would become the driving force of the anti-immigration crusade. Davenport was a scientist who gave credibility to the eugenics movement and was in the process of being tugged in the direction of racism. Grant was a racist whose presumptions of scientific authority would complete the picture.

But first, a World War got in the way.

For the American eugenics movement, the immediate effect of the conflict that ignited Europe in the summer of 1914 was the indefinite postponement of the Second International Congress of Eugenics, which was to have taken place in New York, Fairfield Osborn presiding. At the same time, for the immigration restriction movement the war in Europe inserted an unexpected, if temporary, victory into the long line of restrictionist defeats: the flow of immigrants was stanched.

With the first sinking of a British merchant ship in October, German submarines powerfully aggravated the perils of transatlantic crossing. The Hamburg-American Line and other steamship companies saw their fleets dragooned into military service or seized in enemy ports. In the first full year of war, immigration to the United States plummeted nearly 75 percent. But the war was bound to end at some point, and the prospect of swelling masses of refugees in Europe, homeless and in many parts of the continent stateless, loomed large. The intense anti-German feeling that would be unleashed with American entry into the war in 1917 also lay in the future (however near), but the consequences of armed savagery have a way of turning heads and changing minds. More than a year before the United States entered the conflict, even as immigration numbers were dropping radically, the restriction cause found support in surprising places. In the *New Republic*, which he had cofounded two years earlier, twenty-six-year-old Walter Lippmann described "the sinister effect upon our national life" wrought by immigration. The Harvard-trained son of German Jews, Lippmann believed in "a scientifically managed society run by a public-minded clite," wrote his biographer Ronald Steel; in this instance he urged that elite to support restriction—an argument that led Joe Lee to send Lippmann a letter welcoming him aboard the restriction express. (He didn't stay there; Lippmann jumped to the other side as the restriction-ists' arguments became more obtuse and hate-filled.) The war even compelled the conversion of as devoted an advocate of open doors as James Curley, the fiery Bostonian whose speeches against the literacy test had made him a hero to antirestrictionists. (In a single sentence in one congressional speech, Curley had called the test "vindictive," "insidious," "iniquitous," and "barbarous.") Terrified by the spread of infectious diseases caused by deteriorating conditions in Europe, Curley called for the complete suspension, for five years, of *all* European immigration.

Undeterred by the war's deferment of the international congress, American eugenicists instead replaced it with a domestic event. The 1914 Race Betterment Conference in Battle Creek had proved such a success that its sponsors, taking their celebration of eugenic doctrine to a national stage, stepped forth with a renewed version in San Francisco, to coincide with the 1915 Panama-Pacific International Exposition. As with other world's fairs of the era—Chicago in 1893, St. Louis in 1904—the Pan-Pacific, conceived to celebrate the completion of the Panama Canal, seized the nation's attention. Close to five million Americans viewed the Liberty Bell on its way west for a special appearance at the fair (140,000 turned out for a single six-hour whistle stop in Denver), five million more saw it on the way back home, and during its five months' residency at the Pan-Pacific nearly two million fairgoers paid it homage.

The starry-eyed optimism and unashamed exuberance of a world's fair proved an ideal setting for the second Race Betterment Conference. The meeting's impresario, J. H. Kellogg (of the eponymous corn flakes), was an early devotee of Sylvester Graham (of the eponymous cracker), and eventually extended the latter's belief in vegetarianism and naturopathic medicine into what Kellogg called "biologic living." (He also extended his dietary innovations to the invention and promotion of peanut butter.) The sanitarium he built and ran in Battle Creek had become nationally famous by the turn of the century, and after ceding control of the family cereal business to his brother Will in 1905, Kellogg devoted the rest of his long life to evangelizing his esoteric philosophy. An ideology of health built upon various forms of abstinence (not only alcohol and tobacco, but also coffee, tea, condiments, and most dairy products), some singular medical innovations (chiefly "rational hydrotherapy"), and a hopeful dedication to human progress, biologic living fit in to the premises of eugenics as firmly as a plug fits a socket. The world had a desperate need, Kellogg said, for "a real aristocracy made up of Apollos and Venuses and their fortunate progeny."

In its planning and execution, Kellogg's conference fit just as neatly into the atmospherics of the fair. Pan-Pacific organizers proclaimed a "Race Betterment and Eugenics Day" and scheduled a "pageant procession" through the fairgrounds featuring what one newspaper called "a company of tall men" joined by "a picked body of soldiers," as well as a contingent of centenarians and assorted parade floats designed to vivify principles of hygiene and temperance. Press attention for the eugenics conference was keen. Kellogg declared that coverage in "the leading newspapers" added up to "more than a million lines" of copy, a good portion of it devoted to his announcement of the creation of a "Eugenic Registry." Under the direction of a board that included among its members Charles Davenport, David Starr Jordan, and Luther Burbank, the registry was designed to launch what Kellogg called "the beginning of a new and glorified human race" that would someday inhabit a world where "hospitals and prisons will no longer be needed, and the golden age will have been restored as the crowning result of human achievement and obedience to biologic law."* He thought a "new species of man" could be created in just six generations.

But it was Jordan, his interest in eugenics only sharpened since his visit with Mary Harriman at Arden back in 1910, whose comments at the conference were more timely and more telling. Jordan had been removed from his Stanford presidency in 1913 (victim of a palace intrigue engineered by university board member Herbert Hoover), and subsequently turned his attention to the cause of world peace. Now, almost exactly one year after the onset of World War I's unprecedented carnage, he took the platform at the Race Betterment Conference to preach a secular sermon on "Eugenics and War"—to make the case that wars kill off the best, leaving the future to the genetically worst, a result that came to be described as "dysgenic."

Jordan's arguments could not have been more thoroughly eugenic had they come from Galton himself. In war, Jordan said, after the "best ones are slaughtered . . . the Nation breeds from the second best," and in time "a continual killing off at the upper end and a continual breeding from the lower end" will destroy a nation. It happened in Rome, where after centuries of war "only cowards remained," causing the great empire to plunge into decline and death. The Boston newspaper that had wondered why New England seemed bereft of great figures like Emerson and Thoreau and Oliver Wendell

---

* Kellogg had ready access to his Eugenic Registry Board: Jordan, Davenport, and Burbank periodically put themselves under Kellogg's care at the Battle Creek Sanitarium, as did several other eugenicists and their supporters, including Irving Fisher and Madison Grant.

Holmes, said Jordan, could have found the answer etched into the marble tablets on the somber walls of Harvard's Memorial Hall: the names of the college's Civil War dead, the fine young lads who never had the chance to sire the great men New England needed today.

"The men that make the Nation, that give it its tone, its quality," Jordan said, are those of "superior strains—large in bone, large in strength, large in endurance, large in moral character, large in intelligence, large in personality—large in any of the virtues or in any of those things that make man stand out pre-eminently from other men." Jordan's belief in those "superior strains" and their current endangerment was not entirely new. He had been giving speeches like this for years, at least as far back as 1909, but the prominent stage of the Pan-Pacific Exposition proved a powerful amplifier.

Elements of Jordan's reasoning had been floating around in eugenicist circles for decades. Charles Darwin had made similar points. "The finest young men are taken by the conscription or are enlisted," Darwin had written in 1871, in *The Descent of Man*. "They are thus exposed to early death during war, are often tempted into vice, and are prevented from marrying during the prime of life. On the other hand the shorter and feebler men, with poor constitutions, are left at home, and consequently have a much better chance of marrying and propagating their kind."

But Darwin also said it was imperative to extend sympathy to the constitutionally less fortunate; to do otherwise, he insisted, threatened "deterioration in the noblest part of our nature." In the four decades that followed, however, Darwin's sympathy had been supplanted by a colder calculation, rooted either in the presumed dispassion of scientific and historical analysis that Jordan offered or in the jagged terrain of enmity, contempt, and fear. Or, eventually, both.

The following year J. H. Kellogg picked up where he had left off. Battle Creek was not San Francisco, and the fiftieth anniversary of the sanitarium that had, along with corn flakes, made the small Michigan city famous was not the Panama-Pacific Exposition. Still, for Dr. Kellogg and his Race Betterment Foundation, the sanitarium's jubilee celebration in October 1916 was a confirming event. Two governors, two U.S. senators, and a fistful of congressmen joined the several hundred invited guests, all of them sanitarium alumni—people who had come to Battle Creek in years past for Dr. Kellogg's regimen of vegetarianism, whole grains, and enemas.

On the jubilee's opening night seven bands and twenty-three floats led a torchlight parade two miles long that culminated in a double display of fireworks: first the variety that lit up the evening sky, and then a commemorative oration by the highly combustible William Jennings Bryan, the three-time presidential candidate who had just embarked on a postpolitical career devoted to fighting for alcohol prohibition and against evolution.

Bryan may have been America's foremost fundamentalist, but his was not the most striking religious address offered during Kellogg's three-day jubilee. That came from a man who believed in evolution as thoroughly as Bryan did not and who could not have been more different from Bryan in style and substance: Charles Davenport. He titled the speech "Eugenics as a Religion." It ran through a little Galton, a little history, a few philosophical points, then landed on the one thing he said every religion needed: a creed.

Davenport's testament of faith began, "I believe in striving to raise the human race, and more particularly our nation and community, to the highest place of social organization, of co-operative work and of effective endeavor." It concluded with a pledge of commitment to race betterment. And it included this: "I believe in such a selection of immigrants as shall not tend to adulterate our national germ plasm with socially unfit traits." The storm of applause that followed suggested that the world of eugenics was ready for Madison Grant.

*   *   *

"WARM-HEARTED, SYMPATHETIC AND HELPFUL, [Madison]
Grant was born in 1865 for the very evident purpose of originating
the New York Zoological Society in 1895." The author of those
words, William T. Hornaday, had good reason to admire Grant:
Hornaday was the director of the Zoological Society and its prize
property, the Bronx Zoo, for thirty years. Zoo employees were similarly admiring. They once gave the man who conceived the zoo—and,
for four decades, served it with generosity, loyalty, and unstinted
energy—a silver cup honoring "heaven-sent Madison Grant."

The Bronx Zoo may be Grant's most visible monument, but
it's hardly his only one, not even in New York. Eager to make the
zoo accessible by automobile, Grant was the driving force behind
construction of the verdant Bronx River Parkway, a pioneering piece
of urban design. At the American Museum of Natural History on
Manhattan's West Side, a Grant's caribou (*Rangifer tarandus granti*)
today stands stuffed and proud in the Hall of North American Mammals. Across the continent in northern California, in a redwood grove
ninety miles south of the Madison Grant Forest and Elk Refuge, the
world's fifth-tallest tree looms over a dedicatory plaque at its base:
a memorial salute to the three men who saved this extraordinary
natural specimen and thousands of others like it—Carnegie Institution president John C. Merriam; Fairfield Osborn; and the man
who initiated the effort to protect the redwoods, Madison Grant.
Horace M. Albright, one of the organizers (and later the second
director) of the National Park Service, needed just eight words to
summarize Grant's devotion to the wild world: "No greater conservationist than Madison Grant ever lived," he said.

Nor no greater foe of immigration.

There was no contradiction in Grant's utter dedication to the
preservation of America's natural environment and his perfervid
opposition to immigration. He was, in his own skewed and unseemly
way, an idealist. He believed in the America of his forefathers—a
glorious nation, pure and bountiful and uncorrupted. People from

southern and eastern Europe were as dangerous as the commercial interests who trained their covetous eyes on forests that could be felled and on mountaintops that could be mined.* Like so many other anti-immigration activists, Grant was by many measures a progressive, suspicious of large corporations and repelled by machine politics. In 1894 he worked for the successful reform campaign of New York mayoral candidate William L. Strong, who appointed Grant's friend Theodore Roosevelt police commissioner. Devoted to Roosevelt, Grant supported the ex-president's third-party candidacy in 1912. He even had a personal fondness for Theodore's distant presidential cousin, and though Franklin Delano Roosevelt turned in a political direction he couldn't abide, Grant didn't let that soil their friendship or his acknowledgment of what he called Roosevelt's "great achievements." Nor did Roosevelt turn on him, even after the blossoming of Grant's reputation as a xenophobe and anti-Semite. Their letters to each other were addressed with the most intimate salutation employed by men of their time and class: "My dear Madison," "My dear Frank."

Meeting Madison Grant for the first time, someone who knew nothing of his views of race and ethnicity couldn't help being drawn to this tall, handsome, and elegant man ("a lighthouse of fashion," said a friend). Gifted with an agile wit, a charming smile, and a sonorous voice, he was as personable in social settings as he was savage in his pursuit of an ethnically pristine America. Grant's amiable self-confidence came across not as arrogance but as a kind of gentle and genteel purity. When he visited Andrew Carnegie to ask for a $100,000 donation to fund pensions for the Bronx Zoo

---

* At times Grant could sound like an impassioned twenty-first-century environmental activist, as in this excerpt from an article he wrote in 1925: "We have killed all the wild game animals, we have cut down most of the forests, we have exhausted vast areas of virgin soil, we have polluted our streams and are destroying our coast fisheries, we have torn open the sides of the mountains for minerals, and are digging up our coal and draining off our oil at a prodigious rate." He blamed it all on an unholy amalgam of corporate greed and cheap immigrant labor.

staff, Carnegie told him to count him in for $10,000. Grant politely declined the donation; it simply wouldn't do. As he left the room, an abashed Carnegie called him back and said he was good for the full $100,000.

One of Grant's many admirers said he had "all the independence of a well-groomed musketeer." Financially, that independence was never in question. Although he didn't inherit his mother's fortune until he was fifty—it was a brimming pot of real estate gold that produced an annual income (in 2019 dollars) of roughly $600,000— Grant sailed through his first five decades on a cushion of wealth embodied in the family's Long Island summer place, Oatlands. There, a crenellated castle built by his maternal grandfather sat amid a lush, parklike paradise of espaliered pear trees, enormous rhododendrons, and imported cedars that eventually became the Belmont Park racetrack. Never married, Grant did not move out of the family's city home on East Forty-Ninth Street until he was past sixty. Even then, the bonds of kinship held him close: Madison and his brother DeForest took connecting apartments one block east, on Park Avenue. Madison also took along his six personal servants.

Like many of his social class in that era, Grant benefited from an education both private and personal, supervised by tutors at home and amplified by frequent European trips (he recited the *Iliad* while sitting with his father "on the crumbling walls of Troy," a friend said). He spent several years of his adolescence studying amid the baroque splendor of Dresden (a common educational destination for wealthy young men in the latter half of the nineteenth century, among them Henry Adams, Theodore Roosevelt, and Robert Ward of the Immigration Restriction League). Then came Yale and Columbia Law School, and a few years of legal practice, before he abandoned his career for an undiluted dedication to the preservation of America's natural wonders and, soon enough, its undiluted bloodstream.

In Grant's social world his views were no secret; he felt no need to conceal them. "His was not a nature to forgo a thrust for fear of a riposte," his friend the mammologist H. E. Anthony once said. This obdurate candor was put to a test when Grant was nominated for membership in the Century Association in 1912. Endorsing his friend's candidacy in a letter to the club's admissions committee, Fairfield Osborn first recounted some of Grant's accomplishments as a conservationist and the breadth of his interests as an amateur scholar. Then he turned to his character. He said Grant was "a gentleman and an agreeable companion," but he did add a sentence acknowledging what members of the committee likely knew: "Mr. Grant has a very positive way of expressing himself," wrote Osborn, "and his strong views on certain questions, like Catholicism and the Hebrew race, have made him some enemies."

Not enough enemies, however, to keep Grant out of the Century, where he remained a member for the next twenty years, nor to embarrass his fellow crusaders or dim their undying ardor. "In the tundras of the north," a particularly word-drunk associate would write in tribute to Grant after his death in 1937, "where the sun gods are on guard, men will gather around the flame in the soapstone and tell tales" of the man who tried to "save our land from alien hordes."

Madison Grant's relatives destroyed a lifetime's mountain of mail and memoranda after his death; he wanted no letters to survive. He also had no wish to tell his own story himself. "I have no present intention of writing an autobiography," Grant told Zoological Society director William Hornaday, when he was in his sixties. "It is too much trouble and, besides . . . the things of real interest and importance would probably have to be omitted." No one, not even Grant's superb biographer, Jonathan Spiro, could possibly decode this cryptic reference.

But the "strong views" Osborn mentioned in his letter to the Century's admissions committee are preserved in the files of Grant's many correspondents and in a few other venues beyond the reach of his drive to obliterate his intimate past. The Jews of the Lower East Side, Grant told Elihu Root, were a "curse . . . draining off into this country [from] the great swamp" of Jewish Poland. The Bolshevists, he wrote in the introduction to an associate's book, had "Semitic leadership and Chinese executioners." Trying to persuade Theodore Roosevelt to support the literacy test, he expressed his doubts whether the "dwarfed and undersized Jews," who were "totally unfit physically," had "the moral courage for military service." The United States was fast becoming "a dumping ground for Italians," he wrote in a magazine article. That was around the same time he offered his only criticism of his intellectual progenitor, the archracist Count Gobineau. Though he was "a pioneer in race eugenics," wrote Grant, Gobineau was "greatly impaired by his devotion to the Papacy."

Jews may have attracted more of his venom than Catholics, but Grant didn't really see them as separate threats, leaping to new imaginative heights when he warned the essayist and novelist John Jay Chapman of the threat posed by "the Catholic Church under Jewish leadership." The two groups, he believed, were cut from the same genetic cloth: southern and eastern Europeans, he insisted, were "half-Asiatic mongrels." In his desperate wish to rinse any stain from the reputations of great men, Grant, though an atheist himself, felt the need to insist that Jesus wasn't Jewish—in fact, he argued, Christ was crucified *because* he wasn't Jewish.* And in the difficult case of Christopher Columbus, he made an argumentative leap that carried him far beyond the boundaries of any known logic: "Columbus, from his portraits and from his busts, whether authentic or not, was clearly Nordic."

Five critical words in that sentence reveal the underlying foundations of Grant's polemics. That four-word jaw-dropper at the sentence's heart—"whether authentic or not"—showed his unem-

---

* Jews and Jewishness plagued Grant even at home: however proud he was of his many hunting trophies, he regretted the "Jewish cast of nose" that taxidermists gave his moose heads.

barrassed willingness to invent evidence where none existed. And the resounding word right before the period—"Nordic"—was the Grant invention on which he built his fame and his influence.

In historian John Higham's phrase, Grant was "the man who put the pieces together." The pieces were eugenics and xenophobia; the resulting amalgam was scientific racism as a political creed. Grant's assembly of those pieces no doubt accelerated that April 1914 evening at the Half Moon, when heredity was the topic and Edwin Conklin, Charles Davenport, and Fairfield Osborn were parties to the discussion. So was the fabulously wealthy Moses Taylor Pyne, who spent most of his life pouring his enormous inherited fortune (sugar, banking, railroads) into the treasury of Princeton University, which he loved deeply and at length; he sat on its board for thirty-six years and never missed a meeting. Pyne also played a significant role in the development of the university's distinctive "collegiate Gothic" architectural style, which Princeton's supervising architect described as a response to "the call of inextinguishable race memory" and an expression of "ethnic continuity." (The university's president at the time agreed. Princeton's architecture "declared and acknowledged our derivation and lineage," said Woodrow Wilson.) The handsome Princeton dormitory bearing Pyne's name was not terribly far from the Osborn Clubhouse—a facility for Princeton athletes built with funds provided by Pyne's fellow member of the Class of 1877. Pyne had sponsored Madison Grant's candidacy for membership in the Century Association that Fairfield Osborn had endorsed. The three men formed a tidy triangle of shared interests.

Charles Scribner, Class of '75, had no buildings named after him, only a room in the university's library. But he did have a publishing house—he was one of the two Charles Scribner's Sons commemorated in the firm's official name—and by May of 1916, almost exactly two years after the Half Moon dinner, Madison Grant had completed a book he called *The Passing of the Great Race*. By the time Osborn wrote to Charles Scribner to urge him to read Grant's "very suggestive study" about "the part that the three dominant races of Europe have taken in history," the publisher was predisposed toward it. Scribner already knew about the manuscript—he'd had the opportunity to discuss it with Pyne and Grant at the Half Moon's spring 1916 dinner. He was eager to read it.

By early June, Grant had finished his revisions. Before the month was over Scribner accepted his book and sent Grant a contract. He also turned the manuscript over to a young editor, recently promoted from the firm's advertising department, who ushered it into print in a bare five months. The rest is history—and anthropology, and ethnology, and genetics, almost all of it pathologically distorted.

The essence of the manuscript that excited Scribner and his colleagues is the notion of the "Nordic" as "the white man par excellence," member of a genuine "master race" facing extinction. Employing the concept of three European races that had been elucidated by William Z. Ripley in 1899, Grant refined it by judging each not simply by physical characteristics—head shape, height, skin coloring—but qualitatively, the Nordic prevailing in nearly all respects over the lesser Alpine and Mediterranean. (Another tweak was a tacit acknowledgment of the intensifying anti-German feeling as the United States stood on the brink of World War I: "Nordic" was Grant's substitution for Ripley's "Teutonic.") "These races," Grant wrote, "vary intellectually and morally just as they do physically. Moral, intellectual, and spiritual attributes are . . . transmitted unchanged from generation to generation." These attributes were, in a Mendelian sense, unit characters. And in a Galtonian, eugenic sense, they were sabotaged by careless breeding across "racial" lines. It was a distortion of both Ripley and Galton, but at the same time it was a hugely significant leap: eugenic concern about inferior individuals could be applied with equal conviction to inferior races.*

Grant described the Nordics—fundamentally, the people of northern Europe and the British Isles—as "a race of soldiers, sailors, adventurers, and explorers, but above all, of rulers, organizers, and aristocrats." They dominated the other races by right. "Most ancient tapestries," he wrote, "show a blond earl on horseback and a dark haired churl holding the bridle." Tall, fair, and blue-eyed, blessed with "a narrow and straight nose," the Nordic male (he hardly mentions women at all) was noted as well for bravery, chivalry, and "race pride." The Mediterraneans may be superior in the arts, he acknowledged, but "the Nordic invaders of Italy had absorbed the science, art, and literature of Rome," and therefore could be granted full credit for "the splendid century that we call the Renaissance." Despite the noisome presence of all those dark little southern Italians—corrupted, he believed, with African blood, dangerous because of their "political incapacity and ready resort to treason"—Nordic dominance "persists to this day, and is the backbone of modern Italy." Anything of value in Italy quite clearly arrived with those Nordic invaders: "Dante, Raphael, Titian, Michael Angelo, Leonardo da Vinci were all of Nordic type."

How did Grant know this? Partly from his great faith in his "close inspection of busts or portraits." He also may have picked it up out of admiration for Houston Stewart Chamberlain, whose similar alchemical skills had turned Marco Polo, Francis of Assisi, and Galileo into Germans. But Grant also drew upon an acrid hash of human history just as tendentious (and even more arcane) than his genetic postulates. "In Hindustan the blond Nordic invaders forced their Aryan language on the aborigines, but their blood was quickly absorbed in the darker strains of the original owners of the

---

* Grant had a peculiar notion of how interracial breeding—really, breeding of *any* kind—actually worked. He was relieved, he wrote, that most white-black miscegenation took place in the coupling of a white man with a black woman, for "the reverse process would, of course, have resulted in the infusion of negro blood into the American stock."

land." In France "the process of exterminating the upper classes was completed by the Revolutionary and Napoleonic wars, [which] are said to have shortened the stature of the French by four inches; in other words, the tall Nordic strain was killed off in greater proportions than the little brunet." Like David Starr Jordan, Grant believed World War I to be dysgenic, gravely imperiling what he variously called "the fighting Nordic element," "the tall Nordic strain," or "the blond giant,"* and thereby leaving "the little dark man" victorious. And for those without Grant's presumed familiarity with less well known "races," he reached beyond even remotely familiar groups into the almost comically obscure. He expounded on the migrations and linguistic paths of Dravidians and Esths and Tchouds. He dilated on intermarriage in the Solutrean Period. He explained how the Visigoths and the Jutes, the Varangians and the Suevi, and innumerable, unknowable, and improbable others "swept through history." How could such apparent erudition not be impressive?

Grant's variations on the racial past, which took up more than half of the book, were interpretations either historical (even if he was no historian) or anthropological (he was even less an anthropologist), both offered in service of a single, dominant theme: desolation lay in wait for the Nordics. The invasion of America by lesser tribes had placed the blade of a knife against the Nordic throat. "These immigrants adopt the language of the native American; and they are beginning to take his women," he wrote. And that same native American, by adopting the "suicidal ethics" of open immigration, is welcoming the "exterminati[on of] his own race."

It was in those "suicidal ethics" that Grant found the eugenic punch line to his polemic—a punch line that, in a way, granted special status to all those stunted, dark-haired Alpine and Mediterranean "churls": "Whether we like to admit it or not," he wrote, "the result

---

* These were all echoes of Houston Stewart Chamberlain's descriptions of the Teutonic ideal: "the golden hair . . . the gigantic stature . . . the lofty countenance . . ."

of the mixture of two races, in the long run, gives us a race reverting to the more ancient, generalized and lower type. The cross between a white man and an Indian is an Indian; the cross between a white man and the negro is a negro; the cross between a white man and a Hindu is a Hindu; and the cross between any of the three European races and a Jew is a Jew."

Grant's book didn't cite Henry Cabot Lodge, who, when he introduced the literacy test back in 1896, had invoked both Nordic imagery ("They came upon Europe in their long, low ships . . .") and the dangers of diluting the American bloodstream ("if a lower race mixes with a higher, history teaches us the lower will prevail"). But on the last page of *Passing*, Grant forcefully made Lodge's central point even more clearly than Lodge ever had: "The maudlin sentimentalism that has made America 'an asylum for the oppressed,'" he concluded, is "sweeping the nation toward a racial abyss."

*   *   *

THE PASSING OF THE GREAT RACE is not mentioned in A. Scott Berg's prizewinning biography of the great editor Maxwell Perkins, who was a thirty-one-year-old junior editor when Charles Scribner handed him Grant's manuscript in the summer of 1916. Neither is Grant himself mentioned, even though Perkins was Grant's editor for the original edition and three later revisions of *Passing*. Nor was his encounter with Grant a momentary involvement that Perkins soon outgrew. Seventeen years after their first collaboration—after Perkins had won his enduring reputation as F. Scott Fitzgerald's editor and Ernest Hemingway's—the two men came together for another book, *The Conquest of a Continent*, that was even more extreme in its defense of America's "purity of race" and "Nordic nobility."

In 1916 Perkins was only beginning to get enthusiastic about Grant's mash-up of the eugenic theories of Galton, the ethnic categorizations of Ripley, and the immaculate racism of Gobineau and Chamberlain. Just out of Harvard in 1907, he had taught English to Jewish immigrants from Russia and Poland at a Boston settlement house. He had found his way to Scribner's through an introduction provided by his Harvard teacher, the Brahmin archconservative Barrett Wendell, who introduced the young man to Charles Scribner with the most exalted of Boston accolades: "I have known and admired all four of his grandparents." Now, at the start of what would become the most storied career in American publishing history, he was steering into print a volume that would brand Scribner's as the publishing home for many of America's leading proponents of scientific racism. Perkins was editor to many of them.

Perkins and his colleagues launched *Passing* as "a history of Europe written in terms of the great biological movement which may be traced back to the teachings of Galton." A publicity brochure described Grant as a "scientist, savant, traveler, and trained observer [who] is exceptionally qualified for this work." By contributing the book's preface, Fairfield Osborn lent his reputation as a scientist, as a museum director, and as the author of several popular books to his old friend. A promotional piece mailed to the membership of the Immigration Restriction League asserted that "the inrush of lower races is threatening the very blood of our country," and, to press the point, offered this pointedly italicized warning: "*These races will not be raised to our standards; we will sink to their standards.*" A Scribner mailing to the firm's individual customers described Grant's book as a "scientific" study of the threat "from [the] unchecked influx of non-Nordic races."

Then as now, publishers do not customarily disassociate themselves from the views of provocative authors when they publish their books, but they often construct a wary hedge ("In his sure-to-be-controversial book . . ."). The marketing effort emanating from the fourth floor of the firm's Fifth Avenue "cathedral of books" didn't even hint that others might disagree with Grant and his racial fantasies. The men of Scribner's were all in.

Less than two weeks after Charles Davenport swore his oath to the eugenically inspired restriction of immigration in Battle Creek, *The Passing of the Great Race* got its public liftoff courtesy of the *New York Times*, which unfurled a strutting two-page spread in its Sunday magazine. The reader could slog through the piece—largely a dutiful précis of the book's contents—or simply pick up all the relevant signals from its visual presentation. A schematic map of Europe showed the early "expansion of the Nordics." On the facing page, another map revealed the more recent "encroachment of Mediterraneans and Alpines on Nordics." A rather forbidding photograph of Grant loomed over both, beneath the headline WILL THE BRUNETTE RACE ELIMINATE THE BLOND? (Grant was neither—he was unheroically bald, with gray temples). High starched collar, opulent mustache exquisitely trimmed, no hint of his customary playful half smile or the ironic glimmer that usually played in his eyes (though black-and-white printing didn't reveal it, they were brown, and not the blue he so idealized)—Grant looked stern, assured, even imperial: a man prepared to rule over both maps.

The first meaningful ripples of response to the book came from his friends and associates. One, from his longtime friend and fellow clubman Theodore Roosevelt, was particularly gratifying: "The book is a capital book; in purpose, in vision, in grasp of the facts our people most need to realize," the ex-president wrote. "It shows an extraordinary range of reading and a wide scholarship . . . and all Americans should be sincerely grateful to you for writing it." Grant and his publisher were grateful in return, and with the ex-president's permission used his words to tout subsequent printings of *Passing*.

Reviews were prominent, but mixed. The *New-York Tribune* called the book "a remarkable study, of direct bearing upon one of the greatest problems of the future of our country," and in Boston the *Transcript* couldn't contain itself: "This is a book to be read and considered by thinking men among us . . . a warning which should be heeded before it is too late . . . [Grant's] earnestness and profound learning attest its importance." But in London the *Times Literary Supplement* flatly dismissed Grant's evidence as "incorrect," and in American academic journals even somewhat sympathetic scholars were distressed by its "debatable assumptions," "questionable evidence," and "extreme statements." Nonetheless, the very same writers noted the book's "dignity and coherence," and said it "should be studied by all who are interested in the future of our country." Their reaction was a suggestion of the power of the distorting lens that many in the era's academic establishment looked through: bad scholarship alone was not enough to discredit a claim to virtue.

Two pieces in leading opinion journals formed a symmetrical frame for the book's reception. One, unsigned, appeared in *The Nation*, the venerable weekly then owned by Oswald Garrison Villard—pacifist, suffragist, cofounder of the NAACP, grandson of the great abolitionist William Lloyd Garrison, and hardly the archetype of the progressive xenophobe. But you wouldn't know it from the editorial on *Passing*. "Madison Grant has brought to bear distinct qualities of originality, conviction, and courage" in his book. Its few mistakes or overstatements were "humanly natural accompaniments" to such a "pioneer presentation." It was "admirable," it was "intelligent," and it presented "an historical concept of truths of racial evolution which as a whole is unanswerable."

The *New Republic*, however, proved eager to answer Grant's arguments, in the process rendering them limp and inconsequential. In its selection of a reviewer, the magazine brought out the heavy artillery: Franz Boas. His review of *Passing*, titled "Inventing a Great Race," was unrelenting, a tightly argued and authoritative critique punctuated by a series of sledgehammers. The book was built on "fallacies," and Boas enumerated them. He said its concept of heredity was "faulty," and explained its errors. The book's analysis was constructed "naively," its evidence was "haphazard," its historical reconstructions "fanciful," its opinions "dangerous." Because "a man so eminent" as Fairfield Osborn had lent his credibility to the book with his enthusiastic preface, the dangers were compounded. Boas tore apart the accuracy of Grant's maps. He ridiculed his linguistic analyses. He hardly paused to take a breath.

Grant could not have been surprised, or even upset. One of his most enthusiastic boosters, biologist Frederick Adams Woods of MIT, would obligingly note that most of *Passing*'s negative reviews were "signed by persons of non-Nordic race." (Woods's own theories included the notion that the Nordic mind was biologically incompatible with Bolshevism.) The ease with which Grant and his followers batted away criticism of the book, it seemed, was itself biological.

The Passing of the Great Race was a modest commercial success. Max Perkins assured Grant that it was "undoubtedly one of the most successful books addressed to the thoughtful public" published in 1916, but its real impact lay a few years in the future. The war had not only put the brakes on immigration, it soon focused the nation's attention not on the foreigners who had earlier clamored at the gates but on those whom American troops were battling in the trenches of northeastern France. A more successful edition published a few years after the war brought Grant the sort of popular acclaim he cherished—for instance, the letter from a newspaper publisher and politician from Portland, Oregon, who attributed his recent stock market successes to *Passing*: as a result of following its "first principles," Leslie M. Scott explained in a letter to Grant, he no longer invested in securities issued by "any but members of the 'great race.'" Now, *that* was an endorsement! Grant was so pleased he forwarded Scott's letter to Osborn.

Yet even in 1916, the publication of *The Passing of the Great Race* put the bridge connecting the anti-immigration movement to the eugenicists firmly in place. In his preface, Osborn said the eugenic view of race that informed every page of *Passing* "is not a matter either of racial pride or racial prejudice. It is a matter of love of country . . . based upon knowledge and the lessons of history." A letter Grant received from a man he had met two years earlier at a Half Moon dinner expressed his own love of country. Action was imperative, wrote Charles Davenport. He wanted to know "what can be done to secure our nation" from the "threatening danger" of unchecked immigration.

Chapter Eight

A Carnival of Exclusion

J ust three months after the publication of *The Passing of the Great Race*, the literacy test—so long in gestation, so central to the restriction cause—at last became law. Madison Grant was quick to take credit. "I am told that my book played a very important part in the final passage," he wrote to Charles Davenport. He could even say he predicted the bill's enactment, after a fashion: in *Passing*'s last chapter, Grant had declared that as soon as the "facts" of ethnic differences were "appreciated by lawmakers . . . a readjustment [of law] based on racial values" was inevitable. But the "readjustment" that arrived in 1917 had little to do with Grant. His greatest impact would play out over time, in restrictive stratagems as yet unimagined. In 1917 the winds of war were powerful enough to place the literacy test in the law books with hardly any help at all.

As the United States stood poised to send its young men into battle against European foes, some form of restriction appeared inevitable. Two years earlier, shortly after Woodrow Wilson's veto of the literacy test had been sustained, Louis Brandeis—not yet on the Supreme Court—told an audience of Jewish professional men celebrating the test's defeat that it would return. "We are celebrating not a victory, but an escape. The danger remains," Brandeis said. Invoking Macbeth, he warned his audience that "we have 'scorched the snake, not killed it.'" It did not take long for the snake to reappear, abetted to some degree by the chief scorcher when Wilson embarked on a war-driven assault on "hyphenated Americans." The 128 Americans who died in the U-boat attack on the *Lusitania* in May 1915 were neutrals, yet they had been slaughtered by German torpedoes. That December, some sixteen months before the United States entered the war, the president used his annual message to Congress to assault those immigrants "who have poured the poison of disloyalty into the very arteries of our national life" and called for "such creatures of passion, disloyalty, and anarchy" to be "crushed out." Wilson directed his calculated rage at people of German extraction, including American citizens who had been "welcomed under our generous naturalization laws."

Wilson's reelection campaign the following year would wave a virtual flag of neutrality emblazoned with the slogan "He Kept Us Out of War." But reports of cruel atrocities against civilian populations continued to filter back from the war, aggravating American suspicion of unfamiliar Europeans. The armies of the sprawling Austro-Hungarian Empire—more than three million men gathered in polyglot legions of Slovaks and Czechs, Slovenes and Romanians, Bosnians and Croats and Serbs—stood shoulder to shoulder with the Germans. The roar of nationalistic popular opinion drowned out the pleas of immigration advocates. Restriction sentiment was rampant.

When the literacy test was reintroduced in Congress in early 1916 as part of a larger immigration bill, the House passed it overwhelmingly; the Senate expressed its own resounding support after the November election. Somewhat surprisingly, given the way Wilson's administration had been whipping up native antipathy toward Americans of questionable loyalty, on January 29, 1917, the president again slapped down the bill with a veto. Less surprisingly, given the historical moment—the U.S. declaration of war against Germany and Austria was just weeks away—"a heretofore subservient legislature" (said Madison Grant) declared itself master, and on February 5

THE AMERICANESE WALL, AS CONGRESSMAN BURNETT WOULD BUILD IT.

UNCLE SAM: You're welcome in — if you can climb it!

Raymond O. Evans cartoon, 1916, as the bill was being debated.

overrode Wilson's veto. Charles Warren, the IRL cofounder whose career had taken him to Washington several years earlier, recorded the event in his diary. With the judicious discretion of a presidential appointee (Warren was an assistant attorney general under Wilson), he wrote only this: "Immigration Illiteracy bill passed over President's veto after 24 years of work by Immigration Restriction League."

The new law gave Lodge and his allies both less and more than they had sought. The difficulty of the test had been softened, and it no longer applied to individuals under sixteen, nor to women accompanied by a literate husband or adult son. However, the new law scooped up any number of other provisions the restrictionists had been discussing for years. It extended the prohibition of Chinese immigration to virtually all South and East Asians.* It codified some thirty classes of excluded undesirables, adding members of revolutionary organizations and those suffering from "constitutional psychopathic inferiority" to the old list of epileptics, lunatics, and the tubercular. The measure also granted the federal government broad authority to deport alien radicals who had somehow made it into the country, even if they'd acquired their radical beliefs long after their arrival.

Altogether, the Immigration Act of 1917 appeared to be a restrictionist's dream. Lodge seemed at last content. After twenty-four years' service, he resigned his seat on the Immigration Committee, completing the longest continuous tenure on a committee in Senate

---

* It is a measure of the general attitudes toward Asians that they were actually barred from citizenship through naturalization, at the time a privilege afforded only to whites (through the Nationality Act of 1790) and blacks (through the Nationality Act of 1870, a product of Reconstruction). The principle, later upheld by the Supreme Court, was so embedded in law and practice that in 1907, for instance, Theodore Roosevelt's attorney general could say that "under no construction of the law can natives of British India be regarded as white persons," and thus they were ineligible for naturalization. The previous year he had made a similar declaration about the ineligibility of the Japanese.

history. He soon turned his attention to a bigger fight, namely World War I, which he saw as an opportunity to display American might and to crush a European foe. He engaged in a literal fight as well, when an antiwar protester accosted him in his Capitol office and Lodge punched him in the jaw.

Lodge was a sedentary sixty-seven-year-old; his vanquished foe was a thirty-six-year-old minor league baseball player. Even in victory—the Senate approved the declaration of war two days later—Lodge was no more understanding of opposing views than he had been during all the years he had been on the losing side of the literacy test battle. In the last phases of debate on the 1917 law, a pro-immigration congressman had urged the bill's proponents to consider the virtues immigrants brought to America and even dared to argue that "the old New England Yankee stock can thank God today that a new infusion of immigrant blood is saving it from itself." Lodge, of course, couldn't possibly see it that way. The new law, in his view, provided a last chance to preserve the New England he so cherished. Years earlier he had declared that the people of New England had been "set apart from the rest of mankind for a particular work in the world." Years later a political foe saw it differently: the world of Henry Cabot Lodge, he said, was "a museum of wax figures which were not to be touched."

At long last routed by the restrictionists, the pro-immigration lobby could at least find some solace in one critical section of the 1917 law: refugees from political and religious persecution were given a waiver. They didn't have to pass the literacy test.

As czarist actions against the millions of Jews trapped in the vast Russian Empire escalated in the previous decade, several organizations had managed to squeeze a special exemption for political and religious refugees into most immigration legislation that made its way to a congressional vote. But when House and Senate conferees reconciled their separate versions, the refugee exemption was invariably tossed out. Wilson said its absence from the 1914 bill was one of two reasons, along with the literacy test, that provoked his veto. But when he vetoed the 1917 Immigration Act, the literacy test was the only offender; for the first time the refugee exemption had made it into the final measure, and when Congress overrode the president's veto, this single, ameliorating provision gave the antirestrictionists an unexpected consolation prize.

If one individual could be credited with carrying the refugee exemption into the law books, it was New York lawyer Louis Marshall. President of the American Jewish Committee from 1912 until his death in 1929, Marshall had led the refugee exemption campaign from its onset, and its success planted him firmly at the head of the pro-immigration movement. Considering his origins, Marshall was a somewhat improbable leader for the various Schiffs and Sulzbergers and others who had lined up in opposition to the restriction campaign. Unlike nearly all of the German Jewish grandees, Marshall was born poor. His father had arrived from Germany with ninety-five cents in his pocket and had settled in upstate New York only after finding work on an Erie Railroad construction gang. The son—dazzlingly intelligent, uncommonly ambitious, equally industrious—rose quickly from his inauspicious roots. Marshall graduated from Syracuse High School fluent in three languages and literate in two more (Latin and Greek). He soon apprenticed himself to a local law firm and in time found his way to New York City, where he succeeded as a corporate lawyer, widely respected and handsomely compensated. A lifelong Republican who found the populist branch of the Democratic Party "dangerously disorderly," Marshall was equally suspicious of Republican progressives, whose ideas he considered "half-baked." He knew Theodore Roosevelt (although he didn't much care for him), was nearly appointed to the Supreme Court by William Howard Taft, and would come to know Warren G. Harding well enough to "dash off" (Marshall's term) notes to the president when the mood struck.

A Louis Marshall note was an awe-inspiring thing, simultaneously revealing the intricate workings of a first-class mind and the bloated pomposity of an enervating bore. If Marshall could say it in five words, he'd use ten, or fifty. Ricocheting in tone between the unblushingly grandiloquent and the impenetrably pedantic, notes and letters and position papers flowed in ever-rising floods from his office in downtown Manhattan, his home on East Seventy-Second Street, and his grand Adirondack retreat. He could coin a phrase— he used "affirmative action" as early as 1913—and he could smother one in gibberish. Responding to a professor of economics who had challenged the pro-immigration position, Marshall wrote that the professor's argument "presents to my mind an irrefragable reason against the provision in the present law regarding the examination of intending immigrants overseas." He disapproved of the term "melting pot," explaining at length why he preferred "electrolytic powers" as the proper metallurgical metaphor for the process of assimilation. One of Marshall's "dashed off" notes to Harding ran to nearly a thousand words. More formal letters could surpass ten thousand.

Marshall's conservative brand of Republicanism was thoroughgoing. He was an adamant supporter of states' rights, fought a constitutional amendment outlawing child labor, considered referendum "a most vicious principle," and loathed rent regulations, which he called "dangerous invasions of private individual rights." Where he diverged from his usual political allies was on the immigration issue and anything else that affected the status and condition of Jews, both in Europe and the United States. Departing substantially from the attitudes of uptown friends who wished to help the eastern European Jews so long as they could be kept at arm's length, and from his own early reluctance to welcome the newcomers, Marshall came to adopt a motto he invoked repeatedly: "Nothing Jewish is alien to me." He proved this daily, in his work and in his private life. His mother could recite *Ivanhoe* in German; Marshall made a point of learning Yiddish.

It was in 1913 that Marshall won his first converts to the refugee cause, when he persuaded Representative John L. Burnett, the Alabaman who chaired the House Immigration Committee, and Senator William Dillingham, the Vermonter who had led the immigration commission, that the plight of the Russian Jews merited special consideration. But it was Marshall's unrelenting bombardment of Congress with long-winded letters, massive legal briefs, and position papers baroque in detail and wearisome in length that inserted the refugee exemption into the veto-proof 1917 bill, in the statutory language Marshall had provided. One comparatively ecumenical prorefugee group had based its campaign in part on the patriotic assertion that "the rights of political asylum" were rooted in the American Revolution. On the other hand, Marshall acknowledged, some senators believed the exemption had specifically been intended to "give a preference to Russian Jews." As immigration laws tightened in the years ahead, it was a preference that, to the most zealous restrictionists, would become first an irritant, and then a provocation.

The executive committee of the Immigration Restriction League met in Boston four days after the 1917 Immigration Act became law, both literacy test and refugee exemption intact. If league members were concerned about the refugee exemption, it apparently didn't trouble them overmuch. Prescott Hall gave his colleagues a brief and Hallishly dutiful account of the previous month's events in Washington. In his official minutes of the meeting, though, he displayed what was for him an improvisatory flair: he recorded the sentence about the veto override in red ink.

James Patten was more effusive. "I have been a mere agent in your hands," he told Joe Lee—either modestly, obsequiously, or both—"trying to help you do something which you patriots [believed] ought to be done for the good of your country and your fellow man." In the *Journal of Heredity*, the official publication of the American Genetic Association, Robert Ward offered his thoughts to the community he had been reaching toward for years: "The new law," he wrote, "is, in its essentials, a eugenic measure." He also called it "perhaps the most comprehensive and satisfactory [law] ever passed by Congress."

Perhaps it was—but that was not enough for Lee. Less than a week after the override, the man who had been the IRL's chief benefactor almost since its creation told a friend that the overall price tag had reached more than $100,000—roughly $2 million in 2019 dollars—but the law's enactment was "worth at least a thousand million to the country." Still, at the moment of greatest triumph for the league and its increasingly broad collection of allies, he had a suggestion for another member of the executive committee, Richards Bradley: "Now is the chance for some of those schemes you thought we ought to try instead of the literacy test." As in his life as a civic reformer, Lee did not rest on his victories; he sought to compound them.

The league desired new schemes because, after more than twenty years of unstinting commitment and effort, its leaders had come to recognize the literacy test's central irony: it encouraged the education of the immigrants they wished to keep out. Such irony made them sour. In a letter he sent out to the full IRL membership on behalf of the executive committee, Prescott Hall acknowledged the legislative victory but underscored the sinister prospect lurking within it: "It is probable," he wrote, "that primary schools will be presently established in many parts of Europe . . . so that the reading test, while improving the quality of immigration, is likely to diminish in value as a means of restriction as time goes on."

It was quite a statement: Hall was unembarrassed to admit that the literacy test was not about literacy at all, and the IRL had known it all along. As far back as 1902, league officials had worried that the test could boomerang. Charles E. Edgerton, who had preceded Patten as the IRL's Washington representative, warned Hall that "with the increase of popular education in Europe, races which would now be excluded [by the test] would be admitted after a few years." Minutes of a 1914 executive committee meeting included the baleful news that the Italian government was "spending millions on their schools in the past month in view of the pending bill." At the same moment that Joe Lee was establishing the Boston school system's commitment to immigrant education—he had just secured sight and hearing tests for the city's schoolchildren—the organization he funded regarded improved education in Europe as a threat. They may have been inconsistent, but the literacy test advocates were not necessarily wrong. Over the several decades of the "new immigration," illiteracy rates in Italy alone dropped from nearly 70 percent to roughly 23 percent.

One month after the veto override, it was no surprise to find Harry Laughlin and the *Eugenical News* acknowledging that the literacy test was not a "pure" solution and calling on Congress to take more definitive action. The same month, the IRL had in hand the first draft of a bill that would limit not only the presumed quality of immigrants but their very numbers. Shortly thereafter Hall sent William Dillingham a plan setting specific numerical standards— quotas—for "different racial groups." Immigrants from northwestern Europe would not be constrained by any limit, but the annual total allowed into the United States from eastern and southern Europe would be slashed by 70 percent.

Thus began the next phase of the restrictionists' legislative strategy. As it happened, it was Dillingham himself who had first put forth a rough quota idea in 1911. Three years later the Dillingham Commission's leading academic expert, economist Jeremiah W.

Jenks, raised the notion with Joe Lee and began to push the IRL in the direction of a quota plan. For support he turned to Rev. Ernest M. Stires, rector of St. Thomas's, the loftiest of Manhattan's high Episcopal churches, its congregation a plush collection of Vanderbilts and other prominent families. Stires said he was convinced that he could arrange "an avalanche" of letters and telegrams directed to Washington "from hundreds of Episcopalian churches" summoning support for a quota law. Jenks thought it an excellent idea; he believed it might "counteract very decidedly the very active propaganda being made against restriction by two other groups or religious bodies." This was undoubtedly a reference to Jews, of course, and to Catholics, who the next year would see a pontifical council inscribe responsibility for the welfare of immigrants into the Code of Canon Law.

By May 1918 the IRL had produced a Numerical Limitation Bill that would make eastern and southern Europe's rise to literacy irrelevant—a bill designed in part, said an IRL document, to counteract "the spread of elementary education in the backward countries of Europe and western Asia." The bill would cap immigration from every country at a fixed percentage of people from those nations already in the United States, whether the descendants of, say, Italians (who had been arriving since roughly 1880) or the English (who had had a head start of two and a half centuries to multiply their numbers). "Hebrews of all countries" would be "regarded as a single race or people." Another internal IRL document explained that the bill would "discriminate in favor of immigrants from northern and western Europe." House committee chairman John Burnett assured Hall that a "numerical plan" of some sort was the best path forward.

All this activity demonstrated the brimming confidence that lifted the IRL and its allies after so many years of frustration. Restriction advocate Henry Pratt Fairchild—socialist as well as sociologist—hailed the IRL in an academic article as "the most influential agency" in the passage of the literacy test. Hall went even further. He told Lee, "The League is now all powerful at Washington. . . . No bill as to immigration can be passed if we object, while any bill we favor has a good chance of passage."

It was precisely this eventuality that had earlier led the leaders of one antirestriction organization to anticipate the passage of the literacy test with a darkening gloom. It was not difficult "to understand that the Test is a disguise," their statement read. "Its advocates care little about Literacy or Illiteracy. What they desire is an entering wedge for later and more drastic legislation." The result, the writers predicted, would be "a carnival of exclusion."

*   *   *

FOR MADISON GRANT and various other paladins of the new scientific racism, World War I posed two problems. First, there was the matter of its dysgenic aspects, so persistently stressed by David Starr Jordan in the years before the conflict began. Edward A. Ross, preparing his introduction to the first widely adopted eugenics textbook, wrote of the war, "Owing to this immeasurable calamity that has befallen the white race, the question of eugenics has ceased to be merely academic." More than two million British and German soldiers—deadly enemies, racial kinfolk—had died. Implicitly accepting Grant's version of ethnic history, Harvard philosopher Josiah Royce declared that the Germans bore "the mark of Cain" for murdering their British brothers.

The second problem the war created for the scientific racists was linguistic in nature. For all the pleasure and pride the enactment of the literacy test brought Madison Grant, the war compelled him to further sanitize his increasingly famous book by deleting the slightest hint of admiration for anything German. Just as *The Passing of the Great Race* had miraculously transformed William Z. Ripley's Teutonics into Nordics in 1916, a new edition two years later expressed a startling discovery about the now hated German hordes. Echoing ideas championed by William S. Sadler, a Chicago physician who may have been the only person ever to train with both J. H. Kellogg and Sigmund Freud, Grant assured readers that the barbarity of modern Germany was an expression of a population that was not Nordic at all or even Teutonic, but "very largely Alpine." Most of the Nordics, he argued, had been killed off in wars long past. In a newspaper interview, Grant's friend Fairfield Osborn, who had written a new preface to the 1918 edition of *Passing*, was even more emphatic: modern Germany had been corrupted by "barbaric blood" of "Asiatic ancestry."

Grant also sustained a personal blow delivered by his old friend Theodore Roosevelt. The former president exploded in rage at Grant's suggestion that New Englanders and southerners were the best among America's soldiers. As the war fueled his own broad (if bellicose) brand of patriotism, Roosevelt had recently placed the country's heterogeneous populace in the generous category of what he considered "a new and separate nationality." Roosevelt told Grant that the best American soldiers "exactly represent the melting pot idea," and specifically cited a decorated half-Jewish soldier from Cincinnati he had met: the young man was "exactly like any Yale, Harvard or Princeton boy of the oldest Colonial stock." With his usual Rooseveltian vigor and directness, he also said that a Grant friend who believed in the superiority of "native Americans" was "an addle-pated ass."*

However much Grant had been injured by this last, stinging communication from a man he perhaps admired more than any other, he could find abundant solace in the new persona that *Passing*'s reception had established for him: recognized scholar. The *San Francisco Chronicle* called him "a thoroughly qualified ethnologist."

---

* After the former president died in his sleep just seven days later, Vice President Thomas R. Marshall said that "Death had to take Roosevelt sleeping, for if he had been awake, there would have been a fight."

The National Research Council, which had been authorized by President Wilson to coordinate scientific activity during the war, named him to its select Anthropology Committee. Charles Davenport invited Grant to join the Eugenics Record Office's Board of Scientific Advisors. As the years progressed Grant gained not only wider recognition but the silvery glow of a scholar's credentials as well. In 1920 the *Saturday Evening Post* lauded "authorities of Mr. Madison Grant's standing." By 1922, in the journal of the American Association for the Advancement of Science, he had become "Dr. Madison Grant." And so it would continue over the years, as "Dr. Grant" became a "distinguished zoologist" and eventually, in a respectable academic book published nearly a century after *Passing*, "sociologist Madison Grant."

In 1918 Grant joined with Davenport, Osborn, and Ellsworth Huntington, who taught economics and geography at Yale, to found the Galton Society. Its purpose was the study of "racial anthropology" by a scholarly membership (in Grant's words) "confined to native Americans who are anthropologically, socially, and politically sound." The four founders agreed that the best way to pursue their studies was by asserting exclusive responsibility for determining which candidates for membership met their exacting criteria: no one could join the Galton Society, they decided, without the personal approval of its charter members. Grant's intimate association with the members of the society (there were rarely more than twenty-five of them) did more to provide him access to credentialed scientists than any appellation or attribution ever could. Whatever their political views, Davenport and Osborn were both notable scholars in their respective fields, and though Huntington was mostly a popularizer, he did have a PhD from Yale and a seat on its faculty.

Over the years the founders of the Galton Society would welcome a constellation of American scientists into their fellowship.

They included such long-familiar habitués of eugenicist circles as David Starr Jordan, now retired from Stanford, and the polymathic Yale economist Irving Fisher, who had replaced Franz Boas on the American Breeders Association's immigration subcommittee when Boas had refused to endorse the recommendations of Prescott Hall and Robert Ward. They were joined by the comparative psychologist Robert M. Yerkes, whose name is memorialized at the Yerkes National Primate Research Center in Atlanta; paleontologist John C. Merriam, president of the Carnegie Institution of Washington for nearly two decades; and Princeton psychologist Carl C. Brigham, the father of the Scholastic Aptitude Test. Every one of them was an expert in his field (if not in the field of racial anthropology). Every one of them would become a critically important figure, either as enabler or advocate, in the spread of scientific racism and its application to the immigration issue.

After its initial meeting at Osborn's imposing mansion on Madison Avenue, the Galton Society moved its activities across Central Park to Osborn's westside domain: the fifth-floor sanctum of the American Museum of Natural History reverentially known as the Osborn Library. Located at the end of a long corridor lined floor to lofty ceiling by cabinets packed with zoological, botanical, geological, and paleontological specimens, overlooking Central Park to the south and east, and ringed on three sides by a balcony suspended over glass-fronted cherry bookcases—the library could have been a movie set for a meeting of distinguished scholars. Only one object betrayed the specific interests of this particular group: the portrait of Francis Galton, commissioned by Grant, that Osborn had hung on the wall.

In a sense, the society's monthly meetings were daytime, business-dress versions of the Half Moon Club's gatherings, with its substantially overlapping membership, the same proudly declared exclusivity, the same glossy veneer of scholarship. Members of what Jonathan Spiro has called the "interlocking directorate" of scientific racism and immigration restriction recognized little distinction between the social mode and the ideological one. Perhaps the only meaningful difference between the Half Moon Club and the Galton Society was the fact that for the latter, race was the stated subject not just every so often, but always.

That was fine with the Galton Society's host. Renowned as a paleontologist, respected as director of what was fast becoming the world's foremost natural history museum, Fairfield Osborn often deprecated anthropology's claim to scientific respectability; he once characterized the entire discipline as merely "the gossip of the natives." But he made an exception for the Galton Society's racial anthropology. This was demonstrated most clearly at another meeting, when Osborn offered a declaration that could have been the group's credo. "I am convinced," he said, that the "spiritual, physical, moral and intellectual structure" of individuals is based on "racial characteristics."

*　　*　　*

AROUND THE TIME that Mary Harriman, writing in her diary, recorded her acquisition of "another charming Copley" (her taste in paintings, as in most things, was both refined and conventional), she made note of her annual Christmas party in the Arden village church for the estate's workers and their families. All told, she wrote, 65 men, 25 women, and 188 children received "their Xmas handshake, gloves, and candy from me."

The seigneurial nature of Harriman's relationship to her employees and their families provided a convenient opportunity for her explorations of the byways of eugenics. There were three schools on the property's seventy square miles, and Harriman had all the students at one of them take a Binet-Simon intelligence test. One child, she reported, was normal. Another was abnormally bright. All the others, she found, were deficient. Her conclusion: "One need not go to Virginia to find very many poor whites, I am sorry to say."

The testing vogue permeating the eugenics movement owed much of its spread to Henry Goddard, who had begun to make his mark even before publication of *The Kallikak Family*. The very first issue of the Eugenics Record Office *Bulletin* was a reprint of a Goddard piece on heredity. By the second issue, in 1911, Goddard was contributing to a discussion of "Methods of Collecting, Charting and Analyzing Data." By this point, he had tested some two thousand children—the entire school population of a single New Jersey town—and used the results to adapt the Binet-Simon intelligence scale for American use. The next year saw publication of his Kallikak book and the year after that a testing project in the New York City public school system, which led Goddard to announce that fifteen thousand of the city's students were feebleminded. That captured attention. But it was another series of tests Goddard was conducting at the same time, on Ellis Island, that would deliver to the anti-immigration movement a very large helping of the essential nutrient it so desperately craved: scientific evidence.

The historical case against Henry Goddard has by and large ended in a mistrial—or perhaps it hasn't even ended. But there is no question that much of his work was severely flawed. *The Kallikak Family*, in particular, was soiled by shoddy techniques and corrupted by his, and Elizabeth Kite's, built-in prejudices. And just as the arresting example of Martin Kallikak's good descendants and his bad ones seduced those who wished to believe the book's lessons, so did Goddard's work on Ellis Island provide fresh ammunition for restrictionists who had picked up the eugenic flag.

Goddard had been invited to Ellis Island by the Public Health Service to determine if he could devise a method of identifying mentally deficient immigrants that was more reliable than the eyeball test in use at the time (basically, does this man *look* normal?). In 1913 as many as 5,600 immigrants came through Ellis Island on a single day.* They disembarked from the barges that had collected them shipside in New York Harbor, then waited in long, snaking lines and cramped holding pens for their turn to be examined by medical staff. The Ellis Island doctors were there not to cure ailments—tuberculosis and trachoma were prime suspects—but to diagnose them and thus deny entry to the afflicted. The "ever-changing stream of humanity," wrote one of the examining physicians, provided "a fascinating realm for study of the great questions of economics and eugenics." The same doctor couldn't help but note the "changing and deteriorating character" of the immigrants he saw. This, he said, made restriction both "justifiable and necessary."

Goddard, it was assumed (by Charles Davenport, who admired his work greatly, as well as by the Public Health Service), would find a way to make mental defects as discernible as physical ailments. No one assumed this with more confidence than Goddard himself. In most respects a gentle and modest man beloved both by colleagues and by foes—"the dearest man on earth," one of his critics acknowledged—Goddard could become vainglorious when the virtues of the Binet-Simon intelligence test were challenged. Convinced of the test's "supreme merit," he could dismiss criticism with a sigh that was nearly a smirk: anyone who doubted its value or accuracy, he once said, could "only arouse a smile and a feeling akin to that which the physician would have for one who might launch a tirade against the value of the clinical thermometer."

Goddard had no thermometer, no stethoscope, not even the frightening buttonhooks Ellis Island's medical examiners employed to turn up immigrants' eyelids in the search for trachoma. He relied only on testers he had trained and on Binet protocols he had adapted. His version of the intelligence test—recognizing shapes, memorizing rows of numbers, and the like—was largely language independent

---

* By this point nearly 70 percent of all immigrants were entering the country at Ellis Island; the remaining 30 percent were processed at eighty-one other immigration stations on the nation's borders and coasts.

and thus appropriate for the throngs arriving day after day, ship after ship, from country after country.

The Goddard study was the first credentialed testing effort specifically intended to evaluate the intelligence of the new immigrants. The thousands of index cards haphazardly collected by the young women of the Eugenics Record Office, Goddard's loose investigations into the presumably Mendelian fate of the two Kallikak families—all this work, however deficient by scholarly standards, nonetheless provided ballast to a eugenic theory of individual heredity. It did little, however, to address the influence of heredity on the nature of entire ethnic or racial groups. The sociological observations of Edward A. Ross may have carried the weight of his impressive academic credentials, but not even the most zealous restrictionist could truly make the case that his work was based on anything more substantial than Ross's rhetorical gifts. Madison Grant's manic charge through all of human history may have had the appearance of science and may have been accepted as such by those who dearly wished to believe it; over time it would definitely form the faux-intellectual foundation for the restriction argument. But the necessary accessories of science—the certifying minutiae of equations, statistics, *facts*—did not exist. Despite the success the restriction movement finally achieved with the literacy test, it still had to contend with a contrary (but persuasive) characterization of immigrants that could have been applied to all who had crossed the Atlantic (or Pacific) since the first English colonists arrived in the last decades of the sixteenth century. "Beaten men from beaten races" had been a useful trope, but the counterargument, best summarized by the outstanding immigration historian Alan M. Kraut, still lingered: "Weak, beaten men and women do not undertake transoceanic journeys to far-off lands, unless they are herded aboard ship at gunpoint." Far from being inferior, the immigrants, in this view, had special qualities of enterprise or ambition, or at the very least hardiness.

Even scientists revered by the eugenics movement had been expressing versions of this argument since the 1860s. In *The Descent of Man*, Darwin himself said he considered "the wonderful progress of the United States . . . the result of natural selection." Ten or twelve generations of "the more energetic, restless and courageous men from all parts of Europe," he explained, summoned exceptional inner resources to move "to that great country, and there have succeeded best." Francis Galton believed that "exiles are on the whole men of exceptional and energetic natures." Another man of science put it this way: "The most active, ambitious and courageous blood migrates. It migrated to America and has made her what she has become," he wrote in 1911. "Weaker minds were left behind."

The author of this last observation, put to paper before he was seduced by the notion of a race-based eugenics, was Charles Davenport. Then science marched forward.

Henry Goddard's Ellis Island testers selected something less than 200 immigrants from the hundreds of thousands who waited in the endless lines that season. ("Something less" will have to do, for in various contexts Goddard placed the number at 191, or 177, or "about 165.") Some candidates for testing were rejected because they were obviously intelligent, others because they were so apparently defective. "Apparently" did not mean "definitely": staff physician Howard Knox tested a man Goddard's colleagues had dismissed as mentally deficient because of his peculiar head shape ("simian reversion type with stigmata including malformation of helix"). Then Knox discovered that the man was fluent in three languages.

Something about the aftermath of Goddard's Ellis Island adventures suggested that he wasn't fully confident about his findings. In 1914 he published a book arguing that feeblemindedness was a leading cause of crime and indicating that it was a heritable "unit character," but he made no mention of the Ellis Island studies he had completed

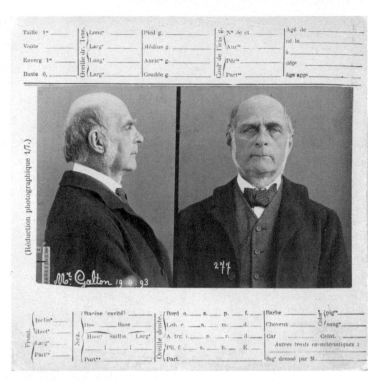

Francis Galton's obsessive categorization of personal data led him to subject himself to the equally detailed scrutiny of other scientists.

In a despairing poem, Prescott Hall of the Immigration Restriction League enumerated the new immigrants: "toiler, beggar, thief and scum."

Around the time that Henry Cabot Lodge posed for John Singer Sargent, he wrote that race prejudice has "ceased to be harmful" and in fact had "very real value."

4

The immigrant boys in this 1909 Lewis Hine photograph learned English in schools that received Joe Lee's very public support. They couldn't have known he was also for three decades the anti-immigration movement's most generous benefactor, fearful of America becoming "a Dago nation."

5

6

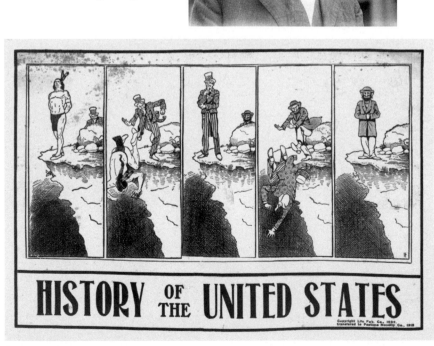

HISTORY OF THE UNITED STATES

Originally a magazine illustration, this anti-Semitic cartoon was reprinted as a postcard in 1913.

Charles Davenport (left) considered national eugenics a religion, with many of its tenets based on the research of Harry Laughlin (below, left) and his young fieldworkers—research described by a prominent British eugenicist as "careless," "inaccurate," and "irresponsible."

Mary Harriman, the richest woman in America, said she financed Davenport and Laughlin to prevent "the decay of the American race."

The pro-eugenics *Medical Review of Reviews* hired four vagrants to demonstrate on Wall Street in 1915. The picture's original caption said the signs the men were paid to carry asked "some very pertinent questions."

Franz Boas, here posing for an American Museum of Natural History diorama about the Kwakiutl tribes of British Columbia, was America's foremost anthropologist, and the eugenicists' greatest foe. Prescott Hall, who had no anthropological training, belittled him after Boas refused to endorse a blatantly racist report Hall had cowritten: "Very few Jews have any manners," he told an associate.

12

"HER SON"
$4000 prize Statue by Miss Nellie Walker
Courtesy Chicago Art Institute

Who will be the Mothers of Coming America?

—

The American Woman is Rapidly Becoming Ugly

Prof. Ross has proved it. When the low immigrant is giving us *three babes* while the Daughter of the Revolution is giving us *one* it means the Gibson and Harrison Fisher Girl is vanishing. Her place is being taken by the low-browed, broad-faced, flat-chested woman of lower Europe. If this continues it means a progressive loss of racial excellence, intelligence and power.

Imbecility and Genius are both Inherited.

Only opportunity will bring out inborn genius, but imbecility **always shows.**

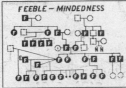

Pedigree collected by Dr. H. H. Goddard.
The black ones are all feeble-minded.

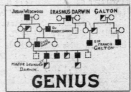

■ Means Fellow of Royal Society.
■ Means Eminent in Science. Pedigree collected by Mr. and Mrs. Whetham of England.

Imbecility is increasing. Great men are decreasing

COIT B
Cleve

WHITE BUREAU
Boston

13

Advertisements for Albert E. Wiggam's Chautauqua speeches featured the "proof" supplied by Edward A. Ross (left).

15

Madison Grant (left) said southern and eastern Europeans were "half-Asiatic mongrels" and disparaged "the Catholic Church under Jewish leadership." H. Fairfield Osborn, the celebrated director of the American Museum of Natural History, endorsed his best friend's views and lent them scientific authority.

Margaret Sanger told Harry Laughlin that her campaign for birth control and his for eugenics "should be and are the right and left hand of one body."

Scribner editor Maxwell Perkins was celebrated for publishing F. Scott Fitzgerald and Ernest Hemingway; at roughly the same time, he was editing and promoting books by the most prominent scientific racists, including Madison Grant and Lothrop Stoddard.

The *Saturday Evening Post*'s Kenneth Roberts (left, with novelist Booth Tarkington and industrialist Atwater Kent, in Kennebunkport, Maine) led the magazine's relentless campaign against the southern and eastern European immigrants, whom he called "the scum of the world, vermin-ridden and useless."

Before his 1924 bill came up for a vote, House Immigration Committee chairman Albert Johnson offered a warning: "If the Jewish people combine to defeat the immigration bill . . . their children will regret it."

Kansas fairgoers were offered instruction in the eugenic merit of native-born whites. The sign at right was meant to prove their superiority to immigrants and American blacks.

When Eugen Fischer—colleague to Davenport and most of the other American eugenicists—became rector of the University of Berlin in 1933, he declared, "What Darwin was not able to do, genetics has achieved. It has destroyed the theory of the equality of man."

the previous year. In 1915 he published an analysis of a young man named Jean Gianini, who had killed his schoolteacher, but did not raise the question of whether Gianini was an immigrant (Goddard did, however, assert that he was an imbecile, and "we know also that he is a masturbator"). At Davenport's suggestion Paul Popenoe, editor of the *American Breeders Magazine*, twice offered to publish Goddard's immigrant study, and twice Goddard declined. It was not until the end of 1916, more than three years after he had concluded his work on Ellis Island, that he revealed any of the results of his investigations, when he discussed them at a professional meeting. He did not actually publish them until September 1917, seven months after the literacy test was enacted.

Still, immigration restrictionists who had picked up the cause of scientific racism and no longer believed the literacy test an adequate barrier could not have dreamed of better results—which is to say, more shocking, more damning, and more fully aligned with their arguments. "One can hardly escape the conviction," wrote Goddard, "that the intelligence of the average 'third class' [i.e., steerage] immigrant is low, perhaps of moron grade." How low? His initial results indicated that 83 percent of the Jews were either "morons" (mental age eight to twelve) or "imbeciles" (mental age three to seven). Italians came in at 79 percent, Hungarians at 80. Rattled by what seemed to be highly unlikely results, Goddard put them through an additional statistical screen and managed to conclude that his calculations were off by a factor of two—it was really only 40 percent, all told, who could be considered feebleminded. Yet more alarming, if less noticed (it was buried among the tables and charts that trailed behind Goddard's narrative), was a column of numbers showing that only six of the nearly two hundred who were tested could be considered "normal."

Such results defied logic, but they were good enough for the restrictionists. Editors of *The Survey*—the leading social work journal of the day, funded in part by Joe Lee—claimed that the 40 percent figure was sufficient to prove that if a visitor to Ellis Island selected one person at random from "the great mass of 'average immigrants,'" then "you would very likely have found that your choice was feeble-minded." It was as simple as that.

Except that it wasn't. What *The Survey* and other Goddard boost-ers failed to acknowledge was the suffocating blanket of qualifications and caveats Goddard used to cushion his bombshell. He and his colleagues were "inadequately prepared for the task," he wrote. It was a study "not of immigrants in general but of six small highly selected groups." The results, "meager as they were," could be considered "so difficult of acceptance that they can hardly stand by themselves as valid." He acknowledged that "persons who have never had a pen or a pencil in their hands, as was true of many of the immigrants," would understandably have trouble copying an image, as the test required. Asking someone who has never had to work with numbers to repeat a string of six digits, he added, was like asking an Amer-ican to repeat six words in Greek; it was, consequently, "not a fair test." The entire study, its author cautioned, "makes no attempt to determine the percentage of feeble-minded immigrants in general or even of the [ethnic] groups named." It was a study, essentially, of testing *techniques*, not a conveyance of meaningful results.

Even more crucial than Goddard's doubts about his methodology was the gist of his conclusion. He noted that most of the immi-grants came from impoverished environments. He pointed out that immigration from Italy and eastern Europe had been going on for years, yet the United States had seen no perceptible increase in the proportion of the feebleminded of foreign ancestry. If indeed the immigrants were mentally deficient, he said, "we have two practical questions: first, is it hereditary defect or; second, apparent defect due to deprivation. If the latter, as seems likely, little fear may be felt for the children." Or, presumably, for the precious American bloodstream. About this, *The Survey* and others promoting the results of Goddard's testing were silent.

*   *   *

THE RESTRICTION MOVEMENT'S ABILITY to proceed without the slightest caution arose not solely from the prejudices that swelled the breasts of its leaders. They were buoyed as well by victory (on the literacy test), by a wave of patriotic hypernationalism (the Wilson administration's demonization of "hyphenated Americans"), and most of all by the ongoing rise of eugenic consciousness in American life. According to a federal study, the number of articles on eugenics appearing in the popular press had tripled between 1909 and 1914 alone, capturing more space, wrote John Higham, "than on the three questions of slums, tenements, and living standards combined." Publishers of a popular sex manual (pro-abstinence, anti-spooning, and very concerned about the inevitable palsy and deafness brought about through "self-pollution") elevated its appeal by promising "Scientific Knowledge of the Law of Sex Life and Heredity or EUGENICS." In a speech to his colleagues titled "Jewish Eugenics," Max Reichler, a young New York rabbi, said the Talmud idealized "a race in body and in spirit, pure and undefiled, devoid of any admixture of inferior human protoplasm." Supreme Court justice Oliver Wendell Holmes Jr. offered an unwitting preview of the majority opinion he would write twelve years later in *Buck v. Bell* authorizing involuntary sterilization of inmates in state institutions. Social improvement, Holmes wrote in 1915, could come only through "trying to build a race. That would be my starting point for an ideal for the law." (The great advocate of individual liberty also asked an associate, "Doesn't the squashy sentimentality of a big minority of our people make you puke?") Movie theaters played a film called *The Black Stork*, "a eugenic love story."

At the same time, eugenic ideas continued to spread through the academic world. At Boston University, eugenics education was provided by the School of Theology. At the University of Oregon, the course catalog explained that the class in eugenics addressed not just "positive" eugenics but "negative measures for race improvement" as well. MIT's course explored "recent experimental advances in the study of biometrics, heredity and eugenics." The Harvard version was taught by a sternly skeptical geneticist, but a faculty colleague, Dr. Dudley A. Sargent, expressed his conviction that young people might well choose their mates by how well they dance with each other. When two people find a common bond on the dance floor, he said, "they should either announce their engagement forthwith, or break away. There are such things as rhythmic affinities." An ironic and (no doubt unintended) double meaning crept into the description of the eugenics course at Colorado Agricultural College. It was "offered to women students in the upper classes."

In many classrooms, eugenics and immigration met in the pages of *Applied Eugenics*, by Paul Popenoe and Roswell Hill Johnson. Johnson, of the University of Pittsburgh, was a biologist of modest academic accomplishment who had trained at Cold Spring Harbor (he was the researcher who had been held rapt by the enormous mass of hibernating beetles imported from eastern Washington). Popenoe, the thirty-year-old editor of the American Breeders Association's magazine, was a resourceful and ambitious young man who decades later would create and preside over the "Can This Marriage Be Saved?" column in the *Ladies' Home Journal*—according to the publisher, "the most popular, most enduring women's magazine feature in the world." Popenoe's interest in finding marital means to accomplish eugenics ends was long a preoccupation: in 1924 he wrote a paper titled "An Examination of Eugenic Celibate Motherhood." (Don't ask.)

Applied Eugenics quickly became the leading textbook in its field, racing through four printings in six years. The book was helped along by Edward A. Ross, whose introduction lent the authors both his academic credibility and his feverish, race-inflamed ideology: "The fear of racial decline [today] provides the eugenist with a far stronger leverage than did the hope of accelerating racial progress." Like Ross, the authors were committed progressives. They argued for the eugenic virtue of outlawing child labor, which would take away the poor's incentive to breed. They supported the idea of inheritance taxes. Popenoe and Johnson even extended a generous hand to immigrants, expressing the belief that "some of these ignorant stocks [from eastern and southern Europe], in another generation and with decent surroundings, will furnish excellent citizens." Then, in the very next sentence, the hand struck with the force of a punch to the gut: "But taken as a whole [these] fecund stocks"—beset by "illiteracy, squalor and tuberculosis, their high death-rates, their economic straits"—could not be considered decent "eugenic material."

Published expressions of support for eugenics and opposition to immigration reached their zenith—or, perhaps more accurately, their nadir—in *The Right to Be Well Born* by William Earl Dodge Stokes, the extremely dissolute heir to three extremely large fortunes. Professionally, Stokes developed real estate on the West Side of Manhattan; personally, according to a family history, his interests were seducing young women and breeding horses. His book, which he said he wrote in "the spare hours of my vacation" at his stud farm in Kentucky, was chatty, unsupported by evidence (he bragged that he hadn't read Mendel because he preferred to remain "unbiased by other views"), and deranged. He pointed out that in the horse breeding business, "unfit" horses are rendered impotent, and money isn't wasted on sanitariums "to keep them alive at public expense." He praised Charles Davenport, Mary Harriman, and David Starr Jordan; quoted from Eugenics Record Office reports; and described a dreamed-of eugenic paradise, where a "working girl" would choose a husband not by how nicely he dances or how well he dresses, but by going to a Public Records Hall to learn where a potential mate ranks on a eugenic scale of A to F. Wrote Stokes, "If the males of laboring classes were compelled to have their own Registry, like the Clysdales [*sic*], Percherons, and other heavy draft Registries, and submit to a microscopic examination of their life germs . . ."—presumably, their genes—"there would be no need for labor agitators . . . to bring on strikes and such things." Even better, "honest labor" would no longer "be assessed to pay for hired assassins to kill judges who render decisions that are not satisfactory to the laboring unions, or to pay attorneys to defend them or witnesses to prove alibis. These are all little things," Stokes acknowledged, "but they count up to quite a sum at the end."

Among his other vacation-inspired musings on "the rotten, foreign, diseased blood" pouring into the country was Stokes's appraisal of Jews, whom he called "this admirable race"—admirable, apparently, because they marry within their group to preserve their "money-getting qualities." A few years later Stokes told Charles Davenport that he had proof that Abraham Lincoln was the son of "a Jew from Portugal with Mother a Scotch Jewess," and that a lock of Lincoln's hair also showed evidence that he was "Oriental." Davenport generally kept Stokes at arm's length but was always polite to him, accepted periodic donations from him, and at times even joined him for dinner. When *The Right to Be Well Born* was published, the ERO's *Eugenical News* pronounced it "full of good ideas."

A more substantial and much more influential recruit to the eugenic cause in this period of its blossoming growth was Margaret Sanger. A century after she first engaged with the subject, Sanger's connection to eugenics is still hotly contested, chiefly in the ceaseless debate over abortion. Twenty-first-century opponents of abortion rights assail the founder of the American family planning movement (who invented the term "birth control" in 1915) for having a wild-eyed commitment to the eugenic sterilization of the undesirable, and they condemn her specifically for what some claim was her engagement in a campaign to "exterminate the Negro population." Sanger's defenders note, correctly, that this hideous phrase, placed in the context in which she wrote it, had an altogether different meaning,* and that Martin Luther King himself praised "her courage and vision."

Nevertheless, there is no question that Sanger not only advocated the eugenics cause, she actively promoted many of its basic precepts and welcomed alliances with its most visible proponents. She told Madison Grant she would find it a "great pleasure" if he agreed to speak at her American Birth Control Conference. She told Harry Laughlin that the two movements—eugenics and birth control—"should be and are the right and left hand of one body." She welcomed *Applied Eugenics* coauthor Roswell Johnson and other academic eugenicists to her board. She endorsed the position of a California biologist who contended that birth control was "the solution to the Japanese problem" on the West Coast and, wrote historian Linda Gordon, she "put together statistics about immigrants, their high birth rates, low literacy rates, and so forth, in a manner certain to stimulate racist fears."

One especially resonant statement often attributed to Sanger ("More children from the fit, less from the unfit—that is the chief issue of birth control") wasn't uttered or written by her at all; the editors of *American Medicine* coined it in a lengthy editorial that was later reprinted in *Birth Control Review*. But Sanger's own words provide ample evidence of her affirmative support for eugenics. In a 1921 essay in *Birth Control Review* she wrote that "the campaign for Birth Control is not merely of eugenic value, but is practically identical

---

* Those who label Sanger a racist cite a letter she wrote to a colleague in 1939 in which she said, "We don't want the word to go out that we want to exterminate the Negro population." On its own the phrase can suggest that she and her allies had exactly that goal in mind and wished to keep it secret. However, the anti-Sangerites who quote it often fail to note that they have cut the sentence in half and have avoided any reference to the context. Sanger and her organization were starting an effort to bring birth control clinics to black areas in the South, and she hoped that local pastors would help them distinguish their effort from the contemporaneous movement for involuntary (and frequently racist) sterilization. Her full statement reads, "The minister's work is also important and he should be trained, perhaps by the Federation, as to our ideals and the goal that we hope to reach. We don't want the word to go out that we want to exterminate the Negro population, and the minister is the man who can straighten out that idea if it ever occurs to any of their more rebellious members."

in ideal with the final aims of Eugenics." The following year, under the title "The Cruelty of Charity," she attacked the idea of providing medical and nursing care to poor families, all but summoning the ghost of Herbert Spencer to make her point: "Fostering the good-for-nothing at the expense of the good is an extreme cruelty." In 1926, declaring herself "glad to say that the United States Government has already taken certain steps to control the quality of our population through the drastic immigration laws," she sounded like Henry Cabot Lodge. Expressing her concern for "the bloodstream of the race," she sounded like Fairfield Osborn. In her autobiography, published in 1938, Sanger took on the voice of Edward A. Ross (whose support she had eagerly sought), lamenting the fact that immigration laws had not barred "defective" individuals before 1907: "Had these precautions been taken earlier," she wrote, "our institutions would not now be crowded with moronic mothers, daughters, and granddaughters." And one of the slogans she eventually adopted for the American Birth Control League—"To breed a race of thoroughbreds"—could have come straight from the febrile fantasies of W. E. D. Stokes.

There are two explanations, equally plausible, for Sanger's engagement with the eugenicists. First, a review of her associations during her career suggests that she was strategically promiscuous, her commitment to her own cause so single-minded that she would ally herself with anyone, or any group, that might support it. The second explanation is embedded within the reality that eugenic theory itself was inherently dependent on birth control—that is, on the planning and limitation of reproduction. In the years when eugenics loomed large in American political and intellectual life, the two explanations could coexist very happily.

*　　*　　*

THE BRUTAL EUROPEAN COMBAT that raged through 1917 and nearly all of 1918 was, Edward A. Ross acknowledged, "an immeasurable calamity." But Ross managed to find the bright side: "Rooted prejudices have been leveled like the forests of Picardy under gun fire." What Madison Grant had called "mutual butchery and mutual destruction between Nordics" now provided eugenicists with an urgent argument: only they could save the race.

The most important attempt to seize opportunity from the war and make use of it to promote eugenicist ideas—and, in time, their ethnic implications—was engineered by Robert Yerkes. Building a career at Harvard, where Charles Davenport had been one of his teachers, Yerkes had become an acknowledged expert in psychobiological research and the study of animal behavior. It could be said that some of the greatest triumphs of twentieth-century scientific exploration were made possible by an event, wrote Yerkes, that "at the time of its occurrence, seemed to be an unimportant incident in the course of my scientific work—the presentation of a pair of dancing mice to the Harvard Psychological Laboratory." The book about his experience with the mice and their offspring, *The Dancing Mouse*, helped establish the study of laboratory mice as an experimental standard throughout the universe of behavioral science.

When the book was published, Yerkes was a thirty-one-year-old junior instructor in comparative psychology. By forty-one, he was president of the American Psychological Association. He was also an advisor to the Eugenics Record Office and a member (along with Davenport and Mary Harriman) of the eugenics branch of the National Committee on Prisons. Soon he would receive an invitation that would place him at the precise intersection of eugenics and immigration restriction: membership in the Galton Society. Then the army came calling.

Unlike the surprise gift of the dancing mice, the research opportunity that World War I presented to Yerkes did not strike him as an "unimportant incident." He had seen the possibilities as the United States moved toward war, arguing that intelligence testing could help the army with the worthy task of identifying officer candidates. This gave him the chance, as historian James W. Reed has written, "to demonstrate that psychology possessed valuable technology for social management." It was a precise expression of the progressive ideal: science in the service of society. Said the archprogressive Joe Lee around this time, "I am a believer in science." It was a belief both genuine and, now, convenient.

As the military ramped up mobilization once war had been declared, so did Yerkes. Picking up the raveled ends of H. H. Goddard's confused Ellis Island research, Yerkes knit them into coherence not by studying the presumed intelligence of another couple hundred subjects, but by turning his attention to a rather larger pool: nearly 1.73 million army recruits, all made available to Yerkes and his colleagues by the U.S. government. Within weeks commissioned a major, he traveled to New Jersey to plan a program with Goddard, Lewis Terman, and other testing specialists. Two hundred psychologists were put through the necessary training at Fort Oglethorpe in northern Georgia, then dispatched to conduct tests at thirty-five army bases. Some higher officers were annoyed (one general called the testers "pests"), and many others became convinced that the point of the entire testing effort was not to serve the military but to advance the testers' own interests. They were not entirely wrong.

"Theoretically," Yerkes once said, "man is just as measurable as a bar of steel." Given the way his results would be put to use, his use of "theoretically" was disingenuous; by this time, promoters of eugenics like Yerkes had moved miles past mere theory. The military recruits who took his tests—one (called the Beta test) for the illiterate, based on the sort of shapes-and-numbers exercises Goddard had used at Ellis Island, the second (Alpha) for those who could read—were his new dancing mice, and a cruel choreography placed them at stage center in the immigration debate.

The Alpha test consisted of 212 questions divided into eight sections: synonyms/antonyms, arithmetical reasoning, analogies, and the like. It's difficult to imagine a plausible argument that it was an indicator of innate intelligence to know, for instance, whether "altruistic" and "egotistic" had the same meaning or opposite ones. Or whether it measured anything remotely meaningful to ask, say, a Polish immigrant who'd been in the country for just a few years to make a coherent sentence out of the scrambled words "External deceptive appearances are."* But no fair person could possibly have believed that the multiple-choice questions in the general information section of the Alpha test were a valid measure of anything at all—anything, that is, except the ease with which one could make a genuinely intelligent person who was unfamiliar with American culture appear to be a dolt. Two or three examples should suffice—but, as with salted peanuts, you can't stop with just a couple:

1. **The Overland car is made in . . .**
   Buffalo   Detroit   Flint   Toledo

2. **The Wyandotte is a kind of . . .**
   horse   fowl   cattle   granite

3. **Bud Fisher is famous as an . . .**
   actor   author   baseball player   comic artist

4. **Velvet Joe appears in advertisements of . . .**
   tooth powder   dry goods   tobacco   soup

5. **Marguerite Clark is known as a . . .**
   suffragist   singer   movie actress   writer

Could this possibly have been taken seriously? Viewed today, the unfairness of these questions is mind-boggling. But it should

---

* At Fort Devens in Massachusetts, Yerkes's associates produced a separate test strictly to determine literacy. Among the series of yes/no questions were some so baffling they almost seem to be Zen koans: "Are intervals of repose appreciated?" "Are scythes always swung by swarthy men?" "Are textile manufacturers valueless?"

have been so in 1918. If this test indicated innate intelligence back then—intelligence independent of one's educational, economic, and cultural background—presumably it would do so today. This wasn't an intelligence test; it was a current events quiz.*

In asserting the scientific validity of such tests, were Yerkes and company naifs, or fools, or scoundrels? The answer had to wait a few years—after the National Academy of Sciences published the results of the army testing in an 890-page doorstop crammed with statistics, charts, tables, formulas, and other impediments to comprehension, and after a few wealthy immigration restrictionists sponsored a project to sift the results by "race." The answer would then become obvious: scoundrels.

Decades later, the tests that Goddard and Yerkes conducted are universally regarded as worthless. Charles Davenport's reputation among scholars, on the other hand, depends to some extent on what discipline they practice. Botanists and zoologists recognize his substantial contributions to their field. Geneticists acknowledge the early studies but condemn the four-decade infatuation with eugenics that followed. Historians hold a variety of views, but one that crops up again and again was expressed most firmly by Elazar Barkan in *The Retreat of Scientific Racism*, published in 1993. Barkan proclaimed Davenport "the most prominent racist among American scientists."

This conclusion isn't really accurate. Davenport abetted the scientific racism movement, and he benefitted personally from his connection with it. But for him racism was nowhere near the impelling engine that it was for so many of his fellow travelers in the xenophobe universe. Even when he addressed the "selection of immigrants" in his "Eugenics as a Religion" speech in Battle Creek, he confined himself to the selection of individuals, not ethnic groups. As late

---

* Correct answers: Toledo, fowl, comic artist, tobacco, movie actress.

as 1918, both his correspondence and his published work is free of anything resembling the racialized invective of Henry Cabot Lodge, Joe Lee, or Prescott Hall, much less Madison Grant or Edward A. Ross. He indulged in occasional ethnic stereotyping, particularly about Jews—"though we love them, they nauseate us" because of their "individualism"—but his language was no more caustic than the expressions of normative anti-Semitism uttered by Eleanor Roosevelt. The noted anthropologist—and eugenicist—Harry L. Shapiro, the son of immigrant Polish Jews, remembered Davenport as "a very nice fellow" who was "temperate" on racial issues, nothing like the committed scientific racists. When his daughter Millia married a Jew, Davenport expressed only "surprise." In 1919 one ERO class of eight researchers included four named Teitelbaum, Silverberg, Klein, and Silver; it seems probable that at least some of them would have been unlikely to sign on to the work of an institution burdened by a reputation for anti-Semitism—or, for that matter, recruited by a director who allowed anti-Semitism to shape his environment or his actions.*

But Davenport's fixation on the eccentric data that the ERO collected and his zealous efforts to fit this mountain of dross into tidy eugenic compartments led him to prowl distant precincts of respectable science. From his study of "wayward girls," he somehow determined not that women became prostitutes for economic reasons or because they were forced into it by predators; instead, he was convinced that erotic tendencies were inherited. Had his name not been on its title page, his *Naval Officers: Their Heredity and Devel-*

---

* The most frequently cited evidence supporting Barkan's position is a sardonic (and offensive) comment Davenport included in a 1925 letter to Grant: "Our ancestors drove Baptists from Massachusetts Bay into Rhode Island but we have no place to drive the Jews to. Also they burned the witches but it seems to be against the mores to burn any considerable part of our population. Meanwhile we have somewhat diminished the immigration of these people." The comment is certainly repugnant, especially considering the literal burning that lay ahead in the flames of the Holocaust, but it is impossible to read this letter and believe that Davenport was being in any way literal.

opment (where, through the study of biographies and pedigrees, he made the discovery that ethnic groups with "sea lust" were genetically impelled to live near seacoasts) could easily have been dismissed as a clumsy parody of Galtonian thinking and techniques. *Naval Officers* revealed two unexceptional truths: sons often pursue the careers of their fathers, and scientists can fall in love with their own theories. In Davenport's case, in the years immediately after World War I, his ideas were put to a critical test.

In 1918 Mary Harriman decided to cede financial responsibility for the Eugenics Record Office, which since its inception had been dependent on her largess. The houses the staff lived in, the laboratories they worked in, the acres upon acres of orchard and sheep meadow dotted with tents set aside for summer trainees—all this she turned over to the Carnegie Institution of Washington. It wasn't that she had ceased to believe in Davenport or his work. She declared her abiding support by supplementing the gift with a $300,000 endowment, which more than doubled her investment up to that point (in 2019 dollars, her total commitment surpassed $12 million). At sixty-seven, she was simply taking another step in a general process of divestment. If she could sign over the deed to Arden and its thousands of acres to her twenty-four-year-old son Averell, as she had done a few years before, she could certainly step away from continuing financial responsibility for the ERO.

The Carnegie Institution was the obvious choice to assume control. Davenport had continued his directorship of the institution's Station for Experimental Evolution in Cold Spring Harbor even as he and Harry Laughlin built up the adjacent ERO. But however much Harriman's magnanimity was appreciated by the illustrious Carnegie trustees (among them Henry Cabot Lodge and Elihu Root), the institution's president, geophysicist Robert S. Woodward, proved skeptical of eugenics. Woodward came from the world of hard science, and some of Davenport's proposed areas of study were softer than a feather.

Almost from the moment the Carnegie Institution acquired the ERO, the office's future—which Davenport saw as his own future— appeared to be in peril. The war was barely over when Davenport told Woodward he wished to travel to Europe with zoologist Clarence Cook Little to discern the "attitude of the remaining population [in the Balkans and Poland] toward remaining at home, or on the contrary, migrating to America." Woodward didn't thrill to the idea of two biologists conducting survey research (in which they had no meaningful experience) in languages and lands utterly unfamiliar to them. He turned them down flat. He also told Davenport he considered eugenics "a peculiarly dangerous" subject. He worried about "the best interests" of the institution. Woodward particularly criticized the *Eugenical News* as a "semi-popular, almost juvenile journal," filled with "objectionable features" that were ripe for ridicule. "I do not mean to discourage amateurism or dilettantism," Woodward said. "The only thing on which I insist is that neither is for us."

Davenport was rocked by Woodward's assault. A quarter century later, a colleague remembered how Davenport usually responded to external judgment: "High praise was eagerly received; adverse criticism tore down his defenses and allowed the specter of inferiority to stare him in the face." In this instance he defended himself by invoking what was, for him, the highest authority: the ERO, he said, wanted only to "give the word 'eugenics' a connotation as high as . . . Galton himself could have wished." That was probably little solace to Woodward, who continued to challenge Davenport right up to the date of his own retirement at age seventy-one in late 1920.

But Woodward's successor, John C. Merriam, looked upon eugenic studies with the benign gaze of a doting grandparent. He was a respected paleontologist, best known for his excavations in the La Brea Tar Pits, which had brought the Ice Age into view in twentieth-century Los Angeles. He was also an intimate friend and associate of Madison Grant and a fellow member of the Boone & Crockett Club, the Half Moon, and the Galton Society. The two men worked side by side as cofounders (with Fairfield Osborn) of the Save-the-Redwoods League. Merriam was also one of the close associates to whom Grant sent his manuscripts for prepublication comment and criticism. Merriam told his friend he approved a second revision of *The Passing of the Great Race* "most heartily."

Davenport could only delight in the prospect of a new boss with such associations, attributes, and attitudes. The most propitious augury for Davenport's future, and the future of the Eugenics Record Office, was specific to their work: Merriam's belief in eugenics, as he would later declare, was "unequivocal." And it freed Davenport to continue his labors in the eugenics cause, with the Carnegie Institution's backing, for the rest of his professional life.

As adamant as Merriam, though ideologically his opposite, was Franz Boas, still the leading scientific voice countering the eugenicist chorus through the late 1910s. But World War I dented Boas's authority. Whether he was indeed pro-German during the early years of the war is an unresolved historical question. That he opposed U.S. entry into the war is certain. Even though he had been an American citizen for nearly three decades, his atavistic attachment to the culture that shaped him was still profound. So was his iron independence: when Columbia undergraduates were asked to report any evidence of their professors' disloyalty during the war, Boas read his students a thorough statement of his ideas and almost dared them to forward them to the university trustees.

The real damage to Boas's standing came a year after the armistice, when he published a statement denouncing anthropologists who, while ostensibly conducting fieldwork, had in fact been government agents. Boas said they had "prostituted science by using it as a cover for their activities as spies." The vehemence of his accusations provided cover for action by his foes. Attacked by Fairfield Osborn, among others, Boas was censured by the American Anthropological Association, stripped of his role in the association's governance, and forced out of his advisory position with the National Research Council.

Though the circumstances were singular, the action against Boas was not, tied as it was to the rising rage against foreign influences of all sorts. It was a storm whipping out of control, propelled across the nation by an intensifying fear of radicalism. A labor market saturated by hundreds of thousands of returning veterans, and simultaneously contracting because of the end of government spending on ships, munitions, food, uniforms, medicines, flags, drums, fifes, and all the other accessories of war, induced a police strike in Boston, a general strike in Seattle, and terror bombings in Cleveland, Pittsburgh, Philadelphia, and other cities. Housing and job shortages provoked violent race riots across the country as disgruntled whites took out their rage on African Americans. Thousands of radicals (and suspected radicals) were rounded up in the "Red Raids" of 1919 and 1920. Hundreds were deported. Henry Cabot Lodge, finally recognizing the inadequacy of his literacy test, told Prescott Hall that new anti-immigration legislation was "of great importance," necessary "to prevent a flood of Bolsheviki" entering the country. Madison Grant, looking ahead, predicted the collapse of the Russian Revolution, which would precipitate a "great massacre of Jews, and I suppose we will get the overflow unless we can stop it." One congressman, a former newspaperman from Grays Harbor, Washington, named Albert Johnson, claimed the Soviet Union was smuggling one hundred Bolshevik agents into the United States from Mexico every day. People engaged in the restriction movement had reason to pay attention to Johnson: earlier the same year he had become chairman of the House Committee on Immigration.

Even more than in the news columns, changing views could be measured in the nation's editorial pages, and Prescott Hall, ailing and housebound in Boston, found sufficient energy to do the measuring. In Washington three daily newspapers, he reported, had all moved from a pro-immigration position to the restriction camp. So had the

Boston Globe, the *Detroit Free Press*, and the *Chicago Tribune*. In New York the *Herald* jumped sides, as did the *Times*. It was time to "shut the gates," the *Times* editorialized in the summer of 1919, because "there are already too many Bolsheviki and bourgeois-exterminators here now." A year after that, the *Times* bought not only Lodge's arguments, but even Madison Grant's. The "latest gospel of the historians," the paper said, is that "the determining factor in human affairs is race."

In late 1920 Grant wrote to Charles Davenport, a frequent correspondent since the founding of the Galton Society. Grant was preparing to visit Washington to meet with Albert Johnson of the Immigration Committee, and he hoped Davenport could provide him with some talking points. At the time, Davenport had nearly completed his conversion to scientific racism. His uneasy relationship with Robert Woodward at the Carnegie Institution had unnerved him; at the same time, his engagement with Grant and the other "racial anthropologists" in the Galton Society had pulled him toward their views. Unreservedly zealous in his promotion of eugenic ideas, he eagerly sought alliances of convenience; anxious and fretful by nature, he required—and found—comfort in the certitudes of true believers. A few months before Grant told him about his planned meeting with Johnson, Davenport was still teetering. "Can we build a wall high enough around this country, so as to keep out these cheaper races," he'd asked Grant, "or will it only be a feeble dam which will make the flood all the worse when it breaks?" In the next sentence, he implicitly denied the very existence of "cheaper races," arguing for "better selection" of immigrants of all races. By the evidence, he was confused. Davenport advised Grant before his meeting with Johnson to stress the need to know "the facts" about immigrants and their genetic background.

Facts in genetic matters remained elusive in 1920, decades before science cracked the code of the human genome. But "facts" gathered by Davenport's methods were readily available, and no matter how irrelevant or misconstrued or flimsy they were, they could make for a sturdy edifice when presented by a credentialed expert brandishing seemingly authoritative data.

Soon Davenport would indicate how the facts would carry the day, at a 1921 scientific conference commemorating the American eugenics movement's full merger with the immigration restriction crusade. "People do not have heated discussions on the multiplication table," Davenport told the assembled experts. "They will not dispute quantitative findings in any science." For the eugenicists and the immigration restrictionists, the quantitative findings were almost ready for their moment.

Chapter Nine

The Coming of the Quota

The armistice in November 1918 that brought peace to Europe ignited renewed warfare on the restriction issue in the United States. The drastic reduction in immigration that World War I had provoked came to an end. In 1918 only 110,000 immigrants arrived in the country; 1920 saw the arrival of 430,000. Henry Cabot Lodge, his literacy test in the books, turned most of his attention (and his bilious loathing for Woodrow Wilson) to the campaign against the League of Nations. Albert Johnson, Lodge's replacement as commanding general of the restriction forces on Capitol Hill, turned his toward a new law. As the *Saturday Evening Post* would have it, Johnson believed "the best way to restrict immigration is to restrict immigration."

Before his first term as chairman of the House Immigration Committee was up, Johnson introduced a bill intended to do just that: his Emergency Immigration Act would allow a few exceptions, but otherwise the measure would stop, for two years, *all* immigration. A statement accompanying his bill said that the threat posed by the "misery and want, distress and starvation beyond description" that continued to scour postwar Europe demanded it. Some 74,000 immigrants had come into the country in October 1920, and "more than 75 percent were of the Semitic race." Steamship company officials reported that were there ships available, "they could bring in 10,000,000 immigrants in one year's time." No alarm could have sounded louder, or more urgently.

As the clamor to punish Germany shook the Versailles Peace Conference in the spring of 1919, Charles Gore, Bishop of Oxford, delivered what for him was a surprising sermon. Gore had been among the few British clerics who attempted to tamp down the nationalistic fires that had overheated the war years, but now he admitted that "War has certain very ennobling powers." His acknowledgment of war's virtues may have been uncharacteristic, but it was also tactical, for it set up the sentence that followed: "It is after-war periods which are the curse of the world," he told his parishioners, "and it looks as if the same were going to prove true of this war."

Gore was calling for a more openhearted attitude toward the vanquished Germans. "We know the enemy is no longer the strength of Germany," he said, "but rather its weakness, its starvation, and its despair." In Britain he turned out to be as prophetic as he was empathetic, but he was largely ignored. Across the ocean, however, his dismay about the postwar period was put to use by a young Harvard PhD from Brookline, Massachusetts, named Lothrop Stoddard, in a book titled *The Rising Tide of Color Against the White World-Supremacy*. Stoddard had the rhetorical gifts of an orator, the productive energy of a combustion engine, and theories of racial differences and distinctions as crudely honed as Madison Grant's. His book framed the postwar period as a time of reckoning. The war, he wrote, had been "nothing short of a headlong plunge into white race-suicide." Franz Boas called Stoddard's book "vicious propaganda." Edward A. Ross called it "masterful." With consequences of the Russian Revolution threatening from abroad, and domestic labor militancy, anarchist bombings, and racial conflict playing luridly on the American mind, it was Ross's view that carried the agitated, frightened, doom-soaked day.

As Stoddard recalled it, the idea for the book that made his reputation arrived as a literal bolt from the blue. He had given up a brief legal career to become an academic, and then deserted academia for a career in journalism. After receiving his doctorate in 1914, he published three books of little distinction and smaller impact. By the end of the world war he was thirty-five years old, writing a column on foreign affairs ("Egyptian Unrest," "The Macedonian Tangle," "The Difficulties of Peace") for a business magazine and living with his mother in an apartment at the western end of Seventy-Second Street in Manhattan. He had broken off at least one romantic relationship for fear of alienating Mary Stoddard (she "was always irked at any of my love episodes," he would remember). Then came the fateful bolt. Sitting in his study, gloomily contemplating what he called "the rotten foundations" of the postwar world, Stoddard was gazing at his sweeping view of the Hudson River and the broad expanse of sky stretching above it when the argument, shape, content, and title of *The Rising Tide of Color* seized him in a galvanizing instant. Working furiously, he completed the manuscript in three months. Stoddard's first book had been published by Houghton Mifflin, the next two by Century. This one, however, would find a happier home.

Madison Grant had made his way to Charles Scribner's Sons through the courtesy of his friend Fairfield Osborn, who not only shared that ineffable Princeton connection with the firm's eponymous president but had also been published by him. Stoddard's path was simpler, even if much more crowded. Charles Scribner's experience with *The Passing of the Great Race* had become a gold-plated invitation to the nation's leading eugenic polemicists and, in turn, many of its most prominent immigration restrictionists. They responded with missionary zeal. By the early 1920s, the distinguished publisher of Henry James, Edith Wharton, Theodore Roosevelt, and F. Scott Fitzgerald had enhanced (or, if you prefer, degraded) its distinguished list with an all-star team (or, if you prefer, police lineup) of scientific racists. Each deserves his own introduction:

- Seth K. Humphrey, an inventor and gentleman explorer who argued in his *Mankind: Racial Values and the Racial Prospect* (Scribner, 1917) that individuals should be required to qualify for licenses granting them the privilege to breed.

- Charles W. Gould, a New York lawyer whose *America: A Family Matter* (Scribner, 1920) bore a chapter epigraph declaring that "A mongrel people never attain real prosperity"; who argued that "the marriage of an educated and refined white man with a beautiful South Italian peasant girl [could] put the children back in the stage of intellectual development many hundreds of years"; and who was hailed in a rapturous encomium on the front page of the *New York Times Book Review*—written, conveniently, by Madison Grant.

- William McDougall, a pioneering British psychologist newly arrived at Harvard, whose *Is America Safe for Democracy?* (Scribner, 1921) claimed—by the publisher's own description—that because of "immigration and the tendency toward race suicide among the upper classes, extinction threatens the race which conceived of and made the United States the great republic that it is." McDougall's book also argued that qualities as nebulous as willpower were racially determined.

- Edward M. East (*Mankind at the Crossroads*, Scribner, 1923), a Harvard plant geneticist who in his book's preface seemed to condemn the idea of eugenics promoted by some Scribner authors, calling it a "honey-pot for the dilettante and the amateur," but near its end described a dark and desperate future if the twenty-five million Americans of "scrub stock" continued to reproduce.

- Ellsworth Huntington of Yale (*The Character of Races*, Scribner, 1924), the Galton Society cofounder who declared himself "so profoundly convinced of the importance of eugenics that my whole outlook upon life has been changed and broadened by it."

And in the same catalog in which Scribner announced a reprint of Stoddard's *The Rising Tide of Color*, it approvingly quoted a *New-York Tribune* review of Charles Conant Josey's *Race and National Solidarity* (Scribner, 1922). The Dartmouth professor's book, the paper said, was a brief "in favor of the permanent domination of the white race." How could its editor *not* send a copy along to the man who had started it all, Madison Grant?

Or had it all been started by the editor himself? For it was Maxwell Perkins who brought Josey's book into the world, as well as Lothrop Stoddard's, and Ellsworth Huntington's, and various others of the species. In his Perkins biography, Scott Berg wrote that the famous editor "sought out authors who were not just 'safe' . . . but who spoke about the new values of the postwar world." In the scientific racists and other anti-immigrationists, he found plenty. He may have been a young and altogether anonymous editor when Charles Scribner dropped Grant's manuscript on his desk in 1916, but his growing renown in the 1920s as the foremost book editor of his era did not deter Perkins from his extended commitment to many of the scientific racists, most especially Grant and Stoddard.

Perkins was somewhat uncomfortable with Grant, who endlessly sought his attention, his assistance, and his approval. But in Stoddard, who was almost exactly Perkins's age (they were thirty-six and thirty-five, respectively, when they met), the editor found a friend and collaborator with whom he sustained amiable relationships both personal and professional for decades. "You can tell as much about a book by talking to the author as by reading a manuscript," Perkins liked to say, and in Stoddard he found an author with whom he was entirely comfortable. In their correspondence, they were "Dear

Max" and "Dear Lothrop." Over a span of eight years beginning in 1920, Maxwell Perkins published seven of Lothrop Stoddard's books. A few of the titles suggested what was on Stoddard's mind, and on Scribner's: *The Revolt Against Civilization. Racial Realities in Europe. Re-Forging America.* The editor later welcomed his author's return to Scribner in 1935 with *Clashing Tides of Color*, a reprise of the book that had come racing down the Hudson to Stoddard's riverside apartment on that clear autumn day in 1919.

Massachusetts-born and -bred, Stoddard was deeply rooted in the same seventeenth-century New England soil (and imbued with the same early-twentieth-century New England worldview) that nurtured the men of the Immigration Restriction League. His friendship with Grant brought him an introduction to Perkins, membership in the Galton Society, and public certification (via Grant's introduction to *Rising Tide*) of his restrictionist and eugenicist bona fides. Stoddard didn't have to make the case for Nordic superiority; thanking Grant in the preface to the book, he allowed that as Grant had "admirably summarized the biological and historical background," he himself could now apply it to the current world crisis.

The Rising Tide of Color, much more so than *The Passing of the Great Race*, was aimed at a popular audience. Grant had been desperate to establish scholarly credentials with *Passing*, littering his book with esoteric voyages into the presumed linguistic history of the Middle East, detailed descriptions of long-forgotten ethnic conflicts in the steppes of central Asia, and other similarly obtuse excursions into historical and anthropological arcana. Stoddard had nothing to prove. He wished only to persuade his readers that worldwide catastrophe was in the offing, and that the central conflagration would be ignited by race. By "race," Stoddard meant the characteristic that distinguished his own people not just from Asians and Africans, but from the "hordes of immigrant Alpines and Mediterraneans, not to mention Asiatic elements like

Levantines and Jews." On reading Stoddard's manuscript, Perkins was immediately enthusiastic and told Grant—who would write its introduction—that "it has an excellent chance of making a marked success."

Deploying Bishop Gore's apprehensive view of the postwar period for his own purposes, Stoddard struck at precisely the right moment. His concept of World War I as "the White Civil War" ("an internecine death-grapple of unparalleled ferocity," he elaborated) "opened up revolutionary, even cataclysmic, possibilities." Such as: Worldwide revolution. Race suicide. "Mongrelization." Stoddard foresaw the end of "white political control," "white political dominion," "white solidarity," "white domination," and "white political mastery." He conjured images that might have come from the era's popular fiction ("Through the bazaars of Asia," he wrote, "ran the sibilant whisper, 'The East will see the West to bed!'"), and he deplored the "inveterate altruism" behind disease control, sanitation, and other palliatives that reversed "the enormous death-rate which in the past has kept colored races from excessive multiplication." He quoted Grant, he quoted Edward A. Ross, and he quoted Prescott Hall. And for any readers disinclined to acknowledge the authority of such allies, he cited W. E. B. Du Bois's ominous 1915 prediction: a "War of the Color Line [that] will outdo in savage inhumanity any war this world has yet seen. For colored folk have much to remember and they will not forget." Stoddard had done his homework.

It was audacious, but it was also effective. *Rising Tide* became a bestseller, sweeping through fifteen separate printings in four years. The book was very publicly endorsed by Woodrow Wilson's successor, Warren G. Harding, whose 1920 campaign rested on an advertising slogan that would reverberate politically for the next century: "America First." The *New York Times*, in an unsigned editorial titled "A New Basis for History," declared that "Stoddard's presentation is as sane and measured as it is dramatically effective," and hailed the book's contribution to the "defense of what is precious in the Nordic inheritance." The IRL added Stoddard to its executive committee ("He is well up on racial questions," Prescott Hall assured Joe Lee, and "is rather well known"). And at one point in Stoddard's soaring flight into American consciousness, Charles Scribner paused to write to Madison Grant, as if in thanks: Grant's book had been "a pioneer," the publisher said, "for the race question has now become a favorite."

A few years later the heft of Stoddard's cultural impact was suggested in a book by another Perkins author. In the opening pages of *The Great Gatsby*, Scott Fitzgerald invoked Stoddard to demonstrate the narrowness of Tom Buchanan's worldview. Fitzgerald retitled *The Rising Tide of Color* and gave Stoddard a different name, but those were thin disguises: the book became *The Rise of the Colored Empires*, and Stoddard became "Goddard" (an interesting choice, seemingly acknowledging the author of *The Kallikak Family*). The books Tom reads "are all scientific," he heatedly insists to Nick Carraway. "This fellow"—Goddard/Stoddard—"has worked out the whole thing. It's up to us, who are the dominant race, to watch out or these other races will have control of things." Turning to Daisy and her friend Jordan Baker, Tom defines their shared place in the world. "This idea is that we're Nordics. I am, and you are, and you are, and . . . we've produced all the things that go to make civilization—oh, science and art, and all that. Do you see?"

Scribner's was hardly alone in its promotion of scientific racism in the postwar, post–literacy test years. Throughout the culture, many saw all too clearly what the inarticulate Tom Buchanan perceived but was unable to describe. At the same time that Sinclair Lewis was satirizing the growing eugenics mania in *Main Street* (as he would again in *Arrowsmith*), Willa Cather was publishing stories portraying

Jewish immigrants as almost subhuman.* Edgar Lee Masters, whose *Spoon River Anthology* had been a sensation in 1915, published "The Great Race Passes," a poem setting Grant's hypotheses to grotesque tropes that could have come straight from Thomas Bailey Aldrich's "Unguarded Gates." Masters begins by hailing "the Vikings who . . . / became the bone of England / And the fire of Normandy, / And the will of Holland and Germany, / And the builders of America." Then he gets to his point:

> On State Street throngs crowd and push,
> Wriggle and writhe like maggots.
> Their noses are flat,
> Their faces are broad,
> Their heads are like gourds,
> Their eyes are dull,
> Their mouths are open—
> The Great Race is Passing."

Grant was delighted by the poem, but a poem—even one by a writer as popular as Masters—was only a poem. Just as gratifying to Grant (and to Stoddard), and more effective in reaching the American public, were the words—tens of thousands of words, torrents of words, words as shiny and as slashing as a harpoon—that hailed their cause in the mighty pages of the nation's foremost periodical, the *Saturday Evening Post*.

---

* An example: In the short story "Scandal," published in Cather's 1920 collection *Youth and the Bright Medusa*, one character describes Siegmund Stein, a penniless immigrant who has risen to great wealth: "He is one of the most hideous men in New York, but it's not at all the common sort of ugliness that comes from over-eating and automobiles. He isn't one of the fat horrors. He has one of those rigid, horselike faces that never tell anything; a long nose, flattened as if it had been tied down; a scornful chin; long, white teeth; flat cheeks, yellow as a Mongolian's; tiny, black eyes, with puffy lids and no lashes; dingy, dead-looking hair—looks as if it were glued on."

It is hard to overstate the dimensions of the *Post*'s influence in the 1920s. Television didn't exist, radio was still an infant, newspapers were local. Among magazines, which were the nation's only shared source of news, culture, and information, the *Post*, edited since 1899 by the courtly George Horace Lorimer, was preeminent both in circulation and in a sort of mass-market prestige. It published the most popular (and some of the finest) writers of the day, including Fitzgerald, Lewis, and Cather, as well as Ring Lardner, Theodore Dreiser, and Jack London. In 1916 Lorimer discovered a twenty-two-year-old illustrator named Norman Rockwell, whose covers for the magazine would fashion America's fondest image of itself. The "Henry Ford of American literature," as Lorimer was once called, was inarguably the nation's most important editor.

By the time the United States entered World War I, Lorimer had ushered the magazine through nearly two decades of solid (if stolid) success. But the war and its aftermath struck Lorimer, as it had Lothrop Stoddard, with life-changing force. Formerly internationalist and moderate, Lorimer and his magazine jumped onto the nativism steamroller and then seized the controls. Unchecked immigration became his obsession, and his magazine became its most potent foe. Lorimer tipped his hand in a 1920 editorial titled "Self-Preservation," where he wrote that "The rank-and-file of these assimilated aliens still live mentally in the ghetto or as peasants on the great estates." At the time, this was garden-variety xenophobia. But the clue that the *Post* would become a hothouse for the most virulent anti-immigration rhetoric was Lorimer's pointed use of "assimilated": even after they were absorbed into everyday American life, these newcomers remained pariahs.

A year passed before Lorimer found a way to articulate his conviction that the deficiencies of the immigrants were not merely cultural but were embedded in the inalterable permanence of biology. In April and May 1921 he published a remarkable series of unsigned editorials that laid down the principles behind the policy the *Post* would pursue in the immigration debate—uncompromisingly, relentlessly, above all effectually.

As much as anything, the series was defined by Lorimer's suggestion that a monument to Gregor Mendel might be in order. The editor's enthusiasm for the work of a long-dead Moravian friar was predicated on a gross distortion of Mendel's ideas ("he supplied the data that have enabled scientists to study intelligently the beginnings of our racial degeneration"). Even more egregious was the arrant falsehood he shamelessly offered in the editorial of May 7, 1921: Mendel, the *Post* said, had issued "authoritative warnings" that must be heeded lest America "forfeit our high estate and join the lowly ranks of the mongrel races." Mendel had written about the color of flowers on pea plants. "Mongrel," "races," "authoritative warnings" (or any kind of warning at all)—these were no closer to Mendel's concerns, and no more connected to his studies, than was the 1921 American League pennant race.

Predicated on a lie, the rest of Lorimer's arguments were inevitable. "Scientific writers" had disproved "the rose-colored myth of the . . . magical melting pot." He urged "every American" to read *The Passing of the Great Race* and *The Rising Tide of Color* and heed "their clear ring of truth," based on "recent advances in the study of heredity and other life sciences." One week later, he called for limiting immigration to individuals "from those races that are fitted biologically for assimilation," said "race character is as fixed a fact as race color," and contended that recent immigrants were "infected stock" whose presence threatened a "sterilizing effect" on "our fine old stock." This last idea, he said, came from Prescott Hall—"a high authority on the subject."

In the same issue in which Lorimer kicked off his hyperventilated series of eugenics-based arguments against immigration, he published a piece of reportage by a man he was developing as his own high authority on the "infected stock." Years later Kenneth L. Roberts would become one of the nation's most popular novelists, author of the historical sagas *Northwest Passage* and *Oliver Wiswell*.

But as a thirty-five-year-old writer at the *Post*, he was an exceptionally potent weapon in the immigration battle. Sent by Lorimer to Europe several times to describe the immigrants waiting at the eastern and southern European gates ("the defeated, incompetent and unsuccessful"), Roberts would over time provide the eyewitness accounts that were meant to confirm the eugenicist theories. "We have been waiting for you for over a quarter of a century," Robert Ward of the IRL told him, "and that's a good long time."

A few months before Lorimer articulated the *Post*'s position, just as Johnson's new restriction bill was inching its way through Congress, a signed column in *Good Housekeeping*, of all places, made clear that eugenics and immigration restriction were two sides of the same xenophobic coin. "It is a duty our country owes itself to require of all those aliens who come here that they have a background not inconsistent with American institutions," said the writer, himself a New Englander of Norman stock. "It would be suicidal for us to let down the bars for the inflowing of cheap manhood." Then, reaching for the clincher, he declared that "There are racial considerations too grave to be brushed aside for any sentimental reasons. Biological laws"—*biological laws!*—"tell us that certain divergent people will not mix or blend," and "the dead weight of alien accretion stifles national progress." The *Good Housekeeping* essayist was neither a reporter like Roberts nor an experienced polemicist like Lorimer. He was Calvin Coolidge, about to be sworn in as vice president of the United States.

*　　*　　*

IN THE LAST MONTHS OF 1920, as debate began on a new immigration restriction law that would leap past the literacy test in ambition and severity, Prescott Hall, the one man who had devoted more of his life to the restriction cause than any other, was dying. Robert Ward continued to teach at Harvard, and Joe Lee's myriad philanthropic activities (on the one hand the Harvard Glee Club, on the other a black church at the bottom of Beacon Hill) remained as endless as his energies and as apparently undiminished as his bank account. Hall had persevered, long ago giving up his law practice to devote his life to immigration restriction. But his collection of ailments, now aggravated by a debilitating bout of pleurisy, had rendered him almost entirely bedridden. He continued the work that had consumed him for nearly three decades mostly through the mail. Whatever progress he and his associates had made over their long journey, he could not escape a generalized despair. "I don't believe a democracy can do anything well," he told a colleague. "Down to 1840 we were practically an aristocracy."

But the rather-less-than-aristocratic Albert Johnson, who boasted that he had moved west because he wasn't interested in living among New England's "Puritans and pedants," was up to the task that Hall felt he had not completed. In the first of his six terms as House Immigration Committee chairman, Johnson had not only corresponded at length with Hall to solicit suggestions on pending legislation but also met with Madison Grant, dined with IRL lobbyist James Patten, and enlisted an "expert eugenics agent" to guide the committee through the imposing scientific thickets they would soon need to navigate. His choice was Charles Davenport's protégé, Harry H. Laughlin.

In 1905, after failing to win appointment as school superintendent in the metropolis of Centerville, Iowa (population 5,200), Harry Laughlin confided in his mother. However disappointed he was, Laughlin said, he chose to look "always on the bright side of life." He was twenty-five years old. Five years later Laughlin exited his quiet labors in the agriculture department at the Missouri Normal School in Kirksville and entered a radically brightened life on Long Island's North Shore, appointed—anointed, really—by Davenport to join him in the quest for a eugenic future. The following year he was sitting side by side with the scientists of the American Breeders Association, serving as secretary to the ABA committee studying "the best practical means for cutting off the defective germ-plasm in the American population." In 1913 the wealthiest woman in America, Mary Harriman, rewarded Laughlin with a three-month European vacation. The next year the *Kirksville Journal* gushed about the hometown favorite son, whose job "brought [him] into frequent contact with great scientists like Edison and Alexander Graham Bell." After editing the *Eugenical News* for a time, he took a leave of absence to add some heft to his threadbare résumé. Earning his doctorate in biology at Princeton, he became the fully credentialed "Dr. Laughlin." His dissertation was a study of mitosis in onion root tips.

By then Laughlin had already become the nation's foremost authority on, and most prominent advocate for, eugenic sterilization. In that letter to his mother all those years before, he had written, "If I can't be great, I can certainly do much good." He might have reversed the terms. Among the anti-immigrationists, sterilization advocates, and scientific racists who were his comrades and collaborators over the next quarter century, Laughlin indeed became great, while doing quite the opposite of good.

Which is not to say that he was without more generous inclinations. He praised the liberal constitution promulgated by Germany's Weimar Republic, believed in women's rights, supported universal free education, and was earnestly antiwar. The only good thing that came out of World War I, he believed, was the League of Nations. Beginning before the war and continuing for decades, he devoted countless spare hours to promoting the idea of world government, on more than one occasion drawing up extremely detailed, and dreamily rose-colored, proposals that he sent in vain to editors of the nation's leading magazines. ("This scarcely seems to us *Atlantic* material" was a typical response.) The preamble to his model world constitution began, "WE, the Sovereign People of Earth, drawn into close contact by the growth of civilization . . ."; it proceeded to encourage "cultural contact and trade with our fellow communities." It's true that one of his later proposals called for an elected world parliament apportioned so that one United States ballot would count the same as twenty-five from India, but by then Laughlin had become so thoroughly committed to racist ideology that it's surprising he granted Indians any voting rights at all.

Immigration first showed up on Laughlin's professional agenda in 1914. That year, while making his public debut at the first Race Betterment Conference in Battle Creek, Laughlin met Robert Ward, who waved the IRL flag in a speech titled "Race Betterment and Our Immigration Laws"; the two men would collaborate productively for more than a decade. But it was Laughlin's work with the Breeders

MEANS PROPOSED FOR CUTTING OFF THE SUPPLY OF HUMAN DEFECTIVES AND DEGENERATES

I. LIFE SEGREGATION

II. STERILIZATION

III. RESTRICTIVE MARRIAGE

IV. EUGENIC EDUCATION

V. SYSTEM OF MATINGS

VI. GENERAL ENVIRONMENTAL

VII. POLYGAMY

VIII. EUTHANASIA

IX. NEO-MALTHUSIAN DOCTRINE

X. LAISSEZ-FAIRE

Which of these remedies shall be applied? Shall one, two, several or all be made to operate.

What are the limitations and possibilities of each remedy?

Shall one class of the socially unfit be treated with one remedy and another with a different one?

Shall the specifically selected remedy be applied to the class or to the individual?

What are the principles and the limits of compromise between conservation and elimination in cases of individuals bearing a germ-plasm with a mixture of the determiners for both defective and sterling traits.

What are the criteria for the identification of individuals bearing defective germ-plasm

What can be hoped from the application of some definite elimination program?

What practical difficulties stand in the way? How can they be overcome?

Harry Laughlin identified nine courses of action that could be used to confront the problem of "defectives and degenerates," and one passive alternative that was obviously unacceptable.

Association's "defective germ-plasm" committee that propelled him into the very heart of the immigration debate.

The most shocking part of Laughlin's report to the Breeders Association called for the annual sterilization of "culls," his term for the least desirable 10 percent of the population. He sanitized the process with a label both antiseptic and chilling: "continuous decimal elimination." The report's central conclusion—"Society must look upon germ-plasm as belonging to society and not solely to the individual who carries it"—suggested an obvious corollary: the new immigrants were pulling the "germ-plasm" in the wrong direction. Soon he came up with the numbers that brought him before Albert Johnson's Immigration Committee in 1920 and that would set Congress on its final path to the conclusive immigration laws looming ahead.

In the 1890s, employed as a journalist in Missouri and Connecticut and the nation's capital, Albert Johnson had no designs on a political career. While working for the *Washington Post* in 1898, he was offered the chance to move west and become managing editor of the *Tacoma News*. Arriving in the burgeoning Pacific Northwest, where the coming of the railroads had turned the region's vast forests into a treasure house for the lumber industry, he hadn't any inkling of what lay in his future. "How could I imagine," he would recall, that "I would be elected to congress with restriction of immigration the chief plank in my platform?"

Johnson—garrulous, self-confident, and at the same time self-deceiving—had always taken great satisfaction in his productive commitment to the restriction cause and to the way he had pursued it. "I am proud to say," he wrote, "that as far as I was concerned, no part of that campaign was conducted with any feeling of malice against any of the various races of the world." Perhaps he didn't consider it malicious that he had spent much of his public life striving to bar all immigration from Asia. And perhaps he had forgotten that he had asserted, during his first campaign for Congress, "that the greatest menace to the republic today is the open door it affords to the ignorant hordes from Eastern and Southern Europe."

Apart from his support for woman suffrage and a somewhat peculiar determination to move the United States from the Fahrenheit scale to Celsius, Johnson was no progressive. He believed in a strong tariff, resisted federal conservation efforts, and in 1912 did not waver in his loyalty to William Howard Taft when Theodore Roosevelt's walkout split the Republican Party in two. He did, however, swear by Roosevelt's "doctrine of the strenuous life," and from the moment of his arrival in Tacoma he strenuously bulled his way into public prominence. In 1909 he became editor, publisher, and owner of the *Daily Washingtonian* in the timber country of the Olympic Peninsula, and three years later started the *Home Defender*, by its own description "a monthly newspaper devoted to a denunciation of radical, revolutionary socialism." From both platforms he threw rhetorical grenades at the Asian immigrants who had settled in the area in the late nineteenth century and, he believed, had taken jobs from Americans. Johnson's blood boiled at the prospect of yet more Asians arriving in the Pacific Northwest, and then nearly vaporized with the rise of the Industrial Workers of the World as the "Wobblies" brought their radical labor tactics to the region. In a speech he delivered in 1912 he railed against "anarchy, free love, [and] the IWW," as well as an unlikely movement he called "organized atheism." He invoked treason, sedition, and the threat of armed revolution. He also attacked local socialists for canceling their subscriptions to his paper.

That was the year Johnson first ran for Congress. It was also the year he made the connection between European immigration and radicalism, and this new discovery fueled his campaign and would shape his entire tenure in Congress. Up until that point, he would recall, he had only "made a study [of] Oriental immigration." But then a Russian immigrant working as a telegraph operator in the

Washingtonian newsroom clued him in: revolution was coming to Russia, the telegrapher said, and its perpetrators would take "the last dollar of the rich and kill the poor by the millions." Johnson had discovered, he said, "a prophecy, as well as a plank" for his congressional campaign.

Advancing his candidacy in the pages of his newspaper and a series of speeches, Johnson attracted praise from as far away as Boston, from a man he had never heard of, representing an organization he had never encountered. "I am sorry to confess that I did not know of the Immigration League," Johnson wrote to an admiring Prescott Hall, adding: "I assure you that I shall proceed along the lines marked out and do all I can for the restriction of undesirable immigration."

Albert Johnson met Harry Laughlin, who would provide the intellectual fuel Johnson believed he needed for the next big push toward immigration restriction, in 1920. Laughlin, who loved show-and-tell, would also provide the visual aids suitable for photo opportunities and for explaining complex numbers to innumerate congressmen. He could assemble a chart to demonstrate any point he wished or a graph to make it seem scientifically authoritative. The fat file of lantern slides he used to illustrate his speeches and other public appearances included images of Mendel, Darwin, and Galton; pedigree charts for families of musicians, families of geniuses, families of epileptics; illustrations of "a typical American head," "Filipino Girl with two extra limbs," "The Roosevelt Smile," "a North Dakota Dwarf and his sister." When immigration was the subject, he would show pictures of "Poles at Ellis Island," a chart mapping "Intermarriages of Nationalities in New York City," a table demonstrating the "Approaching Extinction of the Mayflower Descendants."

In the spring of 1920, as the forty-year-old Laughlin prepared to travel to Washington to testify before Johnson's committee for the first time, eugenics continued to acquire academic credibility. In late March the nation's scientific establishment, in the form of the august National Research Council, granted formal authorization to the American Museum of Natural History to host a Second International Congress of Eugenics, under the direction of Fairfield Osborn, president, and Madison Grant, treasurer. That same year, "besieged with requests for information" about his army intelligence tests, Robert Yerkes and a colleague published an abridged version of his official report for the lay reader; the book was shepherded into print by publisher Henry Holt, a longtime supporter of the Immigration Restriction League who had earlier published Charles Davenport and Prescott Hall. The eugenic moment had arrived.

Laughlin was presented to Johnson's committee as a representative of the Eugenics Research Association, which Davenport had founded in 1913 specifically for the scholarly study of eugenics (the organization's devotion to scholarship, however, was fleeting: only five years later, Madison Grant became its president). For much of his two days before the committee, Laughlin unspooled a series of assertions concerning "the physical, mental and moral qualities" of immigrants. Finding a contemporary application for the social Darwinist principles Herbert Spencer had laid out more than half a century earlier, he declared that charity extended to the eugenically inferior was "biologically unfortunate" because it "bolstered up individuals who under a lower civilization would have perished." Laughlin explained that "the character of a nation is determined primarily by its racial qualities," and that "because immigrant women are on the average more fertile" than the native-born, their genetic material threatened, over time, to dominate. His charts purported to demonstrate that the foreign-born population of state institutions was disproportionately higher than their presence in the population at large. He recommended adding "general shiftlessness" to the list of conditions (such as trachoma and tuberculosis) that guaranteed the automatic rejection of immigrants.

Laughlin's array of charts and calculations and interpretations did not take into account the relative education or income levels of the foreign- and native-born. Nor did he trouble himself to determine whether the children of the foreign-born were as likely to be institutionalized as their parents, which would have been a somewhat more meaningful measure of genetic predisposition. Neither did Laughlin consider the possibility that mentally or socially "deficient" members of wealthier, more settled families were likelier than recent immigrants to be cared for at home or to reside in private rather than public institutions. Laughlin's mode of analysis, one contemporary critic would later charge, was "as unsubstantial as a mirage."

But for the chairman of the Immigration Committee it was right on the money, and Johnson decided to appoint Laughlin the committee's official "expert eugenics agent." For the next decade Laughlin would be the most visible advocate of eugenics in the entire nation. He would repeatedly testify at length before Johnson's committee, elaborating on studies he had conducted on its behalf. He took his place beside Grant, Davenport, and Fairfield Osborn in the living pantheon of eugenic thinkers when he was granted membership in the Galton Society. Secretary of Labor James J. Davis authorized him to take a six-month trip to Europe to study immigration at its source, and gave him untrammeled access to U.S. consular offices across the continent. Using congressional franking privileges, Laughlin solicited mountains of information from across the nation, collecting, collating, and codifying the data to support his arguments. And just as his work would prove critical to the 1927 Supreme Court decision in *Buck v. Bell* establishing the state's right to sterilize "defective" individuals living in state institutions, Laughlin's long labor for the House Immigration Committee enabled him to exert similar influence on the nation's immigration laws—particularly those that would grant admittance to newcomers based not on who they were but on where they came from.

Presiding over his committee's hearings, Albert Johnson was unfailingly polite, even to those advancing views contradicting his own. His were the investigative habits not of a prosecutor but of a former newspaperman. Inoculating himself against charges of closedmindedness, he made certain that there were a few pro-immigration congressmen on his committee—at first one from each party—and generally treated them, and the witnesses they invited to testify, with respect, or at least its facsimile. But however broad his inquiries and however varied the testimony he elicited, Johnson not only never flinched from the position that had first brought him to Congress, he allowed it to harden into a purity that the previous generation's congressional restrictionists had never attained.

Thus did the House Immigration Committee in December 1920 report out what Johnson called an "Emergency Act" that would simply stop immigration, from all countries, for two years. There were exemptions, and they seemed reasonable enough to everyone but the most hardened xenophobes. These included blood relatives of American citizens; certain skilled laborers and professionals; that long-sacrosanct category, domestic servants; and, perhaps most obviously, noncitizen soldiers who had served in the U.S. military during the world war. Yet at roughly the same time that the Johnson bill was macerating in Congress, a lawsuit making its way toward the Supreme Court threatened to throw the immigration status of at least some returning soldiers into shadowy territory. The suit actually challenged much more than a right of return for aliens who had served in the armed forces. What was at stake was the definition of who was white.

Even though the plaintiff in *Thind v. United States* was not a European, his case illuminated the national mood of the moment. Bhagat Singh Thind, a high-caste Sikh from the Punjab, arrived in the United States in 1912 to further his education at the University of California (he was a devotee of Whitman, Emerson, and Thoreau). Six years later he was among the nearly half million alien residents who had enlisted in the American war effort. Just before his honorable discharge as a sergeant in December 1918, Bhagat Thind was sworn in as a U.S. citizen. He wore his army uniform to the ceremony.

But four days later Thind's naturalization was summarily revoked. Immigration officials contended that he was neither white (as required by the Nationality Act of 1790) nor black (as mandated by Reconstruction legislation eighty years later), and was thereby ineligible to claim the precious gift of citizenship, which continued to be denied to Japanese, Chinese, and other Asian immigrants.* A three-year trek through the labyrinthine naturalization system and the federal courts followed. In 1922, in the rare Supreme Court ruling that privileged African Americans above other groups, the court found that among the non-native-born, citizenship was open only to whites and "persons of African descent." The following year, a unanimous court determined that Thind was a) neither, and b) out of luck.

The reach toward "whiteness" was not confined to south Asians. In 1910 Louis Marshall had urged his congressional ally, the Bohemian immigrant Adolph Sabath, to fight a restriction bill that would bar entry to immigrants who were not racially eligible for citizenship. A series of court cases had already raised the question of whether Jews (and, Marshall could have added, Syrians, Turks, and Armenians) were white. There had been no definitive determination that they were not, but the very fact that the courts were juggling the issue alarmed him. "It would be most unfortunate to establish any color test, either of immigration or naturalization," Marshall told Sabath. "That would involve questions of anthropology and ethnology, as to which there is tremendous conflict."

The conflict had only intensified in the years since, especially among those who accepted the theories Madison Grant had presented in *The Passing of the Great Race.* In an Alabama case, a black man who

---

* The citizenry had not remained entirely white and black; children of Asian immigrants who were born in the United States attained citizenship by birthright.

married an Italian woman was convicted of violating the state's anti-miscegenation law, then found surprising absolution when the conviction was vacated by an appellate court's provocative declaration: "The mere fact that the testimony showed this woman came from Sicily can in no sense be taken as conclusive evidence that she was therefore a white woman." IRL lobbyist James Patten described Armenians as "mongrelized Orientals," and Lothrop Stoddard constantly referred to eastern European Jews as "Asiatic." Prescott Hall hung a more precise label on the Bolshevik leadership: "Asiatic semites."

As the effort to attach Asian nationality to eastern and southern Europeans pushed them yet deeper into the unhappy territory of Otherness, Johnson's Emergency Act marched forward on a path cleared by an explosive State Department document. Provided at Johnson's request by Wilbur J. Carr, a career official who headed the Consular Service, it changed the language of the immigration dialectic, sanctioning nationality-specific ethnic imprecations that may have been in common usage among the scientific racists but in recent years had only rarely blemished open congressional debate.

The State Department's diplomatic service was a province of the eastern elites, its training grounds Harvard and Yale, its genealogy Protestant, its viewpoint blinkered. In the words of one of its members, the diplomatic service was "a pretty good club"; according to another, it was "a small group of 'Christian gentlemen' with large purses and narrow minds." Carr was a somewhat different sort. The son of a southern Ohio farm family, his Harvard was the Commercial College of the University of Kentucky, his Yale the shorthand and typing classes at Chaffee's Phonographic Institute in upstate New York. After he joined the State Department as a clerk in 1892 he earned a law degree. Like Albert Johnson, Carr had "native American" genes; like Johnson's, Carr's had not been polished to an aristocratic gleam in the privileged institutions of the Northeast. The two men quickly developed a close working relationship.

Carr was an eager ally. The document he delivered to Johnson on

December 4, 1920—"in accordance," he said, "with your request this morning"—was couched as a collection of "paraphrases of statements in regard to immigration received from officers of this Government who have visited the countries mentioned." State Department officials had found the following:

In Sicily: prospective immigrants who "are inimical to the best interests of the United States. . . . For the most part they are small in stature and of a low order of intelligence."

At the docks in Rotterdam: Polish and Russian Jews "filthy, un-American and often dangerous in their habits."

In Warsaw: "filthy and ignorant and the majority are verminous."

In Danzig: "all" the prospective immigrants encountered there are "decidedly inferior . . . physically, mentally, and morally," and "constitute a menace to the health of all with whom they come in contact."

Nearly everywhere American consuls found "socialistic" ideas and "Bolshevik sympathizers" and "political and labor agitators." Only in Turkey did Carr's source evince no fear of radicalism. "The emigrants from this part of the world," reported the man in Constantinople, "are exclusively raw laborers, waiters and servants who are intellectually incapable of being dangerous."

It may be idle to speculate on the nature of the inquiries these government officers conducted in the cities they visited. But what kind of study might someone like, say, Felix Cole (Harvard '10), the U.S. consul general in Warsaw, have conducted to determine "the general characteristics of aliens emigrating to the United States"? The Carr report described the Polish contingent—by the report's estimate, 90 percent Jewish—as "mentally deficient," "physically deficient," "abnormally twisted," "economically undesirable," and "socially undesirable." Did Cole and his associates conduct surveys? Employ public health investigators? Take personal histories? How much time did the American summarizing the crowds in Danzig devote to his visit to the docks? How many emigrants did he interview in the bleak delousing center outside of town before arriving at the determination that "all" of them were morally questionable? In their final statement, the officials reporting from Poland openly acknowledged the central assumption that preceded their investigation and hovered over it like an inescapable shadow: "The unassimilability of these classes politically is a fact too often proved in the past to bear any argument."

There it was, reproduced in House Report 1109, 66th Congress, 3rd Session, issued from the Government Printing Office—an official document from the Department of State that, in its assignment of both specific and generalized deficiencies to particular ethnic groups, essentially confirmed what the scientific racists had long argued. And the Immigration Committee's accompanying report added an immediate warning: in a freighted shot at American Jewish aid societies, the committee cited a source indicating that "225,000 Hebrews" from Poland alone "have been furnished this year with funds for passage to the United States." That horrifying (and almost certainly imaginary) number was 50 percent more than in the peak year of the European Jewish exodus—and it did not include prospective immigrants from Russia, or Austria, or Romania, or Lithuania, or any of the other centers of European Jewry.

On the House floor, Representative Ira Hersey of Maine pulled out Thomas Bailey Aldrich's "Unguarded Gates" for what had become its ritual reading, then added a coda: "The war is ended. The hour has arrived when the United States must protect itself from these alien races." Then Johnson spelled it out: "We do not want Japanese, Chinese, Hindu, Turk, Greek, Italian, or any other nationality until we can clean house." The *Congressional Record* added the exclamation point: "[APPLAUSE]."

Within days a Philadelphia newspaper warned that "the most extraordinary, hopeless, destitute and pathetic emigration" was en route to America and blamed "certain racial groups" for opposing restriction legislation. The *Boston Post* reprinted most of the Carr report and said Johnson had warned that the majority of these "undesirables" would "locate in cities, making housing conditions more congested and increasing the present unemployment." Representative J. Will Taylor of Tennessee provided his own quotation from the Aldrich poem and then elaborated with his personal description of the immigrants who threatened the nation's unguarded gates: "a heterogeneous hodgepodge, polyglot aggregation of aliens, most of whom are the scum, the offal, and the excrescence of the earth." Robert Ward of the Immigration Restriction League produced an essay that took its facts and its inevitable argument directly from the House report. Albert Johnson told a newspaperman that the State Department had proven the existence of a "real emergency," and then he conjured up imagery to accompany the proof: fleets of ships steaming across the Atlantic "with immigrants hanging over their edges" and steerage passengers "fed from troughs like swine." The *New York Times*, irked by foot-dragging in the Senate, joined Wilbur Carr's chorus: "The need of restriction is manifest," the paper's editorial said. "American institutions are menaced." It warned of "swarms of aliens" who were bringing "diseases of ignorance and Bolshevism" along with the familiar "loathsome diseases of the flesh." The House was the people's branch of Congress, said the *Times*, whereas the dawdling Senate was proving to be "the unpopular branch," responding not to the wishes of the public but "to the interests of private capital."

This last was a fruitful charge, especially when coupled with an older one. The two assaults—on big industry, and on the organized efforts of American Jews—were efficiently yoked together during congressional hearings when Representative John C. Box of Texas attacked the Inter-Racial Council, at this point the most potent lobbying group fighting the bill. The IRC's leadership, said Box, included industrialist Pierre S. Du Pont (the archetypical representative of one set of pro-immigration villains) and Louis Marshall (who had become a virtual synecdoche for the second set). The IRC's dues-paying membership (average assessment: the 2019 equivalent of $35,000 per year) was overwhelmingly composed of industrial employers hungry for cheap labor, among them Allegheny Steel, Colt Firearms, and General Motors. Further, said Box, the IRC's individual members include many whose "very many names I can not pronounce," and then he proceeded to stumble his conspicuous way through a few of them: "Auerbach, Baroti, Budilovsky, Dadakis . . ." The offending names, he said, represented but "a trifling fraction of the list of their racial membership."

As if the hearing room were a stage and the dialogue a carefully laid-out script, Box's Texas colleague Thomas L. Blanton interrupted at exactly the right point: "Is it any wonder, then, that this splendid piece of legislation has been sidetracked and held up?" Completing their duet, Box replied with a slur appended to a sneer: "It is not any wonder, but it is an ominous thing if the will of the American people is to have to give way to influences like these."

By the spring of 1921 congressional whittling had reshaped Johnson's bill. The two-year suspension had been replaced by an idea that had been batted around in restrictionist circles for years. Now, in addition to a sharply lowered annual ceiling on total immigration, the bill provided for something never before imposed on European immigrants: a nation-by-nation quota.

Race arguments grounded in eugenic theory were a central aspect of the debate. Calvin Coolidge's anointment of racial eugenics in *Good Housekeeping* led the way. Madison Grant, who had already made a pilgrimage to Warren G. Harding's front porch in Marion, Ohio, to meet with the incoming president, then went to Washington to join the lobbying effort. In the pages of the *Saturday Evening Post*, Kenneth Roberts was ready at the ramparts on behalf of both Johnson (who, he said, many years later, "took an almost paternal interest in me") and Wilbur Carr (who was merely "a good friend"). To date, Roberts had largely confined himself to slurs ("A few feet of macaroni and a small but highly developed cheese make a day's ration for almost any south Italian"). Now he turned his *Post* dispatches toward science, citing the findings of "biologists and ethnologists" to alert readers to the "streams of undersized, peculiar, alien people" who were "oozing slowly but ceaselessly" across the Atlantic—so different from "the tall, blond, adventurous people from the northern countries of Europe" who had made America what it was. Princeton zoologist Edwin Conklin took to the pages of the publishing house's respected monthly, *Scribner's Magazine*, to lay out the inevitable consequences wrought from "amalgamation of superior hereditary types" with the "inferior races." The nation, he said, was already burdened with "forty-five millions, or nearly one-half of the whole population, [who] will never develop mentally beyond the stage represented by a normal twelve year old child."

The drumbeat for the Johnson bill became deafening. The State Department issued another consular report ("subnormal . . . not the Europeans of a sturdier day . . . parasites"). A military attaché in Berlin leaked a report indicating that 70 percent of the "undesirables" were neither children nor elderly: they were, he said, "ready to breed." As the final vote neared, the *Philadelphia Inquirer* threatened that "disaster will surely overtake the United States" if the bill did not pass. And lest Congress ignore the arguments that had brought it to the brink of effective restriction, the official voice of the *Saturday Evening Post* snapped the somnolent back to attention. There, beneath the etching of Benjamin Franklin that adorned the *Post*'s editorial page, the magazine endorsed the work of Madison Grant and Lothrop Stoddard. "Thirty years ago science had not perhaps sufficiently advanced to make us fully aware of our dangers," said America's most influential periodical. Now, however, it had.

The legislation Warren G. Harding signed into law on May 19, 1921, did not extend the refugee exemption, the one small victory that Louis Marshall and his associates had achieved in 1917. If the exemption had indeed been intended, as Marshall had speculated, "to give a preference" to Russian Jews, by this point there was small appetite for such a preference; the Senate voted it down by a crushing 60–15. Bearing few limitations save for its tenure (it was due to expire July 1, 1922) and the handful of exemptions (relatives of citizens and so forth), the bill cruised into law. The Senate approved the final language by a staggering 78–1, with 17 abstentions. Over in the House, they didn't even bother to conduct a recorded vote; it passed by acclamation. President Harding signed it without blinking.

For the battered antirestriction forces, defeat was made all the more brutal by the final terms of the measure. It was true that Johnson's call for a complete halt to immigration had been excised from his bill in its journey toward passage. But what had been substituted was in a way far worse. A complete halt might have been extreme, but it would also have been impartial. Instead, the bill's system of national quotas was aimed, by its very design, at specific ethnic groups. Now, wrote Louis Marshall, this new system "bases the right of immigration on the nationality of the alien seeking admission, and not on his physical, moral and mental qualifications." That had long been the burden imposed on Asians. For Europeans, this was a first.

The quota system was designed to operate under the ceiling of a general exclusion: the number of immigrants allowed entry, which had averaged 1,035,000 in the five years preceding the war, was cut to a maximum of 355,000 per year. Then came the specifics: the number of individual slots allotted to each country was set at 3 percent of the number of people born in that country who were already in the United States in 1910. Representative Isaac Siegel of New York suggested that the 1920 census would be a fairer standard, but Albert Johnson would entertain no such argument. Since 1910, he said, there had been so much immigration from eastern and southern Europe (in his preferred euphemism, "certain countries") that it would distort his intent. If they used the 1920 census (with its higher proportions of Italians, Greeks, Russian Jews, and other suspect groups), he said he would have no choice but to slash the 3 percent quota to a yet lower percentage.

The consequences of the 1921 Emergency Immigration Act were immediate. The 3 percent rule cut immigration from Poland by 70 percent, from Yugoslavia by 74 percent, from Italy by a breathtaking 82 percent. Smaller tributaries of the immigrant stream were similarly stanched: 28,503 Greeks arrived in 1921 but only 3,457 were allowed through the gates in the first post-quota year.

The bill may have been only temporary, but combatants on both sides knew that the ground had shifted. Louis Marshall blamed the consular reports, "reeking with hatred, prejudice, and contempt against the Jews." Madison Grant, for his part, considered the quota system a way to favor Nordics at the expense of "Jewish tailors and Greek banana vendors."

In Boston, the stalwart leaders of the Immigration Restriction League rested, if only for a moment. They had been trying to guard the gates longer than anyone else, and though they recognized that leadership of the national restriction movement had passed from Beacon Hill to Capitol Hill, they nonetheless had reason not just for celebration, but for remembrance. Nine days after the quota act became law, Prescott Hall died. Although he and his wife had moved into a house directly across Mount Vernon Street from Joe Lee's a few years earlier, the two men—one thoroughly engaged with the world around him, the other an obsessive driven by his commitment to a single cause—had never been personally close. But Lee's memorial tribute was not stinting in its appraisal of Hall's contribution: he had "probably done more to affect for the better the future of this country than almost any man of his generation," he wrote. "Without him the gates would still have been unguarded and the deterioration of our human standard would still be at the flood."

One month before Hall's death, as the quota bill sped toward enactment, he had written to his old comrade Robert Ward, who had been at his side for the full twenty-seven years of the IRL's existence. "I guess my work is about over," wrote Hall. "The rest of you will have to keep it up." And so they would, with a variation on the new quota system that would elevate scientific racism to the level of established law and bind it into place for more than forty years.

Chapter Ten

Science Is Our Polestar

As the White Star liner SS *Canopic* steamed into Boston Harbor on June 6, 1921, the 12,000-ton ship, its main deck longer than a football field, appeared to be completing just another voyage in its longtime role as a mainstay of White Star's Mediterranean service. In 1907, on an outbound voyage, the *Canopic* had carried Henry Cabot Lodge and his Dillingham Commission colleagues to Naples for their fact-finding tour of southern Italy. In 1917 it began three years' wartime service for the Royal Navy, and in 1920 it rejoined the company's peacetime fleet. White Star was especially proud of its first- and second-class service—brochures boasted of oak-paneled dining salons, Chippendale writing desks, smoking rooms set aside "for devotees of 'My Lady Nicotine'"—but had long bragged as well about improvements below the promenade deck. "Third class (steerage no longer)" read the upbeat brochures, and they were partly correct. Though still confined belowdecks, the poorest of the immigrants on many White Star ships now slept in one large hall and ate in a separate one.

But whatever relative pleasures were enjoyed by the third-class passengers on the *Canopic*, they were rendered meaningless when the ship arrived at Commonwealth Pier on this mild early-summer Monday. Under a temporary rule authorized by the Emergency

Immigration Act, which had become law just two weeks earlier, the Port of Boston's June quota for Italian immigrants had been set at 300. Passengers bearing Italian passports were not allowed to disembark. The ship's manifest recorded 1,040 passengers in third class alone. For four days the immigrants remained aboard, restless and uncomprehending. Friends and relatives who had preceded them gathered by the hundreds on the pier, driven, said one Boston paper, by "resentment against the holding of immigrants at the very gates of the Land of Promise." At the same moment, anarchists Nicola Sacco and Bartolomeo Vanzetti, Italian immigrants both, were on trial for murder in nearby Dedham. Reporters relayed rumors of a possible physical assault on the ship. Two hundred police reserves were brought in to contain the seething crowd.

In Washington, Albert Johnson considered the circumstances. The *Canopic* had departed Naples before the quota had gone into effect. Few could challenge Johnson's commitment to restriction, so his recommendation to make a onetime exception for immigrants who had been at sea when the quota countdown began was broadly accepted. Police began to move the passengers to a temporary detention facility where they would stay until the new protocol could be made official a few days later. The screams of the terrified passengers, convinced they were being jailed, provoked the crowd that had massed on the pier. It was a murderously hot day. Panic ensued—an "uncontrollable frenzy," wrote one observer. Adults fainted, children wailed. A dramatic photograph of a young girl being dragged from the *Canopic* appeared on the front page of the *Boston Post*. Even Robert Ward of the Immigration Restriction League considered Johnson's position "humane," though regrettable. He blamed White Star (as well as "various hyphenated societies") for the episode.

Kenneth Roberts, on the other hand, showed no such softening. Spending the summer at his home in the seaside Maine town of Kennebunkport, the *Saturday Evening Post*'s celebrated expert on immigration welcomed an interviewer from the *Boston Herald*. A few days later, beneath an eight-column screamer of a headline (DANGER THAT WORLD SCUM WILL DEMORALIZE AMERICA), the paper gave Roberts the opportunity to describe immigrants like those who had been aboard the *Canopic*. "It is the very slime of Southeastern Europe that is clamoring to get over here," he said, "the scum of the world, vermin-ridden and useless." If they continue to come, he added, "God help the United States." Lothrop Stoddard read the interview and wrote Roberts to congratulate him on "the fine work you are doing for our race." Neither man was likely aware that the small steamer that carried the *Canopic*'s passengers to the detention center was named the *Mayflower*.

The *Canopic* misadventure was only a harbinger of what was to come. The brief fifteen days between Harding's signature and the effective date of the new law's strictures had afforded no time for putting procedures into place, let alone the quotas themselves. And in a misguided attempt to manage the rate of immigration, those quotas, when established, were allocated by month. Thus was the annual allotment of 42,057 Italians (not even 15 percent of the 296,414 who had entered the United States in 1914, the last prewar year) translated to a monthly quota of 3,500. The huddled masses aboard the *Canopic* were tempest-tossed not just because of the 300-person limit imposed at the Port of Boston, but because ships that had arrived in New York three days earlier had already landed the entire month's Italian allotment for *all* entry ports. Lest Albert Johnson's ad hoc exception for the *Canopic* immigrants be misunderstood, immigration officials immediately declared "that henceforth all excess-quota aliens would be denied admission and deported." The southern and eastern Europeans were not the only ones forced to submit to the ruling. When the eighth immigrant from Luxembourg reached Ellis Island on the first day under the new system, the commissioner general of immigration ordered his deportation: that country's June quota was seven.*

The entire transatlantic passenger trade had been turned upside down. Under the law, immigrants rejected at American ports would have to return to Europe at the shippers' expense (not that it was very much expense: third-class compartments were often empty on many eastbound crossings, and the cost of food was negligible in any case). But three thousand people who had begun to travel overland from Poland to Belgium in the weeks before the law's enactment were stranded at the Antwerp docks. In Cherbourg, White Star and the Cunard Line jointly announced plans for a mammoth hotel designed to accommodate as many as 2,500 left behind whenever monthly quotas were used up. The Hamburg-American Line warned its shareholders that its passenger service had been crippled by "ongoing legal stipulations on immigration." The SS *Kroonland* departed Belgium with just 230 people aboard; three pre-quota months earlier, it had carried more than 700 in steerage alone.

That first summer of the emergency quota initiated the "Immigrant Derby," a high-stakes game of chicken that endured throughout the act's life, especially in New York Harbor. The likeliest way a ship could assure entry for its passengers was to pause in unprotected waters outside the three-mile limit a few days before the end of the month, then dash in ahead of the competition when the month's last midnight arrived and the immigrant count began anew. Like contestants in a yacht club regatta, captains of competing ships would jockey for position—as many as twenty on a single evening—trying to maneuver their massive vessels as if they were racing craft, then sprint (if a fifteen-thousand-ton steamer could be said to sprint)

---

* Luxembourg's quota was so small because Luxembourg was so small. On the other hand, the entire continent of Africa was allotted just 122 spaces. When the minister from Liberia learned that his nation's quota was exactly one half of one person, the *New Republic* breathed a sigh of caustic relief: "he luckily obtained a ruling" allowing admission of his candidate "without amputation."

for the goal line at the harbor's narrow entrance, roughly where the Verrazzano-Narrows Bridge would be erected nearly half a century later. At midnight on August 31, 1921, two Greek ships, the *King Alexander* and the *Acropolis*, began their race toward the Land of the Free, chuffing and steaming, each passenger's future (and possibly each captain's job) dependent on a combination of seamanship and harbor traffic. Winning by a scant two minutes, the *King Alexander*'s passengers were admitted, filling the entire Greek quota for September. The immigrants aboard the *Acropolis* were ordered deported, and the crew of the lumbering ship prepared for its dolorous return voyage to Athens. Even Immigration Commissioner Henry Curran called this monthly race "a fiendish prospect, unique in history, unique in its unintended cruelty."

"Immigrant Derby" wasn't the only coinage arising from the ritual. The sympathetic *American Legion Weekly* called the process "choosing Americans by horsepower." And the *New Republic* had a bitterly ironic term for unfortunates like those aboard the *Acropolis*: "surplus Greeks." But there was never a surplus of Britons or Germans, Norwegians or Danes or Swedes. Great Britain's 1921 quota was 77,342. Greece's was 3,294. And when the first fiscal year under the Emergency Immigration Act came to its end, the British quota was left with nearly 35,000 slots unfilled.

*   *   *

JUST AS THE IMMIGRATION SYSTEM began to settle into its newly constricted form, its alteration was memorialized, and its intent amplified, by an event convened in New York. The headline in the *New York Times* for September 25, 1921, couldn't have been more direct, or more precise: EUGENISTS DREAD TAINTED ALIENS, it read, and the chain of subheads trailing beneath made the point abundantly clear for anyone who might have missed it: "Believe Immigration Restriction Essential to Prevent Deterioration of the

Race Here," then MELTING POT THEORY FALSE, in turn followed by "Racial Mixture Liable to Lower the Quality of the Stock—Prof. Osborn's Views."

Fairfield Osborn could not possibly have disagreed with the paper's characterization of the event he had staged specifically to emphasize, credentialize, and in the end apotheosize the views of the racial eugenicists. From the moment in 1920 when the National Research Council authorized Osborn and Madison Grant to play host to the war-delayed Second International Congress of Eugenics, the two old friends had seized control of the invitation list, the program, and the message that would place the congress and its not-remotely-hidden agenda on front pages across the country.

It's impossible to imagine a pair of collaborators more congenial and more like-minded than Osborn and Grant. Since they had initiated their series of joint ventures a quarter century earlier—the Half Moon Club, the Save-the-Redwoods League, the Galton Society, among others—they had spoken virtually daily. William Hornaday, the Bronx Zoo's longtime director, said the two men "pulled together like the best team of horses." When Grant killed a previously unidentified caribou species on one of his many hunting expeditions in Alaska, he gave it the taxonomic name *Rangifer tarandus osborni*. A man who wore his atheism proudly, Grant would occasionally enlist Osborn, the famous paleontologist—he had named *Tyrannosaurus rex*—to help him disprove religious mythology; together they determined that a relic displayed in a Manhattan church was not a fragment of the wrist of St. Anne but the femur of a chicken. Every Saturday when they were both in town, they would meet at the Bronx Zoo, which Grant all but considered his own property and where he had installed Osborn as president of its parent organization, the New York Zoological Society. Most weeks they had meetings at the American Museum of Natural History as well, for Osborn tightened his grip on *his* domain by placing Grant on committee after committee—especially the committee that chose the museum's trustees, which Grant chaired for years. Grant was even willing to fulfill Osborn's express wish to find "an agreeable Hebrew" to join the museum's board; their choice was Felix Warburg, whose father-in-law and business partner, Jacob Schiff, filled the same role on Grant's board at the Bronx Zoo.*

For all their similarities of breeding, ideology, and wealth (Osborn was heir to a railroad fortune), the two men were in manner very different from each other. You could see it in their photographs: Grant elegant and slightly rakish, Osborn as puffed up as a Yorkshire pudding. Where Grant was always cordial and usually charming, Osborn was arrogant, vainglorious, and condescending. One scientist called him "enormously pompous," another preferred "incredibly pompous." In the warm-weather months, starting in April, Osborn often worked from Castle Rock, his thirty-four-room turreted chateau on a promontory above the Hudson River opposite West Point, some forty miles north of his official domain at the museum. Several times a week, two secretaries would board a train in Manhattan at 6:30 a.m.—sometimes only to bring the mail—and spend the day in an outbuilding, on call, until they were dismissed and sent on their way late in the afternoon. The magnitude of Osborn's Olympian self-regard was best described by a museum official who worked for him for more than a decade: "He wouldn't carry anything himself, not even an envelope," the official remembered. "If he wanted a memorandum taken from his fifth-floor office to his second-floor office, one of his secretaries would call a messenger [and] the two men—Osborn and the messenger—might go down in the same elevator."

Back in 1909, shortly after Osborn began his quarter century in command of the Natural History museum, he told his friend

---

* Warburg was not particularly agreeable in 1923, when he called Osborn's preface to a new edition of *The Passing of the Great Race* "scandalous" and "shameful," and demanded that a committee of the board investigate the matter. The committee found "there was no need for anyone to feel offended," and a compliant Warburg remained on the board another ten years, when he was succeeded by his son.

Grant he hoped to make the museum "a positive engine" for the "propagation of socially desirable views." By 1920, as the ravages of war began to recede into the past and as confidence in eugenic thinking was rising toward its apogee, Osborn and his engine were ready for takeoff. Grant was not the only ally beside him at the controls as he planned the Second International Congress of Eugenics. Advising him on matters scientific was Charles Davenport. Harry Laughlin was director of exhibits, Lothrop Stoddard director of publicity. The chairman of the Reception Committee was Mary Harriman, who provided financial support as well.

If the makeup of the event's leadership suggested that this was to be a conference of the already converted, Osborn confirmed it in his private correspondence. Desperately wishing to adorn the congress with the shiniest names in genetics, evolutionary biology, and anthropology (even if he had no intention of allowing any of them to hijack the proceedings), he aimed high. He enlisted Leonard Darwin (an invitee himself) in the effort to secure William Bateson, but was flabbergasted when the eminent geneticist declined the invitation; Bateson said he wanted to keep his pure science (genetics) permanently isolated from an applied science (eugenics) that he had never supported.* At Davenport's urging, Osborn even invited Franz Boas, with whom he had maintained cordial relations dating back to Boas's tenure at the museum.

But Osborn was playing a cynical game. One of the most prestigious names on his list was Thomas Hunt Morgan, whose revolutionary work on chromosomes, already well advanced, would win him the Nobel Prize. Osborn was beyond solicitous in his invitation to Morgan, whom he knew to be dubious about eugenics in principle and who considered many of its advocates unscientific practitioners of "social propaganda." Osborn addressed Morgan's concerns directly:

---

* Bateson believed "alliances between pure and applied science are as dangerous as those of spiders, in which the fertilizing partner is apt to be absorbed."

he wanted, he told him in a carefully worded letter, to give the eugenics congress "a thoroughly scholarly tone and ward off the cranks and faddists who have been fluttering around this subject." Gaining rhetorical momentum, Osborn insisted that "I will have nothing to do with the Congress unless it is kept on a thoroughly scholarly, anti-fad, and anti-crank basis." The forthcoming public announcement of the congress, he concluded, "will inspire the right kind of people . . . and send a chill into the marrow of the cranks."

The following week Osborn dashed off a note, attachment enclosed, to Charles Davenport: "You will be amused, I think, in reading my letter to Morgan."

Of course Davenport would be amused. Both he and Osborn were scientists of sufficient attainments to know that the elementary promises of eugenics—eliminating the unfit, improving the species, purifying the race—were catnip for the gullible, the moonstruck, and the rabid. Crackpots of the W. E. D. Stokes variety came along as part of the deal. But Osborn seemed less concerned with screwball monomaniacs who might seize eugenic theory and disfigure it than with those who simply didn't belong in the same room with him. Preparing the copy for the invitations to the congress's opening reception, he insisted on requiring "evening dress." "People will come *if it is a privilege*," he wrote to Davenport, "and we must carefully guard against cranks and curiousity seekers." By Osborn's standard, a crank was evidently someone who didn't own white tie and tails.

In fact there's plenty of evidence that Osborn knew that Grant, for whom evening dress was virtually daily wear, was himself a crank. At various times Osborn acknowledged to others that his dear friend was biased, and he chastised Grant directly for scholarly lapses, sloppiness, and intellectual bullying. When ethnologist Robert Lowie, a Boas protégé, wrote a savage review of a new edition of *The Passing of the Great Race*, Grant was apoplectic. He told Osborn that Lowie was an "anthropological bolshevist," probably part of a "Jew socialist" academic conspiracy. Osborn's response: "There is much truth in Mr. Lowie's criticism; your book requires rewriting from beginning to end." Grant did not always take Osborn's criticisms kindly, nor did Osborn appreciate Grant's peevish resistance. "Just a line to beg you not to use your sledgehammer methods with me," Osborn told Grant in 1920. "I know you do not mean to do so, but you talk to me just as you would to a Bronx Park contractor." Osborn knew better than to wholly accept Grant's pie-eyed view of human history and evolution. He just chose not to let it bother him.

So there Grant stood, elbow to elbow with the reigning monarch of the eugenicist world as Osborn opened the doors of the Natural History museum to congress delegates on September 22, 1921. Osborn's insistence on evening dress gave the opening reception the appearance of a society ball, which was altogether appropriate. For Grant, the congress was a kind of highbrow coming-out party. Despite all the press references to him as "Dr. Grant," despite his membership in all the Galton Societies and Eugenics Research Associations, nothing compared to being the second-ranking officer of the greatest assemblage of eugenicist scientists ever convened. For Osborn, whose leadership of the museum had taught him the finer points of public relations, it was the opportunity to apply a final, certifying stamp of academic credibility to what he considered the most critical issue facing America. Half a year earlier, Calvin Coolidge's call for adherence to "biological laws" in the shaping of immigration policy marked the marriage of eugenics and immigration restriction. Osborn's congress would be the marriage's public consummation.

Delegates came from all over the United States, and also from Great Britain, France, Norway, Italy, Cuba, the Kingdom of Siam, and several other countries. Among the congress's financial patrons, in addition to Grant, Osborn, and Mary Harriman, were Alexander Graham Bell, J. H. Kellogg, and Herbert Hoover, the secretary of commerce. Members of Harriman's reception committee included

Mrs. Alexis Carrel, whose husband was a Nobel Prize winner in medicine, and Mrs. Harry Payne Whitney, whose yet more impressive credential (in New York at least) was her marriage certificate, which marked the merger of two of the city's royal families, the Whitneys and the Vanderbilts. Among the various receptions and tours (Bronx Zoo, Cold Spring Harbor) arranged by the committee, one particular highlight was a Sunday excursion to Castle Rock, high above the Hudson in Putnam County. Chartered buses were the usual mode of transportation for the other events, but as highway access to Osborn's country estate was less than ideal, delegates and spouses had to be ferried to and from Castle Rock by private railroad car. Several years later, the announcement of a new highway that would make a trip to Castle Rock easier didn't please Osborn at all. He told Grant "to my consternation" that "the new Westchester Parkway will serve to bring thousands more of the East Side Jews into the already crowded beautiful Highlands of the Hudson."

The Second International Congress took over much of Osborn's sprawling museum on Central Park West. In the Hall of the Age of Man, converted into an auditorium for plenary sessions, the stuffed horses on display had to be relocated. But at least the room kept its name. The monumental Forestry Hall, framed by massive Corinthian columns and capped by a soaring recessed ceiling, was renamed Eugenics Hall. For the length of the congress and a month following, Eugenics Hall offered a range of exhibits curated by Harry Laughlin and open to the public. Laughlin said he'd gathered them from a variety of sources, including academics, physicians, social workers, and "scholars and authors of independent means." Docents from the Eugenics Record Office walked visitors through a maze of installations that covered many of the familiar eugenic bases—an exhibit on "Heredity in Epilepsy," another that used the skulls of fetuses to make the case that Negro brains were smaller than those of Caucasians. There was the inevitable display of letters from Galton and Darwin, and an exhibit from Charles Scribner's Sons featuring its brimming shelfful of eugenic offerings (which didn't stop Grant and Lothrop Stoddard from sponsoring booths devoted strictly to their own works). One particular theme, barely hinted at during the First International Congress in London nine years before, was inescapable among the exhibits: "Marriage and Birth Rate in Relation to Immigration"; "Approaching Extinction of Mayflower Descendants"; "Immigration into the United States from Different Countries"; "Growth of United States Population by Immigration and by Increase in Native Stock." The two Eugenics Record Office booths dedicated to race and immigration featured the foreboding declaration, "Whenever two races come in contact for a long period of time, history proves that race mixture follows."

But what might only have been implied by the exhibits in Eugenics Hall was rendered unambiguous when Fairfield Osborn delivered his triumphal welcome speech in the Hall of the Age of Man. It was triumphal because almost everything Osborn said came out that way, and it was triumphal in substance as well—a declaration of victory in the first successful effort to reduce immigration of unwanted Europeans to the United States. Leonard Darwin may have been the evening's featured speaker (having a descendant of Darwin present at any eugenics meeting in 1921 was like displaying a fragment of the True Cross at a meeting of Catholic Pietists), but Osborn used his welcome speech to outline the congress's purposes. "In the United States," he proclaimed, "we are slowly waking to the consciousness that education and environment do not fundamentally alter racial values." With the Emergency Immigration Act, the nation had at last decided to protect itself by "barring the entrance of those who are unfit to share the duties and responsibilities of our well-founded government." And in case anyone was uncertain about the connection between the business of a eugenics congress and the business of the nation, Osborn said this: "The right of the state to safeguard the character and integrity of the race or races on which its future depends is . . . as incontestable as the right of the state to safeguard the health and the morals of its people."

After that, it was as if a centripetal force spun most of the congress's notable events into an irresistible and immutable mass of scientific racism. The Galton Society arranged for members of Albert Johnson's congressional committee to attend the congress, confident that their exposure to eugenic science would result in further restriction. The *Times* reported that every speaker who addressed race questions endorsed the Osborn-Grant position. It was a foreign delegate who made the most stirring case for the eugenic limitation of immigration to the United States. Count Georges Vacher de Lapouge, the author of *The Aryan and His Social Role*, was Grant's close friend, his French translator, and to some degree his mentor. He even looked like Grant, his head just as bald, his sweeping mustache just as shapely, his patrician manner equally integral to his very being. And he certainly thought like Grant. Lapouge brought his speech to its climax with an exhortation Grantian in both its certainty and in its urgency: "America, I solemnly declare that it depends on you to save civilization and to produce a race of demigods!"

Lapouge's call to arms was a message Osborn and his associates would make certain to sustain. After the congress ended, Osborn invited the commissioner of immigration and the chairmen of the two congressional immigration committees to join him for a personal tour of the still-intact exhibit hall. He raised the money to subsidize publication of the congress's complete proceedings. And he asked Irving Fisher, along with Davenport, Grant, and two other dedicated eugenicists, to make a plan to "carry on" the congress's work.

Thus was born the Eugenics Committee of the United States of America, and had there remained any doubt that Osborn's labors were successful, it would have been dashed by the illustrious names that populated the ECUSA's top-heavy letterhead. The Davenports and Grants and Stoddards and Laughlins and other Eugenic Regulars were there, of course, as well as some new academic recruits to the cause. But by now the doors to their movement had swung wide: Surgeon-General H. S. Cumming; Rev. Harry Emerson Fosdick, leader of modernist American Protestants in their battle with the fundamentalists; Adelaide Wolfe Kahn, wife of Otto Kahn, Jacob Schiff's successor as presiding partner of Kuhn, Loeb; William Lawrence, Episcopal bishop of Massachusetts; General Charles E. Sawyer, personal physician to President Harding. And if ever the Regulars wanted to provide proof of the long-desired, hard-won respectability that eugenics had finally attained in America, listed as well was former Harvard president C. W. Eliot.

Eliot had always been an advocate for open gates and an avowed foe of the Immigration Restriction League. His support for various ethnic minorities had been consistent and vocal. But Eliot's confidence in at least one of immigration's by-products had wavered. "The fact is," he would say in a speech a few years later, "and it is perfectly plain, that there has been no assimilation in the United States; and more than that, it isn't desirable that there should be any assimilation or amalgamation of races in the United States." One couldn't be much more eugenic than that.

*   *   *

FEW INDIVIDUALS IN the history of American higher education would exert more influence over a longer period than Carl Campbell Brigham, who would introduce his Scholastic Aptitude Test in 1926. But in the fall of 1921, just weeks after Osborn's congress concluded, Brigham embarked on an exploration of intelligence testing that became nearly as influential in the swelling immigration debate, cementing into place notions of ethnic difference that had been ripening for years.

Psychologist, teacher, bon vivant, Brigham was quick of mind and wit, and swift in his rise to eminence. In 1917, just beginning his career at twenty-six, he met Robert M. Yerkes and was soon enlisted in Yerkes's effort to classify the intelligence of every soldier in the U.S. Army. Commissioned a lieutenant, he administered some of the Alpha tests himself at Fort Dix. After the war's end, he soon became engaged in the effort, arising directly from his work with Yerkes, that would first bring his name and his work to widespread attention.

Brigham was as Princetonian as they come: BA, MA, PhD, and eventually faculty member for more than twenty years. His pedigree was pure as well; according to a colleague he was "a New Englander of New Englanders." His ancestors included passengers on the *Mayflower* and, ten years later, the *Arbella*, the ship that brought John Winthrop, founder of the Massachusetts Bay Colony, to the New World. Something of a rakehell in his early undergraduate years, by the time he received his bachelor's degree he had won recognition as the "most learned" member of his class. But in many respects, he never took himself too seriously. One could encounter characteristic Brigham in his Princeton office, where he'd sit at his desk with a rope tied around his ankle, its other end attached to a wheeled filing cabinet across the room. When he needed something in the cabinet, he'd give the rope a tug, and when he was finished, he'd kick the cabinet away.

In August 1921 Brigham read *America: A Family Matter*, by the New York lawyer Charles Winthrop Gould. The book, published by Scribner the previous year, took the assertions of *The Passing of the Great Race* and amplified them to such a degree one would almost think Madison Grant—one of Gould's closest friends—had written it himself. (From Gould's page 164: "Americans, the Philistines are upon us. Burst the fetters of our unseemly thralldom. Bar out all intruders. Repeal our naturalization laws. Deafen your ears to the clamor of demagogues.") Like Grant, Gould was wealthy, productive, and assured. When Carl Brigham wrote to Gould to say *America: A Family Matter* could "do a great deal to save while it is possible the country for which our ancestors worked so hard and suffered so much and to which we are so attached," the letter initiated a personal and professional relationship between the seventy-three-year-old Gould and the thirty-one-year-old Brigham that would last for the remainder of the older man's life—and, financially, beyond it.

Like Brigham's, Charles W. Gould's blood ran deep in the American past. He was a Winthrop and he was a Saltonstall (a family just as rooted in colonial New England as the Winthrops), and to such roots he attributed virtues unreachable by others. (He insisted that the southern Italians, for instance, had for two thousand years "never produced an outstanding able man.") Widowed at thirty-five, Gould remained single the rest of his life, devoted instead to his law practice, his widely admired collection of art and artifacts, and, enduringly, his "ardent enthusiasm" (as a friend described it) "for the Nordic type." Gould himself put it differently: he considered the immigrant stream corrupting the nation "revolting."

Charles Gould's place on the board of the Metropolitan Museum of Art (alongside Elihu Root and J. P. Morgan, among other members) suggested his stature among the gilded elites of Manhattan. So did his home, located in one of the most prized locations in all of New York, the Washington Square of Henry James. Gould's house was part of "The Row," a collection of Greek Revival gems strung along the square's northern side. Ionic columns framed its front door. The outstanding feature of its back garden was a full-size squash court. Inside the house, a skylight spilled the sun onto an exquisite, sinuous staircase that led to three floors of museum-quality terra cottas from Greece, porcelains from China, Japanese pottery, ancient Egyptian glass. One objet no longer in the house was a bas-relief portrait of Gould's late wife he had commissioned from Augustus

Saint-Gaudens in 1893, portraying her in the dress she wore at their wedding in 1880; he had donated it to the Met in 1915. Apart from his board membership at the museum and a few other engagements, Gould lived mostly as a hermit, wrapped in a cocoon of memory, regret, and resentment.

The house was a dignified setting for the black-tie dinner Gould convened on an October Wednesday in 1921. Charles Davenport, who had praised Gould's book in his address to the Eugenics Congress three weeks earlier, couldn't make it. But Madison Grant, Robert Yerkes, Columbia sociologist Franklin Giddings, and, critically, Carl Brigham, could. Drink was plentiful ("notwithstanding the Volstead Act," Gould confided), the conversation lively. "Though a recluse," the host later told Davenport, "I greatly enjoy the company of brilliant men." On the evening of their dinner, the brilliant men jointly commissioned Brigham, by far the youngest among them, to dive into the ocean of data Robert Yerkes had collected from 1.7 million American servicemen, analyze it with a lens specifically focused on ethnicity and race, and emerge with a book that could make the test's findings as persuasive as they knew they could be. Gould agreed to finance the project himself.

*   *   *

WHILE BRIGHAM AND HIS BACKERS were discussing the Yerkes data in the benign calm of Washington Square, torrents of racial and ethnic mistrust soaked the fabric of American life. Black soldiers who had risked their lives in the trenches of the Marne found lynching unabated in the South. In the North they became unwitting pawns in arguments over immigration policy. With the postwar migration of rural blacks to the industrial North, this fertile new source of cheap labor obviated the need for the imported kind, and the industrial interests who had supported open immigration no longer found it quite as compelling a cause. For Italian Americans, domestic threats became acute. Vigilante mobs attacked an Italian immigrant community in southern Illinois. Relentless newspaper coverage of the six-week-long Sacco-Vanzetti trial served as a daily advertisement for presumed Italian criminality and radicalism. In parts of the West, Armenians, classified as Asians, were barred from owning property. In New England, Harvard president A. Lawrence Lowell, responding to both alumni pressure and his own predilections,

WE CAN'T DIGEST THE SCUM

The anti-immigrant campaign and the anti-radical campaign merged almost immediately after the end of the war. Billy Ireland cartoon, 1919.

tried to impose a hard quota on the admission of Jews.* In Baltimore, biologist Raymond Pearl of Johns Hopkins University—since his appearance at the first Eugenics Congress in London, in 1912, he had become one of the nation's leading interpreters of biological statistics—told a friend that discrimination against Jews "is a necessary move in the struggle for existence on the part of the rest of us. . . . The real question seems to me to come to this. Whose world is this to be, ours, or the Jews'?"

Although specific ethnic insults that Pearl or Lowell—or, for that matter, Joe Lee—might utter in private were rarely said in public, the ethnic vocabulary of eugenics had become normalized and circumspection wasn't necessary. Bloodless euphemisms rooted in *The Passing of the Great Race* provided apparent anthropological authority to replace the coarser language of prejudice. "Mediterraneans" was an evasive way of saying "Italians" or "Greeks" or anything else so precise as to cause specific, nationality-based offense. By 1924 the very word "Nordic," which had had extremely limited use in the American conversation before Madison Grant emblazoned it on his banner, appeared in print more than 150 times as frequently as it had a decade earlier.† Years later the Harlem poet Langston Hughes, cringing at the memory of the jungle-themed exotica put on display in uptown clubs—black dancers in palm frond skirts, shirtless men pounding conga drums—remembered the degrading spectacles as "show nights for the Nordics."

---

* Lowell, who had seen Jewish enrollment more than triple in his fourteen years as president, told one alumnus, "The summer hotel that is ruined by admitting Jews meets its fate, not because the Jews it admits are of bad character, but because they drive away the Gentiles"; he also pointed to the fate of Columbia, which he felt had become similarly unattractive to non-Jews (Jews composed one-quarter of Columbia's entering class in 1918). Angry reactions led the Harvard Board of Overseers to reject Lowell's quota plan, but the admissions office simply put a quota into effect without acknowledging that it existed.

† This datum, courtesy of Google's extraordinary (and extraordinarily fascinating) Ngram Viewer, would be put on steroids by the rise of Adolf Hitler; "Nordic" reached its peak frequency in 1941.

The exalting language of eugenic science was convenient, and it was effective. Lothrop Stoddard declared that "science is our polestar. It is alike our guide for the present and our hope for the future." Margaret Sanger joined Stoddard on the bookshelves with *The Pivot of Civilization*, where she cited Yerkes's army study and its assertions that 47.3 percent of drafted men "are morons."* Raymond Pearl insisted that an experienced animal breeder could produce a "vastly superior" human population within "a couple generations." Kenneth Roberts continued to sound eugenic alarms in the *Saturday Evening Post* and amplified his arguments in his 1922 book, *Why Europe Leaves Home*, where he alerted readers to "the almost invariable breeding out of the Nordics by the Alpines and Mediterraneans." Newspapers reported the call to action issued by Dr. Arthur M. Sweeney, of the University of Minnesota Medical School, who said the nation's threatened racial degradation had to be confronted with the same armaments used to combat "bubonic plague, typhus or cholera," namely "the perfect weapons formed for us by science."

More surprising voices joined the chorus. Editor/columnist William Allen White, the widely admired voice of prairie progressivism, issued a desperate warning in the pages of *Collier's*: "the low breeds of Europe" had formed a "moron majority" that had already overrun American cities. "Another civilization has invaded these shores," he added, predicting a future where one would no longer find "the land of the Pilgrim's Pride" but one seized by invaders. The National Research Council, the most highly credentialed collection of scientists in the country, was moved to appoint a committee charged with measuring the comparative racial value of different ethnic groups, its findings expressly intended to serve as a basis for legislation.

---

* Sanger's admiration for Stoddard went beyond ideology. When New York police attempted to block her from taking the stage to address a birth control meeting in November 1921, she would recall, "Lothrop Stoddard, the author, tall and strong, seized me and literally tossed me up to the platform." Stoddard grabbed a fistful of flowers, thrust them into her hands, and shouted to the crowd, "Here's Mrs. Sanger!"

One of the more bizarre manifestations of the anti-immigration movement's unchecked turn toward eugenic arguments went on display in Washington, DC, in April 1922. Albert Johnson had called hearings on a bill to extend his 1921 legislation another two years, until a permanent quota system could be established. A standing-room-only crowd jostled itself into place behind a rank of newsreel cameras in the House Caucus Room as Johnson's star witness took the stand: the retired vaudeville diva Lillian Russell, former consort of financial buccaneer Diamond Jim Brady. "She was a golden beauty who stampeded men's senses," a friend wrote, and on this day Johnson and his headline-hungry colleagues were ready to be dazzled. Russell's appearances on behalf of Warren G. Harding's election campaign in 1920—in one frenetic three-and-a-half-week stretch, she had given speeches in fifteen states—had led the president to reward her with an assignment as a "special investigator" to look into the immigration question. After a grand tour of European cities (she had a special liking for clothes shopping in the French capital, a practice she called "the Paris cure"), Russell issued her report.

"If congressmen should go abroad they could see the facts as I saw them," she told the panel. "One particular fact is that no good immigration is coming our way." She believed that America was on the ruinous path of ancient Rome, which had been destroyed by "alien infiltration," and recommended a complete halt to all immigration for five years. The newspapers ate it up. Lobbyist James Patten told his IRL colleagues that "all the movies"—the newsreels—were featuring her report.

The extension of the 1921 Act galloped through Senate approval on a voice vote. Two weeks later the House of Representatives was more meticulous in its determination to record the moment. After Albert Johnson saw to the deletion of a refugee exemption approved by the Senate, his colleagues approved the final version 258–26.

The bill that Warren Harding signed in May 1922 was another place-holder. Johnson and his allies, hoping to craft a permanent measure that would protect emigration from Great Britain and Scandinavia while sifting out the verminous hordes from Europe's south and east, had bought themselves two more years to come up with something definitive. The only substantive addition to the 1921 legislation changed the rules for immigration from Latin America, which had remained untouched by the first Emergency Act because western ranchers and farmers valued their migrant workers too highly to hamper their free passage across the southern border. But an unexpected problem had arisen. According to the IRL, an amendment was needed to stop eastern and southern Europeans from "colonizing" Cuba, Mexico, and any other quota-free Latin countries that might be used as a base for subsequent unrestricted immigration to the United States. Brazil, for instance, had taken in eight thousand Italian immigrants in 1920; immediately after the 1921 law went into effect, the annual number leapt toward thirty thousand, any of whom might consider the country a convenient way station on the road to America. The solution contained in the extension legislation blocked immigrants entering the United States from any Western Hemisphere nation unless they had already lived there for at least five years. For Mexican farmworkers (and their seasonal American employers), it was a meaningless hurdle. For Europeans trying an end run around the quotas, it was an enormous one.

In the aftermath of the extension act's passage, Louis Marshall's mood was bleak. "Chauvinistic nationalism is rampant," he told a colleague. "The hatred of everything that is foreign has become an obsession."

Chapter Eleven

6,346,856 Inferior Immigrants

During the months Carl Brigham spent beavering away on the mammoth hoard of data served up by the army intelligence tests, several others drew their own conclusions from the 890 pages of test results that the National Academy of Sciences had released. The *Atlantic Monthly* published a lengthy analysis that led to a frightful verdict: the blood of "inferior" immigrants was destined "to mingle with and deteriorate the best we have." An editorial in the *Missionary Survey*, official publication of the Presbyterian Church, made the case that the test results—"proven accurate by experience"—demonstrated that open immigration was "introducing hundreds of thousands of morons and feeble-minded into our population." Popular lecturer Albert Wiggam announced that "the army mental tests have shown there are, roughly, forty-five million people in this country who haven't any sense." In *The Revolt Against Civilization*, Lothrop Stoddard invoked the results of the army tests to show that "the intelligence level [of immigrants] from northern Europe is far above that of the south and east European countries." Such was the firmness of Stoddard's conviction that the army tests proved northern European superiority that, two years later, Max Perkins advised Stoddard to get in touch with Hans F. K. Günther, who was on his way to becoming the notorious "race pope" of Nazi ideology, to help promote the German edition.

Brigham's views were not far from Stoddard's. But he carried with him a scholarly authority that no one else had yet brought to consideration of the inferiority of certain immigrant groups. He worked on his book about the army data with Yerkes, the test's progenitor, all but perched on his shoulder. Yerkes complained that his army work had been "inexpertly popularized," and he was eager for Brigham to exalt it with an academic treatment. He checked in regularly with editorial suggestions and offered to write the book's introduction. Critically, he persuaded Brigham that it was a tactical mistake to analyze the test results by specific nationality and pointed him instead to more concise (and convenient) racial categories, namely Nordic-Alpine-Mediterranean. The results of his work, Brigham told Yerkes when he finished his first draft, were irrefutable, but that would not render them immune from vigorous assault. He said he approached publication with conviction, but also with trepidation. "I am not afraid to say anything that is true, no matter how ugly the facts may be, and am perfectly willing to stake whatever position I have on the outcome," Brigham told Yerkes. "If [my] Conclusions are published approximately as they stand," he added with rueful humor, "I shall invest everything that I can scrape together on short-term life insurance in the hope of leaving an estate."

Yerkes was glad that Brigham was so certain of his results and so willing to stand behind them. "I predict that your book . . . will make a great stir in the psychological world and far beyond that in the political and sociological," he told Brigham. Yerkes helped initiate the stirring by leaning on Brigham's prospective publisher, Princeton University Press, to rush the book into print "because of its importance in connection with practical immigration problems that are to be considered by Congress during the next few months." In the meantime he congratulated the recently affianced Brigham—he was delighted to learn, he wrote, that "you are engaged to a Nordic lady!"

As Brigham's *A Study in American Intelligence* approached its publication date, another straight-faced inquiry into southern and eastern European deficiency took center stage, courtesy of Harry Laughlin. The energetic Laughlin had had a busy year. He oversaw publication of a compendium of the exhibits from the Second International Congress. He completed his work on *Eugenical Sterilization in the United States*, in which he laid out the model sterilization law that to one degree or another would make its frightful effect felt in thirty states.* And in November he presented the conclusions of a study Albert Johnson had asked him to undertake when Laughlin first signed on as an advisor to the House Immigration Committee in 1920. In his *Analysis of the Metal and Dross in America's Modern Melting Pot*, Laughlin provided exactly what Johnson wanted.

On Sunday, November 12, 1922, the *New York Times Book Review* showcased its take on Laughlin's subject under the unsubtle banner headline FAILURE OF THE MELTING POT. The book under review was *America: A Family Matter* by Charles W. Gould—the same book that had led Carl Brigham to Gould's door. Oddly, the book had been published a full two years before the *Times'* editors got around to it and then proceeded to promote it with such apparent enthusiasm. Congress's impending debate on a permanent immigration law had ripened the moment. Laughlin was scheduled to address Albert Johnson's committee just nine days later.

The book's thesis was tidily summarized by the author's assertion that "the moment we begin to consider the mess of pottage for which we are exchanging our birthright, it becomes revolting." Book review ethics regarding conflict of interest were rather loose in those days: the

---

* In essence, Laughlin's model law and its variations granted the state the right to sterilize, for specifically eugenic purposes, people regarded as genetically inferior who were living under the supervision of the state in prisons, almshouses, mental asylums, and similar public institutions.

author of the *Times* critique, who referred to Gould as "a gentleman of the old stock," was his close friend Madison Grant. Grant's review was very positive about the book, very negative about immigrants, and awash with the sort of anthropological/historical abracadabra that was his metaphorical calling card. Laughlin's credentials were much more substantive, much more imposing: his Princeton doctorate (even if earned for his work on onion roots), his affiliation with the Carnegie Institution, and his numbers—columns of numbers, pages of numbers, mountains of numbers. Gould and Grant relied on analogy, assertion, and principles rooted in Gobineau and other nineteenth-century race theorists. Laughlin's very different approach was reified in a quotation from Lord Kelvin that he kept in his personal files. It was a statement he might well have recited as a daily devotional: "When you measure what you are speaking about and express it in numbers, you know something about it, but when you cannot measure it, when you cannot express it in numbers, your knowledge is of a meagre and unsatisfactory kind."

When Laughlin appeared before the Johnson committee on November 21, he began with a cordial nod to Grant, Gould, and the other amateur scholars riding the eugenic express by dressing the walls of Johnson's hearing room with maps Grant had commissioned for *The Passing of the Great Race*. It made for a grand visual effect. But as Laughlin knew they would be, Johnson and his committee were far more interested in his charts and tables and statistical arcana, which he offered as proof that certain unsurprising ethnic groups were eugenically inferior and therefore dangerous. Laughlin's methodology was simple: he had undertaken an extensive study of the resident populations of 445 public institutions for the "socially inadequate," and then determined whether particular ethnicities—Laughlin knew them only as "races"—were overrepresented relative to their presence in the population at large. To illustrate: if, for unserious instance, 5 percent of the American people were flat-footed but 10 percent of those studied were flat-footed, this would prove that the flat of feet were twice as likely to be institutionalized as the average American.

Laughlin had more crucial criteria in mind, and, category by category, he ticked off the results: Romanians were 41 percent more likely than the average American to be criminal. Italians were 57 percent more likely to be insane. Immigrants from Russia and Poland were more than twice as likely to be tubercular. And so on, a roll call of eye-popping statistics that culminated in the apparent evidence that there was nothing quite so terrible as a Serbian, who was *six times more likely* to be "inadequate" (in any category) than someone of any other ethnic strain—and thus that much more likely to be carrying the perilous genes that would, said Laughlin, "dilute the bloodstream of America."

Three building blocks undergirded Laughlin's imposing statistical construction. He used Daniel Folkmar's dubious 1911 *Dictionary of Races* to sort the institutional population by ethnicity ("...Albanian...Herzegovinian...Russian...Jew...Welsh... Polish"—apparently for clarity's sake, Folkmar appended to that last one a parenthesized "Polack"). He used the categories of individuals barred from entry under the 1917 Immigration Act ("...blind... deformed...epileptic...insane...potentially insane") to classify them by specific deficiency. And the various and increasingly inscrutable mathematical formulae he offered the committee couldn't help but produce appropriate awe. By Lord Kelvin's standards, Laughlin's 133 pages of flyspeck numbers and accompanying commentary indicated that he didn't merely know "something"; on this subject he knew everything. As the hearing neared its conclusion, Albert Johnson, newspaperman turned politician, said, "I have examined Doctor Laughlin's data and charts and find that they are both biologically and statistically thorough, and apparently sound." He also said, "Facts of this nature are the basis upon which the American people must develop their permanent immigration policy."

Johnson wasn't the only satisfied observer. Immigration Restriction League lobbyist James Patten's report to his Boston associates said "Laughlin made a wonderful presentation today . . . a corking study of the alien inmates of public institutions. It will be very helpful." Charles Gould called it "a magnificent piece of work." Using Laughlin's report as bait, Charles Davenport solicited funds to support an expansion of the Eugenics Record Office's work—specifically, to "preserve in the population a high proportion of the excellent Nordic traits by a proper selection of immigrants." Kenneth Roberts told the many millions of readers of the *Saturday Evening Post* that "the findings of Doctor Laughlin of the Carnegie Institution confirm what all students of immigration have known for some time." The essence of that knowledge, Roberts concluded, was simple: "If America doesn't keep out the queer, alien, mongrelized people of Southeastern Europe, her crop of citizens will eventually be dwarfed and mongrelized in return." The Department of Labor was impressed, too: several months later a department document referred to Laughlin as "one of the world's best known scientists."

When Carl Brigham completed his work just a few weeks after Laughlin's bravura appearance before the House Immigration Committee, the men who had made it possible looked toward the public debut of his findings with the giddy anticipation of expectant parents. Late on a December evening in 1922, following dinner at the Union League Club, a sort of after-party at Charles Gould's house on Washington Square brought together a roster of restriction heavyweights. This time Grant, Brigham, and the host were joined by Albert Johnson, Fairfield Osborn, James Patten, and Francis Kinnicutt, an enthusiastic restrictionist whose father was Edith Wharton's friend and her husband's personal physician. The evening's centerpiece was an advance proof of Brigham's just-completed *Study of American Intelligence*. The talk went on for hours. Spirits were high.

From the restrictionist perspective, Brigham's *Study* could have justified fireworks and parades. Given the circumstances of its birth and the backgrounds and predilections of its sponsors, it was hardly surprising that it revealed that Nordics were more intelligent than Alpines, who were more intelligent than Mediterraneans, who were more intelligent—but not much more intelligent—than black people. In the lily-white academic world of 1923, where this sort of arrant racism was almost endemic, Brigham could further argue that European immigration had accounted for two million newcomers who were "below the average negro," thus managing in one sentence to deprecate millions of Americans, both newly arrived and long established. An assertion like this, coming ex cathedra from a member of the Princeton faculty, in a book issued by the university's own publishing division, had headline value.

Brigham's analyses of the army tests, based on fanciful allocations of particular national groupings (he somehow determined, for instance, that Italians were 5 percent Nordic, 25 percent Alpine, and 75 percent Mediterranean) led him to a series of conclusions that, first, "indicate clearly the intellectual superiority of the Nordic race group." And from there he slipped smoothly into the hoary language of the restriction movement, now amplified by his own research: "There can be no doubt that recent history has shown a movement of inferior peoples or inferior representatives of peoples to this country." "According to all evidence available, American intelligence is declining, and will proceed with an accelerating rate as the racial admixture becomes more and more extensive." And, in the book's final paragraph, "The steps that should be taken to preserve or increase our present intellectual capacity must of course be dictated by science and not by political expediency." Supported as his argument was by the book's eighty-four mathematical tables, fifteen charts, and enough jargon-clotted prose to numb a professional statistician, who dared argue?

Brigham was unashamedly grateful to his sponsors. He could

not do justice to Madison Grant, he wrote, because his "entire book should be read to appreciate the soundness of Mr. Grant's position and the compelling force of his arguments." Regarding Charles Gould—"a clear, vigorous, fearless thinker on problems of race characteristics, amalgamation of peoples, and immigration"—Brigham was forthright: Gould "has sponsored this book throughout, has read and re-read all of the manuscript at every stage of its preparation, and is mainly responsible for its contents."

A few years later Gould would be similarly large-hearted about Brigham. "I do not think we have made a mistake in that charming fellow," he told Robert Yerkes. And when the childless Gould died in 1931, he would leave a handsome slice of his fortune to the man whose work had helped tighten the final screws on the scientific case for nationality-based immigration restriction.

In the weeks and months following completion of Brigham's book and the dissemination of Laughlin's bedazzling report—to Albert Johnson's mind "one of the most valuable documents ever put out by a committee of Congress"—the nation hurtled toward an ever-narrower definition of who deserved to be considered American. The year before, Congress had already decided that any American woman "who marries an alien ineligible to citizenship"—that is, an Asian not born in the United States—would have her own citizenship revoked. Then came the Supreme Court's unanimous decision in the Bhagat Singh Thind case, determining that Thind was not white "in accordance with the understanding of the common man." Two months later Secretary of Labor James Davis warned President Harding that nearly half of the fourteen million immigrants who had arrived in the preceding three decades did not even reach "low average intelligence." Two weeks after that, Davis opted for greater precision, telling an audience in Pittsburgh that the army tests had determined that exactly 6,346,856 immigrants were "inferior or very inferior."

Writing in the *New York Times Book Review*, the progressive activist Raymond G. Fuller declared Brigham's book "a sane and sober presentation of certain menacing aspects of our immigration problem." In the *American Economic Review*, Dartmouth professor Charles Leonard Stone hailed the "unusual clarity" of Brigham's findings. Newspapers credentialized Brigham's work in their headlines (INTELLIGENCE LEVEL IN U.S. DECLINING SAYS PRINCETON PROFESSOR). David Starr Jordan, a decade removed from his Stanford presidency but still up to his elbows in the eugenics movement, drew on Brigham to declare that unwanted immigrants were "biologically incapable of rising either now or through their descendants above the mentality of a 12-year-old child." At an anti-immigration rally in New York, Congressman William N. Vaile of Colorado (a member of the House Committee on Immigration) spoke of "unmeltable globs of foreign material" and cited Brigham as he declared that "out of every hundred drafted men born in Poland, only twelve had the average intelligence of the native born white drafted soldier." It was clear, Vaile insisted, that the nation was facing a "racial threat."

But perhaps no one got behind Brigham's analysis more fervently than Fairfield Osborn. Among the aristocratic grandees of Boston and New York who had been steering the anti-immigration movement for nearly three decades, Osborn's scientific credentials were unmatched. And only such prominence could have allowed Osborn to appraise the army tests and Brigham's analyses in quite the fashion that he did at the National Immigration Conference, held in New York as 1923 drew to its close. Under the auspices of the National Industrial Conference Board, some three thousand delegates gathered in the Hotel Astor ballroom to address the pending expiration of the Emergency Immigration Act. Manufacturers, labor leaders, steamship operators; federal officials, social service workers, representatives of foreign governments; "individuals," said the *New York Times*, "prominent in the fields of industry, commerce and government"—they all knew that permanent immigration legislation was coming soon, and they had come to the conference to stake out their positions. Osborn told the delegates his intent was to appraise the issue "in cold-blooded scientific language." He couldn't have gotten much more cold-blooded than this: if the army tests "served to show clearly to our people the lack of intelligence in our country, and the degrees of intelligence of different races who are coming to us," he said, "*I believe those tests were worth what the war cost, even in human life.*" Italics seem appropriate; it's hard to imagine Osborn delivering such a statement without appropriate dramatic effects.

As it happened, the very title of Osborn's speech was nearly as chilling as his dismissive reference to the slaughter of World War I: "The Approach to the Immigration Problem through Science." But neither was as disturbing as a reference to the army tests that appeared elsewhere in the early 1920s, maintaining that the tests had proved that "the Nordic race marches in the vanguard of mankind." So wrote Erwin Baur, Eugen Fischer, and Fritz Lenz, the authors of the definitive German eugenics text, *Menschliche Erblehre und Rassenhygiene* (*Human Heredity and Race Hygiene*). When Congress began debating the new immigration legislation in 1924, the book's second edition was useful jailhouse reading for a thirty-five-year-old inmate in Landsberg Prison in Bavaria, Adolf Hitler.

* * *

AS JOHN B. TREVOR would remember it, despair drove him into the immigration wars. At a meeting of the New York Chamber of Commerce in 1921, he sat by as members debated the Emergency Immigration Act. The forty-two-year-old lawyer was mildly surprised when William G. Willcox, a former president of the New York City Board of Education, spoke against it, less so when the German Jewish community leader Cyrus Sulzberger did. True discouragement set in only when Trevor realized, as he later recalled, that "it was hopeless to really expect businessmen to put the interest of their country first." He determined to travel to Washington, where he knew no one of any political significance, to see what he might be able to accomplish on his own. It was the beginning of a volunteer career in the anti-immigration movement that would last his entire life and eventually earn for Trevor the title "America's alien-baiter No. 1."

It was only partly surprising that Trevor made the trip to Washington with so little connection to the capital's establishment. It was true that he had two Harvard degrees, came from a fabulously wealthy family, and was a natural-born part of the nation's ruling elite. But it was truer still that he was indelibly a New Yorker, and had never felt any particular need to engage in the distant business of national politics. His clubs, his boards (including the almost obligatory American Museum of Natural History), his exalted social world were not just knit into the fabric of upper-class New York—they were the fabric itself. One of his intimates was John D. Rockefeller Jr., who had been a friend since childhood. One of his wife's nearest and dearest was Eleanor Roosevelt.

Trevor could never have supported a complete halt to immigration. When he was in his early twenties, only two of the ten household servants who lived on the third floor of Glenview, the twenty-six-room family home presiding over the Hudson River from a bluff in Yonkers, were American citizens. Almost needless to say, the servants were English, Irish, Swedish—the kind of immigrants who might someday melt without notice into the native population without spoiling the broth. When Trevor and his wife returned from their yearlong honeymoon abroad, they moved into a brand-new limestone mansion in the Beaux-Arts style on the east side of Manhattan, across the street from Andrew Carnegie's enormous chateau and closer to Trevor's downtown law office (which happened to be next door to the office of his friend Madison Grant).

As disengaged as his social and professional life might have been from the immigrant chaos of lower Manhattan, Trevor nonetheless knew the crowded polyglot streets from previous experience and intense observation. As an army captain during World War I, he was in charge of military intelligence for New York, which mostly meant—at least in his view—identifying and pursuing anarchists and other radical elements on the Lower East Side. Trevor's neighborhood-by-neighborhood "Ethnic Map of New York City," which he created while he was in the army, could have been looked at as sociology—or, as he intended it, as a warning: he said his map identified the neighborhoods likeliest to breed armed rebellion. Trevor's xenophobia was ecumenical. Before concerns arose about eastern and southern Europeans evading the quota by passing through Latin America, he said it was "just as objectionable" to allow the immigration of "Mexicans and Brazilians, who by the way, are rotten with various diseases not necessary to enumerate, as it is to have the Greeks and Italians (south) pour in on us." As for the Jews, he told Albert Johnson that simply thinking about new waves of Polish Jews coming to the United States gave him "convulsive shivers."

Once Trevor immersed himself in the restriction movement, shivers gave way to action, and a combination of intellect and energy propelled him to the front lines. He belonged there. In the three-decade history of the restriction movement, leadership had been handed off from northeastern Protestant aristocrat to northeastern Protestant aristocrat. Henry Cabot Lodge ran the first leg of the race, abetted by Joe Lee, Prescott Hall, Robert Ward, and the other men of the Immigration Restriction League. Madison Grant picked up the baton and then handed it off to Charles Gould. John Trevor would take the anchor leg of the relay. Abetting the team's efforts throughout was the scientific auxiliary: Charles Davenport, Fairfield Osborn, Carl Brigham. Of all the essential players who were not actually writing laws, only Harry Laughlin, the teetotaling schoolteacher from small-town Missouri, hadn't emerged from patrician roots (although he did claim James Madison as a relative).

These men were all enmeshed in a sturdy web of colleges, clubs, museum boards, and the other familiar way stations that defined the well-cushioned life of the era. When Trevor was in Boston, he'd meet with Lee and Ward at the Union Club. In New York, when the IRL's James Patten was in town, the preferred venue (when it wasn't Charles Gould's house) was the Union League, sometimes the Century Association. Harvard and Yale and Princeton (and occasionally Columbia) shaped their shared values; various museums and zoos and other quasi-public institutions (which they often treated as if they were their own private assets) were the arenas of their civic engagement. They saw their preeminence in every province of their lives as their birthright, and the immigrants who peopled their nightmares were challenging their claim to it. Testifying before Congress in 1924, Trevor was direct: the new immigrants, he said, "cannot point during a period of seven centuries since Magna Charta to any conception of successful government other than a paternal autocracy." He did not add that his own conception of successful government, like that of so many of the restrictionists, was oligarchy.

Like Harry Laughlin, Albert Johnson was ethnically acceptable but in other ways a mismatch in the world of the eastern restrictionists. The very fact that he'd engaged in the rough-and-tumble of northwestern politics for more than a decade was something of a disqualifier (Lodge, by contrast, had risen from the cobbled streets of Beacon Hill to the U.S. Senate before senators were elected by popular vote). Grant hinted to a relative that Johnson's palm needed the occasional greasing to relieve a constant itch for cash, and Trevor thought Johnson drank too much. On at least one occasion during the early years of Prohibition, Johnson concluded a committee meeting by reaching for the bottle of whiskey he kept hidden on a bookshelf behind two volumes of the Dillingham Commission report and offering a toast to his committee's work. Apart from liquor and possibly a little bribery, flattery offered another path to Johnson. Grant engineered his membership in the Galton Society and played a role in Johnson's improbable election as president of the Eugenics Research Association, the supposedly scholarly institution Charles Davenport had started ten years earlier that had since veered toward immigration restriction. At the time of Johnson's election, Davenport had not even met him.

As Johnson initiated the Immigration Committee's work on permanent legislation in December 1923, Grant was nowhere to be seen. Crippled by arthritis, he no longer visited Washington, saving his traveling energy for trips to Dr. Kellogg's sanitarium in Battle Creek and to various spas and resort hotels in Florida, California, and Colorado. Joe Lee engaged with Johnson almost exclusively through Patten, the IRL lobbyist, whom he continued to pay out of his own pocket and who obliged Lee by sending him daily reports on the progress of restriction legislation. Johnson's private secretary would remember that Kenneth Roberts "practically camped in our offices" while the new legislation was being drafted. But when Lothrop Stoddard was invited to testify formally before Johnson's committee, Roberts turned peevish: Stoddard, he told his diary, was "still the same conceited ass."

John Trevor's involvement in drafting the permanent immigration legislation was different in both scale and function. From the moment he first showed Johnson his "ethnic map" in 1921, he became an intimate part of the legislative process, and also of Johnson's thinking process, introducing him to such anti-Semitic literature as Cecile Tormay's unhinged assault on Hungarian Jews, *An Outlaw's Diary* (it was so "intensely interesting," Johnson reported back to Trevor, that he'd read passages aloud to his companions in the train's smoking compartment on a trip west). Trevor often sat in on the unofficial executive sessions of Johnson's House Committee on Immigration—unofficial because two of its members, Adolph Sabath of Chicago and Isaac Siegel of New York (both of them antirestriction Jews) were not invited. Johnson and Trevor wrote to each other constantly, spoke even more often (Johnson was impressed that Trevor could afford so many long-distance calls), and collaborated on draft after draft of what would become the Immigration Restriction Act of 1924. Many of Trevor's suggestions were helpful; one in particular was crucial.

"I spent thirty minutes with the President yesterday on Immigration matters," Johnson wrote to Trevor in February 1924, "and came away from the White House feeling considerably encouraged." Warren Harding, who had died the previous summer, had long been a supporter of immigration restriction. Calvin Coolidge, who as vice president had introduced "racial considerations" and "biological laws" into the official conversation, was if anything even more committed to slamming the doors. Shortly after Coolidge's ascension, Joe Lee told Robert Ward with easy Bostonian familiarity that "Calvin" was "solidly with us." Large majorities in both the Senate and the House were on board, and there was no question that permanent restriction legislation would soon pass and the president would sign it. Only the details remained to be determined.

Trevor's momentous contribution was a feat of legislative imagination that others would claim as their own but that clearly originated with him. Senator David A. Reed of Pennsylvania was among those who insisted this new idea was his, but the weight of the evidence is entirely on Trevor's side. Reed may not have conceived the novel plan, but he did explain its motivation succinctly. The 1921 law, he said, was "entirely unfair to the native-born American" because "he was ignored in the ascertainment of the quotas."

This was undeniable. The 1921 quotas were arrived at by dividing up the immigrant population into distinct percentages: for simplicity's sake, assume that 50 percent of immigrants already in the United States were from country A, 40 percent from Country B, and 10 percent from Country C; if so, then A would be allowed

50 percent of all new immigration, and so on. But what of Reed's absent "native-born"? Where were they in that calculation? If one were only counting immigrants, the native-born were, as an associate said (with Reed's endorsement), "buncoed" and "rooked" and "trimmed out of their fair share."

Trevor had the solution. Under his scheme, which became known as the National Origins plan, *everybody* counted. A commission working under the authority of the secretaries of state, labor, and commerce would determine what percentage of all Americans, not just immigrants, belonged to each national grouping. It wasn't a question of how many people the census revealed as having been born in, say, Great Britain; it was what percentage of the entire population could trace their *roots* to Great Britain. Your family has been in the United States since your forefathers arrived on the *Mayflower*? Check—British. They came in the first few decades after the American Revolution? Check—more than likely British, maybe German. A bit later, possibly Irish. Said David Reed, "75 percent of us who are now here owe our origin to immigrants" from northwestern Europe—and thus 75 percent of all new immigration slots should be reserved for northwestern Europeans. In painstaking detail (even if with questionable sourcing), Trevor compiled a report that presumed to project the final numbers for forty separate nationality groups with unembarrassed precision (an associate somehow determined that the U.S. population included 44,689,278 descendants of "the old Colonial white stock"). "If I do say so myself," Trevor would write many years later, the National Origins plan was "really a *tour de force.*"

The prospective change in the ethnic allocations of European immigration quotas was radical. Based as they were on the 1910 census, the 1921 quotas had allotted 44 percent of entry visas to southern and eastern Europe. The National Origins plan, according to Trevor's enthusiastic computations, would reduce that number not to 22 percent (as David Reed had calculated it), but to 12 percent. As Trevor remembered it, his scheme was anointed when

Frank Kinnicutt told him that Henry Cabot Lodge wished to see him. Lodge was seventy-three. His health was failing. After more than three decades in the restriction vanguard—Trevor was thirteen when Lodge first addressed the issue in Congress—he had heard every argument, considered every plan. Now he examined Trevor's scheme and declared that he'd been looking for something like this for years—something that was, he said, "an answer to all the charges of discrimination" against the benighted hordes of eastern and southern Europe. Lodge and Trevor believed—or affected to believe—that the numbers were impartial.

Who, though, could wait for a cabinet-level commission to do the difficult work of computing the actual origins of ninety-five million white Americans?* As it would turn out, those numbers, and the permanent quotas derived from them, were not finalized until 1928. But as David Reed—patrician, Princetonian, archconservative— prepared to bring the new legislation to the Senate floor, he had a solution in hand.

It had first been proposed in an article that appeared in the cultivated pages of *Scribner's Magazine* by a little-known econom- ics professor at Vanderbilt University named Roy L. Garis. Even though the Garis article appeared in a rival magazine, editor George Horace Lorimer of the *Saturday Evening Post* was more pleased than envious. Garis's was "a very cagy suggestion," Lorimer told Kenneth Roberts. Cagy, perhaps; audacious, unquestionably. Until the complex computations of the National Origins scheme could

---

* Such was the racial tenor of the times that the proposed legislation specifically excluded from the computation "descendants of slave immigrants," which is to say virtually all American blacks. The IRL did not mince words; including descendants of slaves would "open the country to an African invasion." Another feature of the National Origins scheme: forty years of discrimination against Asian immigrants had left them and their progeny composing a scant 0.2 percent of the population.

330 | THE GUARDED GATE

be completed, it would be fine to rely on declarations of nationality enumerated in the census to determine quotas. But, Garis argued, the quotas should be based not on the census of 1920, or even the 1910 numbers that had been used for the Emergency Act of 1921, *but on the census of 1890*—as Lorimer put it, "that being a year Nordic immigration was still strong and low-grade stuff hadn't begun to come to us in volume."

Never mind that Garis supported his argument with fanciful "facts" that Lillian Russell had uncovered on her "special mission." Never mind as well that even so fervent a restrictionist as John Burnett, the Alabaman who had preceded Albert Johnson as chairman of the House Immigration Committee, had in 1918 argued that even using the census of 1910 as any kind of measuring rod in the immigration debate would be unfair because it was already so dated. What Garis suggested and Reed brought to the Senate floor was a set of statistics compiled thirty-four years earlier. Opponents pointed out that the 1920 census numbers were both available and appropriate; that the 1910 numbers, already in use, might be a reasonable compromise; that the 1900 numbers . . . actually, no one even suggested the possibility of 1900, already twenty-four years distant in the rearview mirror.

To Garis, Lorimer, and Reed, such concerns were irrelevant; they loved the math. By using 1890 as the base year—before the sudden torrent of immigrants from Italy and Poland and Russia and all the other places spewing forth what Kenneth Roberts called "hordes of the most undesirable people in Europe"—they would get exactly what they wanted. In the last year before the 1921 quotas were put in place, 222,496 Italians passed through the gates. In the first post-quota year, that number had been sliced to 42,159. But if that was brutal, then Roy Garis's numerical guillotine was barbarous: only 3,912 Italians a year—barely 1.7 percent of the pre-quota figure—would be allowed to find the brighter future they sought in America's once welcoming arms.

In the House, a nearly apoplectic Adolph Sabath, whose Bohemian accent had still not moderated in his seventeen years representing the heavily ethnic west side of Chicago, was outraged; relying on the 1890 census, he said, was "deliberately discriminatory." Albert Johnson was unmoved; Sabath, he wearily confided to a friend, was elected "to represent districts located in Europe." Over on the Senate side of the Capitol, David Reed simply shrugged. "I think most of us are reconciled to the idea of discrimination," he said at one hearing. "I think the American people want us to discriminate." All he was looking for, he said, was "which is the more plausible, the more reasonable, and the more defensible method of attaining that end." To Reed, the Garis plan was plausibility itself. To use the 1910 census, he maintained, would be "a great discrimination against us, the American born." In truth, for many restrictionists only one other plan could have been more plausible, more reasonable, more defensible. "Dear Cabot," Joe Lee wrote to Lodge with cousinly familiarity, "I don't know why we shouldn't discriminate, but if it is a sin, I think the proper thing would be to suspend all immigration."

During the early skirmishes surrounding the 1924 Immigration Act, the restrictionists who had brought science into the discussion were peacocks in full display. Madison Grant told the readers of the *North American Review* that the nation had undergone "a great change of public opinion" about the "jumbled-up mass of undigested race material" that had threatened the nation's future. Harry Laughlin was introduced to an audience of British eugenicists as "the great American watchdog whose job it is to protect the blood of the American people from contamination and degeneracy." The *New York Times* granted nearly a full column on its editorial page to what the paper called PROFESSOR OSBORN'S POSITION ON THE IMMIGRATION QUESTION (Osborn's own title was "Lo, the Poor Nordic!"). His statement, in the form of a letter to the editor, was less a "position" than it was a sonorous hymn to the once threatened race that might now be pulled back from the brink of extinction. Nordic virtue was so apparent to Osborn that he found it in the most unlikely (and useful) places, drafting into the clan every southern or eastern European luminary worth claiming. By a miraculous combination of presumed genetics, wishful thinking, and a direct lift from a letter he'd received from Grant, Osborn annexed to his tribe a surprising set of Nordics: Giotto and Donatello, Kościuszko and Pulaski, Lafayette and Napoleon, Rodin and Racine and Richelieu. Using Grant's exact words, Osborn, man of science, repeated his friend's dazzling claim that "Columbus, from his portraits and from his busts, authentic or not, was clearly of Nordic ancestry."

How could he write such a sentence and not be embarrassed by its appearance in the *Times*? By this point, the scientific racists were so impervious to challenge that they had ceased to be concerned about the reliability of their assertions. More crucially, neither could they be embarrassed, or chagrined, or even put on notice by the growing number of intellectually powerful attacks on Brigham, Laughlin, the Yerkes test scores, and the entire eugenic interpretation of ethnicity.

Over a period of months, the negative reviews of Brigham's book in the scholarly press outweighed the positive. He was criticized for relying on the general information portion of the tests—those questions about where cars were built, or who appeared in tooth powder advertisements. (His feeble attempt at a preemptive response in the book: "the intelligent person has a broader range of general information than an unintelligent person.") His likening the intelligence of "Alpine" and "Mediterranean" immigrants to the American Negro was ludicrous without taking into consideration the relative educational opportunities for either group; how else could one explain that northern blacks had scored higher on the army tests than whites from Mississippi, Arkansas, and Kentucky? Several critics pounced on his most outlandish assertion, one that he had devised to forestall charges of ethnic prejudice: that because recent immigrants scored worse on the tests than earlier arrivals had, the newcomers were a provably worse cut of humanity than those relatively fine folk who had come to the United States ten or twenty years earlier.

Brigham blamed this decline on his conviction that European countries were exporting "lower and lower representatives of each race"—that they were, by implication, selecting their worst and shipping them to America. But he had made the most elementary of errors, failing to recognize that someone who had taken the test after living in the United States for two decades would inevitably perform better than someone assessed after only five years in the country. His response to this charge was less a defense than an inadvertent guilty plea: "If the tests used included some mysterious type of situation that was 'typically American,' we are indeed fortunate, for this is America." Therefore, Brigham concluded, "inability to respond to a 'typically American' situation is obviously an undesirable trait." Responding in *Science* magazine, the journal of the American Association for the Advancement of Science, sociologist Kimball Young dismissed Brigham's very premise as the product of "an antiquated, outworn and mythological race hypothesis."

Harry Laughlin's science fared even worse than Brigham's. Among the many critics of his *Metal and Dross in America's Modern Melting Pot* report, none was more thorough, more pointed, or more damning than the man whose judgment, Laughlin acknowledged, had to be taken "most seriously," Herbert Spencer Jennings.

Jennings may have been preordained by his first and middle names to engage with the social and sociological implications of science (it was a family calling: his physician father's admiration for the great theorists of mid-nineteenth-century England led him to name Herbert's brother after Darwin). Jennings came by his authority through his outstanding and original scholarly work as zoologist, psychologist, and geneticist. Laughlin had additional reason to respect him: Jennings had trained at Harvard under Charles

Davenport, who had nudged him toward experimental biology; he'd even rented a room in Davenport's Cambridge house. The two men remained close, and Jennings's interest in eugenics—at least in its earliest American phase—was genuine. When he was honored by his admiring colleagues in 1921, Davenport was the main speaker.

Jennings's pedigree was impeccable, his ethics unimpeachable, his reputation formidable. And when the editor of the *The Survey* asked him to write about Laughlin's report, he was well inclined toward it, telling the editor that from what he'd already seen, Laughlin "presents a pretty strong case." Combined with Brigham's data, he explained, "it will furnish strong arguments for restrictive legislation." But six months later, after intensive study of Laughlin's methods, his data, and his conclusions, Jennings was not simply unpersuaded. He was appalled.

Even before his review appeared in print, a distressed Jennings sent a detailed critique to the Eugenics Committee of the United States of America. He was a member of its advisory council, yet he had little reason to hope that the organization would withdraw its support for Laughlin's findings. The gilt-edged ECUSA had emerged from the Second International Congress held at Osborn's museum in 1921 to become the public face of the eugenics movement. It also had yoked itself to restriction when its leaders appointed Laughlin, Robert Ward, and Madison Grant to a committee specifically charged with garnering support for the pending immigration legislation.

Jennings's article in *The Survey*—"'Undesirable Aliens': A Biologist's Examination of the Evidence Before Congress"—appeared in December 1923. It was unrelenting, as was his subsequent appearance before Johnson's committee the following March. He made the obvious point that Laughlin, by confining his study of the "socially inadequate" to public institutions, had failed to count equally deficient individuals who were in private institutions—almost certainly people from families with means, who were far less likely to be foreign-born. Laughlin had also completely ignored (as someone weaned on the Eugenics Record Office's *Trait Book* would) any environmental influences at all—not just poverty and lack of education, but the burden, Jennings wrote, of living "under the heavy handicap of ignorance of the language, customs and laws" of a new country. Most egregiously, Laughlin had lumped together all nine of the disabilities he had studied into one overall number to show a ranking of genetic virtue that put native-born Americans in first place. It was a statistical manipulation that had sailed past Johnson and his committee. According to Laughlin's own data, immigrants from Great Britain, for instance, were *more* prone to feeblemindedness than those from Italy, Romania, or the Balkans—but that was a finding far removed from Laughlin's bottom line. Only when all nine of the report's listed deficiencies were combined on a single numerical scale were people of British origins shown to be genetically sounder than Scandinavians, who topped the French. Then came the long list of nations who were below the immigrant median: Italy. Russia and Poland. Greece. Bulgaria. And, finally, the woebegone Serbia.*

Taking dead aim at Laughlin's statistical manipulations, Jennings noted that individually, "in five of the nine categories—in feeblemindedness, epilepsy, deafness, blindness and deformity—the foreign born are superior to the natives born of native parents." The reason was almost comically obvious: for more than a decade, existing immigration laws had specifically barred individuals in each of those categories from entry. Even eugenicists, it seemed, would have to acknowledge that laws already in place were doing a decent job of genetic culling—by judging the qualities and characteristics of the individual, and not of his or her ethnicity.

But no such acknowledgment was forthcoming. When the officers

---

* Laughlin and his sponsor had ready explanations for the relative absence of American blacks in state institutions. Johnson believed that their living conditions "are so low that dependence does not show itself." At the time, that was a relatively plausible, if cruel, explanation. Laughlin's, however, was ridiculous: "the dependent or inadequate Negro is taken care of by the plantation."

of the ECUSA ignored Jennings's private entreaty, he suggested to a colleague that the group's "unscientific procedures" were an embarrassment and that the true aim of the organization—its letterhead still sparkling with impressive names—was "Nordic propaganda." Increasingly frustrated by the yawns that greeted him when he engaged the ECUSA and when he testified before Johnson's committee, Jennings took to the pages of *Science* magazine, where he recapitulated his argument and conclusively labeled Laughlin's central findings "illegitimate and incorrect." Albert Johnson and his committee could not have been as unmoved by the criticism if they had stuffed their ears with cotton, placed blindfolds over their eyes, and shut down the brain lobes that processed logic, reason, and evidence. "Don't worry about criticism, Doctor Laughlin," Johnson told him at the end of Laughlin's return engagement before the House Committee. "You have developed a valuable research [*sic*] and demonstrated a most startling state of affairs. We shall pursue these biological studies further."

In December 1923, less than half a year into his unexpected presidency, Calvin Coolidge delivered his first Annual Message to Congress. "America must be kept American," he said. "For this purpose it is necessary to continue a policy of restricted immigration."

Over the next five months, on and off, Congress debated the permanent Immigration Act, a.k.a. the Immigration Restriction Act, a.k.a. the Johnson-Reed Act—by any name the most comprehensive barrier to immigration in the nation's history, both then and ever since. Total immigration would be restricted to 155,000 a year. Nation-by-nation quotas were set at 2 percent of the United States' foreign-born (or derived) population from any given country, as enumerated in the census of 1890. During hearings conducted by his committee, Johnson treated antirestriction witnesses with the easy cordiality of a man playing an unbeatable hand. The opposition never had a chance.

One of the primary reasons for Johnson's confidence was his

perception of division in the American Jewish community, for three decades the restrictionists' most potent foe. On one side stood Louis Marshall and his allies, who did not cede an inch. Assaulting theories and expertise paraded by Grant ("not a real scientist, after all"), Marshall dismissed the anthropological arguments with slicing irony: if the Nordics were under so dire a threat, how superior could they possibly be? "I wondered why this fabled race was so frail and fragile. If it did disappear, it is not very complimentary to the Nordic to say he permitted himself to be wiped out by inferior races." Then again, Marshall mused, there was another possible reason: "If [the Nordic race] never existed, of course, it could easily disappear."

But not all Jewish leaders who came to testify shared the absolute conviction of Marshall's determined resistance. The threat of brutal quotas led several to temporize. Some even displayed an unseemly acceptance of certain aspects of Grant's racial theories. Both Joshua Kantrowitz of B'nai Brith and William Edlin, editor of one of the leading Yiddish dailies, said they would bar the immigration of Japanese and Chinese. Edlin threw in Hindus—at the time a catchall term for South Asians, Hindu or not—as well. Judge Bernard Rosenblatt, a stalwart of the American Zionist movement, offered an argument that could have come straight from Charles Gould or Prescott Hall: "When you talk about the races that built America you are talking about the races of Europe, the white races," he said. He argued that the Jews were among "the races that can be assimilated," and therefore merited the committee's approval.* Rosenblatt acknowledged that restriction creates "a sense of injustice"—but if those restricted were "the Asiatic," he testified, it would be entirely

---

* To some eugenicists and immigration restrictionists, this was a reasonable argument, even if they took it to unreasonable ends: the chief medical officer of the Public Health Service told Prescott Hall in 1912 that "intermarriage can solve the problem to the ultimate satisfaction of both Jew and Gentile," and that "in the process of extermination [the Jew] will bequeath a rich legacy to the people with whom he intermarries." Even Harry Laughlin believed that "three per cent Jews in the United States evenly distributed would not leave a serious imprint of their qualities on the American stock."

acceptable. During debate on the House floor, even Fiorello La Guardia of New York, who represented what might have been the most polyglot district in the nation, added his endorsement of Asian exclusion. Adolph Sabath, who had voiced his support for "Asiatic and Mongolian" restriction a decade earlier, was crippled either by his uneasy grasp of English or by an oxymoronic logic: "To discriminate is our right," he declared, "but when we discriminate we ought to discriminate fairly."

The bill's opponents, most of them representing urban districts in the North, did their best during the final floor debates. Representative Charles A. Mooney of Ohio criticized the "fifth-rate extension lecturers," newspaper editorialists, and magazine editors who promoted Nordic theory "with scientific exactness." He also quoted Franz Boas to demolish both the exactness and the science. (Boas had continued to fight the eugenicists in the press and in academic journals, and by offering advice and counsel to congressional antirestrictionists.) John J. O'Connor of New York called Laughlin's *Metal and Dross* report "the greatest joke book that has been published during this session of Congress," and urged members to take notice of the first five letters of Laughlin's surname. James A. Gallivan of Massachusetts said that the Nordics were "the ancestors of every American who is identified with the Ku Klux Klan," and took a specific swing at the IRL—"the corpse of the Loyal Coalition in the city of Boston lift[ing] itself from its bankrupt grave." (Gallivan dodged a real swing when the archrestrictionist Elton Watkins of Oregon threw a punch at him on the House floor.) When La Guardia asked J. Will Taylor of Tennessee for literacy statistics in his state and in Kentucky, Taylor—who had earlier called immigrants "scum" and "offal"—had no room to retreat. So he exited the discussion with a leap toward the preposterous: "We have no illiteracy in Tennessee and Kentucky."

But La Guardia fared less well in a similar tangle with an Appalachian restrictionist a few days later, their exchange and the House's reaction a sharp summary of the mood of the day. Once again comparing the literacy of the immigrants in New York to rural Kentuckians, La Guardia provoked Representative John Marshall Robsion to rise in fury. Robsion's defense of his constituents included hosannas to the quality of their schools, their devotion to "the old-time religion," and their fortunate freedom from the "black hand organizations" and "Tong wars" that presumably terrorized La Guardia's multiethnic Manhattan district. He finally moved from defense of Kentuckians who "suckle their Americanism and their patriotism from their mother's breasts" to game-clinching offense: "I resent the gentleman's insolent, infamous, contemptible slander against a great, honest, industrious, law-abiding, liberty-loving, God-fearing patriotic people." The chamber exploded in applause. The chair denied La Guardia's request for permission to respond. The debate moved on. According to one eyewitness, "The House had had its thrill."

In truth, it had many. When the bill's supporters had control of the floor, the debate was infused with the language of scientific racism. "The primary reason for the restriction of the alien stream," said Representative Robert E. Lee Allen of West Virginia, "is the necessity for purifying and keeping pure the blood of America." John N. Tillman of Arkansas declared America "orientalized, Europeanized, Africanized, and mongrelized" by immigration, and concluded his oration by rolling out Thomas Bailey Aldrich's "Unguarded Gates," now in its thirty-second year on the restrictionist hit parade. Robert L. Bacon of New York was succinct: How could one argue with "scientific results"?

It was all a hyperinflated display of presumed expertise on the part of men who were not experts, preaching the lessons of a science that was not science, justifying prejudices too ugly to be acknowledged. During the Senate debate, one member invoked a fatalistic explanation of how "scientific legislation" often emerged from the marriage of science and politics: "Scientific legislation," it had been said, was "legislation where the legislator pretended to do one thing while he is in reality trying to do another."

Of all the restrictionists' political opponents, none had been more forthright in identifying the true motives behind the Johnson-Reed bill than Emanuel Celler, a thirty-four-year-old freshman congressman from Brooklyn. The American-born son of prosperous Jewish parents, a graduate of Columbia and its law school, Celler comported himself with a steely dignity and confronted the bill's proponents with the focus, the language, and the intent of a prosecutor. It was Celler who solicited Herbert Jennings's testimony before the Johnson committee, and during floor debate he read some of Boas's work into the record. He assaulted the restrictionists' reliance on the army tests and the Laughlin study, which he called "a vicious report . . . redolent with downright and deliberate fallacies." He dismissed Madison Grant's work as "dogmatic piffle." And—critically—he did not euphemize when attacking the restrictionists' obvious intent: to affect, he said, "the rankest kind of discrimination . . . set up against Catholic and Jewish Europe."

Few listened. If even Samuel Gompers was lifting the eugenic banner, accusations of discrimination were rendered moot. The labor leader, himself Jewish, had always been an opponent of unchecked immigration but had long relied on economic arguments rather than racial ones. But in an article titled "America Must Not Be Overwhelmed," published as Congress debated the Johnson-Reed bill, Gompers announced his belief that "THE PERSISTENCE OF RACIAL CHARACTERISTICS"—both "*mental* and *moral*"— could render the process of Americanization futile. The capitals, and the italics, were his.

In the end, the final version of the bill passed with ease: 308–62 in the House, 69–9 in the Senate. (Like previous legislation, it included a set of exemptions for certain professionals, family members, and the like.) But months earlier, Albert Johnson had been annoyed by some parliamentary obstacles thrown in his path by the opposition, and he had briefly dropped his mask of affable confidence. In a lengthy and contentious conversation with a correspondent from the Jewish Telegraphic Agency, "he seemed much agitated and aroused," the reporter wrote. Among other things, Johnson said this: "If the Jewish people combine to defeat the immigration bill as reported by the Committee, their children will regret it."

There had never been even the slightest chance that the Jews—and the Italians and Greeks and Bulgarians, the Romanians and Poles and all the other groups targeted by the quota act—could defeat the bill. And for their children, their fate sealed by the obstinacy of law and the weight of history, that turned out to be far more regrettable than they, or Johnson, or anyone else involved in this saga could possibly have imagined.

Chapter Twelve

Without Foundation

On an April Sunday in the spring of 1924, a headline atop an article by Senator David Reed stretched across a full page of the *New York Times*: AMERICA OF THE MELTING POT COMES TO END. Only two months later the end became palpable to Secretary of Labor James Davis, when he visited Ellis Island and marveled at what looked, he said, "like a deserted village."

Of course it did. The Immigration Restriction Act of 1924, which depopulated Ellis Island as if by epidemic, marked the culmination of three decades of agitation and debate. The "carnival of exclusion" that the antirestrictionists had feared had reached its climactic moment.

A year later, Immigration Commissioner Henry Curran would say these immigrants were "of a better kind than have come here for twenty years." His explanation could not have been simpler: "They are better by reason of our new immigration law; the cause and effect are direct."

Whether the new immigrants were indeed "better" was debatable. Without question, though, they were fewer, vastly fewer. For decades the immigration story had been illustrated with stirring imagery: crowds jamming the decks of incoming ships (seen as liberty-loving new Americans by some, filthy intruders by more), families clutching the small valises and cloth bags containing everything they had not left behind (similarly perceived). But the Johnson-Reed Act changed that; now the tale was best told not with the emotional power of pictures but with the cold exactitude of numbers. They may appear dull and inanimate, but those numbers, if one makes the effort to absorb them, are breathtaking.

In 1914, the last year before the tumult of war disrupted the immigrant flow, more than 1.2 million Europeans had entered the country. Then the 1921 law instituted the first numerical cap, limiting total immigration to 368,000. The 1924 law sliced it further, to no more than 160,000. But all-inclusive numbers, as harsh as the may seem, are only prologue, for it is in the country-by-country enumeration that this particular drama found its resolution. The lands composing most of the Russian Empire sent 189,198 people to the United States in 1921; four years later, immigration from the primary successor nations (the Soviet Union, Poland, Lithuania) was reduced by the Johnson-Reed Act to a bare 7,346. Some 222,260 Italians entered the country in 1921; in 1925, under the new regulations, only 2,662 were admitted. Even these numbers do not fully illustrate how the larger immigration map had tilted. In the five years leading up to the war, the primary sources of southern and eastern European immigration (Italy and the Russian Empire) accounted for 35 percent of all new arrivals, whereas the chief northern and western European sources (Great Britain, Ireland, Germany) claimed just 12.6 percent of new admissions. Post-quota, those proportions were more than inverted—they were utterly transformed. The same southern/eastern grouping saw its share of new immigration cut by 90 percent; the northern/western percentage was more than doubled. Basing the quotas on the 1890 census—the census that had preceded most of the "unwanted" immigration—had worked with the precision of a diamond cutter.

Apart from the larger groups, the Scandinavians and French benefitted, while the Slavs and "Syrians"—the catchall term for a large chunk of the Muslim world—suffered. But as if it were an intentional demonstration of the cruelty of the 1890 cutoff, nothing matched the lacerating punishment visited upon Greeks who were trying to find their way to America. As severe as were the limits confronting the Italians and the eastern Europeans, the quotas did reflect the stable, if modest, stream of immigration from those countries in the years preceding 1890. But Greek immigration to the United States didn't accelerate meaningfully until after the turn of the century, when economic hardship and intensifying conflict with the Ottoman Empire led many Greeks to look westward. In the decade leading up to 1890, fewer than 2,000 Greeks entered the country (by way of comparison, more than a quarter of a million arrived from Italy in the same period). By 1914 the open door welcomed as many as 46,000 Greeks in a single year, but that was too late for a quota based on the 1890 census. The merciless mathematics of the quota limited Greece (a nation of more than five million people) to the statutory minimum that had been established for countries as tiny as Andorra (population 5,231): exactly one hundred souls a year.

This was what the anti-immigrant forces had wanted all along: a device that would hold the door open for those of their own ethnic heritage and nail it shut for those they despised. The restrictionists' fingerprints were all over the Johnson-Reed Act, but to charges of discrimination they could claim, however unconvincingly, that their hands were clean, for nowhere in the act's nearly ten thousand minutely detailed words could one find the terms "Italy" or "Italian," "Russia" or "Jew," "Greece" or "Greek," or any other proper-noun descriptors of the European peoples or nations the bill had targeted. At a dinner where Mary Harriman was honored with the Gold Medal of the National Institute of Social Sciences—an award whose future winners would include such figures as Jonas Salk, Henry Kissinger, and Golda Meir—Fairfield Osborn gave Harriman credit for the work of "two really great men," Harry Laughlin and Charles Davenport. They had helped lay the foundation, Osborn said, for the "wise, deliberate, well-informed action" that resulted in the "exclusion of citizens we cannot welcome to our country." Thanks to Harriman, he concluded, "We are tending toward the selection of the best, the exclusion of the worst."

Albert Johnson took his victory lap in New York, where he wanted to rest for a while. He asked John Trevor if he could spare a room. He said he wanted to spend time with Trevor, Charles Gould, and especially Madison Grant ("I would enjoy to the keenest degree listening to him," he told Trevor). Two months later, concluding his term as president of the Eugenics Research Association, Johnson traveled to Cold Spring Harbor for its twelfth annual meeting, where he addressed the gathered geneticists, biologists, and other scientists on "The National Immigration Policy." One ERA member wrote him afterward to say, "Honorable Sir, if we had more Congressmen interested in science as you are, we would in time have a country based on scientific facts."

Henry Cabot Lodge, ailing and rapidly aging at seventy-four, died six months after the Johnson-Reed Act was signed into law. One of his last statements on the subject was in his usual, unabashed public voice: the law was "a very great measure," he said, "one of the most important if not the most important congress has ever passed."

To say the battle was over would discredit the victors' continued vigilance. Madison Grant may have called the new law "an amazing triumph," but he also saw lingering weaknesses. For one thing, he believed that questionable types from countries with healthy quotas were nervily escaping rigid examination by "travelling second, or even first class." He also worried about Jews who "object to being exactly identified" and consequently "change their names [so they can] go freely back and forth."* The executive committee of the Immigration Restriction League remained on alert as various aspects of Johnson-Reed manifested themselves after its enactment. "Your committee does not believe in resting on the ground already gained," they had declared not two weeks after Coolidge signed the bill into law. "The enemy is still very much alive."

But the enemy didn't have a chance. After three strenuous decades of pushing their cause toward their hard-won victory, the restrictionists needed to do nothing more than play steady defense. As one IRL supporter would tell Joe Lee, "It is only necessary to defeat movements of repeal. The burden of proof is on the anti-restrictionists." The antis were like medical officials facing an epidemic armed with nothing but aspirin, barely able to keep the xenophobic fever from spiking further. Determined to silence discussion of any alterations to the now established National Origins principle, Albert Johnson threatened to cut the quotas in half. He also proposed a constitutional amendment denying citizenship to the American-born children of aliens. To Trevor, Johnson suggested a further step, as diabolical as it was imaginative: all new arrivals would be required to have a valid passport. But because the United States did not have diplomatic relations with the Soviet Union, the passports of immigrants from Russia, Lithuania, Ukraine, and all the other Soviet states would per se be invalid.

John Trevor pushed forward for further restriction through two organizations he dominated, the Citizens Committee on Immigration Legislation and the American Coalition of Patriotic Societies. The

* In New York, the *Tribune* had reported that the courts had disallowed the wish of sixteen Kannofskys to become Kenyons, and a Pavlovsky was not allowed to become a Pawley. Philadelphia courts were more lenient, letting Harry and Myrtle Kabatchnick change their surname to Cabot. This led to an alteration of the familiar Boston quatrain, "And this is good old Boston, / The home of the bean and the cod, / Where the Lowells talk only to Cabots / And the Cabots talk only to God." The new version replaced the last two lines with, "Where the Lowells have no one to talk to, / Since the Cabots speak Yiddish, by God."

latter's primary goals, he said, were "to save the Immigration Act of 1924" and serve as "a watch-dog against pernicious legislation" in the battle against "pacifists and communists." Trevor's organizations attracted the usual suspects, including Laughlin, Grant, Charles Gould, and those old Boston warriors from the Immigration Restriction League, Robert Ward and Richards Bradley. Though several among them were capable of supporting the groups' activities, Trevor largely financed them out of his own pocket—buttressed by secret support from his old friend John D. Rockefeller Jr. Liberal, internationalist, the very exemplar of modern Christian charity, Rockefeller showered Trevor with contributions, each accompanied by words of praise for "the splendid work you are doing," "this important enterprise," "because I believe in the far-reaching value of the work." But in none of those letters did Rockefeller mention the *nature* of the work. Nor, by prior agreement with Trevor, did his name ever appear on any list of contributors. Most tellingly, in no way was his support visible: Rockefeller's money (the 2019 equivalent of more than $150,000 a year) came not from his usual accounts but in the form of cashier's checks, anonymous and untraceable.

In his 1928 presidential campaign, New York governor Al Smith (half Irish, one-quarter German, one-quarter Italian) opposed the National Origins policy and the use of the 1890 census. So, to a degree, did his victorious opponent, Herbert Hoover. But it made no difference. Emigrants from quota-limited nations were compelled to look elsewhere. Long a favored destination for emigrating Italians, Argentina saw its incoming numbers from Italy increase just as the U.S.-bound route was closed. Jews, too, flocked to Argentina, which maintained an absolute open-door immigration policy through the 1920s. They found Brazil even more welcoming: between 1926 and 1930, Jewish immigration to Brazil, largely from Poland, tripled from that of the previous five years and increased tenfold relative to the last five years before passage of the 1921 Emergency Act. Because of the five-year residency requirement enacted in 1922, Brazil was no longer a layover on the way to America. It was a destination.

Among other manifestations of the restrictionists' triumphalist mood was the intensification of anti-Asian activity. The Johnson-Reed Act abrogated Theodore Roosevelt's "Gentlemen's Agreement" with Japan, imposing on the Japanese a quota so low it could only be considered ridiculous: the same minimum quota of one hundred immigrants a year allotted to the tiniest countries of Europe was applied to every Asian nation, no matter how large.* Worse, because Asians not born in the United States were excluded from citizenship, the hundred-person-per-country limit improbably accommodated only whites (or blacks) from Asian nations; Johnson had told Grant he liked the idea because "it could eliminate Japanese and other Orientals without the use of any words" specifically targeting them. Historian Mae M. Ngai's description is succinct: Congress had "created the oddity of immigration quotas for non-Chinese persons of China, non-Japanese persons of Japan, non-Indian persons of India, and so on."

The era's extravagantly liberated race hatred was also the only explanation for the federal government's interest in hunting down people of Indian origin and stripping them of their citizenship, a cathartic purge that began in the aftermath of the Supreme Court's decision in the *Thind* case. Among the individuals who met this fate was Vaishno Das Bagai, a San Francisco shopkeeper originally from India who was denaturalized in 1928 after thirteen years in the United States, seven as a citizen. "I came to America thinking, dreaming and hoping to make this land my home," Bagai wrote in a letter he sent to the *San Francisco Examiner*, ". . . but they now come to me and say, I am no longer an American citizen." It was not just a letter to the editor; it was Bagai's suicide note.

* The Japanese government's alarmed opposition to the invalidation of the agreement—its ambassador to the United States had warned of "grave consequences"—was a major accelerant in the downward spiral in U.S.-Japanese relations that would plummet to its fateful conclusion at Pearl Harbor in 1941.

For advocates of the open door, the only positive glimmer in the nativist frenzy was a particularly perverse law enacted by Congress in 1928. American women abroad who had lost their citizenship by marrying aliens were now allowed to return to the United States outside of the quota—but only if they had been widowed or divorced.

* * *

THE EUGENICS MOVEMENT, running mate to the anti-immigration crusade, was similarly ascendant in the midtwenties. It took its most malign form in Harry Laughlin's continuing campaign for eugenic sterilization. The American practice of involuntary vasectomy or tubal ligation of prisoners, mental asylum inmates, and others "under state control" had first become sanctioned by law in Indiana, in 1907. Other states followed suit; opponents organized; proponents lobbied. Then, in 1924, just weeks before eugenicists were to celebrate the adoption of the Johnson-Reed Act, a version of Laughlin's model sterilization law was adopted by Virginia. Three years later, in *Buck v. Bell*, a near-unanimous Supreme Court, including Louis Brandeis, signed on to a notorious decision by the great liberal jurist Oliver Wendell Holmes Jr. upholding the Virginia law. "Three generations of imbeciles is enough," Holmes famously wrote. By 1970 at least sixty thousand Americans had been compelled to submit to the surgeon's legally sanctioned knife.*

Eugenic thinking in forms both mundane and grand increasingly stained the definition of America. "If you visit the United States," the French academician André Siegfried wrote after a 1925 tour,

---

* The court's one dissenting vote came from Associate Justice Pierce Butler. He wrote no opinion, nor did he describe his view in any surviving documents. However, it's not unreasonable to think that Butler, the court's only Catholic, was motivated at least in part by his religious beliefs, which would not countenance any kind of birth control. Before the court arrived at its decision, Holmes told another justice, "Butler knows this is good law. I wonder whether he will have the courage to vote with us in spite of his religion."

"you must not forget your Bible, but you must also take a treatise on eugenics. Armed with these two talismans, you will never get beyond your depth." The chief evangelist brandishing the second talisman was the American Eugenics Society, a sort-of-successor to the Eugenics Committee of the United States of America. The AES evinced less concern with immigration—by this point, it didn't really have to—than with a wide array of domestic issues. Its board and its advisory committee were versions of the ECUSA's, but where the ECUSA had focused most of its attention on Congress and other political arenas, the AES pursued broader aims, employing a wide range of propaganda techniques to spread its gospel. New funding for these efforts came from photography innovator George Eastman, who contributed the 2019 equivalent of more than $150,000 a year, and from John D. Rockefeller Jr., who for several years was good for half that much.

The AES's most popular endeavor might have been the Fitter Families exhibitions it sponsored at innumerable county and state fairs. These successors to the Better Babies events of the previous decade offered marionette shows meant to explain Mendelian genetics, posters declaiming such slogans as "Some People Are Born to Be a Burden on the Rest," and eugenic lessons from "Cho-Cho the Health Clown." The most thrilling moment at each fair was the selection of eugenically superior families, a ritual all but guaranteed to win prominent coverage in local newspapers. Physical and "psychometric" examinations conducted by such experts as Dr. James Naismith (the inventor of basketball) and noted psychiatrist Karl Menninger determined the winners. "While the stock judges are testing the Holsteins, Jerseys, and whitefaces in the stock pavilion," said one of the originators of the Fitter Families program, "we are judging the Joneses, the Smiths, and the Johnsons." Newspaper photographs showed the winning families—always smiling, unusually hearty, usually blond—receiving a bronze medal inscribed "Yea, I have a goodly heritage." The quotation was from Psalms; the medal's design, showing a classically dressed couple passing a torch to a robust child, was executed by Madison Grant.

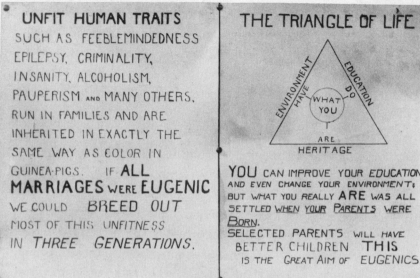

A poster from a Fitter Families event in Kansas, 1926.

Other AES efforts included essay contests on various topics. One competition addressed the decline in Nordic fertility, another—specifically for sermons—recognized such finalists as Harry H. Mayer, a Kansas City rabbi of German origin, who told his congregants, "May we do nothing to permit our blood to be adulterated by infusion of blood of inferior grade." Leaflets headlined "What I Think About Eugenics" carried ringing endorsements of AES efforts (from W. H. P. Faunce, president of Brown University: "To neglect eugenics today is to neglect the whole future of humanity and to insure catastrophe"). The AES's presence at the 1926 Philadelphia world's fair, an event dedicated to the sesquicentennial of American independence, featured a sign that turned the viewer's attention from the nation's past to its future: "How long are we Americans to be so careful for the pedigree of our pigs and chickens and cattle—and then leave the *ancestry of our children* to chance or blind sentiment?" A display of flashing lights at another AES exhibit illustrated the consequences of heedless breeding: "a high grade person" was born every seven and a half minutes, fairgoers learned, a mentally deficient one every forty-eight seconds. The AES's full-time executive director, a former orchard-supply salesman from Massachusetts named Leon F. Whitney, wrote *A Eugenics Catechism*, which the organization distributed in schools and churches across the country. A sample dialogue from the *Catechism*: "Q. Why sterilize? A. To rid the race of those likely to transmit the dysgenic tendencies to which they are subject. To decrease the need for charity of a certain form. To reduce taxes. To help alleviate misery and suffering. To do what Nature would do under natural conditions, but more humanely. Sterilization is not a punitive measure. It is strictly protective."

Beyond the AES, a variety of individuals and institutions of disparate politics grew ever bolder about declaring their eugenic faith. The state of Oregon had a eugenics commissioner, charged with locating the socially deficient and isolating them. The progressive education journal *School and Society* published an article describing a eugenic society so exquisitely stratified that even though some people would only be "fit to be hewers of wood," they would be so perfectly fit they would necessarily be "expert hewers." Margaret Sanger, intensifying the symbiotic alliances she had forged with eugenicist organizations and activists, now invoked the army intelligence tests to further her cause and hailed the results of the new immigration law's efficacy in the struggle "to control the quality of our population." Writing in the *Birth Control Review* under the headline A SOCIALIST'S VIEWPOINT, Norman Thomas found "reason for alarm in the high birthrate of definitely inferior stock." C. W. Eliot, long retired from the Harvard presidency but still a visible and influential public voice, may have been a stalwart supporter of open immigration, but eugenic ideology had come to cramp his view of the melting pot.

Though he despised the Jewish quota imposed by his Harvard successor, Lawrence Lowell, Eliot based his personal campaign against assimilation on an insistence that American society would be best off if the Irish married only the Irish, Jews married only the Jews, and so on, the alternative being "a state of things to be dreaded." He even adopted an unsubstantiated canard that bounced around the eugenics community for years: "You know that it is well determined by the biologists that the Jewish race is to an extraordinary degree pre-potent, that is, if a Jew marries a woman of another race, in two, at any rate in three generations, all the children will look like Jews, all of them."

In academic circles one of the most bizarre examples of eugenic thinking was an exploration along the shores of positive eugenics that was engineered by AES advisory council member Lewis Terman. His continued work on intelligence testing (particularly his development of the standard Americanized version of the Binet-Simon intelligence test) had greatly enlarged Terman's public profile and his scholarly influence. Seeking to determine, among other things, the heritability of genius, he initiated an influential and long-lived longitudinal study officially called *Genetic Studies of Genius*, and colloquially known as the Terman Study of the Gifted. (Nearly one hundred years later, psychologists and other investigators were still making use of—and arguing about—Terman's data.) A 1926 by-product of the study could have been the direct offspring of both Francis Galton's earliest work and the specious mini-biographies published in the *Eugenical News*. Working from a list of "1,000 men of unquestioned eminence" that another researcher had compiled—largely by measuring space granted to them in biographical dictionaries—Terman and his associate Catharine Morris Cox contrived to determine the IQs of nearly three hundred historical figures, relying on sources equally questionable (memoirs by relatives, contemporary biographies) and standards equally risible ("parental standing," "pure-mindedness," "neatness, accuracy, attention to detail").

Entitled *The Early Mental Traits of 300 Geniuses*, this was the study that set the seventeen-year-old Galton's IQ at nearly 200. Given Terman's substantial credentials and the imprimatur of the Stanford University Press, news coverage was ensured; one account began, "Giving 301 of the geniuses of history an intelligence test is the latest feat of scientists at Stanford University." The book was a lamentable example of how the eugenics mania had pushed scholarship to the realm of the berserk: Young John Quincy Adams's IQ, the researchers concluded, was 165 (he got points for becoming his father's private secretary at fourteen), Lincoln's only 125. Robert E. Lee weighed in at 130, U. S. Grant at a mere 110. And so it went, Charlotte Brontë (one of the very few women in the book) 155, Robert Burns 130, Hernán Cortés 115. Cervantes (105) was marked down because his father was "a medical practitioner of little authority and without the training of a physician." Raphael was adjudged to have had an IQ of 110 as a seventeen-year-old, but his "precocious power as an interpreter of human character," among other things, lifted him to 150 by the time he was twenty-six. Robespierre began adulthood at 135 but matured to an imposing 145; it was hard to know from the Terman-Cox study whether he gained or lost points for engineering the slaughter of innocents.

But for all its ascendancy, eugenic thought was not without increasingly notable detractors, including some who had earlier bought into, and in a few particularly influential cases had promoted, some of its central tenets.

After the enactment of the Johnson-Reed Act, Herbert Jennings, whose critique of Harry Laughlin's work had failed to influence the immigration debate in Congress, renewed his correspondence with Irving Fisher, the Yale economist who was chairman of the AES's predecessor organization, the Eugenics Council of the United States of America. Jennings had been engaged in the academic study of eugenics for years. In 1921 he was part of the organizing committee for Osborn's Second International Congress of Eugenics. He supported the eugenic sterilization of "defectives." His friendship with Charles Davenport went back a quarter of a century. But Jennings had been rattled by the way Fisher and the other members of the ECUSA executive committee—among them Fairfield Osborn, Madison Grant, and Davenport—had ignored his plea to disavow their endorsement of Laughlin's grievously inaccurate and dishonest testimony.

Jennings now told Fisher that he had come to realize that the ECUSA's reason for being was the dissemination of propaganda. He said that having an advocate of "Nordic supremacy"—Grant—as chairman of the immigration committee was especially egregious. "It is on these grounds," he told Fisher, "that I have decided not to renew my membership" in the group.

Fisher tried to dissuade him. "Our committee did succeed in getting into the public consciousness the idea that an important principle for sifting immigrants should be eugenics," he wrote. "In the end . . . the thought is being held by millions of people who never thought of it before." Without eugenics, Fisher concluded, America was "certain to go to hell." Jennings, unmoved, told Fisher he had finally chosen to heed the words of William Bateson: "No man of science can afford to have anything to do with a Eugenics Society."

The next important scholar to distance himself from a race-based version of eugenics was Jennings's Johns Hopkins colleague Raymond Pearl, one of the original researchers on Davenport's staff at Cold Spring Harbor and an outspoken advocate of eugenics for nearly two decades. (It was Pearl who in 1918 had told an associate that discrimination against Jews was "a necessary move in the struggle for existence.") The venue Pearl chose for his recantation was the *American Mercury*, the iconoclastic, grenade-launching monthly edited by his close friend H. L. Mencken. Setting aside his personal distaste for Jews and other immigrants, Pearl explained in his *Mercury* article how he had come to see that the bright promises of the early eugenicists had devolved into "a mingled mess of ill-grounded and uncritical sociology, economics, anthropology, and politics, full of emotional appeals to class prejudice, solemnly put forth as science." He invoked Plato, cited Mendel, and elucidated the discoveries of modern geneticists, including Jennings: "Superior" people often have "inferior" children, Pearl argued, and vice versa. Trying to change the "race" would take unimaginable generations of planned reproduction. Environmental influences are often more potent than genetic ones. "The orthodox eugenists," he argued, "are going contrary to the best established facts" of modern genetics. As a young scientist, Pearl had affirmed Galton's call to lift eugenics to the level of national religion. Now he found the public advocacy, the "legislative enactments," and the "moral fervor" of the entire movement to be "as outworn and useless as the rind of yesterday's melon."

Around the same time, leading academic institutions began to move away from any broad acceptance of eugenics. Harvard, notably, rejected a large bequest from the estate of surgeon J. Ewing Mears, who had wanted to underwrite a department of eugenics. At Columbia, Franz Boas had become the dominant figure in the anthropology department—in all of American anthropology, actually—and Darwin medalist Thomas Hunt Morgan, who had long believed eugenics was supported by "no real scientific evidence," dominated the university's genetic research. Morgan soon extended his influence by founding a department of genetics at Caltech.

In 1928 another insider delivered a blow to the eugenics movement when Henry Goddard, whose Kallikak study had been so influential and whose coinage of the word "moron" had been so useful, declared, "I think I have gone over to the enemy." His retraction was by no means complete, but an essential part was categorical: "It may still be objected that moron parents are likely to have imbecile or idiot children. There is not much evidence that this is the case. The danger is probably negligible. At least it is not likely to occur any oftener than it does in the general population." At another point, commenting on the works of Grant and Stoddard, he demurred forcibly: "The difference in humans," his notes read, "is *intellectual* not *racial*."

Finally, what might have appeared to be the knockout punch came from someone far more important to the anti-immigration movement than Goddard. Nine years after the fateful dinner on Washington Square that made him the willing cat's-paw of Madison Grant and Charles Gould, Carl Brigham declared that *A Study of American Intelligence*—the book they had sponsored, that Brigham had used to vault himself into national prominence and that had provided the most imposingly credentialed justification for the theory of genetic differences expressed by nationality—was wrong.

No lightning bolt of recognition prompted Brigham to recant. Two years after the new law narrowed the immigration portal to a faintly perceptible sliver, he expressed the concern that "any system of geographical selection is a stupid one when applied to picking an individual." He said he wanted to allow "persons of outstanding promise or talent" to enter the country, irrespective of quotas. The following year he declined Lewis Terman's request to speak at a conference on intelligence testing; wrote Nicholas Lemann in his book about Brigham and the Scholastic Aptitude Test, Brigham "saw that the movement was dominated by those who began with their conclusions and then set out to do research that proved them."

Then, in March 1930, Brigham made his repudiation of his own work complete, in the pages of *Psychological Review*, his profession's most prominent academic journal. His reasons were manifold: No entirely fair test, he maintained, could be applied to individuals brought up in different homes, much less in different countries. The language of testing was inexact, even malleable, and would necessarily be apprehended differently by different people. Because intelligence was not a single, unitary, inheritable trait, there was no effective way of quantifying it. He had based his book's combustible conclusions on Yerkes's army tests, but given what he now knew, "that study with its entire hypothetical superstructure of racial differences collapses completely." In the years ahead, Brigham would continue his assault. "The 'native intelligence' hypothesis is dead," he wrote in 1934. "It is ridiculous to claim that any test score is related" to genetic inheritance, he told the *New York Times* four years later. The concept of IQ itself, at least insofar as it was a pure measure of something embedded in a person's biological makeup, was "fallacious."

But it was in that 1930 article in *Psychological Review* that Brigham had made his convictions clearest and his repudiation of his own work definitive. Back in 1923, when discussion of permanent immigration legislation was at full boil, he had said that his data "clearly indicate the intellectual superiority of the Nordic race group" and that the decline of American intelligence "will proceed with an accelerating rate as the racial admixture becomes more and more extensive." In 1930, however, addressing "comparative studies of various national and racial groups," he concluded with this: "One of the most pretentious of these comparative racial studies—the writer's own—was without foundation."

The shock contained in Brigham's knockout punch was that it shocked no one—it was a phantom, making contact only with a void, its impact on policy and public debate negligible. The well-matched pair of beliefs that had combined to initiate a radical change in the makeup of the American population—eugenics and an ethnically biased nationalism—continued their dominance, fully embedded in the prevailing cultural reality. Witness the comments of diplomat George Kennan early in his distinguished career as an independent voice in the American foreign policy establishment. Looking at the state of the nation and the planet, he wrote, "Nothing good can come out of modern civilization, in the broad sense. We have only a group of more or less inferior races incapable of coping adequately with the environment which technical progress has created. This situation is essentially a biological one. No amount of education and discipline can effectively improve conditions as long as we allow the unfit to breed copiously and to preserve their young."

Kennan, at the time third secretary of the American legation in Riga, Latvia, confided these thoughts to his diary on July 13, 1932. Less than three weeks later, just five hundred miles to the southwest, in Berlin, the Nazi Party won a plurality of seats in the Reichstag.

*   *   *

THE MONSTROUS VILLAINY of the extermination camps was nearly a decade in the future when Adolf Hitler assumed the German chancellorship in January 1933. But no one who had paid attention to his rise could have been surprised by the malignant policies and programs that metastasized in the early years of Nazi rule. It was a long and ominous list: Brutal laws eviscerating the rights of Jews. The establishment of "genetic courts" with the authority to order involuntary sterilization of those found eugenically wanting. Euthanasia policies that mandated the state-sponsored murder of tens of thousands. Heinrich Himmler's *lebensborn* program, which bred his elite SS troops with teenage girls of suitable Aryan pedigree, then subsidized the upbringing of their eugenically propitious progeny.

Each of these was a radical perversion of Francis Galton's original theories, as seen through racist lenses provided by Arthur Gobineau and Houston Stewart Chamberlain. The very idea of eugenics as social policy had at last been transformed into the national religion that burned so brightly, and fatefully, in Galton's dreams. At a 1934 rally, Hitler's deputy, Rudolf Hess, declared that "National Socialism is nothing but applied biology," and no one, in Germany or elsewhere, could plausibly argue otherwise—even if the particular biological principles invoked by the Nazis were hateful, and rotten, and wrong.

But the celebration of the "Nordic Ideal" that prefigured the doom of millions did not rely solely on this perverse form of Galtonism. It located, and earnestly acknowledged, some of its roots in the politicized American expression of eugenics. Walter Schultze had been associated with Hitler even before the Munich Beer Hall Putsch of

1923. He was a physician, an educator, and a ranking member of the fearsome SA—the storm troopers. In an article that appeared in a Nazi publication just before the party took control of the government, Schultze called for German geneticists to heed the example of the United States. Its immigration laws and the sterilization campaign, he wrote, had demonstrated that in America, "racial policy and thinking have become much more popular than in other countries."

To Nazi eugenicists who soon moved into positions of power, this was not exactly a news bulletin. In the hallowed pages of *Mein Kampf* (first published in 1925, just one year after the passage of the Johnson-Reed Act), Hitler saluted the United States as the "one state in which at least weak beginnings toward a better conception of [citizenship] are noticeable"—among them, "simply excluding certain races from naturalization." A decade later the official Nazi *Handbook for Law and Legislation* would specifically cite American immigration law as a model for Germany. And another volume published in Germany the same year as *Mein Kampf* provided further American-made inspiration for the Nazis: *The Passing of the Great Race*. ("It seems strange that after a silence of about seven years there should be this sudden excitement in Germany over my book," Madison Grant had told Maxwell Perkins while Hitler's supporters were agitating for their leader's release from prison in 1924.) Hitler studied *Passing* enthusiastically, cited it in speeches and other writings, and at the time of his suicide in the Berlin bunker in 1945 still owned a copy of the original German edition, "warmly inscribed" to him by its German publisher.*

Party ideologist Alfred Rosenberg was another Nazi enthralled by Grant. If Rosenberg's *The Myth of the Twentieth Century* was, as

---

* Several historians and other scholars have noted that Leon Whitney of the American Eugenics Society claimed in an unpublished memoir that Grant once showed him a personal letter from Hitler thanking him for writing *Passing*. Another memoirist—Grant's brother's stepson—asserted that Uncle Madison was proud that Hitler had *banned* the book. The former seems somewhat more likely to be true than the latter, but not by much.

sociologist E. Digby Baltzell described it, the Nazis'"new testament," it came with its own set of American prophets: Rosenberg encouraged the United States—"the magnificent land of the future"—to "proceed with youthful strength to set up the new idea of the racial state, such as some awakened Americans have already apprehended, like Grant and [Lothrop] Stoddard." The Nazi "race pope," Hans F. K. Günther, had the same heroes, calling Grant and Stoddard the "spiritual fathers" of immigration laws that should be a model for Nazi Germany. In Günther's *The Racial Elements of European History*, he featured a photograph of a noble bronze bust of Grant that had been commissioned by Fairfield Osborn. *Racial Elements* was published in 1927, three years after Maxwell Perkins had suggested to Lothrop Stoddard that "Guenther and his crowd are the best people" to help promote *The Revolt Against Civilization*.

*   *   *

CHARLES DAVENPORT WAS PRESIDENT of the Third International Congress on Eugenics that convened in New York in the summer of 1932. Much had happened in the eugenics world since the previous congress eleven years earlier, but Davenport's prominence had not diminished, even if his influence had begun to lessen. He was sixty-six years old. His laboratories and his data collection operation at Cold Spring Harbor remained eugenic shrines. But he had ceded a great deal of authority to Harry Laughlin and had reluctantly agreed to the selection of Dr. Clarence G. Campbell, a prominent Manhattan socialite and an even more prominent anti-Semite, as president of the Cold Spring–based Eugenics Research Association.

By the time the world's eugenicists gathered once again in Fairfield Osborn's museum that August, the intellectual movement Davenport had launched three decades earlier had completed its maturation process. The evolution of American eugenics seemed, in retrospect, to have been almost preordained, its grand claims having proven to be as useful in practice as they had been unsupported by fact—applied biology at its most pernicious. The progressives who had promoted the eugenics cause had mostly abandoned it, and reactionaries like John Trevor, Charles Gould, and Clarence Campbell had stepped into the breach. Busts of Galton and Darwin flanked the entrance to the congress's meeting rooms, but the scientific racists and their camp followers had the current historical moment on their minds. Grant, Laughlin, Leon Whitney, and Campbell—a majority of the congress's managing committee—were high in the saddle. Davenport was their stooge, apparently oblivious to the explosive situation in Germany in that troubled summer. He said he missed the presence of several of his German colleagues, including the anthropologist Eugen Fischer, who was the lead author of *Human Heredity and Race Hygiene*, and German psychiatrist Ernst Rüdin. When Rüdin was elected to succeed him as president of the International Federation of Eugenic Organizations, Davenport wrote to his old friend Alfred Ploetz, founder of the German Society for Racial Hygiene. Sharing the news of Rüdin's election, Davenport couldn't have been more direct: "Personally," he told Ploetz, "I am very glad the Federation is under the *Leitung*"—the management—"of a German."

By then, German eugenicists and their American counterparts had been intricately involved with one another for more than two decades, sharing research, reading and commenting on each other's books and articles, building personal relationships by correspondence and sometimes face-to-face. Now their connections would be tested by the Nazis' assumption of power and their passionate attachments to some of the most basic elements of the eugenic faith.

As the leading figure in American eugenic science, Davenport had engaged the Germans as far back as 1908, when he exchanged information on the heritability of hair and eye color with Fischer, and again in 1911, when he began a correspondence with Rüdin, who was assembling materials for a eugenics exhibit. The transatlantic relationships flourished along with each man's career. When Fischer

became head of the Kaiser Wilhelm Institute, the German coun-
terpart to Davenport's domain in Cold Spring Harbor, Davenport
traveled to Berlin for its official opening. Rüdin and Davenport met
in 1923 at an international eugenics conference in Vienna, and Rüdin
made a pilgrimage to Cold Spring Harbor in 1930.

There is nothing in either Fischer's or Rüdin's extensive correspondence with Davenport that suggests thoughts tending toward
the Hitlerian. The question of whether it was hardened conviction or
mere opportunism that impelled Fischer and Rüdin to play critical
scientific roles in the Nazis' institutionalized brutality was mooted
by their actions. In 1932 Rüdin wrote to Davenport lamenting the
difficult situation for eugenic research in Germany—but less than
a year later he was the primary author of a Nazi sterilization law
directed, he would say, at "valueless individuals." The same year,
Fischer was collaborating with Davenport on studies of human
hybridization through race-crossing—but within six months of
Hitler's ascension he was named the rector of the University of
Berlin, and in his inaugural address declared, "What Darwin was
not able to do, genetics has achieved. It has destroyed the theory of
the equality of man."

In a 1933 speech to Nazi doctors Hitler said, "I cannot do without
you for a single day, not a single hour. If not for you, if you fail me,
then all is lost." Both Rüdin and Fischer would more than oblige
him. "Only through [Hitler's] work," said Rüdin, "has our 30-year-
long dream of translating race hygiene into action finally become
a reality." The feelings were mutual. When Hitler marked Rüdin's
sixty-fifth birthday in 1939 by awarding him a medal for his notable
accomplishments, Interior Minister Wilhelm Frick hailed him as "the
indefatigable champion of racial hygiene and meritorious pioneer of
the racial-hygienic measures of the Third Reich." Fischer penetrated
even farther into the fetid corners of Nazism. In 1941 he was guest
of honor, along with the rabid Hans Günther, at the opening of the
Institute for the Investigation of the Jewish Question, in Frankfurt.

And in 1943, as the smoke and horror from the death camps darkened the continent, Fischer identified eugenic theory as a central pillar of Nazi philosophy: "It is a rare and special good fortune for a theoretical science to flourish at a time when the prevailing ideology welcomes it," he wrote, "and its findings can immediately serve the policy of the state."

As early as 1928 Charles Davenport had begun—privately—to turn away from the racialized version of eugenics, even as he studied miscegenation and related subjects. Writing to Leonard Darwin about an international genetics conference he had attended, he expressed his dismay over the influence of racial theorists. "Inferior and superior races were spoken of and the superiority of the Nordic race emphasized," he wrote, complaining that such arguments were "not objective and merely an expression of personal opinion." In 1930 he would not allow the *Eugenical News* to publish a letter Grant had received from Hans Günther, and the following year he advised a young demographer—Fairfield Osborn's nephew, as it happened—that "we have very little precise information" on the inheritance of human traits and "are only slowly understanding the way in which the genes control development."

Davenport could still lapse into the retrograde language of the restriction movement. He despised Franklin Roosevelt, and in the bleakest days of the Great Depression he lifted a Spencerian cudgel, telling an associate that welfare agencies were a "force crushing out civilization." He never severed his associations with Grant, Osborn, and Laughlin. But neither did Davenport follow his German colleagues into their romance with Nazism. His correspondence with Eugen Fischer stopped in July 1933, with Ernst Rüdin two months later. He did contribute to a festschrift in Fischer's honor in 1934, but his article was a brief and innocuous discussion of physical traits in developing fetuses—leg length, breadth of nasal cartilage, and the like; similar engagements in the 1930s indicated a blandly naive willingness to believe that scientific inquiry among German eugenicists was distinct from Nazi policy. He generally retreated from the political issues in which he had earlier been enmeshed, and made clear to associates that what was happening in Germany was a series of "shocking violations of elementary human rights." In 1933 he provided a scholarly home for the young German Jewish geneticist Curt Stern, who had decided he could not safely return to Berlin. Writing to Franz Boas in 1935, Davenport joined an effort to help a German Jewish biometrician remain in the United States, and he enlisted Boas in at least one similar case a few years later.

Still, as remnants of the American eugenics movement took up Nazism as their own cause, Davenport—unlike several of his old allies in the scientific racism movement—did not reconsider his own contributions, witting or otherwise, to a movement that had turned in so horrifying a direction. Raymond Pearl may have held on to his own ethnic prejudices, but in his 1927 recantation he divorced them from scholarly claims. Three years later Carl Brigham's abject retraction had been the intellectual equivalent of public self-flagellation. Then the rise of Hitler compelled even Edward A. Ross, the flamboyant Wisconsin sociologist who had coined "race suicide," spoken of "race superiority," and blithely enumerated the specific "racial" traits of some seventeen different nationalities, to disown the most noteworthy phase of his career. His introduction to Popenoe and Johnson's *Applied Eugenics*, where he had so firmly expressed his "fear of racial decline," did not appear in the 1935 edition. Instead, in a memoir published the next year, Ross said he had awakened "to the fallacy of rating peoples according to the grade of their culture." Recalling his 1904 description of "beaten members of beaten breeds," Ross disowned it: "I rue this sneer," he wrote. With time and reflection, he continued, he had "gained insight and sympathy until my heart overleapt barriers of race." Now, "far behind me in the ditch lies the Nordic Myth."

But Davenport never publicly disavowed scientific racism. He either didn't recognize his own role in the rise of racialized eugenics or couldn't allow himself to acknowledge it. The simple promises of eugenic theory that had excited him as a young scientist continued to thrill him, but also to blind him.

As the aging Davenport receded into the background, and as the sound of goose-stepping boots echoed from across the ocean, the American eugenics movement became a Hitlerite fifth column. Leon Whitney, still the paid director of the American Eugenics Society, hailed Nazi plans to sterilize four hundred thousand Germans and called Americans working toward similar goals "far-sighted." The Eugenics Research Association, now controlled by Clarence Campbell and Harry Laughlin, extended membership to both Rüdin and Fischer just as both men proclaimed their public support for the savagely anti-Semitic Nuremberg Laws and other Nazi depredations. In the *Journal of Heredity*, Paul Popenoe, the coauthor of the standard eugenics textbook, published an article praising Hitler—"though a bachelor"—for his program of "race betterment through eugenic measures."

By the time Davenport retired from the Carnegie Institution in 1934, at sixty-eight, he was a relic, an ancient tree from the garden of eugenic Eden. He told a colleague that "eternal change, rather than order, is heaven's first law." But the actions of three men who had never for a moment struggled with the connection between eugenics and racism disproved Davenport's heavenly law. Fairfield Osborn, Madison Grant, and Harry Laughlin had not changed at all. The rise of Hitler only confirmed them in their belief that they had long been marching in the right direction.

Osborn had recruited Campbell, his friend and neighbor, into the movement and had tapped him for leadership when the Eugenics Research Association was looking for a new president. ("Nothing is going to stop the Germans in squelching the Jews," Campbell once told Grant, "and they are going to treat them RIGHT.") In 1934 Osborn traveled to Frankfurt to accept an honorary degree from the Johann Wilhelm Goethe University, well into the official *Säuberung* —"cleansing"—of Jews from the faculty. When a British scholar challenged the increasingly evident anti-Semitism in the Galton Society and the *Eugenical News*—now in the hands of the Nazi sympathizers and only tenuously connected to the Carnegie Institution—Osborn bristled: because American newspapers were controlled by Jewish advertisers, he said, "they tell our people all that is bad about Nazism and omit all that is good." He encouraged zoologist William K. Gregory, his right-hand man at the American Museum of Natural History, to see for himself, urging him to travel to Germany "and freely mingle with these wonderful people who have so much to teach us." By that point the Nazis had already burned twenty-five thousand "un-German" books (including those by Osborn's former colleague Franz Boas), banned all political parties, and excluded Jews from the civil service.

Much as he might have liked to, Madison Grant couldn't travel to Germany to observe in person the practical application of his theories. His arthritis had worsened to such a degree that he was frequently confined to a wheelchair. But Grant's passions had not dissipated at all, and his engagement with German racists blossomed long distance. In 1933, returning to Scribner and Max Perkins, he published *The Conquest of a Continent*, an application of his race theories to the history of North America. One of Scribner's promotional letters for the book advised readers to recognize that "national problems today are, at bottom, race problems. Herr Hitler has stated that problem for Germany—and is working out his own solution. We in America have our own problem." Grant's book, presumably, provided the American solution. At Grant's request Scribner also sent copies of the book to Alfred Rosenberg, Eugen Fischer, and other prominent Hitlerites. Scribner officials may have been increasingly put-upon by Grant's persistent nagging about sales and promotion, but when the book proved a commercial flop, Perkins lamented that it "deserves much greater success than it has had." He told Grant, "the trouble with reviewers is simply that all of them today happen to be from those races whose prejudice runs counter to the book." A few months later, though, Perkins suggested that there was good news around the corner: reviews in England were certain to be better, he told Grant, because "the Jews are less powerful there than here."

Harry Laughlin, whose stature among the scientific racists rose at the same time that his relationship with Davenport had entered something of a decline, developed warm and productive associations with various agents of Nazi race policy, many of whom he had first connected with during the 1920s, when he was the American herald of involuntary sterilization. A foul stream of articles that might have come directly from the office of Nazi propaganda chief Joseph Goebbels began to fill the pages of the *Eugenical News*, now increasingly dependent on the editorial leadership of Laughlin (and the financial support of Campbell, Grant, and their allies). Articles Laughlin wrote or selected for publication included "Eugenical Sterilization in Germany," which celebrated the Nazi "recognition of the biological foundations of national character"; a reprint of Nazi interior minister Wilhelm Frick's speech on "race hygiene in the service of the State" (said Laughlin, "Dr. Frick's address sounds exactly as though spoken by a perfectly good American eugenicist"); "Jewish Physicians in Berlin" (this was a letter from Alfred Ploetz, who said the many Jewish doctors who had already left Germany had not been "expelled," but had emigrated on their own "because they feared, unjustly, a pogrom"); and a long, enthusiastic review of a book by Hans Günther on "the moral and racial ideals of the New Germany." Clarence Campbell, in "The German Race Policy," hailed Nazi efforts to "attain the greater purity of racial stocks." The journal even reprinted a letter from French race supremacist Georges Vacher de Lapouge to his friend Madison Grant, complaining that things had come to such a terrible pass in France that it was "'raining' German Jews," no doubt because of the Nazis' "splendid example of an attempt at a solution." Several months later, the *News* offered eightieth-birthday greetings to Lapouge, under a headline that described him as A GREAT ANTHROPOLOGIST AND CHAMPION OF THE NORDIC MOVEMENT. In case anyone might wonder to (and for) whom the writers of these articles were speaking in the midthirties, a notice in every issue of the *News* made it clear that the publication was the official organ of the Eugenics Research Association, the Galton Society, and the International Federation of Eugenic Organizations, among others.

When the World Population Congress convened in Berlin in the summer of 1935, Clarence Campbell, representing the Eugenics Research Association, clarified the nature of the American eugenics movement at that unhappy moment. Campbell's recent appointment as president of the Galton Society added further polish to the bona fides he brought to Germany. His address to the congress struck all the resonant notes: "racial instinct," and "racial history," and "racial quality," and "comprehensive racial policy." He praised German anthropologists and saluted Frick, one of the key authors of the Nuremberg Laws. Then, with a toast he delivered at the congress's closing banquet, Campbell made the ERA's implicit position explicit: "To that great leader, Adolf Hitler!" *Time* commented, "The German press reported Dr. Campbell by the yard."

Although he was invited to the University of Heidelberg for its 550th anniversary celebration in June 1936, Harry Laughlin missed his chance to deliver a similar speech. He had told Carl Schneider, the chairman of the university's department of psychiatry who was also a faithful member of the Nazi Party, that he was honored by the invitation but couldn't attend because of other obligations. The event he missed was part academic festival, part historical pageant, part Nazi rally. Bands played, swastikas bloomed. At a black-tie reception in the Royal Hall of Heidelberg's ancient castle, the featured speaker was the reichsminister for public enlightenment and propaganda himself, the notorious Goebbels. A university spokesman declared, "We do not know of nor recognize truth for truth's sake or science for science's sake." The science Germany now sought, he said, was that which was "in accord with the great racial and political task before us."

Laughlin was not the only missing person. A boycott initiated by academics and theologians at Oxford and Cambridge Universities had spread to the United States, in protest of Heidelberg's now completed purge of forty-seven Jewish professors—one-quarter of its faculty. But those Americans who did attend were able to witness the crowning moment of Harry Laughlin's career: the granting of an honorary degree in absentia, in tribute to his role as "the farseeing representative of racial policy in America."

Laughlin didn't actually pick up his diploma until several months later, at a ceremony at the German consulate in New York. But before that, he wrote a letter of thanks to Schneider. Such official recognition, he said, was "a personal honor," but even more it was "evidence of a common understanding of German and American scientists" regarding "the racial endowments and racial health— physical, mental, and spiritual—of future generations." Ten years later, as Carl Schneider was about to go on trial for war crimes, he committed suicide in his jail cell.

Chapter Thirteen

The Train of Consequences

S ometimes the gestures of history are a little too perfect, as
if conceived by a particularly unimaginative writer of cheap
melodrama. One such nod in the direction of the improbable
was initiated on May 14, 1930, when Ernst Rüdin sailed from New
York back to Germany after visiting his friend Charles Davenport
in Cold Spring Harbor. Exactly nine years later to the day, the ship
that took Rüdin home—the SS *St. Louis*—prepared to sail from
Hamburg on a westbound trip that would become known as the
"Voyage of the Damned." (By then Hitler had granted Rüdin his
medal for "racial-hygienic" contributions.) The manifest of the *St.
Louis* listed more than 900 refugees from Nazi terror. When it
reached U.S. waters, the ship was forced to turn away. The 27,300
slots in Germany's immigration quota for the 1939 fiscal year had
already been filled. The *St. Louis* returned to Europe. In Berlin, the
U.S. consul general told Washington there were 125,000 "desperate
people" trying to get to America. In Poland, Russia, and other eastern
nations with far more Jews than Germany, and far smaller quotas,
the situation would become even more dire.

Newspapers and newsreel cameras reported the story of the *St.
Louis*—tragic, ongoing, often lurid—but the American public offered
no wreaths of welcome to the pitiable refugees. The previous year a

Fortune magazine poll showed two-thirds of the American public unwilling to accept any more refugees at all, and among those of larger spirit who were willing to take in any escapees from Nazi brutality, half insisted on an impossible proviso: they were prepared to open a humanitarian crack in the door only if it didn't require raising the quotas. In January 1939, two months after the widely reported Kristallnacht pogrom, another poll asked whether the United States should accept the immigration of ten thousand Jewish children. Sixty percent were opposed. It was a question not asked idly: a pending bill that would have relaxed the quota specifically for twenty thousand German Jewish children died in the Senate. One of those who led the opposition to the measure was John Trevor, who said he wanted "to protect the youth of America from this foreign invasion." Laura Delano Houghteling was rather more direct: "20,000 charming children would all too soon grow up into 20,000 ugly adults," she said. Houghteling was Franklin Roosevelt's first cousin; her husband was U.S. commissioner of immigration. Retired Major General George van Horn Moseley was more precisely eugenic than Houghteling: any refugees who *did* make it to the United States must be sterilized, he said, for "only in that way can we properly protect our future." The editors of *Time* had their finger on a barely stirring pulse. Americans showed "no inclination to do anything for the world's refugees," the magazine said, "except read about them."

Whether the American people connected Nazi race policies to the eugenic arguments they had been hearing for two decades was unknowable. This was not the case, however, among American organizations and institutions connected with eugenicists. Beginning shortly after Hitler's ascension and through the rest of the 1930s, members of one organization after another seemed suddenly to wake from a nightmare they had helped to script. For many, each report of another Nazi law, another Hitler speech, was almost an accusation of complicity. John D. Rockefeller Jr.'s top lieutenant, Raymond B. Fosdick, withdrew from the American Eugenics Society, and by the next year had begun to extricate the Rockefeller Foundation from eugenic projects it had bankrolled. The Eugenics Research Association, whose past presidents included Madison Grant, Albert Johnson, and Clarence Campbell, soon began a radical transformation, remaking itself into an organization that eschewed racial explanations for individual traits. Even the Immigration Restriction League dialed back its race-baiting, in 1934 publishing an anti-immigration tract headed PROBLEM IS ECONOMICAL, NOT RACIAL—a retreat to the disingenuous prolabor pose so unconvincingly struck by Henry Cabot Lodge four decades before. Hollywood showed that it sensed a change in the American attitude toward eugenics with the 1936 release of *College Holiday*, a broad send-up of eugenic mating programs treated with exactly the gravity one might expect from the headliners in its cast: Jack Benny, George Burns, and Gracie Allen.

The American Museum of Natural History, for so long a sort of home stadium for the eugenics movement, began to turn away from its eugenic history when William Gregory broke with his boss and his associates in 1935. For years Gregory was the colleague Fairfield Osborn relied on more than any other, and for at least a time was his chosen successor. He had been a charter member of the Galton Society, and had replaced Charles Davenport as its chairman in 1930. In 1932 he told Madison Grant that critics of *The Conquest of a Continent* were "bitter partisans" who were "protesting piously" against Grant's view of Jews. But Gregory, unlike Osborn or Grant, allowed himself to be awakened. Increasingly appalled by the plight of Jewish scientists in Germany, he was horrified as he watched the *Eugenical News* verge toward Nazism. Resigning from the chairmanship of the Galton Society in 1934, he told Grant that "I cannot approve of your attitude, as well as that of others in the Society, on anti-Semitism and Hittlerism [*sic*] in America." He left the organization altogether the following year and named Osborn, his friend and mentor, as one of those who were "in sympathy with the Hitler government," particularly "its anti-Jewish and pro-Aryan and eugenical" objectives.

Raymond Pearl tried to dissuade Gregory from resigning, insisting that political issues should not stand in the way of science. Gregory told a colleague, "To which the obvious answer is that I did not import the issue, I simply uncovered it." But the uncovering was only temporary. From the 1960s at least until the last few years of the twentieth century, officials at the American Museum of Natural History conspired to hide the museum's ugly connections to a disgraced movement. Researchers were denied access to pertinent archival materials, and when Fairfield Osborn's papers were processed in the late 1990s, the cataloger was instructed not to use the word "eugenics" anywhere in the index to the vast collection.

The last fortress of American eugenics still standing was its birthplace, Charles Davenport's enterprise in Cold Spring Harbor. When William Gregory turned against the Galton Society, he sent copies of his resignation letter to all of its charter members. One of these was John Merriam, the self-described "unequivocal" supporter of eugenics who was president of the Carnegie Institution of Washington, still the chief backer of eugenic research in the United States through its sponsorship of the ERO. Merriam and Madison Grant were close friends and, as cofounders with Osborn of the Save-the-Redwoods League, closer colleagues. Merriam's support for Davenport's research had been constant, even if he at times questioned its scientific merit. Occasionally Merriam worried about the uncomfortable melding of politics and science that showed up in Harry Laughlin's work and the "superficiality" of some of Davenport's inquiries. In 1929 he even convened an advisory committee to monitor the ERO. But Merriam didn't act until after Davenport's retirement in 1934, just as the Nazis' eugenic steamroller struck Merriam and the Carnegie board with embarrassing impact. Merriam reconstituted the 1929 committee, this time to determine the ERO's very future.

The scholars on the committee were unanimous, both in their analysis of the ERO's work and in their recommendations for its future. They found the office's hundreds of thousands of eugenic records, which were the very core of its operations, to be "unsatisfactory for the study of human genetics." The competence of those who had gathered the information (fieldworkers, college students in genetics classes, "casually interested individuals") was at best questionable. Many of the traits the records purported to identify—such characteristics as "loyalty," "sense of humor," "self-respect"—were unmeasurable. Davenport and Laughlin's treasured mountain of data, secure in its fireproof vault in Cold Spring Harbor, they declared useless.

The committee's forward-looking recommendations were equally blunt. The Eugenics Record Office had to divorce itself "from all forms of propaganda and the urging or sponsoring of programs for social reform or race betterment such as sterilization, birth-control, inculcation of national consciousness, restriction of immigration, etc." It needed to sever its by now nominal relationship with the *Eugenical News* immediately. Until the Carnegie board could come to a final determination of the ERO's future, all the activities that had marked its quarter century of cultural, political, and scientific significance should cease. And given the word's connotations in Nazi Germany, the term "eugenics" should be henceforth avoided.

Harry Laughlin, desperate to maintain both his job and what was left of his benighted crusade, turned to Madison Grant, urging him to intervene on his behalf with Grant's old friend Merriam. For all his fantasies of racial purification, Grant knew he and his allies were on the run. He was willing to do what he could, he told Laughlin, but warned him that "any intervention by me might easily prejudice your case."

The Eugenics Record Office did not meet its absolute end until 1940, after Merriam had retired and was replaced by Vannevar Bush, midway through his passage from the academy (dean of the school of engineering at MIT) to government service (presiding over the birth of the atomic bomb as head of the Manhattan Project). By then the office was under the leadership of a new director, Carnegie botanist Albert F. Blakeslee. It was also operating under a new name: the Genetics Record Office. Even the retired Davenport considered the renaming decision "entirely wise," for the connotation of the word "eugenics," he said—with either intentional irony or timid understatement—"has changed in the 29 years since our office was started." Blakeslee wanted to rid the Carnegie Institution of any trace of what had come before, especially the archives of the odious *Eugenical News*. He offered them to the former Eugenics Research Association, now scrubbing its own ignoble history by renaming itself the Association for Research in Human Heredity. The ARHH turned him down flat. Its president believed that the *News* and its sponsors were "thoroughly unscientific." He said that when "Madison Grant and others with similar views" reigned, they promoted discreditable views on race and social class. His organization wanted nothing to do with them or their work.

The ARHH president who determined to rid his organization of any connection to the eugenics movement's past was Frederick Osborn, nephew of Fairfield. The group's organizing meeting was suggestively convened in the office of American Museum of Natural History anthropologist Harry Shapiro. In Cold Spring Harbor the study of genetics continued, but on a path radically different from the one first marked out by Davenport and Laughlin. Unlike the Museum of Natural History, the Cold Spring Harbor Laboratory (as it renamed itself after separating from the Carnegie Institution) hid nothing. It sponsored the publication of books revealing its eugenic past and maintained websites that delved deeply, honestly, and uncomfortably into eugenic history and the laboratory's role in it.

The individuals who had welded together the scientific racists and the immigration restrictionists generally faded into a kind of oblivion, most of them known today only to scholars, or to twenty-first-century xenophobes longing for the old days. (Long out of copyright, *The Passing of the Great Race* was available in at least eight different editions in 2018, and both the book and its author were invoked with reverence on racist websites.) First to go was Frederick Osborn's uncle Fairfield. Osborn had been nudged from his throne at the American Museum of Natural History in 1933. His imperial ways had already marked him as a relic, and his racialized eugenics had rendered him both an irritant and an embarrassment. Back in 1908, when Osborn was appointed head of the museum, Franz Boas congratulated him for "the unequalled opportunity this gives you to advance the interests of science in this country"; as the years passed and his engagement with scientific racism deepened, Osborn's scholarly reputation was so severely damaged that University of California ethnologist Robert Lowie, who had spent two decades on the staff of the AMNH, refused to sign a seventieth-birthday tribute. Osborn's endorsement of Madison Grant's work, wrote Lowie, "puts him beyond the pale as a representative of science." Osborn could dismiss Lowie's attitude, believing that his negative view of Grant arose from a "biased spirit." But when William Gregory resigned from the Galton Society, Osborn could not ignore it. "To err is human, to forgive divine," he wrote to Gregory, seeking absolution. The abashed tone of his letter was as uncharacteristic as if he had been writing in Inuit. Pleading was not Osborn's style, but he had by his own actions put himself in a place where he had no choice. "If I have ever erred in anything I have said about Germany," he told Gregory, "I hope you will forgive me."

Osborn continued to rattle around in the south tower of the ungainly old museum, worked on his monumental study of prehistoric elephants, and then died in his castle on the Hudson in October 1935, at seventy-eight. One front-page obituary called him "the successor to Darwin and Huxley." The lavish three-column piece in the *New York Times* devoted only one sentence to immigration and one more to eugenics. But the *Eugenical News* got straight to the point: "As lover of his country and his race his ideals will long influence the applications of eugenics here and abroad."

In 1971 Princeton's Osborn Clubhouse, which had served as a semiprivate lair for the college's athletes since its eponymous benefactor founded it in 1892, was renamed and repurposed: it became the university's Third World Center, dedicated to "providing a social, cultural, and political environment that was responsive to issues of ethnic and racial diversity." For a suitable memorial, twenty-first-century Osbornites would instead have to visit the Bernard Family Hall of North American Mammals at the American Museum of Natural History, where the caribou once named *Rangifer tarandus osborni* stands in proud display—directly opposite the caribou once known as *Rangifer tarandus granti*. Later research determined that the two species, almost like the men they were named for, were one and the same.

Both Madison Grant and Joe Lee died in the summer of 1937. The historically resonant synchronicity of their famous surnames was a neat coincidence but in no way a representation of their relationship, for throughout the long immigration restriction wars they were always on the same side. But apart from their wealth and their determination to stop immigration from eastern and southern European countries, they had little in common. Lee once went so far as to say that relative to the typical American businessman, he was a Bolshevik. Grant blamed the detestable French Revolution for "the dogma of the brotherhood of man," and used the term "democratic institutions" as an insult.

Although it's not clear whether the two men ever met, they certainly knew each other by reputation. As early as 1916, Lee was aware of the potency of Grant's zeal. Having failed to excite presidential candidate Charles Evans Hughes's interest in the perils of immigration, Lee suggested to a colleague that it was time to unleash Grant on Hughes, as if no other weapon could be as effective. Eight years later, after the passage of the Johnson-Reed Act, Grant praised Lee for financing the Immigration Restriction League "throughout the long period of Egyptian night." The closest they may have come to each other physically may have been in Lee's bedroom in the old house on Mount Vernon Street, where an inscribed copy of *The Passing of the Great Race* enjoyed pride of place on his bookshelf, just a few volumes away from Lee's copy of *Das Kapital*.

In 1933, writing for his Harvard fiftieth reunion class report, Lee proudly acknowledged his decades of financial support for the IRL and noted the league's legislative success. He also expressed the hope that similar restrictions would be applied to Latin America; then, once "the birth of the chocolate races has been put in low, [the] generally American brand of citizen may last for quite a while." Four years later, eulogizing his father in a family publication, Joseph Lee Jr. commemorated his determination "to uplift the psalm of our democratic faith until the poorest immigrant . . . heard the song and found his voice in it." His college friend Richards Bradley, who had been by his side in the IRL for more than three decades, said Lee blamed "racial prejudice," among other dark impulses, for provoking immigration. Not long after Lee's death, when it became clear to Bradley and others that no one was willing to replace him as the IRL's primary benefactor, the league ceased to exist.*

Any lingering memories of Joe Lee's key role in four decades of increasingly xenophobic lobbying and propaganda disappeared as well. The Boston papers eulogized him as if he had been the city's

---

* Its last paid operative, lobbyist James Patten, did not want for replacement clients. Appearing before a Senate committee in 1939 to oppose the measure that would have allowed twenty thousand Jewish children into the country, Patten presented himself as a representative of the Sons of America, the Patriotic Civic American Alliance, the American Citizenship Foundation, and the General Board of Patriotic Societies.

most valuable citizen (which, in many ways, he was). The *New York Times* treated him as a national figure: in neither his lengthy obituary (JOSEPH LEE, EXPERT IN RECREATION, DIES), nor an editorial page encomium to his various good works, was immigration even mentioned.

Irony was a common mode of expression for Joe Lee, and his family provided a large helping of it after his death. In 1947 his grand-daughter Margaret Colt traveled to Italy with a postwar international aid organization—exactly the sort of undertaking Joe would have endorsed. He likely would have been less sanguine about what came next, when she met and married a handsome, charming Neapolitan named Vincenzo Vicedomini. He moved to the United States with his wife, shortened his name to Enzo Domini, sent three kids to college (Boston University and Babson College, not Harvard), and from his base in gritty Danbury, Connecticut, made a success in the food importing business. The same sort of thing happened in the family of Lee's friend and IRL comrade Richards Bradley, who did not live to see his granddaughter (Oberlin, not Radcliffe) marry an attorney named Lionel Epstein (whose parents came to the United States from Russia and Lithuania), nor to see her pass along her husband's surname to his great-grandchildren. The irony isn't that Lee and Bradley had been proven wrong; it's that they were proven right. Exactly what the anti-immigration movement feared came true: a few generations of adaptation, cross-cultural fertilization, and intermarriage had taken their country away from them. They even lost their claim to the term "native American."

The *Times* treated Madison Grant with nearly the same gentle, forgiving (or forgetting) tone it had afforded Lee. The headline would have thrilled him: MADISON GRANT, 71, ZOOLOGIST, IS DEAD. The obituary, as well as three other brief articles—one about his will, two about his funeral (the first previewing it, the second reporting on it)—stuck to the theme of the headline. He founded the zoo, he saved the redwoods, he "discovered many mammals while exploring the American frontier." Any reader thrown off stride by the "zoologist" label trumpeted in the headline would likely have been equally nonplussed by one of the subheads in the piece: "Authority on Anthropology." Deep within the detailed account of his life, one lone paragraph addressed Grant's engagement with both the immigration restriction crusade and the eugenics movement.

The *Times'* careful tiptoe around the uglier aspects of Grant's public and private activities may not have been an accident. Unsettled by the deafening inattention paid to his last book, *The Conquest of a Continent*, Grant had turned in his final years toward shaping the story of his life. He asked Charles Davenport to confirm his role in the founding of the Galton Society. He lobbied hard to get an honorary degree from Yale, and Harry Laughlin initiated a futile letter-writing campaign on his behalf. He solicited an advance obituary from a particularly florid hunting companion ("We shall, like the Norsemen of old, carry him with us to the halls of Valhalla. . . . Like Ulysses of old, he wandered far, but came home to die. . . . He brought with him his mighty bow, and if you want to see where his magic arrows struck, read the Congressional Record"). One imagines he liked it.

Near the end, unable to walk or even to stand, his wanderings truly at their end, alone but for his manservants and his brother, Grant realized that he would have to forgo an event that could have brought together his paired passions—reverence for the natural world and devotion to scientific racism—in a perfect, life-defining union. In his last months he served as one of the American organizers of a three-week extravaganza in Berlin called the International Hunting Exposition, scheduled for the fall of 1937. One of his counterparts in the host country, who invited Grant to join his personal hunting party at the event, was the *Reichsjägermeister*, or Reich Master of the Hunt: Hitler's reliable deputy, Hermann Göring.

Like Galton, like Laughlin, like Gould, like Prescott Hall—like many members of the eugenic chorus so concerned about the genetic future, the never married Madison Grant had no children. He consequently did not leave behind descendants who might marry Italians or Jews.

Harry Laughlin's exit from the stage had already begun by the time he accepted his honorary degree from the Nazis. As the Carnegie Institution's support for eugenic study evaporated in the late 1930s, he was left with nothing but his ties to men like John Trevor and the enduring prejudices they shared. Around the time he started to suffer frequent epileptic seizures—not the most convenient affliction for a eugenicist—Carnegie officials raised the question of retirement. But when Laughlin published the Trevor-financed *Immigration and Conquest* in 1939, calling for an absolute bar on immigration from "alien races [who] tend to resist assimilation in the United States," he assured the end of his Carnegie affiliation. After Vannevar Bush received a copy of the book from Laughlin, with its references to "race decay," "low-grade aliens," and "alien race-loyalty," he told him he couldn't simultaneously work for the institution and play a public role in political debate, and really, Dr. Laughlin, we know how much you care for the future of our country, so how could we possibly expect you to give up that part of your life?

The Carnegie Institution sent Laughlin on his way with an accelerated pension (he was only fifty-nine), a letter of appreciation, a pair of field glasses, and a sigh of relief. A boxcar full of his papers followed him home to Kirksville. He built an ugly faux-colonial home across from the campus of the Missouri Normal School and spent the last three years of his life in his garden—and at the post office, sending out copies of *Conquest by Immigration* to scores of college and university libraries across the country.

On Charles Davenport's seventy-fifth birthday, in 1940, Laughlin sent his earliest mentor greetings that evoked their sunny years together in Cold Spring Harbor. His wife, Pansy, Laughlin wrote, had always made Davenport a box of fudge for his birthday just like the one accompanying his letter, and "placed it on your desk as evidence of our regards and best wishes from the Laughlins." By this point Davenport, too, had been pushed out by the Carnegie Institution. Though he had retired six years earlier, he had retained office space, some staff assistance, and a financial relationship that had enabled external supporters of his research to route their money through Carnegie accounts. When his time came, Davenport did not object. "The attitude of the Institution is entirely understandable," he told the Carnegie officer who informed him that the four-decade connection was over. It is likely he did not know that more than a year earlier another Carnegie official had suggested that Davenport "should be 'bought off' by means of a small grant."

But such knowledge could not have blunted Davenport's perpetual optimism. The same birthday mail that brought Pansy Laughlin's fudge to his home also brought other felicitations that no doubt pleased him even more. It was true that some came from racists (one said he was devoting himself solely "to working along lines that *you* have pointed out"). Many more, though, came from men whose respect he had somehow retained despite his embrace of a science they believed to be dangerous or bogus or both, such as Herbert Jennings and the geneticist Leslie C. Dunn, who had been the most forceful member of the advisory committee that had effectively shut down the ERO. And, meaningfully for a man who had been—and still is—accused of anti-Semitism, many came from such prominent Jewish anthropologists as Melville Herskovits and Ashley Montagu.

And from a friend and colleague who had known Davenport for more than three decades, Franz Boas.*

The year before, Davenport had reflected on his life in his Harvard Class of 1889 fiftieth reunion book. "The machine that goes by my name has almost uniformly worked well and persistently," Davenport wrote. "It has been capable of great thrills and has found especial pleasure in creating and giving the initial impulse to more or less novel undertakings that have had a train of consequences."

"A train of consequences." In truth, to Davenport the train that mattered was a phantom. He was expressing the truism that scientific study yields real-world impact, yet failing to acknowledge the ruinous impact of his own work. In the same month when he was trying vainly to enable the immigration of the Austrian Jewish biologist Hans Przibram (who would die five years later in the concentration camp at Theresienstadt), Davenport recounted the history of the Eugenics Record Office in a letter to Vannevar Bush. Without the example of the ERO, he said, there would have been no Kaiser Wilhelm Institute. "The work of the Record office," he told Bush, "is, therefore, not to be measured merely by its own publications but also by the influence that it has exerted on research in the subject elsewhere."

Even now, Davenport could not acknowledge any connection between the research conducted by Eugen Fischer at the Kaiser Wilhelm Institute and the plight of his friend Przibram, or between Ernst Rüdin's career as a eugenicist and his rise to such stature in Germany that Hitler would honor him for his contributions to Nazi racial policies. For all his success as a biologist, Davenport was unable to see that his endless effort to explain and to promote

---

* Boas's regard for Davenport was such that in a will he drafted in 1924 he instructed his executors to leave all his anthropometric data in Davenport's care. Eight years older than Davenport, Boas died in 1942 during a luncheon at the Columbia Faculty Club. Discussing race and racism with some colleagues, he collapsed in midsentence, fell over backward in his chair, and expired.

and to exalt a eugenic view of the human species had been not only misdirected, but weaponized.

In his last years Davenport's uncanny vigor did not falter. Some of his late work was a reversion to the sort of science he had pursued before he was kidnapped by the promises of eugenics: differences in facial features, for instance, and the mathematical analysis of growth curves. He was ubiquitous in the village of Cold Spring Harbor, serving as a volunteer air warden in the early years of World War II and founding a local whaling museum. He did stay in touch with those studying human genetics and behavior, and in 1942, two years before his death at seventy-seven, he told a colleague he looked forward to a forthcoming conference on individuality. The meeting, he believed, would provide an opportunity to address the effects of heredity versus those of environment—what Francis Galton in 1874 had called "nature and nurture." The two factors "are intimately mingled in bringing about human differences," Davenport wrote, and this important truth "is not generally known by the public." He did not add that his entire life's work had been directed toward the glorification of heredity at the expense of environment—and, worse, a version of heredity disproven, discredited, and disastrous.

Lothrop Stoddard died in 1950, eleven years after the high point of his career. That occurred when he traveled to Germany as a reporter and met with many Nazi luminaries, including Heinrich Himmler ("he laughed easily"), Eugen Fischer and his coauthor Fritz Lenz ("outstanding authorities"), and Hitler himself ("a firm handshake and a pleasant smile"). In 1945, thirteen years after Washington voters sent Albert Johnson into an unwanted retirement, the former congressman did some computations and figured that the two laws he had brought into being—the 1921 Emergency Act and the 1924 act that bore his name—had kept eighteen million Europeans from American shores; he met his end in a veterans' hospital in 1957.

Upon John Trevor's death in 1956, John D. Rockefeller Jr. extolled—privately—"the soundness of his judgment." Trevor's cause did not die with him. When legislation aimed at undoing the Johnson-Reed Act was introduced in Congress nine years later, his son John B. Jr. testified against it, warning that any "conglomeration of racial and ethnic elements" would lead to "a serious cultural decline."

*   *   *

ONE OTHER DEATH concludes this bleak tale of eugenics, immigration, racism, and the corrupting potential of scientific authority. In 1936 Yehoshua Rotenberg, a struggling merchant in the town of Połaniec, in southwestern Poland, wrote to his older brother, whom he had not seen since 1920. That was when Hersh Rotenberg had departed for the United States and begun his new life. Yehoshua remembered it "as if it's been less than a year."

In the intervening years Hersh—now Harry—became a solid citizen in Batavia, New York, near Rochester. At first he worked for a cousin in the furniture business who had preceded him to Batavia; in time he set out on his own, raised a family, and prospered. In Poland things did not proceed as well for Yehoshua. He had five children and a small business, but worried constantly about threats to the Jews of Plontch (as his town was known in Yiddish). "Anti-Semitism is growing by leaps and bounds," he wrote to Harry in 1938. "Young Jews want to emigrate," he said, "but unfortunately the world is completely closed to them." He also said, "More than once, it has occurred to me that we made a mistake in not leaving."

Harry saved his brother's letters, and they read today like footprints left in new concrete just as it is about to dry. Specifics are vague, but the outline remains clear. Hitler hovered nearer and nearer. Across the border in Romania, Jews who had obtained Romanian citizenship just after World War I were compelled to reapply. Jewish businesses in Plontch endured a boycott. Yehoshua's financial circumstances worsened. "It is just like the sorrows of Job," he wrote in 1938. "Everyone wants to leave. There is nothing here."

Though Harry's responses are lost, his efforts on behalf of his brother's family can be inferred from Yehoshua's letters. He consulted lawyers. He traveled to Toronto, perhaps trying to see if it might be easier for his brother to enter Canada. He tried to enlist the support of a U.S. senator. He prepared the necessary papers indicating his ability and willingness to sponsor Yehoshua's family financially, and sent them to Poland. Yehoshua filed the papers with the American consulate.

In April 1939, Yehoshua told Harry, "I know you are eager to know what has happened with the papers you sent. It is not a simple matter." The U.S. consulate, he said, "is inundated." Two months later, American officials informed him that it would take two to three years for the Rotenberg family to secure visas. There were more than 3.5 million Jews in Poland in 1939. Under the National Origins law, the 1939 quota for the entire nation allowed only 6,524 Poles, Jews and non-Jews alike, to enter the United States legally. Writing from Berlin, the American consul general, dismayed by the iron inflexibility of the system, told another official that "we can only be sympathetic and kind; in most cases little practical help can be given." Writing from Plontch, Yehoshua Rotenberg told his brother, "America pities and sends wishes to the Jews." He had hoped for better.

In 1941 Harry received a postcard from his brother. "May God help us and we will rejoice together. I am writing so little, because it isn't possible to write a long letter." That was the year the Germans arrived in Plontch. Soon the town's Jews, and several hundred others rounded up from neighboring shtetls, were confined to a ghetto. In September 1942 the SS knocked on Yehoshua Rotenberg's door. A witness said they took him to the bridge over the Vistula River and shot him. What became of his wife and five children is not known.

Liberty Island, 1965

Had there been no Johnson-Reed Act constraining his escape from doomed Poland, it's likely that Yehoshua Rotenberg would have eluded his fatal destiny and made it to America. He had sufficient funds. He had family in the United States ready to help. And for at least the last six years of his life, he had compelling motivation. Johnson-Reed alone made it impossible for him to act on it.

As it did for so many others. In the last year before the quotas were established, 50,000 European Jews entered the country; unsheathed, the new law worked like a scythe. From 1925 until the beginning of World War II, the number plummeted to an annual average of slightly less than 9,000. Subtract the new number from the old, and straight-line math would presume 41,000 a year who wanted to come but were unable to—in all, some 574,000 people over the fourteen-year period. A more aggressive accounting would recognize that the rise of the Nazis would have accelerated the pace, increasing the total radically, to . . . what? A million? A million and a half?

But speculation calls for caution; sorting through such a grim accounting demands the most conservative math possible. Let's assume that the wheel of history turns at a steady pace, that in the 1930s Hitler merely drew attention to an endemic anti-Semitism that was a perpetual plague across Europe, that the lure of an American future maintained a steady, unwavering glow. Let's begin, then, with those math-measured 574,000. Even if we assume that half of those managed to emigrate to other nations in the Western Hemisphere (it wasn't nearly that many), we're down to 287,000. And let's also assume that the rate of immigration would have slowed anyway during the worldwide depression of the 1930s to, say, only half of its previous rate. And let's further stipulate that half of these remaining 143,500 who might have emigrated were instead stranded in Europe but somehow managed to escape the Nazis. What happened to that last 70,000-plus? Or, just to be even more conservative, make that 50,000. Or even 10,000. No number one can conjure is so small that we can ignore it.

We know all too well what happened. This is not to blame the deaths of perhaps hundreds of thousands on the eugenicists and the anti-immigrationists, on the congenitally xenophobic, or the defensively xenophobic, or the situationally xenophobic. We can contemplate possibility, but we cannot be conclusive; besides, attributing blame to anyone but Hitler and his Nazis can only dilute their responsibility for their unspeakable crimes. But this, surely, is undeniable: because of the 1924 immigration law, many, many people who might otherwise have found their way to Chicago or Boston or Dallas or Batavia, New York, perished instead.

While weighing this awful truth, we can add another portion of woe to the scales: in 1946, at the Nuremberg "Doctors' Trial," the Nazi defendants (including Hitler's personal physician, Karl Brandt) invoked the *Buck v. Bell* sterilization decision in their defense. And *The Passing of the Great Race*. And the Johnson-Reed Act of 1924 itself. When Ernst Rüdin was apprehended after the war, he was quick to cite his extensive collaboration with international researchers as an exculpatory factor.

These men didn't say they were "following orders," in the self-exonerating language of the moment; they said they were following Americans.

The singular position of Europe's Jews in the genocidal crosshairs of the Nazis' final solution will forever require specific attention. But the suffering of others kept out of the United States by the 1924 act demands notice as well. Add the two hundred thousand Serbs killed by Nazi-connected death squads, the seventy thousand executed Greeks, the slaughtered Gypsies and homosexuals, even the millions of Russians who gave their lives in the Red Army or fell to starvation and disease in the streets of besieged Leningrad. Italians under the heel of fascism. Poles caught in the brutal vise of the German and Soviet war machines. Hungarians, Czechs, Romanians. And then go steps further, and add to this desolate roster the Japanese, Chinese, and other Asians permanently barred from entry to the United States for decades, many hundreds of thousands of whom would no doubt have preferred to move to America. How different it might have been.

But change did come—slowly at first, then all of a sudden. The first crack in the dike appeared during World War II when the American wartime alliance with Chiang Kai-shek's Chinese nationalists provoked repeal of the 1882 Chinese Exclusion Act. Through the 1950s, various ameliorative measures opened the doors to people fleeing the eastern European countries that were under Soviet domination. Finally, in 1965, on a bright October day in New York Harbor, Lyndon B. Johnson sat at a desk on Liberty Island and signed a new Immigration and Nationality Act into law. The pack of politicians standing behind him included, among others, Senators Robert Kennedy, Edward Kennedy, and Hubert Humphrey—and the bill's coauthors, Senator Philip Hart of Michigan and Representative Emanuel Celler of Brooklyn. As a freshman congressman in 1924, it was Celler who had risen on the House floor to call the Johnson-Reed Act "the rankest kind of discrimination . . . set up against Catholic and Jewish Europe." Now, forty-one years later, he was the dean of the House of Representatives, and it was his bill that had abolished the quotas, establishing instead a nationality-blind system of immigration.

"Over my shoulders here," Johnson said in his prepared remarks, "you can see Ellis Island, whose vacant corridors echo today the joyous sound of long ago voices. And today we can all believe that the lamp of this grand old lady is brighter today—and the golden door that she guards gleams more brilliantly in the light of an increased liberty for the people from all the countries of the globe."

Eugenic theories of race were long forgotten. Now the racialized policies those theories had helped establish were dead as well. For believers in the promise of the nearby statue, the future of American immigration policy looked as bright as the brilliant sun overhead.

Acknowledgments

In January 1923, when he was sixty, Joe Lee prepared instructions for his heirs and executors. With a few exceptions, he wrote, "there is nothing of value among my written papers, and they all ought to be thrown away in bulk without being looked at."

Happily for scholars and other researchers (though less happily, perhaps, for Lee's reputation), his wishes were ignored. Residing in thirty-eight large file boxes at the Massachusetts Historical Society, Lee's papers define the life, the work, the entire universe of this complicated and wholly original man. They can also stand as a synecdoche for all the thousands upon thousands of original papers and records I drew on as I researched this book. A hundred years from now, when a historian decides to write about, say, the anti-immigration activists of the 2010s, there will likely be no papers to turn to—or, at least, no private papers. A few people may try to make their words live on by carefully preserving the billions of digits that make up their emails and their electronic diaries, but I expect these will be heavily expurgated. People today, I believe, don't want their unfiltered selves made public, even posthumously.

This may have been the case during Lee's life, too, but I suspect there was less impulse to edit. Reading the candid and often unseemly comments of Lee and his comrades, you get the sense that members of the next generation were either great devotees of the gods of history . . . or they simply considered little in their parents' papers to be embarrassing. The immigration restrictionists, the eugenicists, and many of their children believed that their thoughts and expressions and political passions were nothing to be ashamed of. For their descendants today, this may be a little distressing. For historians, it's a godsend.

In addition to the many archivists, scholars, and others mentioned below, there are a few individuals I wish to single out for special thanks. The first two are no longer with us. Half a century ago, John Higham was my teacher at the University of Michigan, and he guided me on the first serious piece of research I ever conducted. He was already, at forty-seven, the most eminent historian of immigration we had. Today, sixteen years after his death, he remains so. I hope I do not defame his reputation by saying that I would like to believe a small portion of his scholarly DNA rubbed off on me.

Robert Sklar was another one of my teachers in the Michigan history department. I was only in touch with John Higham once after leaving Ann Arbor. Bob Sklar and I, on the other hand, became lifelong friends. Sadly, his life was not nearly long enough. Bob died at seventy-four in 2011. I feel his presence in everything I write.

As I began working on this book, I sought out the counsel of Daniel Kevles. Just as Higham's *Strangers in the Land* remains the definitive book on his subject, Dan's *In the Name of Eugenics* is the definitive American work on the entire strange, fate-filled eugenics movement. Dan was generous with his time and with his suggestions. One of the latter was an introduction to Diane B. Paul, an outstanding historian of eugenics, whom I persuaded to read my manuscript in its final draft form. My friend Alan M. Kraut—a strong claimant to Higham's position among contemporary immigration historians— read it as well. Both of these distinguished scholars offered many suggestions and criticisms, all of them valuable. If the reader finds flaws of interpretation or fact in *The Guarded Gate*, it's doubtless because at those specific junctures I foolishly chose to disregard the comments of Diane and Alan. They are hereby absolved of any responsibility for my errors.

Jonathan Spiro, the author of the definitive biography of Madison Grant, also deserves my special gratitude and that of anyone else who chooses to write about Grant. While working on *Defending the Master Race* a quarter of a century ago, Spiro scoured the nation's archives and unearthed hundreds of letters from Madison Grant to scores of correspondents. Despite Grant's express wishes to have his papers destroyed, his private thoughts survive in the files of those he shared them with. Thanks to Jonathan Spiro, they are accessible to future generations of researchers.

Barbara Miller Solomon's *Ancestors and Immigrants*, published in 1956, was the first scholarly book to draw on the available records of the Immigration Restriction League. Maida Solomon gave me permission to examine her mother's personal papers, which include notes on interviews with IRL figures who were still alive when Barbara Solomon was conducting her research in the early 1950s. Other private documents were generously provided to me by Lawrence B. Thompson, whose father was Madison Grant's step-nephew, and by James Rotenberg, who never knew his great-uncle Yehoshua Rotenberg, but who knew how valuable—if heartbreaking—were the letters Yehoshua sent to James's grandfather between 1936 and 1941.

Jean Kaufman led me to James Rotenberg and his family's papers. Anna Kolchinsky translated various documents in German. Edward Jacoby in Boston welcomed me into Joe Lee's house on Beacon Hill; Krystal Loh of New York University allowed me to visit Charles Gould's on Washington Square. Roberto Lebron of the American Museum of Natural History gave me a tour of the offices of Fairfield Osborn and his colleagues, and of the rooms used for the Second International Eugenics Congress. Henry Rosovsky explained how the Jewish quota established at Harvard in the 1920s persisted after its presumed disestablishment. Charles E. Rosenberg provided perspective on the development of the eugenics movement. Alexander Sanger, Margaret's grandson, offered insight into her involvement with eugenics. John Domini, Joe Lee's great-grandson, was similarly helpful with his recollections of his parents and the story of the Lee family's fascinating evolution.

I also benefitted from assistance provided by a number of scholars and researchers whose knowledge of immigration, eugenics, or the individuals who shaped both varied from eminently helpful to absolutely essential. They include Lee D. Baker, Duke University; Gillian Beer, University of Cambridge; Adam Cohen; Regna Darnell, University of Western Ontario; Julio Decker, University of Bristol; Noah Fuller; Aaron Goings, St. Martin's University; David Greenberg, Rutgers University; Diane Kolbe, University of Iowa; John R. Lukacs, University of Oregon; Jason McDonald, Truman State University; Devin Pendas, Boston College; Claudia Roth Pierpont; Brian Regal, Kean University; Neil Swidey, *Boston Globe*; Jack Tchen, New York University; David Ward, National Portrait Gallery; Mark S. Weiner, Rutgers Law School; and Philip K. Wilson, East Tennessee State University. When I began my work on *The Guarded Gate*, Ann Fabian of Rutgers University was an acquaintance; now she's my friend. I'm very grateful for that and for her wise counsel.

Digital archives have eliminated much of the distance between the researcher and his subject. But collections not yet fully digitized require on-site attention. Jill Lepore, Annalise Orleck, and Martha A. Sandweiss kindly led me to some of their superb students, whom I enlisted as research assistants at Harvard, Dartmouth, and Princeton, respectively. My thanks to them and to their students: Robert Henderson, Amy Huprich-Cook, Ryan Low, Julia Marino, Blake Paterson, Will Sherman, Emmet Stackelberg, Anna Strong, and Amy Weiss-Meyer. As I neared the end of this project, I brought in the heavy artillery: the tireless and talented Heather Merrill, who did original research and also helped me with fact-checking.

My own research trips took me to archives in Ann Arbor, Boston, Cambridge, New York, Philadelphia, Princeton, Washington, and the metropolis of Kirksville, Missouri, where I spent a week exploring the papers of Harry H. Laughlin at the Pickler Memorial Library, Truman State University. Amanda Langendoerfer, who supervises the library's special collections, was the ideal guide/host/ interlocutor. I would also like to single out Charles Greifenstein, curator of manuscripts at the American Philosophical Society Library in Philadelphia, and his associate Valerie-Ann Lutz for equally comprehensive assistance—and encouragement—as I immersed myself in the APS's invaluable collections at the beginning of this project, and again and again as I needed to examine additional documents. Gregory Raml was similarly accommodating over the several weeks I spent in the library of the American Museum of Natural History in New York. Not for a moment did he ever display the institutional defensiveness that for decades underscored the museum's discomfort with its own past.

Based on my experience over the past twenty years, I am absolutely unable to write a book without the help of Jeff Flannery, whose grasp of the vast collections of the Manuscript Division of the Library of Congress is matched only by his grasp of the needs, large or petty, of researchers. I am equally indebted to the Wellfleet Public Library, in Wellfleet, Massachusetts. It is a marvelous institution, and its facilities and its staff—especially the astonishing Naomi Robbins—are treasures beyond price. Jay Barksdale and Melanie Locay of the New York Public Library provided me with access to the library's Frederick Lewis Allen Room, enabling me to make efficient and timely use of the library's extensive resources. I met Tom Straw in the Allen Room. Tom was working on a novel that involved eugenics; I hope I was half as helpful to him as he was to me.

I am also grateful to the following archivists and librarians for their assistance: Lizette Royer Barton, Center for the History of Psychology, University of Akron; Kevin Proffitt, American Jewish Archives; Elizabeth Hyman, American Jewish Historical Society; John Strom, Carnegie Institution for Science; David Rosenberg, Center for Jewish History; Timothy J. DeWerff, Century Association Archives; Clare Clark, Cold Spring Harbor Laboratory; Hillary Dorsch, Division of Rare and Manuscript Collections, Carl A. Kroch Library, Cornell University; Tom Ewing and Nick Telepak, Educational Testing Service; Ellen Shea, Schlesinger Library, Harvard University; Marjorie Winslow Kehoe, Alan Mason Chesney Medical Archives, Johns Hopkins University; James Stimpert, Sheridan Libraries, Johns Hopkins University; Elaine Heavey and Sabina Bouchard, Massachusetts Historical Society; Adam Barenbak, Rod Ross, and David Langbart, National Archives and Records Administration; Richard Tuske, New York City Bar Association; Kendra Lightner, Franklin Delano Roosevelt Presidential Library & Museum; Alexandra Eveleigh, Wellcome Library, University College, London; Judy Pitchford, Washington State Library; Hailey Kaylenne Woodall and John R. Waggener, American Heritage Center, University of Wyoming; and Melissa Grafe, Cushing/Whitney Medical Library, Yale University. Mostly everyone at Harvard's invaluable Houghton Library was helpful; I'm sorry to say that one staff member was decidedly not.

At various times through this book's long gestation, I asked some good friends to read portions of the manuscript. They are, nonetheless, still my friends. Suzie Bolotin, Jim Carroll, Nick Delbanco, David Denby, Jim Gaines, Lisa Hendricksson, Jane Isay, Jim Kelly, Arthur Kopit, Allen Kurzweil, Steve Lipsitz, and Rafe Yglesias all made their way through sections of *The Guarded Gate*, and whatever its failings, it is better for their comments. The physical aspects of my long walks with Nick were probably good for me, too; I know the conversation was.

Other similarly valued friends who helped me in this four-and-a-half-year journey provided a range of services (political arguments, comfortable sleeping arrangements, etc.) and goods (chiefly evening martinis) that made the process more efficient, more endurable, and in some cases more enjoyable. I am lucky to know Jerry Barondess, Taylor Branch and Christy Macy, Lizabeth Cohen and Herrick Chapman, Jim Cronin and Laura Frader, Elena Delbanco, Don Fanger and Leonie Gordon, Todd Gitlin, Lisa Grunwald, JoAnn Gutin, Curtis Hartman, Jane Kramer, Robert Jay Lifton, Dick Meyer, Lynn Novick, Biddy Owens, Nancy Palmer, Nancy Rosenblum, Eleanor Schwartz, Scott Sherman, Laura Wulf, and Paul Zolan. I'm also fortunate in my four-decade friendship with Sam Schulman. Though Sam wasn't involved in *The Guarded Gate*, he was connected to and helpful with all my earlier books, and I've never thanked him sufficiently. Here's to you, Sam.

Thanks also to Dana Prescott and her colleagues at the Civitella Ranieri Foundation. Dana invited my wife and me to spend three weeks in Civitella's splendid castle in Umbria, where the wine, the truffles, the porchetta, and the other visiting artists and writers interfered with my work, but not (I don't think) too much.

At Scribner, I am once again indebted to Colin Harrison and his colleagues, particularly Sarah Goldberg, Katie Rizzo, and Nan Graham. Because of the firm's heavy involvement in the promotion of scientific racism in the first third of the twentieth century, its support for my project required a rare form of commitment. In addition to those named above, I would like to thank the recently retired president of the Scribner Publishing Group, Susan Moldow—publisher, friend, and neighbor.

Then there's Team Dan. Ivan Drucker has been tending to my

technological needs for fifteen years. I cannot be sufficiently grateful for his ample skills, his endless patience, and his ability to speak English instead of Techish. My professional relationship and my friendship with Barbara Fox date back to the early 1990s; without her transcription skills, this book would have taken much longer. Liz Darhansoff holds the most senior position in this crew. Liz has been my agent for forty years, my friend for fifty. She's great in both roles.

For more than three decades, Chris Jerome has been wrestling with my most overwrought sentences, in most cases forcing them to submit to her will; if the reader believes Chris has missed some, I assure you that they survive only because of my vanity.

Finally, my family. Becky, John, Xela, Lydia, Luke—thank you for, well, everything (especially, this year, for Oola). My love for all of you is boundless.

—D.O.
Wellfleet, Massachusetts,
October 2018

Notes

C
itations in this section largely reference the books, dissertations, and scholarly articles in the Bibliography that begins
on page 433. For sources that do not directly pertain to the
subject matter of this book and are used only sparingly, the full citation
appears with the note, as do citations for newspapers and popular
magazines. Citations of biographical dictionaries and encyclopedias
refer to the entry of the individual under discussion, except as indicated.
All figures specifically quantifying immigration numbers are taken
from the Statistical Abstract of the United States, except as indicated.

ABBREVIATIONS USED IN NOTES
(*Full descriptions in the Bibliography*)

ACSS	Archives of Charles Scribner's Sons
ANB	*American National Biography*
CAA	Century Association Archives
CBDP	Charles Benedict Davenport Papers
CCBP	Carl C. Brigham Papers
CIWA	Carnegie Institution of Washington Archives
COHP	Columbia Oral History Project
CR	*Congressional Record*
CWEP	Charles W. Eliot Papers
DNB	*Dictionary of National Biography*
EN	*Eugenical News*

ERP	Elihu Root Papers
FBP	Franz Boas Papers
HCINC	House Committee on Immigration and Naturalization Correspondence
HCLP	Henry Cabot Lodge Papers
HCR	Harvard Class Reports
HFOP	Henry Fairfield Osborn Papers
HHLP	Harry H. Laughlin Papers
IRLR	Immigration Restriction League Records
JBTP	John Bond Trevor Papers
JLP	Joseph Lee Papers
LMP	Louis Marshall Papers
NYT	*New York Times*
OCAH	*Oxford Companion to American History*
RFA	Rockefeller Family Archives, Office of the Messrs. Rockefeller
RPHU	Records of the President of Harvard University
SEP	*Saturday Evening Post*

Prologue Ellis Island, 1925

1 Ellis Island conditions: Curran, 287–93. Arnold, 174–75. Kraut, *Huddled Masses*, 16. Alfred C. Reed, "Going Through Ellis Island," *Popular Science*, 1/1913, 5–18. **2** more than 3,000: Moreno, 51. **2** Curran and guests: Henry H. Curran, "The New Immigrant," *SEP*, 8/15/1925, 25. **3** 76 percent, 11 percent: *Annual Report of the Commissioner General of Immigration*, 1925, 8. **3** "ethnological," "electric": CAA, Curran speech introducing La Guardia, 1939. **3** "immigrants of today": Henry H. Curran, "Have We an Alien Menace?," *Collier's*, 7/4/1925, 8. **3** "Biological laws": Calvin Coolidge, "Whose Country Is This?," *Good Housekeeping*, 2/1921, 13–14. **3** "lowly ranks": no author, "The Great American Myth," *SEP*, 5/7/1921, 20. **3** "through science": H. F. Osborn, "Can We Save America?," unpublished, Hellman Papers, Ser. 3, oversize F157. **3** "fundamental": Albert Johnson, "Immigration, a Legislative Point of View," *Nation's Business*, 7/1923, 26–28. **4** "glad to welcome": Curran, *Collier's*, 7/4/1925, 8.

Chapter One The Future Betterment of the Human Race

7 "Protoplasm": Sanger, *Margaret Sanger*, 374–75. **7** "nervous": Riddle, 86. **7** "life of his own": MacDowell, 8. **8** "thrills": Charles Davenport, *Class of 1889, 25th Year*, HCR, 1914, 318–21. **8** unconfident, resentful: MacDowell, 33. **8** "I am deaf": Riddle, 85. **8** papers, boards, memberships: MacDowell, 39–44; Witkowski and Inglis, 53–54. **8** Davenports at Brooklyn Institute: *Yearbook of the Brooklyn Institute*. **9** "chemotropism": Davenport, *Experimental Morphology*, 335. **9** Eliot: CBDP, B36, Eliot to Davenport, 7/30/1894. **10** death notices: Riddle, 79. **10** teaching microscope: CBDP, B66, F: MacDowell, memorial note for Gertrude Crotty Davenport. **10** inveterate walker: MacDowell, 35. **10** "Whenever you can," worms: Pearson, Vol. II, 340, 196. **10** "good fellow": Pearson, Vol. I, 203. **11** "Beauty Map": Galton, *Memories*, 315–16. **11** "Fidget": Francis Galton, "The Measure of Fidget," *Nature*, 6/25/1885. **11** "fleas": Galton, *Inquiries*, 2nd ed., 18. **11** Galton family: galton.org; Pearson, Vol. I, 18. **11** inherit: Haller, 8–9. **12** Galton IQ: Cox, 40–43. **12** 170: Terman,

American Journal of Psychology. **12** French, Scott, *Iliad:* Cox, 40–43; Cowan, v–vi. **12** journey by pony: Pearson, Vol. IIIB, 446. **12** "forehead": Burt, 1. **13** "unusual power": Galton, *Memories,* 11. **13** "white traveler": Galton, *Hereditary Genius,* 339. **13** "dignity": Pearson, Vol. II, 334. **13** medical student: Galton, *Memories,* 37. **13** African expedition: Pearson, Vol. I, 231–32. **14** titles: galton.org. **14** brewing tea: Brookes, 129. **14** 1853: Darwin to Galton, 7/24/1853, at galton.org. **14** "tides . . . insurance": Browne, *Voyaging,* 512. **15** "marked epoch," "ancient": Galton, *Memories,* 287. **15** "fundamental concept": Pearson, Vol. II, 82. **15** "useful reference": Phillips, title page. **15** law of gravity: *DNB.* **16** one in six: Galton, "Hereditary Talent," 159. **16** Aikin, LeSage, Becket: Phillips, 1005, 1042, 1013. **16** Sir *Thomas:* Galton, "Hereditary Talent," 159. **16** Galton's sources: Ibid., 157–66, 318–27. **17** "great eaters": Ibid., 164. **17** mass wedding: Ibid., 165. **17** "oarsmen": Galton, *Hereditary Genius,* 307. **17** Athenians: Ibid., 343. **17** selective breeding: Ibid., 1 (1869 ed.). **19** "high and generous": Ibid., 357 (1869 ed.). **19** "not well received": Diane B. Paul, "Wallace, Women, and Eugenics," in Smith and Beccaloni, 267. **19** "inert": *Saturday Review,* 12/15/1869, 833. **19** "exhale myself": Darwin to Galton, 12/23/1869, galton.org. **19** Some Darwin scholars: See, e.g., Angelique Richardson, "I Differ Widely from You," in Voigts, 17–40. **19** "We now know": Darwin, *Descent,* 111. **20** Clifford: Quoted in Beer, *Darwin's Plots,* 186. **20** fifth edition: Browne, *Power,* 312; wide currency: *OCAH.* **20** Adams: *Education,* 284. **20** "Anthropometric Laboratory": Galton, "On the Anthropometric," 205–18; "On Apparatus," 469–77. **21** other cities: Blacker, 37–38. **21** "nature and nurture": Galton, *English,* 12. **21** "good in stock": Galton, *Inquiries,* 24n. **21** Penn: Robert Ward, "The Crisis in Our Immigration Policy," *The Institution Quarterly,* 6/30/1913, 31. **21** "a new race": Galton, *Hereditary Genius,* 64 (1869 ed.). **21** same notion: Darwin, *Descent,* 168. **21** Bell: Alexander Graham Bell, "Upon the Formation of a Deaf Variety in the Human Race," presented to the National Academy of Sciences, 11/13/1883. **22** "gestation": Woodhull, *Human Body,* 443. **22** "sensuality": Woodhull, *Selected,* 276. **23** denial of "the liberty": Galton, *Memories,* 310–11. **23** "two grades": Galton, *Hereditary Genius,* 339–342 (1869 ed.). **23** paper, Venn: "Abstracts of Papers Communicated to the Seventh International Congress of Hygiene and Demography, London, August 10–17, 1891." **24** other attendees: *British Medical Journal,* 8/15/1891, 315. **24** Galton speech: *Transactions of the Seventh International Congress of Hygiene and Demography.* London: Eyre & Spottiswoode, 1892–1893, Vol. X, 11. **25** Carnegie meeting: Carnegie, *Yearbook,* 1902, xvi, xxi. **25** basic research: Kevles, *In the Name,* 45. **25** earmarked: www.carnegiescience.edu/about/history. **25** "plot of ground": CBDP, B11, F1, Davenport to Trustees, 5/5/1902. **26** "25 years": MacDowell, 19. **26** give up tenure: CBDP, B11, F1, Davenport to Trustees, 5/5/1902. The original draft of the letter included his willingness to give up tenure, which he then crossed out. **26** "better director": MacDowell, 18, Davenport to H. F. Osborn. **26** his qualifications: Ibid., Davenport to John Shaw Billings. **26** Davenport–Galton correspondence: CBDP, B40, 4/6–5/27/1897. **27** "constructors": A. Benedict Davenport, *History and Genealogy of the Davenport Family,* New York: S. W. Benedict, 1851, iii, 12. **27** Young Davenport: CBDP, B16, F: Diaries, 1878; B14, Autobiographical; MacDowell, 39–40. **27** bivalve-hunting: Riddle, 81. **27** dinner, support: MacDowell, 20. **27** trustees granted him: Garland Allen, 229–30. **28** "Yours unworthily," RED LETTER: CBDP, B16, F: Diaries, 1904; MacDowell, 24. **28** "running wild": Charlotte B. DeForest, *Smith College Monthly,* 10/1902, 49. **28** "There was a little": Fogler Library of the University of Maine, Records of the UMaine Laboratory at Lamoine, B1, F41. **29** Mendel: Henig provides an engaging account of Mendel's experiments. **29** Darwin and Mendel's experiments: Vorzimmer, 77–82. **30** soon grasped: Riddle, 83. **30** Davenport's domain: Carnegie, *Yearbook*, 1904, 23, 29; MacDowell, 23. **31** strictly honorary: CBDP, B40, Galton to Davenport, 5/27/1897. **31** sheep experiments: CBDP, B4, Bell to Davenport, 3/11/1904, and continuing through 1914. **31** ABA, "thremmatology": American Breeders Association, *Proceedings*, I (1905), 115, 190. **31** SCIENCE TO MAKE: *Washington Post*, 5/18/1906, 2.

Chapter Two Thrifty, Capable Yankee Blood

33 "harmless": Holmes, "The Brahmin Caste of New England," *Atlantic Monthly*, 1/1860, 92. **33** Papanti's: Marquand, 57. JLP, Box 33, F: Tributes, September 1926, Lee article on Joseph Storrow, *Harvard Graduates' Magazine*, 9/1926. **33** traveling, "complete peace": Marquand, 50. **33** Bostonitis: Adams, *Education*, 419. **34** child of the eighteenth: Ibid., 42. **34** "Had he been": Ibid., 3. **34** "howling": Baltzell, *Protestant*, 92–93. **34** Spain and Morocco: Harap, 1087. **34** "Vesuvius": Samuels, *Selected*, 281. **35** "Warsaw or Cracow," "Indians or the buffalo": Adams, *Education*, 238. **35** same journal: *North American Review*. **35** in *The Nineteenth Century*, Doyle: *A Monthly Review*, 8/1888, 184. **36** "ability": Lodge, "The Distribution of Ability in the United States," *Century Magazine*, 9/1891, 687–94. **36** "common grandmother": Margaret Cabot Lee, 3. **36** opium and slaves: Finding Aid, Cabot Family Papers. **36** George Cabot: Baltzell, *Puritan*, 197. **36** "thin soil": Evan Thomas, 118. **36** Mowry: "Politicking in Acid," *Saturday Review*, 10/3/1953, 30. **37** "disgusted": "Americanisms," *America: A Journal for Americans*, 7/10/1890, 405. **37** Velázquez: Groves, 137–38. **37** wrote weekly: Garraty, 5. **37** "Pinky": Samuels, *Henry Adams* (1989 ed.), 380. **38** "most remarkable": CR, 3/16/1896, 2818. **38** "some Jew": Adams to Lodge, 5/26/1875, in Saveth, 70. **38** "guard our civilization": Lodge, "Restriction," 27–36. **39** "queer species": JLP, B38, F: Genealogy, undated note about Chilton Cabot. **39** *Das Kapital*: JLP, B38, F: List of Books Owned. **39** "not a day": JLP, B5, John F. Moors speech at Twentieth Century Club dinner, 5/8/1936. **39** "founder": JLP, B34, Retirement tribute from Massachusetts Civic League. **39** row house: Sapora, 114. **39** "Difficult Problems": Margaret Cabot Lee, 60. **39** poured large sums: JLP, B39, Joseph Lee donations. **39** forswore: JLP, B5, John F. Moors speech at Twentieth Century Club dinner, 5/8/1936. **39** compelled to take: JLP, B43, F: Joseph Lee Jr. papers about Lee, Memoir by JL Jr. in *Yearbook of the Thomas Dudley Family Association*, 1938, 308. **40** "Expensive Living": Sapora, 109, from Springfield *Sunday Republican*, 3/27/1898. **40** mooring stone: JLP, B5, John F. Moors speech at Twentieth Century Club dinner, 5/8/1936. **40** "helpful": *Boston Globe*, 1/5/1936. **40** "brotherly": *Boston Herald*, 7/29/1937. **40** "whimsical," "original," "life of the party": Mary Coolidge Barton, quoted in Sapora, 100. **40** "Boston's most": Crawford, 286. **40** "personage": Barbara Solomon Papers, B4, F4. Moors unpublished memorial notice. **40** "put the law": Sapora, 164. **41** 74 percent: U.S. Census 1910, 852, 866. **41** "vicious": JLP, Lee to "Blakely," 3/8/1912. **41** "drained": JLP, B2, Nov.–Dec. 1923, Lee to Patten, 12/14/1923. **41** "evil," "Dago," "exclusion": JLP, B1, Apr.–Dec. 1906: Lee to Ward, 12/29/1906. **41** Franklin: Franklin to Peter Collinson, 5/9/1753, *The Papers of Benjamin Franklin, Vol. 4*, digital edition at www.franklinpapers.org. **42** Madison: Zolberg, 58. **42** *New-England Primer*, New York: Beaver, 1750, 23. **42** "Whore": *OCAH* online, "Nativist Movement." **42** Morse: Morse, 70–71. **42** able to elect: Tichenor, 61. **42** denying the vote: Handlin, *Boston's*,

204. **43** Douglass: Tichenor, 37, from Douglass, *My Bondage and My Freedom* (New York: Miller Orton, 1855), 454–55. **43** "thronging": Zolberg, 166. **43** American Emigrant Company: Erickson, 9–10, 24–25; American Emigrant Company brochure, "Statement of the Object and Mode of Operation of This Company," New York: 1865. **44** In western states: Abbott, 139. **44** Hill: Morris, *Theodore Rex*, 599. **44** unlawful: Arnold, 109–13, citing *People v. Hall*, 1854. **44** Supreme Court barred: *Re: Ah Yup*, 1878. **44** "instinctive": Bisland, 138, Lafcadio Hearn to Ellwood Kendrick, 8/1883. **45** "no standard": Gossett, 291. **45** "biped": López, 44. **46** "Reilly . . . Ah-San": Stoddard, *Rising Tide*, 274. **46** Pittsfield: Bluford Adams, 22. **46** total Russian Jewish: Kuznets, 35. **46** cholera epidemic: Handlin, *Uprooted*, 33; Kohn, 197. **47** "Evil Effects": Higham, *Strangers*, 41. **47** 20 percent: Schrag, 24. **47** "American Dublin": Brooks, 7. **47** "ignorance and vice": Keyssar, 119. **47** "blessed garden": Aaron, 260. **47** "higher and pleasanter": Norton and Howe, 254. **48** one foreign-born: Thernstrom, 113. **48** "No sound": James, *American*, 231. **48** Bushee: Woods, 140. **48** "pale babies": Bellamy, 457–61. **49** "Abraham Cohen": Kraut, *Silent*, 208. **49** Jewish doctors: Richard Clarke Cabot Papers, B:29, F: Various correspondence, 1908–1929; Cabot interview, 10/6/1922. **49** Jewish hospital: Linenthal, 36, 373. **49** "no current": Garraty, 1670. **50** "Dude of Nahant," "Lah-de-dah," "Silver Spoon": Schriftgiesser, 57. No, not "Duke" of Nahant, as some sources have it! The term "dude," roughly equivalent to "dandy," attained currency in the early 1880s, as Lodge entered public life. The "Dude" epithet was attached to Lodge firmly enough for his first biographer to use it as a chapter title (Schriftgiesser, Chapter V). **50** "ancestral acres": Solomon, 68. **50** "aristocratic disdain": *ANB*. **50** Bemis: Edward W. Bemis, "Restriction of Immigration," *Andover Review*, 3/1888, 251–64. **51** Lodge article and speech: Lodge, "Restriction"; *CR*, 2/19/1891. **52** "Race pride": Lodge, *Boston*, 210–11. **53** "let loose": *The Nation*, 4/20/1891, 149–50. **53** "Polish society": *NYT*, 2/11/1891. **53** New Orleans: Lodge, "Lynch Law," 602. **53** glass factory: Higham, *Strangers*, 92. **54** APA: Higham, "Mind," 20–21. **54** main address: "Abuses Many," *Boston Globe*, 6/1/1894, 3. **54** downtown Boston: IRLR, Ser. II, Executive Committee Minutes, Vol. 1, 5/31/1894. **54** Noble's: Solomon, 99. **54** initiated: IRLR, Additional Papers, "To the Members of the IRL," 6/4/1924. **54** Winthrop: Ward's mother was a descendant of Richard Saltonstall. **54** "old-time families": Mrs. Prescott F. Hall, xiii. **55** Hall never: Mrs. Prescott F. Hall, xii–xiii, xv, 119–23. **55** "no two": Blodgett, 620. **55** "No generalization": Brooks, 259. **56** Paine: *CR*, 5/20/1896, 5476. **56** Henry Lee: IRLR, F589, H. Lee to Warren, 7/3/1894. **56** John Murray Forbes: *ANB*. **56** "Strictly private": IRLR, F431, Forbes to Warren, 7/16/1894. **57** "old crank:" JLP, B33, F: Leo Tolstoy visit, 1889. **57** requesting copies: JLP, B1, F: 1894–1896. Lee to State Board, 8/15/1894. **57** family money: JLP, B38, F: Financial Statements, 1898. **57** wrote to tell Lee: Sapora, 80. **58** "a society started": JLP, B36, F: Margaret Cabot Lee. **58** "bible": JLP, B1, F: 1894–1896, Hall to Lee, 5/6/1895. **58** "Study These": IRLR, Publications of the IRL, No. 2. **58** "thrifty, capable": *Boston Herald*, Hall to editor, 6/25/1894. **58** personal emissary: JLP, B43, F: Joseph Lee Jr. papers about Lee, Memoir by JL Jr. in *Yearbook of the Thomas Dudley Family Association*, 1938. **58** "sifted few": Holmes, from his poem "Urania," at www.poemhunter.com. **59** "our dear land": Solomon, 87. **59** "educational test": IRLR, Additional Papers, "The Present Aspect of the Immigration Problem." **59** two decades: Garraty, 46. **59** "obvious choice": *ANB*. **59** Walker's article: "Immigration," 133–37. **60** "Where Mrs. Lodge": Adams, *Education*, 354. **60** "repellent": Garraty, 158. **61** LeBon's views: Higham, *Strangers*, 141–

42. **61** Lodge speech: *CR*, 3/16/1896, 2817–19. **62** "bed sheet": Garraty, 61. **62** *"No one," "everybody," "history"*: Lodge, "Restriction," 27–36. **62** "if a lower," "The danger": *CR*, 3/16/1896, 2819. **63** Emerson: *DAB*, "Emma Lazarus." **63** Henry James: Carole Kessner, "The Emma Lazarus–Henry James Connection: Eight Letters," *American Literary History*, Spring 1991, 46–62. **63** Lowell: Harap, 296. **63** Thomas Bailey Aldrich: mark twainproject.org/biographies. **63** venerated: Solomon, 112. **64** "cesspool": Greenslet, 168. **64** "Wide open": www.poemhunter.com. **64** "A-1": Morison, *Letters*, Roosevelt to Lodge, 3/23/1896. **64** "most scholarly": *Boston Advertiser*, 3/17/1896. **65** effigy: *St. Louis Post-Dispatch*, 3/18/1896, 1. **65** Hoar: Solomon, 118. **65** maids, cooks: Hutchinson, *Legislative*, 116–18. **65** Schultheis: IRLR, F820, Schultheis to Prescott Hall, 12/4/1896. **65** Danford: *CR*, 1/27/1897, 1219. **65** Wilson: *CR*, 5/20/1896, 5472. **65** Elijah A. Morse: *CR*, 1/27/1897, 1230. **65** condemned mob: Message to Congress, 12/8/1885. **66** "hardy laboring": Message to Congress, 12/2/1895. **66** Cleveland veto message: 3/3/1897. **66** new president: HCLP, Reel 141, Lodge to Curtis Guild, 2/15/1897. **66** carefully deleted: Morris, *Rise*, 537. **67** "too ignorant": Hutchinson, *Legislative*, 118–24. **67** suspected McKinley: Petit, 29. **67** Hall managed: IRLR, F658, Telegram, J. A. Porter to Hall, 11/14/1898. **67** McKinley might: IRLR, Executive Committee Minutes, 11/23/1898. **67** donated its papers: IRLR, Executive Committee Minutes, 4/1/1899; file memorandum, 10/11/1899. **68** "Enough! Enough!": IRLR, F1082, 5th of 6 folders: undated, in Hall's handwriting.

Chapter Three The Warfare of the Cradle

69 Albert Ballin, steerage: Sorin, 45; Chernow, 103–5. **70** average fare: Nadell, 88. **70** cubic feet: IRLR, F999, William Williams to Prescott Hall, 12/27/1902. **70** cram two thousand, herring: Kraut, *Huddled*, 49. **70** recruiting agents: Nadell, 46–51. **70** In southern Italy: Kraut, *Huddled*, 16. **70** "I welcome": Antonio Mangano, "The Effects of Emigration Upon Italy," *Charities and the Commons*, 1/4/1908, 1329. **70** Oświęcim: IRLR, F1060, 5th of 9, Herbert Sherwood report for National Liberal Immigration League, 7/21/1907. **71** "insidious": HCLP, Reel 141, Lodge to Mr. Hayes, 2/15/1897. **71** "pressing evil": Higham, *Strangers*, 71. **71** "only issue": Gompers, Vol. II, 171. **71** "threats to members": HCLP, Reel 141, Lodge to W. G. Hunneman, 2/1/1897. **71** direct payments: See *St. Louis Post-Dispatch*, 10/2/1913. Rep. Richard Bartholdt had been accepting considerations from two German lines since 1895. **72** North German Lloyd, Claussenius: *Chicago Times-Herald*, 1/28/1897. **72** Guild, Ward: HCLP, Reel 141, Lodge to Curtis Guild, 2/18/1897; Lodge to Ward, 2/20/1897. **72** "so far superior": *Saturday Evening Post*, 5/7/1910, cited in Kenin and Wintle, 496. **73** personal plea: Sachar, 285. **74** almost immediately accepted: Baltzell, *Protestant*, 56; Urofsky, 38. **74** Hall and Brandeis: Hearings of the Subcommittee of Senate Judiciary Committee, 3/8/16, 1312–14. **74** Adler: *Harvard Graduates' Magazine*, 12/1904, 322. Most of those who have written about Adler have expressed uncertainty about his ethnicity. Those willing to take a deep dive on the Internet, however, can trace Adler to Millersburg, Ohio, and a further step will take the investigator to *A Century and a Half of Pittsburg and Its People, Vol. 4*, published in 1908 (and now residing at Google Books). There one finds Adler's relatives among the membership of the city's Congregation Rodeph Shalom. Perhaps this is an example of why the Internet was invented, and why some books take so long to write. **74** Hale: Harap,

713. **74** Emma Lazarus's father: *NYT*, 2/11/207, RE7. **74** "admission of Hebrews": *NYT*, 4/15/1893, 1. **74** Bombay: Spiro, 96–97. **75** bride's family: Dinnerstein, 52. **75** hundred Jews: Peter C. Holloran, *Boston's Wayward Children: Social Services for Homeless Children, 1830–1930* (Rutherford, NJ: Fairleigh Dickinson University Press, 1989), 158. **75** "very Jew," "hung," "appall[ed]": Lash, 214. All three letters were sent to her mother-in-law in the winter of 1918. **75** "frayed raiment": Cook, 390. **76** "immigrant's disease": Hoy, 99. **76** Sulzberger: Glazier, 9, citing "Jews at Summer Resorts," *American Hebrew*, 7/4/1884, 122. **77** "uncouth Asiatics," "gnaw the bones": Sachar, 125. **77** term "kike": For example, see *Seventh Biennial Session of the National Conference of Jewish Charities in the United States*, 1912, 226. **77** "ignorance and depravity": Glazier, 32, citing *American Israelite*, 3/26/1891, 1. **77** "receive [and] disperse," Cotopaxi: Osofsky, 179–81. **78** New Odessa: Sachar, 135. **78** seed money: Ibid., 134. **78** Augustus A. Levey: Glazier, 8, citing *Jewish Messenger*, 9/8/1882, 2. **78** not tolerate: Sachar, 124. **78** In Boston . . . 415 Russian Jews: Fein, 38–39; *Boston Hebrew Observer*, 1/26/1883, 28; 11/23/1883, 4; 3/30/1883, 100. **79** 7,500: Marinbach, 104. **79** Voorsanger: Sorin, 55. **79** Schiff, port of Galveston: Brawley, passim; Kraut, 65; Glazier, 59. **79** sell everything: Marinbach, 24. **80** kosher meals: Glazier, 110. **80** "Large numbers": *Hearings, House Committee on Immigration and Naturalization*, 3/10/1910, 287. **80** "injure the country": Roosevelt, *Selections*, TR to HCL, 3/19/1897. **80** "careful and not": TR Message to Congress, 12/3/1901. **82** Roosevelt was befriended: Morris, *Rise*, 290. **82** who most influenced: Evan Thomas, 77. **82** "observant foot traveler": Shaler, "European Peasants as Immigrants," *Atlantic Monthly*, 5/1893, 647–55. **82** "Jew bankers": Morison, Vol. VI, 556. TR to Anna Roosevelt Cowles, 11/13/1896. **82** "show Russia": Straus, 210. **82** particularly upset: Cannato, 156–58. **83** "a 'settler'": Roosevelt, *Autobiography*, 1. **83** bodyguards: Sachar, 215. **83** "his principles": Aaron, 249. **83** "*de notre monde,*" "our brains": Morris, *Theodore Rex*, 52, 560. **83** large families: Dyer, 148. **83** "most fecund": Ibid., 147. **83** "extinguishment": theodore-roosevelt .com, TR to James Wilson, 2/3/03. **83** "native Americans": See, e.g., IRLR, F832, Prescott Hall to George Shiras, 2/6/1914; CBDP, B42, F: Madison Grant, Grant to Fairfield Osborn, 3/9/1918; JLP, B1, Samuel J. Barrows to Lee, 2/3/1906. **84** "half-filled": Gossett, 243. **84** "warfare": Roosevelt, "National Life and Character," *Sewanee Review*, 8/1894. **84** *Melting Pot*: Dyer, 131. **84** "severest of all": *Outlook*, 4/30/1910, 986. **84** "vicious-ness": theodore-roosevelt.com, speech, 2/13/1905. **84** "whole future": Roosevelt, "Race Decadence," *Outlook*, 4/8/1911, 766. **84** "I, for one": Roosevelt, ibid., 764. **85** "see a white man": Evan Thomas, 140, TR to HCL, 8/13/1896. **85** "melancholy": Dyer, 158, TR to Jordan, 12/12/08. **85** "nice friends": Spiro, 99, quoting Wister, *Theodore Roosevelt*, 66. **85** "vulgar modes": John Stuart Mill, *Principles of Political Economy*, London: John W. Parker, 1849, Vol. 1, 390. **87** "my husband": Spiro, 107. **88** "one is fascinated," "very per-nicious": Ibid., 106. **88** "Everywhere the white races": Gobineau, 456. **88** certain ambiv-alence: Biddiss, *Father of Racist Ideology*, 45, 165. **88** "artistic genius": Carlson, 288, 294. **89** "anthropologically unintelligible": Gossett, 345. For a more recent examination of the genetic meaning of race, see Aravinda Chakravarti, ed., *Human Variation: A Genetic Perspective on Diversity, Race, and Medicine* (Cold Spring Harbor, NY: Cold Spring Laboratory Press, 2014). **89** Gossett notes: Gossett, 82. **90** Adolf Hitler . . . Joseph Goebbels paid: James Joll, "Ravings of a Renegade," *New York Review of Books*, 9/24/1981; Spiro, 112–13. **90** "Physically and mentally": Chamberlain, 542. **90** these sentences, "mongreldom": Ibid., 537, 328. **90** "That Dante is": Ibid., 538. **90** Marco Polo et al.: Spiro,

iii; Gossett, 350. **90** Shaw . . . Churchill: Field, 464, 463. **90** Roosevelt, by then: "The Foundations of the Nineteenth Century," *Outlook*, 6/29/1911, 195–203. **90** Hall, Lee: JLP, B1, Hall to Lee, 7/23/1911. **91** He dismantled: Ripley, 477–85. **91** first page . . . book's end: Ibid., 1, 529. **92** "vulgar": Ibid., 516. **92** "William . . . 'Tonio": Ross, *Old World*, 303. **92** introduced the phrase: Ross, "Causes," 88. **92** Ross description: Hertzler, passim; *ANB*; Greenberg, 37. **93** "raise hell": *ANB*. **93** Ross's firing, AAUP: Menand, 411–12. **93** "Sacramento hardware merchants": Ross, *Seventy*, 69. **93** "hollowness": Hofstadter and Metzger, 437–39. **93** "ruthless," hundreds of thousands: Gossett, 168–69. **94** "reprints," "good repute": Ross, "Capsules of Social Wisdom," *Social Forces*, 12/1948, 186, 188. **94** "higher race": Ross, "Causes," 88. **94** "fuzzy term": Mike Wallace, 84. **94** "lower races": Ross, "Causes," 85. **95** "oxlike": Ross, *Old World*, 285. **95** "deserves the extinction": Ibid., 304. **95** "A Yellow World": Chang, 11. **95** "unfit," "brutalized": Francis A. Walker, "Restriction of Immigration," *Atlantic Monthly*, 6/1896, 822–29. **95** "masses of filth": Walker, "Immigration," 135, 137. **96** inferior: Walker, "Immigration and Degradation," 426. **96** "great majority": Walker, "Restriction of Immigration," 823. **96** *"pride of blood,"* "uncompromising": Ross, "Causes." **96** just as much: Wister, *Roosevelt*, 65–66. **96** "educated and careful," "few or no": "Men of the Month," *The Crisis*, 10/1916, 278. **96** "train and breed": English, 5. **96** 2.02 children: Roland M. Byrnes, "Vital Statistics of Yale Graduates," *Yale Alumni Weekly*, 6/19/1907, 914–16. **96** "had failed": IRLR, F1078, "Copied from The Transcript." **96** Phillips's study: John C. Phillips, "A Study of the Birth-Rate in Harvard and Yale Graduates," *Harvard Graduates' Magazine*, 9/1916, 25–34. **96** "South Italians": Terman, "The Conservation of Talent," *School and Society*, 3/29/1924, 359–64. **97** "Roumanian lady": JLP, B2, Lee typescript, 11/29/1922, "Immigration and the Women's Clubs." **98** 68 percent: Hall, "Italian Immigration," 252. **98** Lee, Brandeis, Frankfurter: JLP, B36, F: Margaret Cabot Lee, Lee to MCL, 6/19/1918. **98** Lourie: JLP, B14, F: BSC, Naming Schools, Lee to "Hugh," 12/1/1914. **98** peddlers and bootblacks: See, e.g., HFOP, B32, F19, Irving Fisher to Osborn, 11/15/1923. **98** "barbarian invasions": IRLR, F1086, clip from *Lexington* (KY) *Herald*, 3/17/1908. **98** Jordan said: Jordan, "Should Present Restriction Laws Be Modified?," *Congressional Digest*, 7–8/1923, 304. **99** complete ban: IRLR, F188, Brown to Prescott Hall, 4/25/1910. **99** *Post* editorial: *Washington Post*, 5/10/1906, 6. **99** Simmons of North Carolina: *Raleigh News & Observer* online, 12/15/2015. **99** "furtive," "bath": Wister, *Philosophy*, 30, 40. **99** social reformer I. M. Rubinow: Ribak, 44–45. **100** seven returning: Kessner, 28. **100** "pig-sty," "conspicuous faults": Riis, 48–49, 53. **100** "inborn suavity": *Boston Evening Transcript*, 7/18/1907. **100** Antonio Stella, Enrico Caruso: Iorizzo, 100; Caruso, 371. **100** Daughters of the American Revolution: Finding Aid, Carr Papers. **101** "Bathe the whole body," "good wages": Carr, 47, 20–21. **101** "immigrant predecessors": Carr, "The Coming of the Italian," *Outlook*, 2/24/1906. **102** Italian Settlement dedicated: *NYT*, 4/30/1944, 46. **102** Messina earthquake, "our experience": LaGumina, 112–13. **102** "duty": IRLR, F343, W. E. Davenport to Hall, 3/7/10. **102** "neglected," "burdens": CBDP, W. E. Davenport to C. B. Davenport, 2/18/1924. **102** His brother Charles: Cinotto, 102–3.

Chapter Four The Kindled Fire

103 out for dinner: COHP, "Reminiscences of William Stiles Bennet," 35–38. **104** "psychical": See Hall, "Experiments with Mrs. Caton," *Proceedings of the American Society for Psychical Research*, 1914, 1. **104** small salary . . . office expenses: IRLR, Ser. II, Executive Committee Minutes, 12/5/1901; JLP, B1, Richards Bradley to Lee, 6/11/1919. **104** "the mainspring": Mrs. Prescott F. Hall, xxv. **104** Republican platform: Higham, *Strangers*, 113. **104** Lee was pleased: JLP, B1, Lee to Lodge, 2/5/1907. **104** "a few patriots": JLP, B2, Patten to Frederick Bigelow, 2/10/1923. **105** personal expense: Sapora, 136; Solomon, 850. **105** They included . . . last appearance: IRLR, F41, letterhead of Purity Society, 2/14/1911; Patten testimony, Senate Immigration Committee Hearings, 7/28/1939. **105** "ablest lobbyist," its liaison: JLP, B1, Lee to Marjory Moors, 8/9/1917. **105** "Jew," "Chink": JLP, B1, Patten to Lee, 11/28/1910; B1, Patten to Lee, 1/11/1913; Patten to Prescott Hall, 1/19/1918. **106** "overwhelmed": JLP, B1, Patten to Lee, 3/8/1906. **106** "patricians of those races": Gossett, 437–38. **106** "In general": JLP, B1, Eliot to R. M. Bradley, 2/7/1906. **107** "letter from God": Urofsky, 457. **107** Lowell petition: Ibid., 445. **107** "no interest": JLP, B1, Bradley to Eliot, 12/19/1905. **107** opposing intermarriage . . . a lot of support: RPHU, B222, F279, *American Hebrew*, 3/19/1909; *Town Topics*, 3/11/1909. **107** He insisted: Henry James, *Eliot*, Eliot to unnamed correspondent, 11/21/1892. **107** "Anglo-American by race": JLP, B28, F: Harvard 1921–1925, Eliot to Lee, 4/10/1924. **107** "more Italian": Solomon, 187. **108** "You and I": Baltzell, *Protestant*, 145. **108** NLIL: Lissak, 197–238. **108** opposing immigration: *Proceedings of the First General Meeting, National Liberal Immigration League*, 3/10/1908, 13. **108** Curley of Boston: Lissak, 228. **108** its first book: Edmund J. James, ed., *The Immigrant Jew in America* (New York: Buck and Co., 1907). **108** league's letterhead: IRLR, F705, JLP, B1, 10/30/1912. **109** "sordid": Wilson, Vol. V, 213. **109** "great people": Link, 383. **109** "Gompers writes": IRLR, F1125, first of four. Eliot to Lauterbach, 2/1/1907, reprinted in pamphlet "Contrary Views on Immigration," National Liberal Immigration League. **109** union label: CWEP, B98, F: NLIL, Eliot to N. Behar, 1/6/1911; Behar to Eliot, 11/13/1912. **109** National Association of Manufacturers: Higham, *Strangers*, 116. **109** "despotism": Suggs, 66–67. **109** plantation: Bertram Wyatt-Brown, "Leroy Percy and Sunnyside," *Arkansas Historical Quarterly*, Spring 1991, 60–84. **109** Percy: *Proceedings of the First General Meeting, National Liberal Immigration League*, 3/10/1908. **110** "vicious types": *Philadelphia Inquirer*, 3/25/1908. **110** "dig our ditches": IRLR, F468, Wickersham to Madison Grant, 12/21/1912. **110** Ross insisted: Ross, *Old World*, 144. **110** bow-and-curtsy: IRLR, F705. **110** "Bible says": IRLR, F705, N. Behar to Hall, 2/26/1907. **111** "group of Jews": IRLR, F338, Hall to R. Fulton Cutting, 1/17/1908. **111** spy for the IRL: IRLR, F468, Hall to Madison Grant, 2/11/1907. **111** "get some Jew": IRLR, F540, O. C. Kidney to Hall, 7/1/1912. **111** head tax, $25: Hutchinson, *Legislative*, 138–39. **112** "best elements": *CR*, 5/23/1906, Sen. Furnifold Simmons, 7294. **112** air space: IRLR, F608, 3rd of 4, Lodge to Prescott Hall, 4/25/1908. **112** Lee could say: JLP, B1, Lee to "members of the immigration committee," n.d. **113** German agent: JLP, B1, Lee to Lodge, 2/26/1916. **113** "uncouth": JLP, B1, Patten to Prescott Hall, 1/21/1920. **113** "wote": Salter, 197. **113** "extraordinary spectacles": *NYT*, 6/16/1907, 7. **113** Cannon roamed: Tichenor, 126. **114** recruited the mayors: IRLR, F1125, first of four, NLIL pamphlet "An Appeal to American Citizens." **114** Gibbons of Baltimore: IRLR, F563, Jesse Taylor fundraising letter, 3/26/1906. **114** promise to Gardner: JLP,

B1, Robert Ward to Lee, 1/10/1907. **114** "disadvantage politically": Roosevelt, *Selections*, 227; Morison, Roosevelt to Lodge, 8/15/1906. **115** "deserving immigrants": JLP, B1, Bennet to NLIL, 2/19/1907. **115** "Cousin Lodge": JLP, B1, Lee to Lodge, 2/5/1907. **115** "old charm," "felicity": James, *American*, 243. **116** ludicrous exercise: IRLR, F1051; see, for instance, meeting of 4/11/1903. **116** his wallet: JLP, B39, F: Donations, IRL, 2/1908. **116** "embodies," "not immortal": Lee letter to editor, *Boston Herald*, 9/3/1900. **117** ONE AMERICAN: *Boston Globe*, 3/31/1908, 5. **117** Mount Vernon Street: Author visit. **117** "VOTED": IRLR, Ser. II, Executive Committee Minutes, 3/30/1908. **117** Alexander Graham Bell: IRLR, F117, Hall to Bell, 3/31/1908. **117** reading list: IRLR, F590, 5/5/1908. **118** Publication No. 51, "wars": Mrs. Prescott F. Hall, n.p. **118** Charles Davenport's Station: Carnegie, *Yearbook*, 1907. **118** "prevent the outbreeding": Johnson, "The Eugenic Aspect of Birth Control," *Birth Control Review*, 1/1922, 16. **118** hilltop, "nostril height": Carnegie, *Yearbook*, 1907, 79, 76. **119** passion fruit, "outside source": Carnegie, *Yearbook*, 1910, 75, 77. **119** "richest woman": *NYT*, 11/8/1932, 21. **119** "distributed among": CBDP, B22, FR: Background, early studies: 1909. **119** "socially fit," "weak," "preventive": CBDP, B125, Davenport to Starr J. Murphy, 7/n.d./1910. **120** that summer was: MacDowell, 29. **120** "group of girls": E. Roosevelt bio, website of Association of Junior Leagues International, ajli.org. **120** carriage uptown, "Eugenia": Donn Mitchell, "Debutantes of the World Unite: The Irrepressible Mary Harriman," www .anglicanexaminer.com. **120** H. Fairfield Osborn: Jordan, 297–98. **121** *Who's Who*: MacDowell, 29. **121** "most 'surely'": CBDP, B84, Mary Harriman (daughter) to Davenport, 2/26/1909. **121** In a will: *NYT*, 11/8/1932, 21; Campbell, 1. **121** "great opportunity," six thousand requests, "become efficient": William Allen, v, 3. **121** "unfortunate ones," "decay of the American": CBDP, B45: Harriman to Davenport, Thanksgiving Day, 11/30/1911. **122** decisions . . . checks: Mehler, 365–66. **122** marble bust: *Arts and Decoration*, 4/1915, 251; catalog, Sotheby's, 2012 Impressionist and Modern Art Sale. **122** "equal to": Carl Gray, in *NYT*, 11/8/1932, 21. **123** called Arden: *NYT*, 9/28/1909, 8; various photographs. **123** Davenport's plans, "fit matings," "monument to the memory": CBDP, B84, Davenport to Harriman, 2/3/1910. In the letter he says his plan required $500,000 a year. The prevailing interest rate in 1910 was 4 percent. **124** "time lost": MacDowell, 29. **124** Rockefeller: CBDP, B125, Davenport to Murphy, 6/7/1910, 7/n.d./1910. **124** Jacob Schiff: CBDP, B84, Davenport to Schiff, 5/25/1910. **124** absolute punctuality, "cloak": Campbell, 1, 46. **124** "Red Letter Day": MacDowell, 29. **125** retard evolutionary progress: Carlson, 196. **125** "feeling around": CBDP, B59, Davenport to Jordan, 5/24/1910. **125** Muir: Campbell, 67–84. **125** "little visit," speech: Jordan, 297–98. **125** "wholesome home life": CBDP, B45, F: Harriman, Jordan to Harriman, 7/22/1910. **126** "doesn't want": CBDP, B59, Jordan to Davenport, 7/20/1910. **126** She sailed: CBDP, B45, Harriman to Davenport, 5/29/1911. **126** prize Holsteins: CBDP, B45, Davenport to Harriman (daughter), 12/5/1910. **126** "uplifting," "broad plans": CBDP, B45, Davenport to Harriman, 6/24/1910. **126** 95 percent: CBDP, B29, "Notes on the History of the Eugenics Record Office." **126** "farseeing": Kuhl, 87. **127** instructor at his alma mater, "most profitable," stop over in Kirksville: Garland Allen, 236–38. **127** "youth and energy": CBDP, B45, Davenport to Harriman, 6/27/1910. **127** few semesters' work: Hassencahl, 50–51. **127** "little papers," family histories: CBDP, B45, Davenport to Harriman, 6/27/1910. **128** "worthless": Garland Allen, 243. **128** "conflagration": CBDP, B45, Davenport to Harriman, 2/21/1911. **128** "Red letter day": CBDP, B45, Davenport to Harriman, 10/1/1910. **129** "well built," encouraged to emigrate: Pearson, Vol. IIIA, 422, 420. **129** told Galton: Pearson, Vol. IIIB, Davenport to Galton, 10/26/1910. **130** "well-assembled machine," "mechanical skill": CBDP, B45, Davenport to 7/20/1910; 7/24/1910. **130** "Seamen know": Davenport and Scudder, 26. **130** his belief that: Kevles, *In the Name*, 48–49. **131** "extreme measures": Davenport, *Fit*, 664. **131** Punnett: Smith and Wehmeyer, 138, 225. **132** If the institutions: Bix, 619. **132** *Trait Book*, "community reactions": *Bulletin No. 6*, Eugenics Record Office, 1919. **132** 3,500 human attributes: CIWA, Genetics, B10, F1: Barbara Burks, "Report of Activities, 11/15/36–6/30/37." **134** "silly old fellow": Garland Allen, 243. **134** "wedding outfit": Eugenics Record Office Records, F36, Field worker files, Hester Ann Aldridge. **134** half a million: Garland Allen, 239. **135** "standing of the nation": CBDP, B28, "The Family and the Nation." **135** "Buffalo Bill": *EN*, 3/20, 16. **135** "insane, feeble-minded": CBDP, B45, Davenport to Harriman, 1/5/1911. **135** "tactful": CBDP, B125, Davenport to Starr J. Murphy, 1/20/1911. **136** "careless . . . inaccurate": David Heron, "Mendelism and the problem of mental defect: A criticism of recent American work," *Questions of the Day and of the Fray*, 1913, 61. **136** listed in *Who's Who*: IRLR, F1072, Prescott Hall affidavit, 6/10. **136** "Harvard Medical School": Committee report, *American Breeders Magazine*, 1912, 249–55. **136** prominent white: Hall, 7/22/1905, in Petit, 154n. **136** union officials: IRLR, F1071, 1/20/1902. **136** particularly risible: IRLR, F1049l, 7/1905. **136** Boston Juvenile Court, new headquarters: Sapora, 114, 119–20. **137** Lee's personal poll: JLP, B1, 11/1905; Ward to Lee, 12/3/1905. **137** Barrows: JLP, B1, Lee to Barrows, 12/13/1905. **138** "public opinion is largely": IRLR, F472: Hall to Charles M. Green, 4/29/1910. **138** Bradford: IRLR, F159, Bradford to Hall, attached "manifesto," 4/28/1910. **138** Maxim: IRLR, F646, Maxim to Hall, 3/9/1910. **138** Wilcox: IRLR, F992, Wilcox to Hall, 3/29/1910. **138** Hall, Ward, Ripley: IRLR, Ripley to Hall, 2/16/1909. **139** "a racial [question]": Ward, "National Eugenics." **139** "general tendency": JLP, B1, Lee to George H. Ellis, 11/11/1911. **139** "Perhaps I ought not": CBDP, B44, Hall to Davenport, 4/14/1911.

Chapter Five Short, Sober, Musical Rapists

141 thirty-five trips: IRLR, table of arrivals, Port of Boston, 1901. **142** 220,000: Iorizzo, 220. **142** "unable to supply": IRLR, F916, 2nd of 2, [E. A. Moffett?] of Dillingham Commission to Prescott Hall, 10/17/1910. **142** socialist Sidney Webb: Kevles, *In the Name*, 74. **142** more than two-thirds: Alderman, 150. **142** "white Australia": Daniels, 33. **142** Wells told: Wells, *Future*, 195–201. **142** "exceedingly abominable": Wells, *Anticipations*, 299. **143** fewer than: Fitzgerald and Martin, 99. **143** "no race," "pure" European: Davenport, *Heredity*, 222, 188. **144** "pathetic and unedifying": Davenport, *Heredity*, quoting Francis N. Balch, 199. **144** "Would you not," "they are sincere": IRLR, F342, Davenport to Hall, 5/20/1911; Hall to Davenport, 5/22/1911. **144** blunt assertion: *Boston Herald*, 6/25/1894. **145** Eugenic Immigration League: Solomon, 150. **145** "comparative capacity": *Boston Evening Transcript*, 6/2/1906, 2. **145** "race selection": JLP, B1, Lee to R. M. DeForest, 2/2/1907. **145** "fitness": JLP, B1, Lee to L. T. Chamberlain, 5/29/1906. **145** "need of more facts": IRLR, F342, Davenport to Hall, 3/23/1912. **146** he proposed: IRLR, F342, Davenport to Hall, 5/20/1911. **146** colleague Robert Ward: Ward, "National Eugenics," 56–67. **146** "lose sight," "oft repeated," "Unless conditions," "mercurial people," "series of visits": Davenport, *Heredity*, 225, 251, 219, 224, 268. **148** "paid agent," related to Emil Boas:

IRLR, F342, Hall to Davenport, 5/22/1911. **148** Emil Boas: Norman Boas, 181. **148** "fat job": IRLR, F342, Hall to Davenport, 5/22/1911. **148** demanded it: IRLR, F342, Davenport to Hall, 11/17/1911. **148** "did more to combat": Gossett, 418. **149** "My ideas have": Boas, "An Anthropologist's Credo," *The Nation*, 8/27/1938. **149** "If I do not": Norman Boas, 15. **149** "unquestionably the greatest": Mitchell, "Man—with Variations," *New York World-Telegram*, 11/1/1937, 29. **149** "easy to be": Painter, 229. **149** comparing the cranial: Brinton, 25–26. **150** speech that shredded: Claudia Roth Pierpont, "The Measure of America," *The New Yorker*, 3/8/2004, 48–50. **150** Brinton insisted: *Science*, 8/30/1895, 249. **150** repeatedly resign: COHP, "Reminiscences of Franziska Boas," 67–68. **150** notable scars: Gossett, 418–19; COHP, Franziska Boas, 25. **150** visit with him: CBDP, B5, 6/13/1910. **151** same obsessiveness: COHP, "Reminiscences of Franziska Boas," 65–68. **151** journalists, "Preposterous!," "icy enthusiasm": Mitchell, *New York World-Telegram*, 11/2/1937, 13. **151** psychoanalysis, "Contemporary Operetta": COHP, Franziska Boas, 40, 13, 34. **151** Lowie, Mead: *ANB*. **152** Worcester incident, "middle-aged Eskimo": Norman Boas, 101–2, 119. **152** flesh stripped: Spiro, 49. **152** Stocking called it: Mike Wallace, 351. **152** "spared the struggle": Norman Boas, 12–13. **153** "label 'reactionary'": Duffy, Hand, and Orth, *The Vermont Encyclopedia* (Burlington: University of Vermont Press, 2003), 106. **153** United States Immigration Commission work: Zeidel, 21–55, 101. **153** "licking envelopes": Lepore, 76. **153** "exhaustive inquiry": Zeidel, 101. **153** "superior," "inferior": Guterl, 45–46. **154** His *Dictionary*: Dillingham, Vol. 5, 3, 11, 18. **154** *Changes in Bodily Form*: Dillingham, Vol. 38; Herskovitz, 39; King, *Making*, 65–69. **154** von Török: Handlin, *Race*, 88. **154** selling skulls: David Thomas, 59–60. **155** "obvious fact": Russell, 255. **155** "no stability": FBP, Boas to Jacob Schiff, 4/12/1909. **156** "exorbitant prices": FBP, Boas to W. P. Dillingham, 6/17/1910. **156** "carefully read": FBP, Schiff to Boas, 6/14/1910. **156** "unrelenting empiricism": Julian H. Steward, in "Alfred Louis Kroeber," National Academy of Sciences Biographical Memoirs, 1962. **156** final report: Dillingham, Vol. 1, 44. **156** Folkmar's . . . "reliable": Dillingham, Vol. 1, 210. **157** "lecture notes": Ward, *Climate: Considered Especially in Relation to Man* (New York: Putnam, 1907), iii. **157** "astral projection": Mrs. Prescott F. Hall, xv. **157** Appalled . . . declined: IRLR, F417, Hall to J. A. Field, 4/28/1912; F143, Hall to Boas, 8/28/1912. **157** "securing laws": CBDP, B1, F:1, American Breeders Association Committee, Ward to Davenport, 12/8/1911. **158** Hall's article: Hall, "The Future of American Ideals," *North American Review*, 1/1912. **158** Alexander E. Cance: IRLR, F226, Cance to Hall, n.d. **158** "any manners": IRLR, F417, Hall to J. A. Field, 4/28/1912. **158** published report argued: *American Breeders Magazine*, 1912, 249–55. **159** "We scientists," "his jester," "all America's streams": *NYT*, "Social Problems Have Proven Basis in Heredity," 1/12/1913, Sec. 5, 10. **159** "Some day we": CBDP, B83, Roosevelt to Davenport, 1/3/1913. **159** Root and Stimson: CBDP, B45, Davenport to Harriman, 11/5/1911. **160** Gertrude Davenport: MacDowell, 28; *NYT*, 1/12/1913. **160** Laughlin play: CBDP, B117, produced 2/2/1912. **160** new ditty: MacDowell, 30. **160** "no Negroes": E. L. Doctorow, *Ragtime* (New York: Plume, 1996), 3. **161** Otto Kahn: Mike Wallace, 299. **161** "desirable elements": Davenport, *Heredity*, 218. **161** "modern studies": IRLR, F342, Davenport to Hall, 10/7/1912. **161** removed Boas: IRLR, F342, Davenport to Hall, 4/18/1912; F948, 5/13/1913. **162** Davenport declined: CBDP, B5, Davenport to Boas, 1/30/1913, 10/11/1913. **162** "great families": *NYT*, "Social Problems Have Proven Basis in Heredity," 1/12/1913, Sec. 5, 10. **162** "defective blood": Hershfield, 102. **162** list of college presidents: IRLR, F1063 (4th of 10). **162** "steady influx": IRLR,

F560, Jordan to Hall. **162** Committee to Study: Hassencahl, 95. **162** a laborer he knew, "very blue": CBDP, B33, W. E. Davenport to C. B. Davenport, 11/26/1914; C.B.D. to W.E.D., 11/28/1914. **163** "day of the sociologist": Ward, "The Crisis in Our Immigration Policy," *The Institution Quarterly*, 6/30/1913, 31. **163** "When power": Mukherjee, 63.

Chapter Six To Hell with Jews, Jesuits, and Steamships!

165 "To play Providence": *The Times* (London), 5/3/1912, 5. **165** wore a badge: Smith and Wehmeyer, 57. **165** "relics": *Catalogue of the Exhibition*. **166** "baby science": First International Eugenics Congress, *Problems*, 13. **166** improbable entombment: Desmond and Moore, 665. **166** "give us courage": First International, *Problems*, 6. **166** "stupidest" member: Browne, *Power*, 333–34. **166** "zealots and cranks": Ludmerer, 54. **166** Montague Crackanthorpe: Gillham, 336. **167** committee members: IRLR, F1115 (6th of 8), announcement of First International Eugenics Congress. **167** Sanger: David Kennedy, *Birth*, 114. **167** Bleecker Van Wagenen: "Century Memorials," CAA, 1922, 26. **167** "obtain wider," "eliminating defective": International, *Problems*, 12–13, 461. **167** "inferior blood": Lombardo, 42–43. **168** "imbeciles," mutability, "injurious effect," "storm of applause": International, *Problems*, 456, 18, 322, 38. **168** Prince Kropotkin, "slums": Woodcock and Avakumonic, 225, passim. **168** fifty servants . . . estate: James R. Miller, ed., *Encyclopedia of Russian History* (New York: Gale, 2004), 789–90. **169** Smith speech: International, *Problems*, 36–39, 484–85. **169** "grasped the heart": Straight, 6. **169** Better Babies Bureau: Rydell, 48–49. **170** "number name": Witkowski and Inglis, 77. **170** refuse to officiate: *NYT*, "Baldwin Pleads for Eugenic Unions," 10/31/1913. **170** person voidable: Kevles, *In the Name*, 100. **170** Fitzgerald, asked: Fitzgerald, *Fie!* **170** Belasco explained: Kimberly Miller, 14. **171** "most approved," "eugenic wife": *NYT*, "Gets Eugenic Certificate," 10/22/1913; *Chicago Examiner*, "Wanted—Eugenic Wife," 10/29/1913, 1; *NYT*, "Wants to Be Eugenic Bride," 11/3/1913. **171** Washington, who harbored: Williams Jr., 61; CBDP, B93, 1/16/1913, Washington to Davenport. **171** *Civic Biology*: Hunter, 265, 413. **172** "Had Jesus been": Wiggam, 110. **172** Rogers wrote: Book review, *Journal of Psycho-Asthenics*, 12/1912, 83. **172** The book was *The Kallikak Family*: J. A. Plucker and A. Esping, eds., "Human Intelligence: Historical influences, current controversies, teaching resources," at www.intelltheory.com. **172** trace their origins, John Woolverton: Smith and Wehmeyer, 188; Zenderland, 180; Goddard, *Kallikak*, 50, 29. **172** "unguarded moment," "Old Horror": Goddard, *Kallikak*, 50, 18. **173** *Kakos*: wiktionary.org. **173** she made judgments: Goddard, *Kallikak*, 73, 77. **174** critical reception: *Book Review Digest*, 1912, 175; *The Dial*, 10/1912, 247; *The Independent*, 10/3/1912, 794. **174** Goddard even found: *Kallikak*, 103. **175** explicitly eschewed: Gossett, 365. **175** "Of one thing": S. J. Gould, 183. **175** "our eye," "wobble," "Queen's plan": JLP, B1, Lee to James Patten, 11/28/1910; Lee to A. Lawrence Lowell, 8/4/1910; Lee to Patten, 3/17/1910. **175** prepare to attack: JLP, B1, Lee to James Patten, 11/28/1910. **176** "expert on nation-building," "My own studies": JLP, B1, Prescott Hall to Lee, 7/30/1910; Lowell to Lodge, copy to Lee, 8/9/1910. **176** primary public concern: Sapora, 164. **176** "pawn my socks": JLP, B1, Lee to Cabot, 2/11/1912. **176** 1896 roster, "lower race": *CR*, 3/16/1896, 2817, 2819. **177** "like to secure": *CR*, 4/18/1912, 4967. **177** Root's clients: Mike Wallace, 38. **177** Root declared: *CR*, 4/18/1912, 4967–68. **177** Borah of Idaho: *CR*, 4/18/1912, 4971. **177** As far back: R. H. Mahany, *CR*, 5/20/1896, 5475. **178** Cleveland had: Veto message, 3/2/1897. **178** Southern senators: Higham, *Strangers*, 166–67. **178** Washington, who insisted: "Races and Politics,"

Outlook, 6/3/1911, 264. **178** "objections to interbreeding": Spiro, 200, quoting IRL to "The Honorable." **179** Agassiz and his followers: Browne, *Power,* 216. **179** "altogether inferior": Morris, *Theodore Rex,* 941, quoting Roosevelt to Owen Wister, 4/1906. **179** biologically related, "live issue": Spiro, 242; ACSS, Author Files 1, B90, F1: Madison Grant to Maxwell Perkins, 5/3/1927. **179** "Asiatic and Mongolian": *CR,* 8/23/1912, 13145. **180** Burnett held back: Tichenor, 135–36. **180** "Hurray": Patten to Robert Ward, 5/10/1912. **180** "my favorite": JLP, B1, Lee to A. Lawrence Lowell, 3/25/1911. **180** crossed out: JLP, B1, Lee letter to the editor, *Post,* 5/14/1912. **180** "suggest racial": JLP, B1, Lee to multiple recipients, 1/1/1913. **181** "instinctively turn": Bailey, 164. **181** found it unimaginable: IRLR, F608 (2nd of 4), HCL to Hall, 5/10/1912. **181** "certain elements": Lowell Papers, B16, F1, Lodge to Lowell, "Personal," 8/11/1910. **182** equally American: IRLR, F1008, Pamphlet, Wilson speech, New York City, 9/4/1912. **182** "doors swinging": LMP, B1, F7, Taft speech, Cambridge Springs, PA, 10/26/1912. **182** "indifference and neglect": *NYT,* "Progressive Aid for Our Aliens," 8/19/1912, 8. **182** Curley . . . representing: Lissak, 215. **182** brochures in 1912: LMP, B1, F7, "The Injustice of a Literacy Test for Immigrants," 26–27. **183** East Room, portion of Kentucky: *NYT,* 2/7/1913, 4; Betty C. Monkman, *The White House: The Historic Furnishings and First Families* (Washington, DC: White House Historical Association, 2000), passim. **183** veto message: Senate document 1087, 2/14/1913. **184** "To hell with": Solomon, 173–74. **184** "arrested for forgery": Beatty, 133–34. **184** Williams of Mississippi: *CR,* 2/18/1913, 3317. **185** "offspring," "Wide open and": *CR,* 2/18/1913, 3315–16. **185** "on the rock": *NYT,* 2/20/1913, 5. **185** Amonson . . . seven-stanza response: *CR,* poem read by Rep. J. H. Moore of Pennsylvania, 2/19/1913, 3421; *CR,* read by Rep. Adolph Sabath, 2/1/1917, 2453. **186** "vague, conjectural": Morris, *Colonel,* 228. **186** "multitudes of men": Wilson, Vol. 5, 212. **186** "corruption of foreign": Wilson, "The Character of Democracy in the United States," *Atlantic Monthly,* 11/1889, 585. **186** "somersault": *CR,* quoted by Rep. Caleb Powers, 2/4/1915, 3031. **186** told allies: IRLR, F608 (2nd of 4), Lodge to Prescott Hall, 3/30/1914. **186** "waves of democracy," "Darwin and Galton": Lodge, *Early,* 3. **187** "blood of the race": Hershfield, 110–11. **187** quadratus muscle: R. B. Bean, quoted in Stocking, 188. **187** Taft's veto: IRLR, F806, 3/4/1913. **188** "cannot fail": *Century,* 10/1913, 952. **188** "He is tackling": CBDP, B44, Hall to Davenport, 10/5/1912. **188** "so keen: *Louisville Courier-Journal,* 10/19/1914, 8. **188** "most illuminating": *Rochester Democrat and Chronicle,* 11/1/1914, 1. **188** "readable style": *NYT Book Review,* 11/1/1914, 477. **188** "morally below," etc.: The excerpts from Ross, *Old World,* quoted here appear consecutively on pages 293, 114, 244, 243, 113, 154, 136 (both "quarrelsome" and "farmers"), 286, 208, 285, 287. **189** offered to travel: IRLR, Ser. II, Executive Committee Minutes, Vol. 3, 3/6/1914. **189** "are immune," "lips thick," "pride of race": Ross, *Old World,* 291, 286, 304. **190** invited advocates: *CR,* 2/4/1915, 3048. **190** sending an emissary: IRLR, Ser. II, Executive Committee Minutes, Vol. 3, 1/15/1915. **190** "not selection": Wilson veto message, 1/28/1915. **190** "Oriental coolieism": Stoddard, *Rising,* 287. **190** "greatest chance": IRLR, F832, Hall to George Shiras. **190** "our Waterloo": IRLR, F401, Patten to Henry P. Fairchild, 2/9/1915.

Chapter Seven Heaven-Sent Madison Grant

195 clubs and societies: *National Cyclopaedia of American Biography* (Clifton, NJ: J. T. White, 1942), 320–21; Spiro, 7–10. **195** "widespread conspiracy": HFOP, B32, F15, C. N. Penfield to Osborn, 10/17/1924. **195** "manly sport": Evan Thomas, 53. **196** Half Moon members, "reserve a cabin": Spiro, 92–93. **196** Half moon rituals, menus, speakers through Ripley: CBDP, B77, F: H. F. Osborn: invitation for 2/5/1925. **197** Conklin, a prominent: Half Moon Club files, MS 1475, New-York Historical Society, Log 1906–1934. **197** "eminent leader," "Director": HFOP, Osborn to Grant, 4/24/1914. **197** "reckless" and "unreliable": Nils Roll-Hansen, "Eugenics and the Science of Eugenics," in Bashford and Levine, 29–30. **197** Flexner, the son: *ANB*. **198** scientific holes: RFA, III 2F, B1, F2: Starr Murphy to John D. Rockefeller Jr., 2/16/1914. **198** "biological consequences": Conklin, 418. **199** Walter Lippmann: *ANB*. **199** "sinister effect": Unsigned, "Americanization," *New Republic*, 1/29/1916, 322. Lippmann's authorship established by subsequent correspondence with Lee in JLP, B1, 1/31/1916–2/14/1936. **199** "managed society": *ANB*. The entry was written by Steel. **199** Lee to send: JLP, B1, Lee to Lippmann, 1/31/1916. **199** single sentence: IRLR, F1120, extract from Curley speech in the House of Representatives, 12/14/1912. **199** complete suspension: *Boston Globe*, 4/7/1915. **199** Liberty Bell: Nash, 122–29. **200** J. H. Kellogg: *ANB*. **200** "Apollos and Venuses": *Los Angeles Times*, 8/8/1915, 6. **200** Description of fair: Rydell, 40–41; Race Betterment Foundation, 5, 144; *Los Angeles Times*, 6/27/1915, 25. **201** "new and glorified": *Los Angeles Times*, 8/8/1915, 6. **201** six generations: Selden, 11. **201** palace intrigue: *ANB*. **201** Jordan's arguments: "Eugenics and War," Race Betterment Foundation, 12–15. **202** 1909: "The Biology of War," *Unity*, 6/10/1909, 231. **202** "finest young," "deterioration": Darwin, *Descent*, 133–34. **203** sanitarium's jubilee, Davenport speech: *The Golden Jubilee of the Battle Creek Sanitarium*, 1916, copy at Bentley Historical Library, University of Michigan; ubhistory.org/storiesandpeople/JI1Kellogg .html. Speech, 64–68. **204** "Warm-hearted," "heaven-sent": Spiro, 38, 50. **204** driving force: *New York Herald Tribune*, 5/31/1937, 10. **204** initiated the effort: IRLR, F:468, Grant to Prescott Hall, 11/22/1918. **204** "No greater": Spiro, 52. **205** "We have killed": Madison Grant, "America for Americans," *The Forum*, 9/1925, 346–55. **205** reform campaign: Spiro, 34. **205** Devoted to Roosevelt: D. G. Brinton Thompson, "A Personal Memory of Madison Grant," n.d. **205** "great achievements": HFOP, B9, F4, 7/20/1933. **205** "My dear": Grant to Roosevelt, 4/28/1928, and Roosevelt to Grant, 5/5/1928, in Franklin Delano Roosevelt Papers. **205** "lighthouse of fashion": George Bird Grinnell, quoted by Spiro, 16–17. **205** Carnegie incident: Spiro, 48. **206** "well-groomed musketeer": William Hornaday, in Hornaday Papers, B112, unpublished autobiography, 11:2. **206** annual income: Thompson, private reminiscence. **206** summer place, Oatlands: "Oatlands," *Architecture*, 10/1918, 297–300. **206** East Forty-Ninth Street, Park Avenue, servants: Spiro, 117, 336; Thompson, private reminiscence. **206** "walls of Troy," "not a nature": H. E. Anthony, "Madison Grant," *Journal of Mammalogy*, 8/1938, 396–97. **207** Osborn letter: Chase, 164. **207** "tundras of the north": F. R. Burnham, "Madison Grant: Charon Beckoned," typescript, Kermit Roosevelt Papers, B106, F1935–1938, in Dean Sage to Roosevelt, 6/17/1938. **207** "no present intention": Hornaday Papers, B13, Grant to Hornaday, 12/13/1927. **208** were a "curse": ERP, B94, F:G1912, Grant to Root, 5/10/1912. **208** "Semitic leadership": Stoddard, *Rising*, 247. **208** "dwarfed and undersized": Petit, 111. **208** "dumping ground": Spiro, 331. **208** "Papacy": HHLP, Grant to Laughlin, 2/25/1933. **208** "Jewish leadership": Baltzell, *Protestant*, 96. **208** "half-Asiatic": Grant foreword in Mrs. Prescott F. Hall, x. **208** atheist himself: Thompson, private reminiscence. **208** moose heads: Grant, "A Canadian Moose Hunt," in G. B. Grinnell and T. Roosevelt, eds., *Hunting in Many Lands* (New York: Forest and Stream Publishing Co., 1895), 104. **208** "Columbus, from":

HFOP, B8, F40, Grant to Osborn, 5709. **209** "the man who put": Higham, *Strangers*, 155. **209** Moses Taylor Pyne: Mike Wallace, 29; Alexander Leitch, *A Princeton Companion*, Princeton University Press, 1978. **209** "race memory," "ethnic continuity," Woodrow Wilson: Ralph Adams Cram, quoted in Maynard, 80–81. **209** Pyne had sponsored: CAA, Century Genealogy. **210** "suggestive study," opportunity to discuss: HFOP, B56, F8: Osborn to Charles Scribner, 5/2/1916. **210** "white man par": Quotations from *The Passing of the Great Race* given here appear consecutively on pages 23, 187, 11–13, 198, 199, 150, 198, 191, 138, 140, 144–46, 143, 191, 191. **211** Grant . . . peculiar notion: *Passing*, 74. **211** Houston Stewart Chamberlain: Gossett, 350; Spiro, 110. **211** "In Hindustan": Grant, *Passing*, quotations continue, consecutively, on pages 63–64, 178, 144, 67, 134, 203, 203, 101, 159, 210, 81, 81, 15–16. **213** "They came," "lower race mixes": *CR*, 3/16/1896, 2818–19. **213** "maudlin": Grant, *Passing*, 228. **213** "purity of race," "Nordic nobility": Grant, *Conquest*, 5, 15. **214** Boston settlement house, Wendell: Berg, 32. **214** "his grandparents": Cowley, 24. **214** "history of Europe": ACSS, Author Files I, B675, F2, 1916 Fall catalog. **214** "scientist, savant": ACSS, Publicity Files, B1139, promotional brochure, 1916. **214** "inrush of lower": ACSS, Publicity Files, B1139, "RVC" letter to IRL members, 11/16/1916. **214** "unchecked influx": ACSS, Publicity Files, B1139, "RVC" letter, 5/1917. **215** public liftoff: *NYT Magazine*, 10/22/1916, 8–9. **215** Roosevelt, was particularly: ACSS, Author Files 1, B675, F3, 1917 Spring catalog, 1. **215** ex-president's permission: Morison, Roosevelt to Grant, 12/5/1916. **215** "a remarkable study": ACSS, Publicity Files, B1139, quoted in catalog brochure. **216** "warning which should": *Boston Transcript*, 12/9/1916. **216** "incorrect": Gossett, 363. **216** "debatable assumptions," "questionable," "dignity": A. B. Show, *American Historical Review*, 7/1917, 842. **216** "studied by all": Carl Kelsey, *Annals of the American Academy of Political and Social Science*, 3/1917, 330. **216** "distinct qualities": *The Nation*, 4/19/1917, 466. **216** titled "Inventing": "Inventing a Great Race," *New Republic*, 1/13/1917. **217** Frederick Adams Woods: Spiro, 159; Woods, "The Racial Limitation of Bolshevism," *Journal of Heredity*, 4/1919, 190. **217** "undoubtedly one of": ACSS, Author Files 1, Perkins to Grant, 4/30/1917. **217** Scott explained in a letter: HFOP, B8, F40, Scott to Grant, 11/27/1922, enclosed in Grant to Osborn, 12/4/1922. **218** "not a matter": Osborn, in Grant, *Passing*, ix. **218** "secure our nation": CBDP, B42, Davenport to Grant, 2/10/1917.

Chapter Eight A Carnival of Exclusion

220 "I am told": CBDP, B42, Grant to Davenport, 2/16/1917. **220** "readjustment [of law]": Grant, *Passing*, 228–29. **220** " 'scorched the snake' ": *Boston Daily Globe*, 4/7/1915, 9. The *Globe* printed it as "scotched"; the quote, with "scorch," is from *Macbeth*. **221** "poison of disloyalty," "welcomed under": David Kennedy, *Over Here*, 24. **221** "subservient legislature": Grant foreword, in Mrs. Prescott F. Hall, viii. **222** "after 24 years": Warren Papers, B10, F4, biographical note, 2/5/1917. **222** Attitudes toward Asians: Attorney General Charles Bonaparte quoted in Ngai, 41. **222** deport alien: Higham, *Strangers*, 202. **222** longest continuous tenure: *Boston Herald*, 3/13/1917. **223** Lodge punched him, baseball player: Garraty, 333–35. **223** "new infusion": Rep. Isaac Siegel quoted in Petit, 120. **223** "set apart": Lodge, *Boston*, 210–11. **223** "museum of wax": William Gibbs McAdoo quoted in Garraty, 128. **224** one of two reasons: Hutchinson, *Legislative*, 163. **224** Louis Marshall: introduction by Oscar Handlin in Reznikoff, x–xliii. **224** He knew Theodore Roosevelt: Reznikoff, 1149. **224** nearly appointed: Handlin in Reznikoff, xvi; JLP, B1, [Patten?] to

Taft, 4/9/1910. **225** "dash off": Reznikoff, 363n. **225** "affirmative action": LMP, B1, F3, n.d. **225** "irrefragable reason": Reznikoff, 218. **225** "electrolytic powers": *NYT*, 4/8/1918. **225** "most vicious," "dangerous invasions," "Nothing Jewish": Handlin in Reznikoff, xiii, xxxviii–xliii. **226** persuaded Representative John L. Burnett, William Dillingham: LMP, B1, F8, Marshall to Dillingham, 1/1/1913; Dillingham to Marshall, 1/4/1913. **226** in the statutory language: LMP, B2, F2, Marshall to James Reed, 4/21/1916. **226** rooted in the American: IRLR, F437: Friends of Russian Freedom to Dillingham, 2/2/1915. **226** "give a preference": LMP, B2, F3, Marshall to Montague Triest, 12/16/1916. **226** red ink: IRLR, F1052, Executive Committee Minutes, 2/9/1917. **227** "mere agent": JLP, B1, Patten to Lee, 2/7/1917. **227** "most comprehensive": Ward, "Immigration After the War," *Journal of Heredity*, 4/1917, 151. **227** "thousand million": JLP, B1, Lee to Marjory Moors, 8/9/1917. **227** "those schemes you": JLP, B1, Lee to Bradley, 2/13/1917. **227** "It is probable": JLP, B1, Hall to "Members of the League," 2/22/1917. **228** warned Hall: IRLR, F381, Edgerton to Hall, 6/11/1902. **228** "spending millions": IRLR, Ser. II, Executive Committee Minutes, Vol. 3, 3/6/1914. **228** sight and hearing: JLP, B14, F: BSC Elections, 1914, "My Great Deeds." **228** Italy alone: Cannato, 435. **228** definitive action: *EN*, 3/1817, 22. **228** would limit: IRLR, F1110, Draft amendment, 3/1917. **228** quotas, slashed by 70: IRLR, F363, Hall to Dillingham, 4/12/1917. **228** in 1911: Handlin, *Uprooted*, 260. **228** Jeremiah W. Jenks: IRLR, F549, Jenks to Lee, 12/10/1914. **229** "an avalanche," "from hundreds," "two other groups": IRLR, F549, Jenks to Hall, 4/21/1914. **229** counteract "the spread": JLP, B1, draft of "Numerical Limitation Bill," 5/1918. **229** "single race": IRLR, F1068, 1st of 4, "Preliminary draft," n.d. **229** "discriminate in favor": JLP, B1, draft of "Numerical Limitation Bill," 5/1918. **229** John Burnett: IRLR, F203, Burnett to Hall, 11/29/1918. **229** "most influential agency": Fairchild, 452. **230** "now all powerful": JLP, B1, Hall to Lee, 3/11/1917. **230** "carnival of exclusion": Industrial Removal Office, *Monthly Bulletin*, 2/1915, quoted in Glazier, 67. **230** "immeasurable calamity": Introduction by Ross in Popenoe and Johnson, ix. **230** "mark of Cain": *Boston Post*, 9/16/1916, 1. **231** Sadler ideas: Sadler, passim. **231** Kellogg, Freud: Martin Gardner, *Urantia: The Great Cult Mystery* (New York: Prometheus, 1995), 36–37. **231** "very largely Alpine": Grant, *Passing*, revised ed., 231–32. **231** "barbaric blood": *Washington Times*, 6/2/1918. **231** "new and separate": *Kansas City Star*, 7/15/1918, quoted in Hall and Ferlege, eds., *Theodore Roosevelt Cyclopedia*, entry "Immigrants—Obligation of." Online at theodoreroosevelt.org. **231** "any Yale": Morison, Roosevelt to Grant, 12/30/1918. **231** Thomas R. Marshall said: William Manners, *TR and Will: A Friendship That Split the Republican Party* (New York: Harcourt Brace, 1969), 320. **231** "qualified ethnologist": *San Francisco Chronicle*, 2/11/1917, 2D. **232** Anthropology Committee: Spiro, 310. **232** lauded "authorities": SEP, 5/7/1921, 20. **232** "Dr. Madison Grant": Robert DeC. Ward, "Some Thoughts on Immigration Restriction," *Scientific Monthly*, 10/1922, 317. **232** "distinguished zoologist": *NYT*, "Madison Grant, 71, Zoologist, Is Dead," 5/31/1937, 15. **232** "sociologist Madison Grant": H. S. Merrill and M. G. Merrill, *The Republican Command, 1897–1913* (Lexington: University Press of Kentucky, 2015), 11. **232** "racial anthropology": Spiro, 305. **232** "confined to native": CBDP, B42, Grant to H. F. Osborn, 3/9/1918. **232** personal approval: CBDP, B40, F: Galton Society. **232** Over the years: Spiro, Appendix D, 394. **233** First meetings of the Galton Society: *Science*, 3/14/1919, 267–68. **233** Osborn Library: author visit. **233** portrait of Francis Galton: HFOP, B8, F38: Osborn to Grant, 12/14/1918; Spiro, 305–6. **233** "interlocking directorate": Spiro, 229. **234** "gossip of the natives": Claudia Roth Pierpont, "The Measure of America," *The New Yorker*, 3/8/2004, 57. **234** "I am convinced": CBDP, B40, F: Galton Society, ms. copy of Osborn, "Research on the Evolution of Man and the Human Species," 6. **234** "charming Copley," "Xmas handshake": Campbell, 72–77. **234** "One need": Ibid., 295. **235** Eugenics Record Office *Bulletin*: Bulletin No. 1, Bulletin No. 2, 1911. **235** two thousand children: Boorstin, 222. **235** fifteen thousand: *NYT*, 2/18/1913, 10. **235** 5,600, nearly 70 percent, "ever-changing stream": Alfred C. Reed, "Going Through Ellis Island," *Popular Science*, 1/1913, 5–13. **236** admired his work: CBDP, Ser. II, B125: Davenport to Starr J. Murphy, 7/n.d./1910. **236** "dearest man": William Healy quoted in Zenderland, 358–59. **236** "arouse a smile": Goddard, "The Binet Measuring Scale of Intelligence," *Training School Bulletin*, 10/1914, 88. **237** "ship at gunpoint": Kraut, *Huddled*, 3–4. **238** Darwin himself: Darwin, *Descent*, 142. **238** Galton believed: Galton, *Inquiries*, 308. **238** "Weaker minds": Davenport, *Heredity*, 211. **238** Ellis Island testers: E.g., Goddard, "Mental," 262; Cannato, 454. **238** fluent in three: Cannato, 253–54. **238** made no mention: Goddard, *Feeblemindedness* (1914). **239** Jean Gianini, "masturbator": Goddard, *Criminal*, 20. **239** Paul Popenoe: Goddard Papers, Popenoe to Goddard, 9/9/1913, 5/21/1914; Goddard to Popenoe, 9/10/1913, 6/22/1914. **239** "hardly escape," 40 percent, considered "normal": Goddard, "Mental," 252, 249. *See also* Kraut, *Silent*, 74–75. **239** funded in part: Sapora, 133. **240** "great mass": "Two Immigrants Out of Five Feeble-Minded," *The Survey*, 9/15/1917, 528–29. **240** qualifications and caveats Goddard used: Goddard, "Mental," 243, 247, 270. **240** "two practical questions": Ibid., 243. **241** federal study, more space: President's Research, 428; Higham, *Strangers*, 150–51. **241** sex manual: T. W. Shannon, *Nature's Secrets Revealed* (Marietta, OH: S. A. Mullikin, 1914), 257–63. **241** "Jewish Eugenics": Reichler, 18. **241** "trying to build": Leuchtenberg, *Supreme*, 18. **241** "make you puke": Lombardo, 164. **241** Boston University, University of Oregon, MIT: CBDP, Ser. II, B116, F: Eugenics & Genetics in Colleges. **242** skeptical geneticist: W. E. Castle, *Genetics*. **242** Dudley A. Sargent: *EN*, 3/1917, 38. **242** Popenoe, "most popular": David Popenoe, "Remembering My Father: An Intellectual Portrait of 'The Man Who Saved Marriages,'" Popenoe Papers, B174, F18, 2. **242** "Celibate Motherhood": HFOP, B43, F10: Program, annual meeting of Eugenics Research Association, 6/14/1924. **242** "fear of racial": Popenoe and Johnson, ix. **243** outlawing child labor, inheritance taxes, "ignorant stocks": Popenoe and Johnson, 368, 353, 139. **243** "excellent citizens": Popenoe and Johnson, 139. **243** William Earl Dodge Stokes: Dodge, 211–15. **243** Stokes quotations: Stokes, 8, 7, 56, 58. **243** He praised Charles Davenport: Stokes, 6, 183. **243** eugenic paradise: 85–86. **244** "rotten, foreign," "admirable race": 48, 174–75. **244** Abraham Lincoln: CBDP, Ser. II, B134, Stokes to Davenport, 2/19/1921. **244** joined him for dinner: CBDP, Ser. II, B134, Davenport to Stokes, 1/10/1924. **244** "good ideas": *EN*, 2/1917, 13. **244** "exterminate the Negro," "We don't want": Margaret Sanger Papers Project, Sanger to Clarence Gamble, 12/10/1939. **245** Martin Luther King: Speech, 5/5/1966, Planned Parenthood 50th Anniversary Banquet, New York, available at thekingcenter.org. **245** "great pleasure," "should be," to her board: Spiro, 194. **245** "Japanese problem": HHLP, C 2-6:14, "Sayings of Others," pamphlet copyrighted by Sanger 1921, quoting E. W. Ritter. **245** "racist fears": Gordon, 281. **245** "More children": *American Medicine*, 3/1919, 123; *Birth Control Review*, 5/1919, 12. **245** 1921 essay: Sanger, "The Eugenic Value of Birth Control Propaganda," *Birth Control Review*, 10/1921, 5. **246** "Cruelty of Charity": Sanger, *Pivot*, 105. **246** "glad to say": English, 40. **246** "bloodstream of the race," "moronic mothers": Sanger, *Autobi-*

ography, 376. **246** eagerly sought: Ross Papers, Reel 14, Sanger to Ross, 3/4/1921, 10/18/1921, 10/20/1921. **246** "thoroughbreds": Chesler, 216. **246** "immeasurable calamity," "Rooted prejudices": Introduction by Ross in Popenoe and Johnson, ix. **247** "mutual butchery": Grant, *Passing*, 200. **247** Yerkes at Harvard: *ANB*. **247** "unimportant incident": Robert M. Yerkes, *The Dancing Mouse* (New York: Macmillan, 1907), vii. **247** also an advisor, member: *EN*, 3/1916, 19, 32. **247** seen the possibilities: CCBP, Yerkes correspondence, 3/28/1917. **248** "valuable technology": *ANB*. **248** "I am a believer": JLP, B1, draft letter to *Boston Transcript*, n.d., early 1917. **248** commissioned a major: Downey, 7–8. **248** necessary training: Marks, 89–90. **248** "pests," not to serve: Kevles, "Testing," 574. **248** "bar of steel": Kevles, *In the Name*, 80. **248** Alpha test consisted: Paul, *Controlling*, 66. **249** At Fort Devens: Yerkes, 284. **250** "most prominent racist": Barkan, 69–70. **251** "they nauseate us": CBDP, B42, F: Joseph J. Gould, 10/?/13. **251** "very nice fellow": RFA, Daniel J. Kevles Papers, B2, F2, Kevles oral history interview with Harry Shapiro, 1984. **251** only "surprise": CBDP, B14, F: Autobiographical; see also www.arthurmoss.com. **251** eight researchers: *EN*, 3/1919. **251** frequently cited evidence: CBDP, B42, Davenport to Grant, 4/7/1925. **251** "wayward girls": Rosenberg, "Charles," 271. **252** Harriman endowment: CIWA, Genetics B9, F8, typescript history by Davenport. **252** deed to Arden: *Boston Post*, 9/16/1916, 1. **253** wished to travel: CIWA, Genetics, B4, F17, Davenport to Woodward, 12/12/1918. **253** turned them down, "peculiarly dangerous," "best interests": CIWA, Genetics, B3, F7, Woodward to Davenport, 2/15/1919. **253** "juvenile journal," "discourage amateurism": CBDP, Ser. II, B106, Woodward to Davenport, 10/15/1919. **253** "High praise": MacDowell, *Bios*, 33. **253** "Galton himself": CBDP, Ser. II, B106, Davenport to Woodward, 10/18/1919. **253** continued to challenge: CBDP, Ser. II, B106, Woodward to Davenport, 12/8/1920, 12/29/1920. **253** Merriam, looked upon: *ANB*. **254** "most heartily": Barkan, 69–70. **254** "unequivocal": Spiro, 314. **254** almost dared them: *ANB*. **254** "prostituted science": *The Nation*, 12/20/1919, 797. **254** Fairfield Osborn: Hyatt, 132. **254** Boas was censured: Norman Boas, 196. **255** "flood of Bolsheviki": IRLR, F608 (4th of 4), Lodge to Hall, 10/18/1919. **255** "great massacre of Jews": Higham, *Strangers*, 306. **255** smuggling one hundred: *New York Herald*, 11/24/1919. **255** nation's editorial pages: IRLR, F1070, 4th of 11, "Friendly and Hostile Newspapers." **256** "shut the gates," "latest gospel": *NYT*, 6/9/1919, 12; 7/11/1920, Sec. 2, 2. **256** "Can we build": CBDP, B42, Davenport to Grant, 5/3/1920. **256** know "the facts": CBDP, Davenport to Grant, 11/27/1920.

Chapter Nine The Coming of the Quota

259 "best way": *SEP*, 5/19/1923, 92. **259** "misery and want," "75 percent," "bring in": House of Representatives Report 1109, accompanying HR 14461, 12/6/1920. **260** Gore speech: Charles Gore, "Diplomacy, Old and New," *The Christian Century*, 5/1/1919, 11–12. **260** "headlong plunge": Stoddard, *Rising*, 179. **260** Boas called Stoddard's: *The Nation*, 12/8/1920, 656. **260** Ross called it: Bachman, 4. **261** a business magazine: *The World's Work*, 1919, 205, 276, 471. **261** apartment at the western, "always irked," "rotten foundations," three months: Bachman, 84, 55. **262** Seth K. Humphrey: *EN*, 11/1917, 92. **262** Charles W. Gould, "rapturous encomium": Charles Gould, 1, 28–29; *NYT Book Review*, 11/22/1922. **262** William McDougall: ACSS, Author Files 1, B675, F6, Scribner Fall 1921 catalog, 19; McDougall, 69–71. **262** Edward M. East: East, vi, 316. **263** Ellsworth Huntington: "What I Think About Eugenics," ca. 1927, pamphlet issued by American Eugenics Society. **263** "permanent domination": *New York Tribune*, n.d., quoted in ACSS, Author Files 1, B676, F4, Scribner 1924 Spring catalog. **263** send a copy: ACSS, Author Files 1, B90, F3, Perkins to Grant, 9/17/1923. **263** "new values": Berg, 41. **263** "You can tell": Cowley, xiii. **264** "admirably summarized," etc.: The excerpts from Stoddard, *Rising*, quoted here appear consecutively on pages vii, vi, 10, vi, 115, 4, 91, 169, 70, 56, 13, xxx, 8. **264** "hordes of immigrant": Stoddard, *Rising*, 165. **265** "marked success": ACSS, Author Files 1, B90, F2: Perkins to Grant, 2/24/1920. **265** Du Bois's ominous: 14. **265** fifteen separate printings: ACSS, Author Files 1, B676, F4, Scribner 1924 Spring catalog. **265** "sane and measured," "defense of what": *NYT*, 7/11/1920, Sec. 2, 2. **266** "well up": JLP, B1, Hall to Lee, 10/10/1920, 10/15/1920. **266** "pioneer": ACSS, Author Files 1, B90, Grant F2: Scribner to Grant, 6/8/1922. **266** *The Great Gatsby*: F. Scott Fitzgerald, *Gatsby*, 12–13. **266** Cather was publishing . . . subhuman: "Scandal," in *Youth and the Bright Medusa* (New York: Knopf, 1920), 185–86. **267** Masters begins: Edgar Lee Masters, *The Open Sea* (New York: Macmillan, 1921), 270–71. The poem was originally published in *Reedy's Mirror*, in 1920. **267** Grant was delighted: ACSS, Author Files 1, B90, F2, Grant to Perkins, 1/20/1920. **268** "Henry Ford": *NYT*, 10/23/1937, 1. **268** "Self-Preservation": *SEP*, 2/2/1920. **269** Gregor Mendel, "rose-colored," "recent advances": *SEP*, 5/7/1921, 20. **269** "fitted biologically," "fixed a fact," "infected stock," "sterilizing effect," Prescott Hall: *SEP*, 5/14/1921, 20. **270** "defeated, incompetent": *SEP*, "Ports of Embarkation," 5/7/1921. **270** "waiting for you": Roberts Papers, B52, Ward to Roberts, 3/23/1922. **270** "require of all those aliens": Calvin Coolidge, "Whose Country Is This?," *Good Housekeeping*, 2/1921. **270** myriad philanthropic: JLP, B39, F: Donations, passim. **271** bout of pleurisy, "an aristocracy": CBDP, B44, Hall to Charles Davenport, 10/1/1920. **271** "Puritans and pedants": Johnson Papers, Scrapbooks, "Some Reminiscences," 4/29/1934. **271** "bright side": HHLP, E 1-1:10, HHL to his mother, 3/1905. **272** "best practical": Ludmerer, 92. **272** "frequent contact": HHLP, E 1-3:5, *Kirksville Journal*, 1/1/1914. **272** onion root tips: Carlson, 2235–36. **272** generous inclinations: HHLP, C 2-2:14, Laughlin, "Eugenics in Germany," *Eugenics Review*, 1/1921. **272** earnestly antiwar, League of Nations: Hassencahl, 46–47. **272** "scarcely seems": HHLP, D 2-1:5, *Atlantic Monthly* editors to Laughlin, 9/21/1917. **272** preamble to his model: McDonald, 390. **273** granted Indians: McDonald, 393, quoting Laughlin to Madison Grant, 6/13/1932. **273** met Robert Ward: Hershfield, 110–11. **274** "decimal elimination": Spiro, 1373. **274** "not solely": Witkowski and Inglis, 167. **274** Johnson elected, "proud to say": Johnson Papers, "Some Reminiscences," 6/17/1934. **275** "greatest menace": Hillier, 199. **275** Apart from his support: Johnson Papers, Scrapbooks, 1913–1914. **275** to Celsius: CBDP, B58, Johnson to Davenport, 11/3/1915. **275** "strenuous life": Johnson Papers, "Some Reminiscences," n.d. **275** "anarchy," "organized atheism": *Home Defender*, 5/13/1912, 2. **275** "made a study," telegraph operator, "a prophecy": Johnson Papers, "Some Reminiscences," 1/14/1934. **276** "I am sorry": Hershfield, 116–17. **276** lantern slides: HHLP, C 2-4:6. **277** "besieged": Yoakum and Yerkes, iii. **277** Laughlin testimony: House hearings, *Biological*, 3–22. **278** "as a mirage": Rep. Emanuel Celler, *CR*, 1/23/1914, 1331–35. **278** in the Galton Society: HHLP, D 2-4:10, W. K. Gregory to Laughlin, 3/20/1923. **278** trip to Europe: HHLP, C 2-3:3, "Report of Harry H. Laughlin for the Months September 1, 1923–June 30, 1924." **279** Singh case: Huping Ling and Allan W. Austin, eds., *Asian American History and Culture: An Encyclopedia* (London: Routledge, 2015), 363; www.bhagatsinghthind.com. **280** the court found: *Ozawa v. U.S.*, 1922. **280** "most unfortunate": LMP, B1, F3, Marshall to Sabath, 2/28/1910. **281** came from Sicily: *Rollins v. State*, Ala. Crim. App. 1922. **281** Patten described: JLP, B2, Patten to Robert Ward, 1/17/1923. **281** Stoddard constantly: E.g., Stoddard, *Racial*, 27; Stoddard, *Re-Forging*, 129. **281** Hall hung: Hall, "Immigration and the World War," *Annals of the American Academy of Political and Social Science*, 1/1921, 190. **281** "pretty good club": Hugh Wilson, quoted in Martin Weil, *A Pretty Good Club: The Founding Fathers of the U.S. Foreign Service* (New York: Norton, 1978). **281** "small group": Stephen A. Schuker, "Pride and Prejudice," *Commentary*, 9/1978. **281** Carr was: *ANB*; Richard Hume Werking, *The Master Architects: Building the United States Foreign Service 1890–1913* (Lexington: University of Kentucky Press, 2015), 88–89. **282** "in accordance," and subsequent quotes in document: Appendix A, House hearings, "Temporary," 9–12. **283** "225,000 Hebrews": House report 1109, House hearings, "Temporary," 4. **283** Ira Hersey, Johnson spelled, "[APPLAUSE]": *CR*, 12/10/1920, 1–7. **283** "most extraordinary": *Philadelphia Public Ledger*, 12/11/1920, quoted in Robert Ward, "The Immigration Problem Today," *Journal of Heredity*, 9–10/1920, 323. **283** "undesirables": *Boston Post*, 12/20/1920, 28. **284** "heterogeneous hodgepodge": *CR*, 12/11/1920, 4563–64. **284** Ward essay: Ward, "Immigration Problem," 323–28. Though this issue of the journal is dated "September–October 1920," the Ward piece is dated 1/1/1921, and the front page of the issue indicated it wasn't published until 3/1921. **284** "fed from troughs": *NYT*, 12/12/1920, 9. **284** "American institutions": *NYT*, "The Unpopular Branch," 2/9/1921, 7. **284** Box . . . attacked, IRC membership: *CR*, 1/8/1921, 1162–63. **284** IRC's dues-paying: House hearings, *Proposed*, 4/22/1920, 127. **285** "trifling fraction," "any wonder": *CR*, 1/8/1921, 1162–63. **285** Grant to Marion and Washington: Spiro, 209. **285** "paternal interest," "good friend": Roberts, *I Wanted*, 149, 180. **285** "few feet of macaroni": *SEP*, "Guests from Italy," 8/21/1920, 11–12. **286** "biologists," "adventurous people": *SEP*, "Points of Embarkation," 5/7/1921, 2, 72. **286** Conklin took: Conklin, "Some Biological Aspects of Immigration," *Scribner's Magazine*, 3/1921, 354–59. **286** "subnormal": *CR*, 4/20/1921, 437–39. **286** "ready to breed": Bendersky, 161. **286** "disaster will": *Philadelphia Inquirer*, 5/6/1921. **286** "fully aware": *SEP*, 5/7/1921, 20. **287** "give a preference": LMP, B2, F3, Marshall to Montague Triest, 12/12/1916. **287** "bases the right": LMP, B2, F5, Marshall to House Committee, undated. **287** Isaac Siegel, Albert Johnson: *CR*, 4/20/1921, 500. **288** "reeking with hatred": Reznikoff, 191. **288** "Jewish tailors": Spiro, 205. **288** Although he and his wife: JLP, B1, Hall's stationery, in Hall to Lee, 10/18/1918. **288** "Without him": Lee, letter to the editor, *Springfield Republican*, 6/3/1921. **289** "guess my work": JLP, B1, Ward to Lee, 4/30/1921, quoting letter from Hall.

Chapter Ten Science Is Our Polestar

291 *Canopic* steamed: *NYT*, 6/7/1921, 3 and 6/12/1921; *Boston Post*, 6/10/1921, 1; 6/11/1921, 4; 6/12/1921, 1. **291** White Star was especially: Two brochures, 1907, at gjenvick.com/Brochures /WhiteStarLine. **292** Even Robert Ward: Ward, letter to the editor, *Boston Herald*, 6/18/1921. **293** the paper gave Roberts: *Boston Sunday Herald*, 6/26/1921, Sec. 2, 1. **293** "fine work": Roberts Papers, B53, Stoddard to Roberts, 7/1/1921. **293** *Mayflower*: *Boston Post*, 6/12/1921, 1. **293** "henceforth all": Wang, 82. **294** Luxembourg's quota: *NYT*, 6/7/1921, 3; Liberia: "Uncle Sam's Turnstile," *New Republic*, 8/17/1921, 314–15. **294** Antwerp docks: *NYT*, 6/17/1921, 1. **294** In Cherbourg: *NYT*, 6/16/1921, 14. **294** Hamburg-American Line: Averell Harriman Papers, B679, F11, Hamburg-American Annual Report, 1921. **294** *Kroonland* departed: *NYT*, 6/17/1921, 1; 3/7/1921, 1. **294** "Immigrant Derby": Curran, 287. **295** Greek ships: *NYT*, "'Quotas' Harass Ship Lines," 10/2/1921, Sec. 8, 12. **295** "by horsepower": *American Legion Weekly*, 12/21/1921, 9. **295** never a surplus: "Uncle Sam's Turnstile," *New Republic*, 8/17/1921, 314–15. **295** EUGENISTS DREAD: *NYT*, 9/25/1921, Sec. 2, 1. **296** front pages across: E.g., *Nebraska State Journal*, 9/28/1921; *Minneapolis Star-Tribune*, 9/27/1921 and 9/28/1921; *El Paso Herald*, 9/21/1921. **296** spoken virtually daily: Spiro, 352. **296** "best team of horses": Hornaday Papers, B112, Ch. 11, 2. **296** *Rangifer*, femur of a chicken: Spiro, 24, 48. **297** "agreeable Hebrew": Hellman, 92. **297** Warburg was not, succeeded: J. M. Kennedy, 216; *NYT*, 5/2/1933, 10. **297** "enormously pompous," "incredibly": COHP, "Reminiscences of L. C. Dunn," 167; Hellman Papers, Ser. 3, F4, Ellis L. Yochelson to Hellman, 2/22/1969. **297** two secretaries: Hellman, *Bankers*, 193–94. **297** "not even an envelope": Ibid., 201. **298** "positive engine": Osborn to Grant, 2/10/1909, quoted in J. M. Kennedy, 154. **298** provided financial support: CBDP, B45, Davenport to C. C. Tegethoff, 6/13/1921. Tegethoff was a financial manager employed by the Harriman family. **298** flabbergasted: CBDP, B77, Osborn to Davenport, 11/22/1920. **298** pure science: CBDP, B3, Bateson to Davenport, 2/11/1921. **298** "alliances between": Bateson, "Commonsense in Racial Problems," *Eugenics Review*, 325, quoted in Ludmerer, 52. **298** Davenport's urging: CBDP, B77, Davenport to Osborn, letter recommending participants, ca. 11/1920. **298** "social propaganda": CBDP, B77, F: H. F. Osborn, Morgan to Osborn, 6/14/1920. **299** "scholarly tone": CBDP, B77, Osborn to Morgan, 7/16/1920. **299** "be amused": CBDP, B77, Osborn to Davenport, 7/21/1920. **299** *"if it is a privilege"*: CBDP, B77, Osborn to Davenport and C. C. Little, 7/31/1921. Emphasis in original. **299** biased, lapses, sloppiness, bullying: Lowie Papers, B12, Osborn to Lowie, 6/6/1922; HFOP, B8, F39, Osborn to Grant, 6/3/1919; Lowie Papers, B7, W. K. Gregory to Lowie, 7/5/1927. **300** "Jew socialist," "much truth": HFOP, B8, F40, Grant to Osborn, 6/5/1922; Osborn to Grant, 6/6/1922. **300** "sledge-hammer": HFOP, B8, F39, Osborn to Grant, 5/28/1920. **300** most critical issue: HFOP, B11, F320, Osborn to Albert Johnson, 12/19/1922. **301** railroad car: American Museum of Natural History Central Archives, F20.3: Invitation and guest list. **301** "my consternation": HFOP, B9, F1, Osborn to Grant, 8/21/1928. **301** Congress took over, exhibits: AMNH Central Archives, F20–20.5, Osborn to F.A. Lucas, 5/6/1921; Laughlin, *Second*, 9, 20–36, 45–59; Spiro, 213–14. **301** "independent means": Rydell, 45. **302** Osborn delivered: Second International, *Eugenics*, 1–4. **303** Johnson's congressional committee: CBDP, B40, F: Galton Society, draft minutes, meeting of 5/5/1925. **303** every speaker: *NYT*, "Eugenists Dread Tainted Aliens," 9/5/1921, Sec 2, 1. **303** Lapouge, "race of demi-gods": Spiro, 214. **303** personal tour: AMNH Central Archives, F20–20.5, Osborn to Frederick A. Wallis et al., 10/11/1921. **303** "carry on": CBDP, B77, Osborn to Fisher, 10/11/1921. **303** ECUSA membership: CBDP, B77, letterhead. **304** C. W. Eliot: Eliot, "A Plea for Jewish Integrity," *Jewish Tribune and Hebrew Standard*, 12/19/1994, clipping in RPHU, B233, F829. **304** Carl Campbell Brigham biography: *ANB*; Leonard Carmichael, "Carl Campbell Brigham 1890–1943," *Psychological Review*, 9/1943, 443; Downey, 5–11. **305** "the Philistines": Charles Gould, 164. **306** "our ancestors worked": CCBP, Gould correspondence, Brigham to Gould, 8/6/21. **306** "never produced": CCBP, Gould correspondence, Gould to Brigham, n.d. **306** "ardent enthusiasm," squash court: Richard Ward Greene Welling, "Charles Winthrop Gould," Century Association, *Yearbook*, 1931. **306** "revolting": Charles Gould, 162. **306** museum-quality: Anderson Galleries, "The Charles W. Gould Art Collection," auction catalog, 1932. **307** black-tie dinner, brilliant men: CBDP, B42, telegram, Gould to Davenport, 10/18/1921, 11/2/1921. **307** "Volstead Act": CCBP, Gould correspondence, Gould to Davenport, 10/18/1921. **307** focused on ethnicity: Spiro, 217. **307** Gould agreed: Brigham, xvii. **308** Armenians, classified: Barkan, 84; Craver, 30–56. **308** alumni pressure: Levine, 154; Dinnerstein, 84. **309** Lowell, who had seen: Dinnerstein, 84. **309** "summer hotel": Lowell Papers, B173, F1056, Lowell to William Ernest Hocking, 5/19/1922. **309** without acknowledging: Author interview with Henry Rosovsky, former dean, Harvard College. **309** "necessary move": Melissa Hendricks, "Raymond Pearl's Mingled Mess," *Johns Hopkins Magazine*, 4/2006. **309** Hughes, cringing: Blom, 107. **310** "is our polestar": Bachman, 22. **310** she cited Yerkes's: Sanger, *Pivot*, 263. **310** "Here's Mrs. Sanger!": Sanger, *Autobiography*, 300–301. **310** "vastly superior": Spiro, 335. **310** "almost invariable": Roberts, *Why*, 47–48. **310** "bubonic plague": Arthur M. Sweeney, "Mental Tests for Immigrants," *North American Review*, 5/1922, 600–612. **310** William Allen White: White, "What's the Matter with America?," *Collier's*, 7/1/1922, 4–5, 18. **310** National Research Council: Stocking, 299. **311** "golden beauty": Marie Dressler, *My Own Story* (Boston: Little, Brown, 1934), 84. **311** fifteen states, "Paris cure": Lillian Russell, "Reminiscences," *Cosmopolitan*, 9/1922, 108, 106. **311** Russell issued her report: *CR*, 4/15/1922, 5557–58, 5562–63. **311** "all the movies": JLP, B2, Patten report, 4/5/1922. **311** Johnson saw to the deletion: Wang, 86. **312** "colonizing": IRLR, Additional Papers, Executive Committee Report, 6/15/1922. **312** Brazil: *NYT*, "Influx of Immigrants to Brazil," 5/8/1921, 35. **312** "nationalism is rampant": Reznikoff, 203–4.

Chapter Eleven 6,346,856 Inferior Immigrants

313 *Atlantic Monthly* published: Cornelia James Cannon, "American Misgivings," *Atlantic Monthly*, 2/1922, 145–57. **313** *Missionary Survey*: "Why We Should Be Alarmed on the Immigration Question," *Missionary Survey*, 5/1922, 326–27. **313** Wiggam announced: *Current Opinion*, 10/1/1922, 512. **313** Stoddard invoked: Stoddard, *Revolt*, 72. **313** get in touch: ACSS, Author Files 1, B173, F5: Perkins to Stoddard, 7/30/1924. **314** "inexpertly popularized": CCBP, Yerkes correspondence, Yerkes to Brigham, 9/1/1922. **314** pointed him, "not afraid": CCBP, Yerkes correspondence, Brigham to Yerkes, 7/16/1922. **314** "I predict": CCBP, Yerkes correspondence, Yerkes to Brigham, 9/1/1922. **314** "its importance": Yerkes to Princeton University Press, 1/1924, in Schrag, 105. **314** "Nordic lady": CCBP, Yerkes correspondence, Yerkes to Brigham, 8/4/1922. **316** Laughlin's book's thesis: Charles Gould, 162. **316** from Lord Kelvin: HHLP, D 2-4:14. **316** maps Grant had: Spiro, 215. **316** Laughlin report: Hearings, "Analysis," esp. 727, 771, 733. **317** "Facts of this nature": Ibid., 1233. **318** Patten's report: JLP, B2, Patten to Robert Ward, 11/21/1922. **318** Gould called it: CBDP, B42, Gould to Davenport, 3/25/1922. **318** report as bait: CBDP, B35, Davenport to Wycliffe P. Draper, 3/23/1923. Draper, heir to a textile fortune, would later be the founder and primary funder of the unashamedly racist Pioneer Fund. He described the days of his life leading up to its founding in his Harvard *Class of 1913, 25th Anniversary Report*: "A dozen years of travel. Shooting jaguar in Matto [*sic*] Grosso and deer in Sonora; elephant in Uganda and chamois in Steiermark; ibex in Baltistan and antelope in Mongolia. Climbing in Alps and Rockies. Pigsticking in India and fox-hunting in England. Exploring in West Sahara with French Mission" (247–48). **318** Roberts told: *SEP*, Roberts, "Lest We Forget," 4/28/1923, 3–4, 158, 162. **318** "best known scientists": King, *In the Name*, 120. **318** Kinnicutt: Cornelia Brooke

Gilder, *Edith Wharton's Lenox* (Charleston, SC: The History Press, 2017), 156. **318** talk went on . . . Spirits: JLP, B2, Patten to Robert Ward, 12/14/1922. **319** than black people: Brigham, 197. **319** Excerpts from *A Study of American Intelligence*: Brigham, 204–10. **320** justice to Madison Grant, Regarding Charles Gould: Ibid., 184, xvii. **320** "charming fellow": CCBP, Gould–Yerkes correspondence, Gould to Yerkes, 11/19/1927. **320** slice of his fortune: Saretzky, "Sponsor," 11. **320** "most valuable documents": Ludmerer, 103. **320** "who marries": López, 90. **320** Third case: *United States v. Bhagat Singh Thind*, 261 U.S. 204 (1923). **320** Davis warned: JLP, B2, Davis to Lee, 9/24/1923, enclosed in Davis to Harding, 4/12/1923; *NYT*, "Davis Favors Tests to Pick Immigrants," 4/28/1923, 15. **321** "sane and sober": *NYT Book Review*, 3/18/1923, 18. **321** "unusual clarity": Stone, "Social Problems and Reforms," *American Economic Review*, 9/1923, 523. **321** PRINCETON PROFESSOR: *Iowa City Press-Citizen*, 6/30/1923, 5. **321** David Starr Jordan: Jordan, "Should Present Restriction Laws Be Modified?," *Congressional Digest*, 7–8/1923, 304. **321** William N. Vaile: American Defense Society Papers, B13, F1, ADS pamphlet report on 11/9/1923 immigration conference. **321** Fairfield Osborn: Osborn, "The Approach to the Immigration Problem Through Science," *Proceedings of the National Immigration Conference, Special Report No. 26*, New York: National Industrial Conference Board, 1923, 8. **321** National Immigration Conference: *NYT*, 11/25/1923, 16; 12/9/1923, 17; 12/14/1923, 20. **322** "vanguard of mankind": Baur, Fischer, and Lenz, 655. The original edition was published in Germany in 1923; the first English translation, cited here, appeared eight years later. **322** Adolf Hitler: Muller-Hill, 8. **322** "it was hopeless": JBTP, B1, F: Origins, unpublished autobiography, 497–99. **323** "alien-baiter": Louis Adamic, "Aliens and Alien Baiters," *Harper's*, 11/1936, 566–74. **323** Trevor biography: *NYT*, obituary, 2/21/1956; Panetta, 145–73; *NYT*, 6/26/1908, 7; Spiro, 203–4. **323** One of his intimates: RFA, III, B118, F884, J. D. Rockefeller Jr. to Mrs. J. B. Trevor, 8/1/1956. **323** wife's nearest: Spiro, 1313. **323** the servants were English: Panetta, 161, 163, 173. **323** downtown law office: Spiro, 203–4. **324** "Ethnic Map": Mike Wallace, 1031. **324** "Mexicans and Brazilians": HCINC, HR68A-F18.1, Trevor to Johnson, 12/6/1923. **324** "convulsive shivers": Trevor to Johnson, 2/18/1927, quoted in Spiro, 203–4. **324** teetotaling schoolteacher, Madison: Hassencahl, 46, 42. **325** Union Club: MacVeagh Papers, B31, F: IRL. **325** Union League: JLP, B2, Patten to Ward, 11/25/1922. **325** Century Association: IRLR, F401, Henry Fairchild to Hall, 3/29/1917. **325** "Magna Charta": *CR*, 4/3/1924, Trevor report, 5469. **325** itch for cash: Thompson, private reminiscence. **325** Johnson drank: Higham Papers, Higham notes on telephone conversation with Trevor, 7/23/1949. **326** Davenport had not: CCBP, Gould correspondence, Gould to Davenport, telegram, 4/21/1924. **326** traveling energy: Various letters from Grant to Albert Johnson et al. **326** continued to pay: Grant to Robert Ward, 5/27/1924, quoted in Solomon, 126. **326** "practically camped": Higham Papers, Peter F. Snyder to Higham, 6/6/1952. **326** "conceited ass": Roberts Papers, B14, F3, Diary, 1/8/1924. **326** Johnson reported: HCINC, HR68A-F18.1, Johnson to Trevor, 6/18/1924. **327** not invited: Higham Papers, Higham notes on telephone conversation with Trevor, 7/23/1949. **327** Johnson was impressed: Higham Papers, Peter F. Snyder to Higham, 6/6/1952. **327** draft after draft: HCINC, HR68A-F18.1, Trevor–Johnson correspondence, 2/24–4/24. **327** "considerably encouraged": HCINC, HR68A-F18.1, Johnson to Trevor, 2/14/1924. **327** "solidly with us": JLP, B2, Lee to Ward, 9/19/1923. **327** weight of the evidence: Reed himself acknowledged it on the Senate floor, in *CR*, 4/3/1924, 5489. See also Johnson–Trevor correspondence, esp. 3/15/1924, and Johnson to Coolidge, cited at Wang, 118fn70. **327** "entirely unfair": *NYT*, Reed, "America of the Melting Pot Comes to End," 4/27/1924, Sec. 9, 3. **328** "buncoed": *CR*, 4/3/1924, Speech by Henry Curran entered into the record by Reed, 5475. **328** "75 percent of us": *NYT*, 4/27/1924, Sec. 9, 3. **328** an associate somehow: Burr, 62, 98. In a letter to the editor (*NYT*, 3/16/1924), Burr argued that the 1790 census should be used as the bill's basis. **328** "really a *tour de force*": JBTP, B1, F: National Origins plan, unpublished autobiography, 502. **329** benighted hordes: Higham Papers, Higham notes on telephone conversation with Trevor, 7/23/1949. **329** "open the country": JLP, B2, IRL, memo relating to Senate debate, 3/12/1924. **329** Garis article: Roy L. Garis, *Scribner's Magazine*, "The Immigration Problem: A Practical American Solution," 9/1922, 364–67. **329** George Horace Lorimer: Roberts Papers, B53, Lorimer to Roberts, 8/29/1922. **330** Burnett . . . argued: IRLR, F203, Burnett to Hall, 12/10/1918. **330** "most undesirable": *SEP*, Roberts, "Lest We Forget," 4/28/1923, 3–4, 158, 162. **330** only 3,912: Garis, cited in Wang, 88. **330** apoplectic Adolph Sabath: Sabath Papers, B1, F10, Sabath to "Dear Colleague," n.d./1924. **331** "located in Europe": Johnson to Hale W. Parish, 4/3/1924, quoted in Hassencahl, 221fn. **331** "are reconciled": Senate hearing, *Selective*, 2/14/1924, 30. **331** "the American born": Spiro, 230. **331** "it is a sin": JLP, B2: Lee to Lodge, 2/13/1924. **331** "jumbled-up": Grant, "The Racial Transformation in America," *North American Review*, 3/1924, 343–52. **332** "American watchdog": HCINC, HR68A-F18.1, text of Laughlin speech to Eugenics Education Society, 1/29/1924. **332** Osborn letter: *NYT*, "Lo, the Poor Nordic," 4/8/1924, 18. **332** preemptive response: Brigham, *A Study*, 28. **332** northern blacks: William Bagley, *Determinism in Education*, Baltimore: Warwick and York, 125. **333** "lower and lower," " 'typically American' ": Brigham, *A Study*, 178, 96. **333** "antiquated, outworn": Kimball Young, review of Brigham, *A Study*, 6/8/1923, 670. **333** brother after Darwin: Barkan, 191. **334** rented a room, main speaker: Ibid. **334** "pretty strong": Jennings Papers, B6, Jennings to Bruno Lasker, 6/20/1923. **334** appointed Laughlin: Wang, 90. In most respects, the membership and leadership of the ECUSA were identical to those of its successor organization, the American Eugenics Society. **334** Jennings's article: Jennings, "Undesirable." **335** Laughlin and his sponsor: King, *In the Name*, 116. **336** "Nordic propaganda": Jennings Papers, B3, Jennings to J. McKeen Cattell, 2/20/1924. **336** "illegitimate and incorrect": *Science*, 3/14/1924, 256–57. **336** "Don't worry": Hearings, *Europe*, 3/8/1924, 1311. **336** "kept American": Message to Congress, 12/6/1923. **337** Marshall testimony: Hearings, *Restriction*, 289–90. **337** Kantrowitz, Edlin, Rosenblatt: Hearings, *Restriction*, 316, 373–74, 387. **337** chief medical officer, Even Harry Laughlin: IRLR, F917, J. G. Wilson to Hall, 2/25/1912; HLLP, Laughlin to Grant, 11/19/1932. **338** Fiorello La Guardia: Schrag, 118. **338** Adolph Sabath: *Los Angeles Times*, "Strict Immigration Bill Easily Passes House," 4/13/1924, 1. **338** Congressional debate quotations, with *CR* page numbers for the first two weeks of April 1924: Mooney, 5910; O'Connor, 5467; Gallivan, 5849 (real swing: *Boston Globe*, 4/8/1924, 1A); Taylor, "no illiteracy", 5871; Robsion, 6254 ("had its thrill": *Los Angeles Times*, 4/13/1924, 1); Allen, 5693; Tillman, 5865; Bacon, 5901. **338** "scientific legislation": *CR*, 4/18/1924, 6639. **340** solicited Herbert Jennings's: Jennings Papers, B7, Jennings to Johnson, 1/8/1924. **340** read some of Boas's: Spiro, 226. **340** "vicious report," "dogmatic piffle": *CR*, 4/8, 3913–15; *CR*, 1/23/1924, 1328–30. **340** PERSISTENCE OF RACIAL: Gompers, "America Must Not Be Overwhelmed," *American Federationist*, 4/1924, 313–17. **341** "much agitated," "If the Jewish": Jewish Telegraphic Agency dispatch, 2/14/1924, reprinted in "Twenty Years Ago This Week," *Detroit Jewish Chronicle*, 2/25/1944.

Chapter Twelve Without Foundation

343 Reed stretched: *NYT*, 4/27/1924, Sec. XX, 3. **343** James Davis: *NYT*, 7/20/1924, 5. **343** Curran would say: "Have We an Alien Menace?," *Collier's*, 7/4/1925, 8. **345** Osborn gave Harriman: HFOP, B10, F6, Speech, 5/14/1925. **346** victory lap: JBTP, Johnson to Trevor, 4/19/1924. **346** "Honorable Sir": HCINC, HR68A-F18.1, William L. Corey to Johnson, 7/24/1924. **346** Henry Cabot Lodge: *NYT*, 5/27/1924, 1. **346** "amazing triumph," "change their names": CBDP, B40, F: Galton Society, draft minutes of meeting, 5/5/1925. **347** Kannofskys, Pavlosky: *New York Tribune*, 8/17/1923, 8. **347** Kabatchnick: Various sources spell the name Kabotschnik, Kabatchnik, Kabakoff, even Kabozizki. I've taken the spelling from court filings signed by both Kabatchnicks. **347** "Your committee": IRLR, Additional Papers, IRL to members, 6/4/1924. **347** "only necessary": JLP, B5, Demarest Lloyd to Lee, 5/17/1928. Lloyd was the son of Henry Demarest Lloyd, the late-nineteenth-century muckraking journalist. **347** Johnson threatened, valid passport: HCINC, HR68A-F18.1, Johnson to Trevor, 5/8/1926. **347** amendment denying: Hutchinson, *Legislative*, 197. **347** through two organizations: RFA, III, B118, F884, Trevor to John D. Rockefeller Jr., 4/2/1928; Hassencahl, 219. **348** "a watch-dog": JBTP, B1, F: Origins, unpublished autobiography, 555. **348** old friend John D. Rockefeller: RFA, III, B118, F884, Trevor to Rockefeller, 3/14/1930; Rockefeller to Trevor, 3/31/1928, 4/21/1929, 3/18/1932, 5/31/1933. Rockefeller's cashier's checks begin 6/17/1927 and repeat annually. **348** Al Smith, Herbert Hoover: Franklin MacVeagh Papers, B31, F: IRL, IRL Executive Commitee Bulletin no. 8, 2/1/1928. **348** found Brazil: Jeffrey Lesser, "Jewish Immigration to Brazil," in Baily and Miguez, 251–52. **349** "grave consequences": Ambassador Masanao Hanihara, quoted in Garraty, 407. **349** "eliminate Japanese": HCINC, HR68A-F18.1, Johnson to Grant, 12/27/1923. **349** "created the oddity": Ngai, 27–28. **349** Vaishno Das Bagai: www.immigrant-voices.aiisf.org/stories-by-author/876 -bridges-burnt-behind-the-story-of-vaishno-das-bagai. **350** particularly perverse law: Hutchinson, *Legislative*, 203. **350** at least sixty thousand: Estimates vary; the most precise, provided by Rebecca M. Kluchin, *Fit to Be Tied: Sterilization and Reproductive Rights in America* (New Brunswick: Rutgers University Press, 2011), is 62,000. **350** "Butler knows this": Leuchtenberg, *Supreme*, 13–15. **350** André Siegfried: Frank, 156. **351** innovator George Eastman, Rockefeller: Spiro, 1436. **351** "Some People Are Born," "Holsteins, Jerseys," bronze medal: Spiro, 185. **351** "Cho-Cho": Rydell, 48–49. **351** James Naismith . . . Karl Menninger: Laura L. Lovett, "Fitter Families for Future Firesides": Florence Sherbon and Popular Eugenics, *The Public Historian*, Summer 2007, 79–80. **352** Harry H. Mayer: Spiro, 186. **352** W. H. P. Faunce: HHLP, C 4-4:3, "What I Think About Eugenics," ca. 1927, pamphlet issued by American Eugenics Society. **352** 1926 Philadelphia world's fair: Kevles, *In the Name*, 62–63. **353** orchard-supply salesman: HFOP, B23, F9, reference letters, January 1924. **353** from the *Catechism: A Eugenics Catechism*, American Eugenics Society, 1926. **353** state of Oregon: CBDP, B40, F: Galton Society, Harry Laughlin in draft minutes of meeting, 5/5/1925. **353** "hewers of wood": W. D. Tait, "Psychology, education and sociology," *School and Society*, 1925, 37. **353** now invoked: Kennedy, *Birth Control*, 114–17. **353** struggle "to control": Sanger, "Function of Sterilization," *Birth Control Review*, 10/1926, 299. **353** Norman Thomas: *Birth Control Review*, 9/1929, 255. **353** C. W. Eliot: "A Plea for Jewish Integrity," *The Jewish Tribune and Hebrew Standard*, 12/19/1994, clipping in RPHU, B233, F829. **354** Terman study: Terman, *Genet-*

ics, 18, 40–43, 87–172. **355** "Giving 301": Article distributed by Science Service, in *Berkeley Gazette*, 12/14/1926, 4; *Charleston* (WV) *Daily Mail*, 1/18/1927, 6, and other papers. **356** "these grounds," William Bateson: Herbert Jennings Papers, B4, Jennings to Fisher, 9/27/1924. **356** "Our committee did": Herbert Jennings Papers, B4, 10/2/1924. **356** Pearl recantation: Raymond Pearl, "The Biology of Superiority," *American Mercury*, 11/1927, 255–66. **357** As a young scientist: *World's Work*, 1/1908, 9823. **357** Mears bequest: *Harvard Crimson*, 5/1/1929. **357** Thomas Hunt Morgan: Quoted in Pearl, *American Mercury*, 11/1927. **357** "over to the enemy": Goddard, "Feeblemindedness" (1928), 219–27. **358** "*intellectual* not *racial*": Zenderland, 327. **358** "any system": Brigham, "Validity of Tests in Examination of Immigrants," *Industrial Psychology*, 6/1926. **358** "movement was dominated": Lemann, 33. **358** repudiation of his own work: Brigham, "Intelligence Tests of Immigrant Groups," *Psychological Review*, 3/1930, 164–65. **359** "hypothesis is dead": Downey, 27. **359** "ridiculous to claim," "fallacious": *NYT*, "Brigham Adds Fire to 'War of the I.Q.s,'" 12/3/1938, 10D. **359** "Nothing good": Kennan, *Diaries*, 78. **360** Rudolf Hess, declared: Kuhl, 36. **360** Walter Schultze had been: Robert S. Wistrich, *Who's Who in Nazi Germany* (New York: Routledge, 2002), 229–30. **361** "policy and thinking": Proctor, 100. **361** "simply excluding": Hitler, 400. **361** *Handbook for Law*: Whitman, 54. **361** "It seems strange": ACSS, Author Files 1, B80, F3: Grant to Perkins, 11/7/1924. **361** studied, cited: Hitler, *kritische edition*, Vol. I, 745, Annotation #22; Vol. II, 1111, editors' introduction to Chapter 3. **361** "warmly inscribed": Ryback, 109. **361** Several historians, Another memoirist: Whitney, unpublished autobiography, 205, American Philosophical Society, Mss.B.W613b; D. G. Brinton Thompson, "A Personal Memory of Madison Grant," n.d. **362** "new testament": Baltzell, *Protestant*, 274. **362** Rosenberg encouraged: Rosenberg, *The Myth of the Twentieth Century: An Evaluation of the Spiritual-Intellectual Confrontations of Our Age*, at aryanism.net, 149. **362** "spiritual fathers": Kuhl, 38. **362** commissioned by Fairfield: HFOP, B8, F39, Osborn to Grant, 1/16/1920. **362** reluctantly agreed: William Gregory Papers, B44, F16, Davenport to Gregory, 2/14/1930. **363** he missed . . . Fischer . . . Rüdin: CBDP, B28, Draft of Davenport speech to Third International Congress. **363** "under the *Leitung*": CBDP, B80, Davenport to Ploetz, 10/1/1932. **364** official opening: CBDP, B14, Diary for 1927. **364** met in 1923 . . . pilgrimage: CBDP, B84, Davenport to Rüdin, 4/10/1923; 2/26/1930; Rüdin to Davenport, 2/1/1930, 4/15/1930. **364** difficult situation: CBDP, B84, Rüdin to Davenport, 8/9/1932. **364** "valueless individuals": Muller-Hill, 31. **364** human hybridization: CBDP, B37, Davenport to Fischer, 1/28/1932. **364** "destroyed the theory": Proctor, 345. **364** "single day": Ibid., 64. **364** "Only through": William Tucker, *The Science and Politics of Racial Research* (Champaign: University of Illinois Press, 1994), 121. **364** Frick hailed, guest of honor, "rare and special": Muller-Hill, 120–23, 15, 61. **365** "not objective": CBDP, B14, Davenport to Darwin, 6/6/1928. **365** publish a letter: CBDP, B42, Davenport to Madison Grant, 10/7/1930. **365** "slowly understanding": CBDP, B77, Davenport to Frederick Osborn, 2/10/1930, 2/14/1930. **365** He despised: Davenport, letter to the editor, *Life*, 6/13/1928, 3. **365** "force crushing": Davenport to Frederick Osborn, 12/23/1932, quoted in Rosenberg, *No Other*, 95. **366** naive willingness: Kuhl, 68–70. I should acknowledge that I interpret the evidence Kuhl presents rather differently than he does. **366** "shocking violations": William Gregory Papers, B78, F18, Davenport to Gregory, 5/7/1935. **366** Curt Stern: Ludmerer, 149–50. **366** enlisted Boas: FBP, Davenport to Boas, 5/31/1935; CIWA, Genetics, B2, F18: CBD to W. M. Gilbert, 6/1/1938. **366** Edward A. Ross: Ross, *Seventy*,

275–79. **367** Leon Whitney: Kuhl, 36, 45. **367** extended membership: Spiro, 367. **367** In the *Journal of Heredity*: Popenoe, "The German Sterilization Law," *Journal of Heredity*, 7/1934, 257. **367** "eternal change": CBDP, B14, Autobiographical #2: Davenport to John C. Merriam, 9/21/1933. **367** recruited Campbell . . . tapped him: HFOP, B4, F12, Osborn to Campbell, 10/14/1925; B9, F1, Osborn to Madison Grant, 6/27/1928. **368** "squelching the Jews": American Defense Society Papers, B8, F5: Campbell to Grant, 9/18/1935. **368** Osborn traveled: Spiro, 370. **368** "all that is bad," "freely mingle": HFOP, B44, F8, Osborn to Charles Singer, 5/28/1935; Osborn to Gregory, 5/25/1935. **368** including those: Norman Boas, 236. **368** confined to a wheelchair: H. E. Anthony, "Madison Grant," *Journal of Mammalogy*, 8/1938, 396–97. **368** "his own solution": HHLP, C 2-1:8, R. N. Fuller of Scribner Bookstore to "those interested in the future of America," 11/1933. **368** At Grant's request, increasingly put-upon: ACSS, Author Files 1, B90, F3, R. V. Coleman to "Miss Wycoff," 10/26/1933; Whitney Darrow to Perkins, 12/13/1933. **369** "deserves much greater": ACSS, Author Files 1, B90, F1, Perkins to Robert Thomas, 8/7/1934. **369** "those races whose": ACSS, Author Files 1, B90, F3, Perkins to Grant, 11/4/1933. **369** "Jews are less": ACSS, Author Files 1, B90, F1, Perkins to Grant, 4/23/1934. **369** something of a decline: HFOP, B12, F38, Laughlin to Grant, 9/30/1933. **369** warm and productive: HHLP, C 4-4:7, Laughlin to Eugen Fischer, 7/31/1935; Fischer to Laughlin, 3/4/1936; B 2-2:6, Ernst Rüdin to Laughlin, 1935 [date unclear]; D 2-2:17, HHL to Fritz Lenz, 10/25/1928–. **369** financial support: HHLP, D 2-5:5, Laughlin to Grant, 11/14/1931; CBDP, B7, F2, Davenport to Campbell, 11/20/1928. **369** "biological foundations": *EN*, 10–11/1933, 89–92. **369** Frick's speech: "German Population and Race Politics," *EN*, 3–4/1934, 33. **369** "Dr. Frick's address": Lombardo, 202, quoting Laughlin to Grant, 1/13/1934. **369** Alfred Ploetz: *EN*, 9–10/1934, 129. **369** enthusiastic review: *EN*, 1–2/1935, 7. **369** Clarence Campbell: *EN*, 3–4/1936, 1. **370** Lapouge to his friend, eightieth-birthday greetings: *EN*, 3–4/1934, 39; 1–2/1935, 4. **370** Campbell speech: Kuhl, 34; *NYT*, 8/29/1935, 8; *Time*, 9/9/1935. **370** University of Heidelberg ceremonies: *NYT*, "Heidelberg's Aim Changed by Nazis," 7/2/1936, 8; HHLP, E 1:3-8, event program. **371** university spokesman, boycott initiated: *NYT*, "Heidelberg Guests See Rule by Nazis," 7/5/1936, Sec. IV, 4; editorial, 7/2/1936, 20. **371** completed purge: Arye Carmon, "The Impact of the Nazi Racial Decrees on the University of Heidelberg," *Yad Vashem Studies*, 1976, 31–141. **371** "farseeing representative": Kuhl, 187. **371** "personal honor": HHLP, E 1:3–8, Laughlin to Schneider. **371** committed suicide: Weindling, 71.

Chapter Thirteen The Train of Consequences

373 Rüdin sailed: CBDP, B84, Davenport to Rüdin, 2/26/1930. **373** *St. Louis*: Ogilvie and Miller, 13, 24. **373** "desperate people": Breitman et al., *Refugees*, 143–44. **374** *Fortune* magazine poll: "The Fortune Quarterly Survey: XIII," 7/1938, 36. **374** another poll asked: Ishaan Tharoor, "What Americans Thought of Jewish Refugees on the Eve of World War II," *Washington Post*, 11/17/2015. **374** "protect the youth": Wyman, 75–78. **374** Houghteling was rather: Daniels, 78–79. **374** Moseley was more: Bendersky, 250. **374** "no inclination": *Time*, 3/4/1940, 16. **375** Fosdick, withdrew: Mehler, 349. **375** extricate the Rockefeller Foundation: Paul, *Politics*, 61. **375** remaking itself: Notice of Special Meeting of Members, 10/25/1938, at www.dnalc.org, document 11607. **375** Even the Immigration Restriction League: JLP, B3, F:IRL, "The Immigration Problem Today," IRL pamphlet 11/1934. **375** chosen successor, chairman: Regal, 193–95. **375** "bitter partisans": William Gregory Papers, B44, F16, Gregory to Grant, 7/25/1932. **375** "I cannot approve": William Gregory Papers, B44, F16: Gregory to Grant, 10/9/1934. **376** "in sympathy," "simply uncovered": William Gregory Papers, B78, F18, Gregory to Wingate Todd, 5/13/1935; Gregory to C. R. Stockard, 5/23/1935. **376** Researchers were denied: In 1965, a museum official rejected a researcher's request for "personal facts about Madison Grant," saying they were generally "uninformative" and Grant's letters at AMNH were mostly written in his role as an officer of the New York Zoological Society; in fact, the Grant records comprise eight bulging folders of frank and revealing correspondence. (AMNH Archives, Biography Files, Charlotte W. Stove to Lewis Fechter, 2/8/1965.) Three decades later, while working on his definitive biography of Grant, scholar Jonathan Spiro was "abruptly and rudely kicked out" of the museum library when officials learned he was "more interested in Madison Grant the eugenicist than MG the conservationist." (Email from Spiro to author, 12/22/2014.) **376** not to use: Author interview with cataloger Eleanor Schwartz, 12/09/2015. **376** uncomfortable melding, "superficiality": Hassenchahl, 328–29; CIWA, Genetics, B4, F18, Merriam, "Confidential Administration Document," 7/6/1929. **376** advisory committee to monitor: Garland Allen, 250. **377** committee were unanimous: L. C. Dunn Papers, B3, Merriam to Dunn, 7/25/1935, A. V. Kidder to Dunn, 8/1/1935. **377** committee's forward-looking: CIWA, Genetics, B8, F9, "Report of the Advisory Committee." **377** "any intervention": HHLP, C 2-1:8, Grant to Laughlin, 11/22/1935. **378** "entirely wise": CIWA, Genetics, B2, F18, Davenport to Bush, 5/8/1939. **378** renaming itself, Shapiro office: Notice of Special Meeting of Members, 10/25/1938, at www.dnalc.org, document 11607. **379** The individuals who, Grant and others: CBDP, B77, Frederick Osborn to Albert Blakeslee, 4/23/1940. **379** racist websites: www.eugenicsarchive.org and www.dnalc.org. **379** "unequalled opportunity": FBP, 2/11/1908. **379** "beyond the pale": Hellman, 196–97. **379** "biased spirit": Robert Lowie Papers, B12, Osborn to Lowie, 6/6/1922. **379** "To err is": HFOP, B44, F8: Galton Society, Osborn to Gregory, 3/23/1935. **379** "successor to Darwin": *New York Sun*, 11/6/1935. **380** one sentence: *NYT*, 11/7/1935, 23. **380** "his ideals will": *EN*, 1–2/1935, 98. **380** Third World Center: www.fieldscenter.princeton.edu. Its current name is the Carl A. Fields Center for Equality and Cultural Understanding. **380** he was a Bolshevik: JLP, B1, Lee to James Patten, 11/30/1918. **380** as an insult: Grant's introduction in Stoddard, *Rising*. **381** unleash Grant: IRLP, F590, 2nd of 2, Lee to Hall, 7/28/1916; F528, unknown to Hughes, 7/29/1916. **381** "Egyptian night": Solomon, 126. **381** on his bookshelf: JLP, B38, F: List of books owned. **381** "chocolate races": HCR, *Class of 1883, 50th reunion*, 189–95. **381** "uplift the psalm": JLP, B43, F: Joseph Lee Jr. papers about Lee, Memoir by JL Jr. in *Yearbook of the Thomas Dudley Family Association*, 1938, 308. **381** Lee blamed: Grant, *Passing*, 14. **381** "racial prejudice": Barbara Solomon Papers, B4, F4, Bradley to Mrs. Joseph Lee, 6/18/1937. **382** his lengthy obituary, editorial page encomium: *NYT*, 7/29/1937, 4, 19. **382** Lee-Domini family: Author correspondence with John Domini, Joe Lee's great-grandson. **382** Bradley-Epstein family: Lionel Epstein obituary at legacy.com, from death notice in *Washington Post*. **382** The *Times* treated: *NYT*, 5/31/1937, 15. **383** He asked Charles Davenport: HFOP, B6, F15, Davenport to Grant, 6/19/1935. **383** He lobbied hard . . . futile: HHLP, C 2-1:8, Laughlin to James Rowland Angell, 2/17/1936; Grant to Laughlin, 12/29/1936, 1/8/1937. **383** particularly florid: F. R. Burnham, "Madison Grant:

Charon Beckoned," typescript, Kermit Roosevelt Papers, B106, F1935–1938, in Dean Sage to Roosevelt, 6/17/1938. **383** International Hunting Exposition: *NYT*, 11/7/1937, 34; Spiro, 385. **384** epileptic seizures: CIWA, Genetics, B5, F11, George L. Streeter to John C. Merriam, 10/26/1937, Albert Blakeslee to Streeter, 11/3/1937. **384** Trevor-financed: HHLP, C 4-3:1, Trevor to Francis K. Stevens, 4/29/1939. **384** *Immigration and Conquest*: Laughlin, 92, 28, 123. **384** Bush received: CIWA, Genetics, B31, F13, Bush to Laughlin, 5/4/1939. **384** accelerated pension: CIWA, Genetics, B31, F13, Bush to Laughlin, 6/1/1939; Laughlin to Bush, 6/22/1939. **384** field glasses: CIWA, Genetics, B5, F10, CIW press release to *Science*, 1/19/1940. **384** sending out copies: HHLP, C 4-5:9. **385** box of fudge: CBDP, B30, Seventy-Fifth Birthday Scrapbook. **385** route their money, "entirely understandable": CIWA, Genetics, B2, F18, W. M. Gilbert to Davenport, 11/25/1939; Davenport to Gilbert, 11/27/1939. **385** "should be 'bought off'": CIWA, Genetics, B2, F18, George L. Streeter to Merriam, 10/19/1938. **385** same birthday mail: CBDP, B30, Seventy-Fifth Birthday Scrapbook. **386** Boas's regard for Davenport: CBDP, B5, Davenport to Boas, 5/28/24. In 1930, as Columbia was starting a department of physical anthropology, he revised his will and sent his papers there. **386** Boas's death: Herskovitz, 120-21. **386** "great thrills": HCR, *Class of 1889, 50th Reunion*, 148–50. **386** Hans Przibram: CIWA, Genetics, B2, F18, Davenport to W. M. Gilbert, 6/1/1938. **386** Davenport recounted: CIWA, Genetics, B2, F18, Davenport to Bush, 6/12/1939. **387** volunteer air warden: Riddle, 92. **387** "not generally known": CBDP, B77, Davenport to Frederick Osborn, 3/12/1941. **387** Stoddard comments: Stoddard, *Into*, 256, 187, 205–6. **387** in a veterans' hospital: John Higham Papers, Johnson to Higham, 7/22/1951. **388** "soundness of his judgment": RFA, III, B118, F884. Rockefeller to Caroline Trevor, 6/1/1956. **388** his son John B. Jr.: *NYT*, "Fund Backs Controversial Study of 'Racial Betterment,'" 12/11/1977, 76. **388** Rotenbergs: Letters, as translated by Miriam Leberstein, provided to author by James Rotenberg. **389** "sympathetic and kind": Breitman and Stewart, 143–44. **389** Yehoshua's death: Dovid Schnipper, trans. Michael Gottlieb, "My Town Plontch," at www.jewishgen.org/yizkor/staszow/sta633.html.

Epilogue Liberty Island, 1965

391 50,000 European Jews, less than 9,000: Schneiderman, 599, 600. **392** "Doctors' Trial": See, e.g., at nuremberg.law.harvard.edu, Karl Brandt document 51, 116–18; also here, defense statement for defendant Wilhelm Beiglboeck, 11150; at *Trials of War Criminals Before the Nuernberg Military Tribunals* (Washington, DC: Government Printing Office, 1949), defense exhibits for defendant Otto Hofmann, Vol. 4, 1159. Additional material in Kuhl, 101–3, and Spiro, 381–82. **392** Rüdin was apprehended: Weindling, 71. **393** Johnson sat at a desk: *Public Papers of the Presidents of the United States*: Lyndon B. Johnson, 1965, Vol. II (Washington, DC: Government Printing Office), 1037–40.

Acknowledgments

395 "nothing of value": JLP, B38, F: Instructions.

Bibliography

MANUSCRIPT COLLECTIONS AND OTHER ARCHIVAL MATERIALS

American Defense Society Papers, New-York Historical Society, New York, NY
American Museum of Natural History, Biography Files and Central Archives, New York, NY
Franz Boas Papers, American Philosophical Society, Philadelphia, PA
Carl Campbell Brigham Papers, Educational Testing Service Library, Princeton, NJ
Papers of the Cabot Family, 1786–2013, Schlesinger Library, Harvard University, Cambridge, MA
Richard Clarke Cabot Papers, Harvard University Archives, Pusey Library, Cambridge, MA
Carnegie Institution of Washington Archives, Washington, DC
John Foster Carr Papers, New York Public Library, New York, NY
Columbia Oral History Project, Butler Library, Columbia University, New York, NY
Charles B. Davenport Papers, American Philosophical Society, Philadelphia, PA
L. C. Dunn Papers, American Philosophical Society, Philadelphia, PA
Eugenics Record Office Records, American Philosophical Society, Philadelphia, PA
Henry Herbert Goddard Papers, Archives of the History of American Psychology, University of Akron, Akron, OH
William King Gregory Papers, American Museum of Natural History, New York, NY
W. Averell Harriman Papers, Manuscript Division, Library of Congress, Washington, DC
Records of the President of Harvard University, Pusey Library, Cambridge, MA
Geoffrey Hellman Papers, New York Public Library, New York, NY
John Higham Papers, Sheridan Libraries, Johns Hopkins University, Baltimore, MD
William T. Hornaday Papers, Manuscript Division, Library of Congress, Washington, DC
House Committee on Immigration and Naturalization Correspondence, RG233, National Archives, Suitland, MD
Immigration Restriction League (US) Records, Houghton Library, Harvard University, Cambridge, MA
Herbert Jennings Papers, American Philosophical Society, Philadelphia, PA

Albert Johnson Papers, Special Collections, Washington State Library, Tumwater, WA

Harry H. Laughlin Papers, Pickler Library, Truman State University, Kirksville, MO

Joseph Lee Papers, Massachusetts Historical Society, Boston, MA

Henry Cabot Lodge Papers, Massachusetts Historical Society, Boston, MA

Records of Abbott Lawrence Lowell, Harvard University Archives, Cambridge, MA

Robert Lowie Papers, Bancroft Library, University of California, Berkeley

Franklin MacVeagh Papers, Manuscript Division, Library of Congress, Washington, DC

Louis Marshall Papers, Center for Jewish History, New York, NY

Paul Bowman Popenoe Papers, American Heritage Center, University of Wyoming, Laramie

Kenneth Roberts Papers, Rauner Special Collections Library, Dartmouth College, Hanover, NH

Office of the Messrs. Rockefeller, Rockefeller Family Archives, Rockefeller Archive Center, Pocantico Hills, NY

Franklin D. Roosevelt Papers, Franklin D. Roosevelt Presidential Library, Hyde Park, NY

Kermit Roosevelt Papers, Manuscript Division, Library of Congress, Washington, DC

Elihu Root Papers, Manuscript Division, Library of Congress, Washington, DC

Edward A. Ross Papers, Wisconsin Historical Society, McIntyre Library, University of Wisconsin–Eau Claire

Adolph Joachim Sabath Papers, American Jewish Archives, Cincinnati, OH

Margaret Sanger Papers, Margaret Sanger Papers Project, New York University, online (see Websites, below)

Archives of Charles Scribner's Sons, Princeton University Library, Manuscripts Division, Princeton, NJ

Barbara Miller Solomon Papers, Schlesinger Library, Harvard University, Cambridge, MA

John Bond Trevor Papers, Bentley Historical Library, University of Michigan, Ann Arbor

Charles Warren Papers, Manuscript Division, Library of Congress, Washington, DC

WEBSITES

American National Biography Online: anb.org

ancestry.com/genealogy/records

Angel Island Immigration Station Foundation: aiisf.org

Carnegie Institution of Washington: carnegiescience.edu

DNA Learning Center, Cold Spring Harbor Laboratory: dnalc.org

The Papers of Benjamin Franklin: franklinpapers.org

The Free Encyclopedia of Washington State History. Washington Department of Archaeology and Historic Preservation: historylink.org

galton.org

Harvard Law School Library Nuremberg Trials Project: nuremberg.law.harvard.edu

Human Intelligence: intelltheory.com

jewishgen.org

livinganthropologically.com

Margaret Sanger Papers Project: nyu.edu/projects/sanger/

mayflowerhistory.com

Almanac of Theodore Roosevelt: theodore-roosevelt.com

Theodore Roosevelt Association: theodoreroosevelt.org
Theodore Roosevelt Center, Dickinson State University: theodorerooseveltcenter.org

PRIVATE DOCUMENTS

Rotenberg, Harry and Yehoshua. Letters.
Thompson, D. G. Brinton. "A Personal Memory of Madison Grant"

BIBLIOGRAPHY

Newspapers, magazines, oral histories, and interviews conducted by the author are cited in the Notes. Books, scholarly journal articles, dissertations, and unpublished papers listed here are identified in the Notes by author's name.

Aaron, Daniel. *Men of Good Hope: A Story of American Progressives.* New York: Oxford University Press, 1961.

Abbott, Edith. "Federal Immigration Policies, 1864–1924." *University Journal of Business,* March 1924.

Adams, Bluford. *Old & New New Englanders: Immigration and Regional Identity in the Gilded Age.* Ann Arbor: University of Michigan Press, 2014.

Adams, Henry. *Democracy: An American Novel.* 1925 edition. gutenberg.org.

———. *The Education of Henry Adams.* New York: Modern Library, 1946.

Alderman, Geoffrey. *Modern British Jewry.* Oxford: Clarendon Press, 1992.

Allen, Garland E. "The Founding of the Eugenics Record Office, Cold Spring Harbor, Long Island, 1910–1940: An Essay in Institutional History." *Osiris,* 1986.

Allen, William H. *Modern Philanthropy: A Study of Efficient and Appealing Giving.* New York: Dodd, Mead, 1912.

American National Biography. New York: Oxford University Press, 1999–.

Anderson, Margo J. *The American Census: A Social History.* New Haven, CT: Yale University Press, 1988.

Arnold, Kathleen R, ed. *Anti-Immigration in the United States.* Santa Barbara, CA: Greenwood, 2011.

Bachman, James Robert. "Theodore Lothrop Stoddard: The Bio-Sociological Battle for Civilization." PhD. diss., University of Rochester, 1967.

Baily, Samuel L., and Eduardo Jose Miguez, eds. *Mass Migration to Modern Latin America.* Wilmington, DE: Jaguar Books, 2003.

Baltzell, E. Digby. *The Protestant Establishment: Aristocracy & Caste in America.* New York: Vintage, 1966.

———. *Puritan Boston and Quaker Philadelphia.* New York: The Free Press, 1979.

Barkan, Elazar. *The Retreat of Scientific Racism: Changing Concepts of Race in Britain and the United States Between the World Wars.* Cambridge: Cambridge University Press, 1992.

Bashford, Alison, and Philippa Levine, eds. *The Oxford Handbook of the History of Eugenics.* New York: Oxford University Press, 2010.

Baur, Erwin, Eugen Fischer, and Fritz Lenz. *Human Heredity.* New York: Macmillan, 1931.

Beatty, Jack. *The Rascal King: The Life and Times of James Michael Curley.* Reading, MA: Addison-Wesley, 1992.

Beer, Gillian. *Darwin's Plots: Evolutionary Narrative in Darwin, George Eliot and Nineteenth-Century Fiction.* London: Routledge & Kegan Paul, 1983.

———. *Open Fields: Science in Cultural Encounter.* Oxford: Oxford University Press, 1996.

Bellamy, Edward. *Looking Backward.* Boston: Ticknor, 1888.

Bendersky, Joseph W. *The "Jewish Threat": Anti-Semitic Politics of the U.S. Army.* New York: Basic, 2000.

Berg, A. Scott. *Max Perkins: Editor of Genius.* New York: Dutton, 1978.

Biddiss, Michael D. *Father of Racist Ideology: The Social and Political Thought of Count Gobineau.* New York: Weybright and Talley, 1970.

Bisland, Elizabeth. *The Life and Letters of Lafcadio Hearn.* Boston: Houghton Mifflin, 1906.

Bix, Amy Sue. "Experiences and Voices of Eugenics Field-Workers: 'Women's Work' in Biology." *Social Studies of Science,* September 1997.

Black, Edwin. *War Against the Weak: Eugenics and America's Campaign to Create a Master Race.* Expanded edition. Washington, DC: Dialog Press, 2012.

Blacker, C. P. *Eugenics: Galton and After.* London: Duckworth, 1952.

Blodgett, Geoffrey. "The Mind of the Boston Mugwump." *Mississippi Valley Historical Review,* March 1962.

Blom, Philip P. *Fracture: Life & Culture in the West, 1918–1938.* New York: Basic, 2015.

Boas, Franz. *Anthropology and Modern Life.* New York: Dover, 1986.

Boas, Norman Francis. *Franz Boas, 1858–1942: An Illustrated Biography.* Mystic, CT: Seaport, 2004.

Bolles, Blair. *Tyrant from Illinois: Uncle Joe Cannon's Experiment with Personal Power.* New York: Norton, 1951.

Boorstin, Daniel. *The Americans: The Democratic Experience.* New York: Vintage, 1974.

Brawley, Edward Allan. *The Galveston Project: An Early Attempt at Immigration Reform.* Palo Alto: Berman Jewish Policy Archive, 2009.

Breitman, Richard, and Allan J. Lichtman. *FDR and the Jews.* Cambridge, MA: Harvard University Press, 2013.

Breitman, Richard, Barbara McDonald Stewart, and Severin Hochberg. *Advocate for the Doomed: The Diaries and Papers of James G. McDonald, 1932–1935.* Bloomington: Indiana University Press, 2007.

———. *Refugees and Rescue: The Diaries and Papers of James G. McDonald, 1935–1945.* Bloomington: Indiana University Press, 2009.

Brigham, Carl C. *A Study of American Intelligence.* Princeton, NJ: Princeton University Press, 1923.

Brinton, Daniel G. *Races and Peoples: Lectures on the Science of Ethnography.* Philadelphia: David McKay, 1901.

Brookes, Martin. *Extreme Measures: The Dark Visions and Bright Ideas of Francis Galton.* New York: Bloomsbury, 2004.

Brooks, Van Wyck. *New England: Indian Summer, 1865–1915.* New York: Dutton, 1940.

Browne, Janet. *Charles Darwin: The Power of Place.* New York: Knopf, 2002.

———. *Charles Darwin: Voyaging.* Princeton, NJ: Princeton University Press, 1995.

Bruinius, Harry. *Better for All the World: The Secret History of Forced Sterilization and America's Quest for Racial Purity.* New York: Vintage, 2007.

Burr, Clinton Stoddard. *America's Race Heritage.* New York: National Historical Society, 1922.

Burt, Cyril. "Francis Galton and His Contributions to Psychology." *British Journal of Statistical Psychology*, May 1962.

Cabot, Richard C. *Social Service and the Art of Healing*. New York: Moffat, Yard, 1915.

Campbell, Persia. *Mary Williamson Harriman*. New York: Columbia University Press, 1960.

Cannato, Vincent J. *American Passage: The History of Ellis Island*. New York: Harper-Collins, 2009.

Carlson, Elof Axel. *The Unfit: A History of a Bad Idea*. Cold Spring Harbor, NY: Cold Spring Harbor Laboratory Press, 2001.

Carnegie Institution of Washington. *Yearbook*. Carnegie Institution of Washington, annual.

Carr, John Foster. *Guide for the Immigrant Italian in the United States of America*. Garden City, NY: Doubleday, Page, 1911.

Caruso, Enrico, Jr., and Andrew Farkas. *My Father and My Family*. Portland, OR: Amadeus Press, 1997.

Castle, W. E. *Genetics and Eugenics*. Third edition. Cambridge, MA: Harvard University Press, 1924.

Catalogue of the Exhibition: First International Eugenics Congress. London: Charles Knight, 1912.

Cecil, Lamar. *Albert Ballin: Business and Politics in Imperial Germany, 1888–1918*. Princeton, NJ: Princeton University Press, 1967.

Celler, Emanuel. *You Never Leave Brooklyn: The Autobiography of Emanuel Celler*. New York: John Day, 1953.

Century Association Yearbook. New York: Knickerbocker Press, annual.

Chamberlain, Houston Stewart. *Foundations of the Nineteenth Century*. New York: John Lane, 1910.

Chang, Li Hung. *A Yellow World*. New York: Frederick Brown, 1900.

Chase, Allan. *The Legacy of Malthus: The Social Costs of the New Scientific Racism*. New York: Knopf, 1977.

Chernow, Ron. *The Warburgs: The 20th-Century Odyssey of a Remarkable Jewish Family*. New York: Random House, 1993.

Chesler, Ellen. *Woman of Valor: Margaret Sanger and the Birth Control Movement in America*. New York: Simon & Schuster, 1992.

Chesterton, G. K. *Eugenics and Other Evils*. London: Cassell, 1922.

Cinotto, Simone. *Making Italian America: Consumer Culture and the Production of Ethnic Identities*. New York: Fordham University Press, 2014.

Cohen, Adam. *Imbeciles: The Supreme Court, American Eugenics, and the Sterilization of Carrie Buck*. New York: Penguin Press, 2016.

Cole, Douglas. *Franz Boas: The Early Years, 1859–1906*. Seattle: University of Washington Press, 1999.

Conklin, Edwin Grant. *Heredity and Environment in the Development of Men*. Princeton, NJ: Princeton University Press, 1915.

Cook, Blanche Wiesen. *Eleanor Roosevelt: Volume One, 1884–1933*. New York: Viking, 1992.

Cowan, Ruth Leah Schwartz. "Francis Galton and the Study of Heredity in the Nineteenth Century." PhD diss., Johns Hopkins University, 1969.

Cowley, Malcolm. *Unshaken Friend: A Profile of Maxwell Perkins*. Boulder, CO: Roberts Rinehart, 1972.

Cox, Catherine Morris. *Genetic Studies of Genius, Vol. II: The Early Mental Traits of Three Hundred Geniuses*. Edited by Lewis M. Terman. Stanford, CA: Stanford University Press, 1926.

Crane, Katharine. *Mr. Carr of State: Forty-Seven Years in the Department of State*. New York: St. Martin's, 1960.

Craver, Earlene. "On the Boundary of White: The Cartozian Naturalization Case and the Armenians, 1923–1925." *Journal of American Ethnic History*, 2009.

Crawford, Mary Caroline. *Famous Families of Massachusetts*. Boston: Little, Brown, 1930.

Curran, Henry. *Pillar to Post*. New York: Scribner, 1941.

Currell, Susan, and Christina Cogdell, eds. *Popular Eugenics: National Efficiency and American Mass Culture in the 1930s*. Athens: Ohio University Press, 2006.

Daniels, Roger. *Guarding the Golden Door: American Immigration Policy and Immigrants Since 1882*. New York: Hill and Wang, 2004.

Darwin, Charles. *The Descent of Man*. London: John Murray, 1871.

———. *On the Origin of Species: A Facsimile of the First Edition*. Cambridge, MA: Harvard University Press, 1964.

Davenport, Charles B. *Experimental Morphology*. New York: Macmillan, 1897–1899.

———. "Fit and Unfit Matings." *Bulletin of the American Academy of Medicine*, 1910.

———. *Heredity in Relation to Eugenics*. New York: Henry Holt, 1911.

Davenport, Charles B., and Maria Scudder. *Naval Officers: Their Heredity and Development*. Washington, DC: Carnegie Institution, 1919.

Davenport, W. E. *Social Settlement Sonnets*. Brooklyn, NY: The Italian Settlement Society, 1935.

Degler, Carl N. *In Search of Human Nature: The Decline and Revival of Darwinism in American Social Thought*. New York: Oxford University Press, 1991.

Desmond, Adrian. *The Politics of Evolution: Morphology, Medicine, and Reform in Radical London*. Chicago: University of Chicago Press, 1989.

Desmond, Adrian, and James Moore. *Darwin*. New York: Norton, 1991.

Dictionary of American Biography. New York: Scribner, 1928–1958.

[Dillingham] Commission. *Reports of the Immigration Commission*. Washington, DC: Government Printing Office, 1911.

Dinnerstein, Leonard. *Anti-Semitism in America*. New York: Oxford University Press, 1994.

Dodge, Phyllis B. *Tales of the Phelps-Dodge Family: A Chronicle of Five Generations*. New York: New-York Historical Society, 1987.

Downey, Matthew T. *Carl Campbell Brigham: Scientist and Educator*. Princeton, NJ: Educational Testing Service, 1961.

Dunn, L.C., ed. *Genetics in the Twentieth Century: Essays on the Progress of Genetics in Its First 50 Years*. New York: Macmillan, 1951.

Dyer, Thomas G. *Theodore Roosevelt and the Idea of Race*. Baton Rouge: Louisiana State University Press, 1980.

East, Edward M. *Mankind at the Crossroads*. New York: Scribner, 1923.

English, Dayanne. *Unnatural Selections: Eugenics in American Modernism and the Harlem Renaissance*. Chapel Hill: University of North Carolina Press, 2004.

Engs, Ruth Clifford. *The Eugenics Movement: An Encyclopedia*. Westport, CT: Greenwood Press, 2005.

Erickson, Charlotte. *American Industry and the European Immigrant, 1860–1885*. Cambridge, MA: Harvard University Press, 1957.

Fabian, Ann. *The Skull Collectors: Race, Science, and America's Unburied Dead*. Chicago: University of Chicago Press, 2010.

Fairchild, Henry Pratt. "The Literacy Test and Its Making." *Quarterly Journal of Economics*, May 1917.

Fein, Isaac M. *Boston—Where It All Began: An Historical Perspective of the Boston Jewish Community*. Boston: Jewish Bicentennial Committee, 1976.

Field, Geoffrey G. *Evangelist of Race: The Germanic Vision of Houston Stewart Chamberlain*. New York: Columbia University Press, 1981.

Fitzgerald, David Scott, and David Cook Martin. *Culling the Masses: The Democratic Origins of Racist Immigration Policy in the Americas*. Cambridge, MA: Harvard University Press, 2014.

Fitzgerald, F. Scott. *Fie! Fie! Fi-Fi!: A Facsimile of the 1914 Acting Script and the Musical Score*. Columbia: University of South Carolina Press, 1996.

———. *The Great Gatsby*. New York: Simon & Schuster, 1973.

Frank, Tibor. "From Nativism to the Quota Laws: Restrictionist Pressure Groups and the U.S. Congress, 1879–1924." *Parliaments, Estates, and Representation*, 1995.

Friedlander, Henry. *The Origins of Nazi Genocide: From Euthanasia to the Final Solution*. Chapel Hill: University of North Carolina Press, 1995.

Galton, Francis. *The art of Travel; or, shifts and contrivances available in Wild Countries*. London: Murray, 1855.

———. *English Men of Science*. London: Macmillan, 1874.

———. *Hereditary Genius: An Inquiry Into Its Laws and Consequences*. London: Macmillan, 1892.

———. "Hereditary Talent and Character." *Macmillan's Magazine*, July 1865 and August 1865.

———. *Inquiries into Human Faculty and Its Development*. Second edition. London: J. M. Dent, 1907.

———. *Memories of My Life*. London: Methuen, 1908.

———. *The Narrative of an Explorer in Tropical South Africa*. London: John Murray, 1853.

———. "On Apparatus for Testing the Delicacy of the Muscular and Other Senses in Different Persons." *Journal of the Anthropological Institute*, 1883.

———. "On the Anthropometric Laboratory at the Late International Health Exhibition." *Journal of the Anthropological Institute*, 1885.

Gardiner, Robin. *The History of the White Star Line*. Hersham, UK: Ian Allen, 2001.

Garraty, John A. *Henry Cabot Lodge: A Biography*. New York: Knopf, 1953.

Gillham, Nicholas Wright. *A Life of Sir Francis Galton: From African Exploration to the Birth of Eugenics*. Oxford, UK: Oxford University Press, 2001.

Glazier, Jack. *Dispersing the Ghetto: The Relocation of Jewish Immigrants Across America*. East Lansing: Michigan State University Press, 2005.

Gobineau, Count A. de. *The Moral and Intellectual Diversity of Races*. Translated by H. Hotz. Philadelphia: Lippincott, 1856. (This is the title of the first American edition of Gobineau's *Essay on the Inequality of Human Races*.)

Goddard, Henry H. *The Criminal Imbecile*. New York: Macmillan, 1915.

———. "Feeblemindedness: A Question of Definition." *Proceedings and Addresses of the Annual Session of the American Association for the Study of the Feeble-Minded*, 1928.

———. *Feeblemindedness: Its Causes and Consequences*. New York: Macmillan, 1914.

———. *The Kallikak Family: A Study in the Heredity of Feeble-Mindedness.* New York: Macmillan, 1912.

———. "Mental Tests and the Immigrant." *Journal of Delinquency,* September 1917.

Gompers, Samuel. *Seventy Years of Life and Labor.* New York: Dutton, 1925.

Goodman, Roger, ed. *The First German War Crimes Trial: Chief Judge Walter B. Beals' Desk Notebook of the Doctors' Trial, Held in Nuernberg, Germany, December 1946 to August 1947.* Salisbury, NC: Documentary Publications, n.d.

Gordon, Linda. *Woman's Body, Woman's Right: A Social History of Birth Control in America.* New York: Grossman, 1976.

Goriansky, Alexander Yale. *Shadows on the Wall: A Brief History of Number 77 Mount Vernon Street.* Boston: The Club of Odd Volumes, 2007.

Gossett, Thomas F. *Race: The History of an Idea in America.* New York: Oxford University Press, 1997.

Gould, Charles W. *America: A Family Matter.* Scribner: New York, 1920.

Gould, Stephen Jay. *The Mismeasure of Man.* Revised and expanded edition. New York: Norton, 1996.

Graff, Henry F. *Grover Cleveland.* New York: Holt, 2002.

Grant, Madison. *The Conquest of a Continent, or The Expansion of Races in America.* New York: Scribner, 1933.

———. *Hank: His Lies and Yarns.* New York: privately printed, 1931. (Published pseudonymously, author's name "The Major.")

———. *The Passing of the Great Race, or The Racial Basis of European History.* Fourth edition, revised 1921. New York: Scribner, 1923.

———. *The Passing of the Great Race: or The Racial Basis of World History.* New York: Scribner, 1916.

Grant, Madison, and Charles Stewart Davison, eds. *The Alien in Our Midst: Selling Our Birthright for a Mess of Pottage.* New York: Galton Publishing, 1930.

———. *The Founders of the Republic on Immigration, Naturalization and Aliens.* New York: Scribner, 1928.

Greenberg, David. *Republic of Spin: An Inside History of the American Presidency.* New York: Norton, 2015.

Greenslet, Ferris. *The Life of Thomas Bailey Aldrich.* Cambridge, MA: Riverside Press, 1908.

Groves, Charles S. *Henry Cabot Lodge, the Statesman.* Boston: Small, Maynard, 1925.

Günther, Hans F. K. *The Racial Elements of European History.* London: Methuen, 1927.

Guterl, Matthew Pratt. *The Color of Race in America: 1900–1940.* Cambridge, MA: Harvard University Press, 2002.

Guyer, Michael F. *Being Well-Born: An Introduction to Eugenics.* Indianapolis: Bobbs-Merrill, 1916.

Hall, Prescott F. "Italian Immigration." *North American Review,* 1896.

Hall, Mrs. Prescott F., comp. *Immigration: and Other Interests of Prescott Farnsworth Hall.* New York: Knickerbocker Press, 1922.

Haller, Mark H. *Eugenics: Hereditarian Attitudes in American Thought.* New Brunswick, NJ: Rutgers University Press, 1963.

Handlin, Oscar. *Boston's Immigrants.* Cambridge, MA: Harvard University Press, 1979.

———. *Race and Nationality in American Life.* Boston: Little, Brown, 1957.

———. *The Uprooted: The Epic Story of the Great Migrations That Made the American People*. Second edition. Boston: Little, Brown, 1979.

Harap, Louis. *The Image of the Jew in American Literature: From Early Republic to Mass Immigration*. Philadelphia: Jewish Publication Society, 1974.

Harriman, E. Roland. *I Reminisce*. New York: Doubleday, 1975.

Hassencahl, Frances. "Harry H. Laughlin. 'Expert Eugenics Agent' for the House Committee on Immigration and Naturalization, 1921 to 1931." PhD diss., Case Western Reserve University, 1970.

Hellman, Geoffrey. *Bankers, Bones & Beetles: The First Century of the American Museum of Natural History*. Garden City, NY: Natural History Press, 1969.

Henig, Robin Marantz. *The Monk in the Garden: The Lost and Found Genius of Gregor Mendel, the Founder of Genetics*. Boston: Houghton Mifflin, 2000.

Hershfield, Rachel Leah. "The Immigration Restriction League: A Study of the League's Impact on American Immigration Policy, 1894–1924." MA thesis, University of Calgary, 1993.

Herskovits, Melville J. *Franz Boas: The Science of Man in the Making*. New York: Scribner, 1953.

Hertzler, J. O. "Edward Alsworth Ross: Sociological Pioneer and Interpreter." *American Sociological Review*, October 1951.

Hess, Stephen. *America's Political Dynasties: From Adams to Kennedy*. Garden City, NY: Doubleday, 1966.

Higham, John. "The Mind of a Nativist: Henry F. Bowes and the A.P.A." *American Quarterly*, Spring 1952.

———. *Send These to Me: Immigrants in Urban America*. Revised edition. Baltimore: Johns Hopkins University Press, 1984.

———. *Strangers in the Land: Patterns of American Nativism, 1860–1925*. New Brunswick, NJ: Rutgers University Press, 2002.

Hillier, Alfred J. "Albert Johnson, Congressman." *Pacific Northwest Quarterly*, July 1945.

Hitler, Adolf. *Mein Kampf*. Translated by Ralph Manheim. London: Hutchinson, 1969.

———. *Mein Kampf: Eine kritische edition*. Munich: Institut für Zeitgeschichte, 2016.

Hofstadter, Richard. *Social Darwinism in American Thought*. Revised edition. New York: George Braziller, 1959.

Hofstadter, Richard, and Walter P. Metzger. *The Development of Academic Freedom in the United States*. New York: Columbia University Press, 1955.

Howe, Irving. *World of Our Fathers*. New York: Harcourt Brace Jovanovich, 1976.

Howe, Mark DeWolfe, ed. *Holmes–Laski Letters: The Correspondence of Mr. Justice Holmes and Harold J. Laski, 1916–1935*. Cambridge, MA: Harvard University Press, 1953.

Hoy, Suellen. *Chasing Dirt: The American Pursuit of Cleanliness*. New York: Oxford University Press, 1995.

Hunter, George William. *A Civic Biology: Presented in Problems*. New York: American Book, 1914.

Huntington, Ellsworth. *The Character of Races*. New York: Scribner, 1924.

Hutchinson, E. P. *Immigrants and Their Children, 1850–1950*. New York: Wiley, 1956.

———. *Legislative History of American Immigration Policy, 1798–1965*. Philadelphia: Balch Institute of Ethnic Studies, 1981.

Hyatt, Marshall. *Franz Boas, Social Activist: The Dynamics of Ethnicity*. Westport, CT: Greenwood, 1990.

International Eugenics Conference. *Problems in Eugenics, Vol. II.* Report of Proceedings of the First International Eugenics Congress, July 24 to 30, 1912. London: Eugenics Education Society, 1913.

Iorizzo, Luciano J., and Salvatore Mondello. *The Italian Americans.* Youngstown, NY: Cambria Press, 2006.

Jacobson, Matthew Frye. *Whiteness of a Different Color: European Immigrants and the Alchemy of Race.* Cambridge, MA: Harvard University Press, 1999.

James, Henry (1843–1916). *The American Scene.* London: Chapman and Hall, 1907.

James, Henry (1879–1947). *Charles W. Eliot: President of Harvard University.* Boston: Houghton Mifflin, 1930.

Jennings, Herbert S. *Prometheus, or: Biology and the Advancement of Man.* New York: Dutton, 1925.

———. "'Undesirable Aliens': A Biologist's Examination of the Evidence Before Congress." *The Survey,* December 15, 1923.

Jimenez, Tomas. *Replenished Ethnicity: Mexican Americans, Immigration, and Identity.* Berkeley: University of California Press, 2009.

Jordan, David Starr. *The Days of a Man, Volume II: 1900–1921.* Yonkers, NY: World, 1922.

Kazin, Michael. *A Godly Hero: The Life of William Jennings Bryan.* New York: Knopf, 2006.

Kenin, Richard, and Justin Wintle. *The Dictionary of Biographical Quotation.* New York: Knopf, 1978.

Kennan, George. *E. H. Harriman: A Biography.* Boston: Houghton Mifflin, 1922.

Kennan, George F. *The Kennan Diaries.* Edited by Frank Costigliota. New York: Norton, 2014.

Kennedy, David. *Birth Control in America.* New Haven, CT: Yale University Press, 1970.

Kennedy, David M. *Over Here: The First World War and American Society.* New York: Oxford University Press, 1980.

Kennedy, John Michael. "Philanthropy and Science in New York City: The American Museum of Natural History, 1868–1968." PhD diss., Yale University, 1968.

Kessner, Thomas. *The Golden Door: Italian and Jewish Immigrant Mobility in New York City, 1880–1915.* New York: Oxford University Press, 1977.

Kevles, Daniel. *In the Name of Eugenics: Genetics and the Uses of Human Heredity.* Revised edition. Cambridge, MA: Harvard University Press, 1995.

———. "Testing the Army's Intelligence." *Journal of American History,* December 1968.

Keyssar, Alexander. *The Right to Vote: The Contested History of Democracy in the United States.* New York: Basic, 2000.

King, Desmond. *In the Name of Liberalism: Illiberal Social Policy in the USA and Britain.* Oxford, UK: Oxford University Press, 1999.

———. *Making Americans: Immigration, Race, and the Origins of Diversity in America.* Cambridge, MA: Harvard University Press, 2000.

Klein, Maury. *The Life and Legend of E. H. Harriman.* Chapel Hill: University of North Carolina Press, 2000.

Kline, Wendy. *Building a Better Race: Gender, Sexuality, and Eugenics from the Turn of the Century to the Baby Boom.* Berkeley: University of California Press, 2001.

Kohn, George Childs, ed. *Encyclopedia of Plague and Pestilence.* New York: Facts on File, 2008.

Kraut, Alan. *The Huddled Masses: The Immigrant in American Society, 1880–1921.* Arlington Heights, IL: Harlan Davidson, 1982.

————. *Silent Travelers: Germs, Genes, and the "Immigrant Menace."* New York: Basic, 1994.

Kuhl, Stefan. *The Nazi Connection: Eugenics, American Racism, and German National Socialism.* New York: Oxford University Press, 1994.

Kunkel, Thomas. *Man in Profile: Joseph Mitchell of* The New Yorker. New York: Random House, 2015.

Kuznets, Simon. "Immigration of Russian Jews to the United States: Background and Structure." *Perspectives in American History*, 1975.

La Guardia, Fiorello H. *The Making of an Insurgent: An Autobiography, 1882–1919.* Philadelphia: Lippincott, 1948.

LaGumina, Salvatore J. *The Great Earthquake: America Comes to Messina's Rescue.* Youngstown, NY: Teneo, 2008.

————. *Wop!: A Documentary History of Anti-Italian Discrimination in the United States.* San Francisco: Straight Arrow, 1973.

Larson, Edward J. *Evolution.* New York: Modern Library, 2004.

Lash, Joseph. *Eleanor and Franklin: The Story of Their Relationship, Based on Eleanor Roosevelt's Private Papers.* New York: Norton, 1971.

Laughlin, Harry H. *Eugenical Sterilization in the United States.* Chicago: Psychopathic Laboratory of the Municipal Court of Chicago, 1922.

————. *Immigration and Conquest.* New York: Chamber of Commerce of the State of New York, 1939.

Laughlin, Harry H., ed. *The Second International Exhibition of Eugenics.* Baltimore: Williams & Wikins, 1923.

Laughlin, Harry H., and Henry F. Perkins, eds. *A Decade of Progress in Eugenics: Scientific Papers of the Third International Congress of Eugenics.* Baltimore: Williams & Wilkins, 1934.

Lee, Margaret Cabot. *Letters and Diaries of Margaret Cabot Lee.* Privately printed, 1923.

Lemann, Nicholas. *The Big Test: The Secret History of the American Meritocracy.* New York: Farrar, Straus & Giroux, 1999.

Leon, Sharon M. *An Image of God: The Catholic Struggle with Eugenics.* Chicago: University of Chicago Press, 2013.

Leonard, Henry Beardsell. *The Open Gates: The Protest Against the Movement to Restrict European Immigration, 1896–1924.* New York: Arno Press, 1980.

Leonard, Thomas C. *Illiberal Reformers: Race, Eugenics & American Economics in the Progressive Era.* Princeton, NJ: Princeton University Press, 2016.

Lepore, Jill. *The Mansion of Happiness: A History of Life and Death.* New York: Knopf, 2012.

Leuchtenburg, William E. *The Perils of Prosperity, 1914–1932.* Chicago: University of Chicago Press, 1993.

————. *The Supreme Court Reborn: The Constitutional Revolution in the Age of Roosevelt.* New York: Oxford University Press, 1995.

Levine, David O. *The American College and the Culture of Aspiration, 1915–1940.* Ithaca, NY: Cornell University Press, 1986.

Lewis, Sinclair. *Arrowsmith.* London: Jonathan Cape, 1925.

Lifton, Robert Jay. *The Nazi Doctors: Medical Killing and the Psychology of Genocide.* New York: Basic, 2000.

Linenthal, Arthur J. *First a Dream: A History of Boston's Jewish Hospitals, 1896–1928.* Boston: Beth Israel Hospital, 1990.

Link, Arthur S. *Wilson: The Road to the White House*. Princeton, NJ: Princeton University Press, 1968.

Lissak, Rivka Shpak. "The National Liberal Immigration League." *American Jewish Archives*, Fall/Winter 1994.

Lodge, Henry Cabot. *Boston*. Third edition. London: Longmans Green, 1902.

———. *Early Memories*. New York: Scribner, 1913.

———. "Lynch Law and Unrestricted Immigration." *North American Review*, May 1891.

———. "The Restriction of Immigration." *North American Review*, January 1891.

———. *A Short History of the English Colonies in America*. New York: Harper, 1991.

Lodge, Henry Cabot, and Charles F. Redmond, eds. *Selections from the Correspondence of Theodore Roosevelt and Henry Cabot Lodge, 1884–1918*. New York: Scribner, 1925.

Lodge, Henry Cabot, and Theodore Roosevelt. *Hero Tales from American History*. New York: Century, 1895.

Lombardo, Paul A. *Three Generations, No Imbeciles*. Baltimore: Johns Hopkins University Press, 2008.

López, Ian Haney. *White by Law*. Revised and updated edition. New York: New York University Press, 2006.

Ludmerer, Kenneth. *Genetics and American Society*. Baltimore: Johns Hopkins University Press, 1972.

MacDonald, Kevin. *The Culture of Critique: An Evolutionary Analysis of Jewish Involvement in Twentieth-Century Intellectual and Political Movements*. Westport, CT: Praeger, 1998.

MacDowell, E. Carleton. "Charles Davenport, 1866–1944: A Study of Conflicting Influences." *Bios*, March 1946.

Manners, Ande. *Poor Cousins*. New York: Coward, McCann & Geoghegan, 1972.

Marinbach, Bernard. *Galveston: Ellis Island of the West*. Albany: State University of New York Press, 1983.

Marks, Russell. "Testers, Trackers and Trustees: The Ideology of the Intelligence Testing Movement in America, 1900–1954." PhD diss., University of Illinois, 1972.

Marquand, John P. *The Late George Apley*. New York: Back Bay, 2004.

Masters, Edgar Lee. *The Open Sea*. New York: Macmillan, 1921.

Maynard, W. Barksdale. *Princeton: America's Campus*. University Park: Penn State University Press, 2012.

McDonald, Jason D. "Making the World Safe for Eugenics: The Eugenicist Harry H. Laughlin's Encounters with American Internationalism." *Journal of the Gilded Age and the Progressive Era*, July 2013.

McDougall, William. *Is America Safe for Democracy?* New York: Scribner, 1921.

Mehler, Barry Alan. "A History of the American Eugenics Society, 1921–1940." PhD diss., University of Illinois, 1988.

Menand, Louis. *The Metaphysical Club: A Story of Ideas in America*. New York: Farrar, Straus and Giroux, 2002.

Mencken, H. L. *Prejudices, Sixth Series*. New York: Octagon, 1977.

Mill, John Stuart. *Principles of Political Economy*. London: John W. Parker, 1849.

Miller, Kimberly A. "Eugenics and American Theatre, 1912–1921." PhD diss., University of Kansas, 2005.

Miller, Richard F. *Harvard's Civil War: A History of the Twentieth Massachusetts Volunteer Infantry*. Hanover, NH: University Press of New England, 2005.

Moreno, Barry. *Encyclopedia of Ellis Island.* Westport, CT: Greenwood Press, 2004.

Morison, Elting E., ed. *The Letters of Theodore Roosevelt.* Cambridge, MA: Harvard University Press, 1951–.

Morris, Edmund. *Colonel Roosevelt.* New York: Random House, 2010.

———. *The Rise of Theodore Roosevelt.* New York: Ballantine, 1979.

———. *Theodore Rex.* New York: Random House, 2001.

Morse, Samuel F. B. *Foreign Conspiracy Against the Liberties of the United States.* Seventh edition. New York: American Foreign and Christian Union, 1855.

Mukherjee, Siddhartha. *The Gene: An Intimate History.* New York: Scribner, 2016.

Müller-Hill, Benno. *Murderous Science: Elimination by Scientific Selection of Jews, Gypsies, and Others, Germany, 1933–1945.* Oxford, UK: Oxford University Press, 1988.

Nadell, Pamela Susan. "The Journey to America by Steam: The Jews of Eastern Europe in Transition." PhD diss., Ohio State University, 1982.

Nash, Gary B. *The Liberty Bell.* New Haven, CT: Yale University Press, 2010.

Nevins, Allan. *Grover Cleveland: A Study in Courage.* New York: Dodd, Mead, 1933.

Ngai, Mae M. *Impossible Subjects: Illegal Aliens and the Making of Modern America.* Princeton, NJ: Princeton University Press, 2004.

Norton, Sarah, and M. A. DeWolfe Howe, eds. *Letters of Charles Eliot Norton.* Vol. 2. Boston: Houghton Mifflin, 1913.

Ogilvie, Sarah A., and Scott Miller. *Refuge Denied: The* St. Louis *Passengers and the Holocaust.* Madison: University of Wisconsin Press, 2006.

Osborn, Henry Fairfield. *Creative Education in School, College, University and Museum: Personal Observation and Experience of the Half-Century, 1877–1927.* New York: Scribner, 1927.

Osofsky, Gilbert. "The Hebrew Emigrant Aid Society of the United States." *Publications of the American Jewish Historical Society*, March 1960.

O'Toole, Patricia. *The Five of Hearts: An Intimate Portrait of Henry Adams and His Friends.* New York: Simon & Schuster, 1990.

Painter, Nell Irvin. *The History of White People.* New York: Norton, 2010.

Panetta, Roger G. *Westchester: The American Suburb.* New York: Fordham University Press, 2006.

Paul, Diane B. *Controlling Human Heredity: 1865 to the Present.* Atlantic Highlands, NJ: Humanities Press, 1995.

———. *The Politics of Heredity: Essays on Eugenics, Biomedicine, and the Nature-Nurture Drive.* Albany: State University of New York Press, 1998.

Pearson, Karl. *The Life, Letters, and Labours of Francis Galton*, Vols. 1–4. Cambridge, UK: Cambridge University Press, 1914–1930.

Pernick, Martin S. *The Black Stork: Eugenics and the Death of "Defective" Babies in American Medicine and Motion Pictures Since 1915.* New York: Oxford University Press, 1996.

Petit, Jeanne D. *The Men and Women We Want: Gender, Race, and the Progressive Era Literacy Test Debate.* Rochester, NY: University of Rochester Press, 2010.

Phillips, Richard. *A Million of Facts.* London: Ward, Lock & Tyler, 1836.

Pleasants, Helene, ed. *Biographical Dictionary of Parapsychology.* New York: Helix Press, 1964.

Popenoe, Paul, and Roswell Hill Johnson. *Applied Eugenics.* New York: Macmillan, 1918, revised edition, 1933.

Pottker, Jan. *Sara and Eleanor: The Story of Sara Delano Roosevelt and Her Daughter-in-Law, Eleanor Roosevelt*. New York: St. Martin's, 2004.

President's Research Committee on Social Trends. *Recent Social Trends*, Vol. 1. New York: Whittlesey House, 1934.

Proctor, Robert N. *Racial Hygiene: Medicine Under the Nazis*. Cambridge, MA: Harvard University Press, 1988.

Quammen, David. *The Reluctant Mr. Darwin: An Intimate Portrait of Charles Darwin and the Making of the Theory of Evolution*. New York: Atlas/Norton, 2006.

Race Betterment Foundation. *Official Proceedings of the Second National Conference on Race Betterment*. Battle Creek, MI: Race Betterment Foundation, 1915.

Rafter, Nicole Hahn. *White Trash: The Eugenic Family Studies, 1877–1919*. Boston: Northeastern University Press, 1988.

Regal, Brian. *Henry Fairfield Osborn: Race, and the Search for the Origin of Man*. Aldershot, UK: Ashgate, 2002.

Reichler, Max, Joel Blau, and David de Sola Pool. *Jewish Eugenics: and Other Essays*. Charleston, SC: Bibliolife, n.d.

Reznikoff, Charles, ed. *Louis Marshall: Champion of Liberty*, Vols. 1 and 2. Philadelphia: Jewish Publication Society, 1957.

Ribak, Gil. *Gentile New York: The Images of Non-Jews among Jewish Immigrants*. New Brunswick, NJ: Rutgers University Press, 2012.

Riddle, Oscar. "Charles Davenport," in *Biographical Memoirs*, National Academy of Sciences, 1949.

Riis, Jacob. *How the Other Half Lives*. New York: Scribner, 1890.

Ripley, William Z. *The Races of Europe: A Sociological Study*. New York: Appleton, 1899.

Roberts, Kenneth. *I Wanted to Write*. Garden City, NY: Doubleday, 1949.

———. *Why Europe Leaves Home*. Indianapolis: Bobbs-Merrill, 1922.

Roosevelt, Theodore. *Theodore Roosevelt: An Autobiography*. New York: Scribner, 1913.

Roosevelt, Theodore, and Henry Cabot Lodge. *Selections from the Correspondence of Theodore Roosevelt and Henry Cabot Lodge, 1884–1918*, Vols. 1 and 2. Edited by Henry Cabot Lodge and Charles F. Redmond. New York: Scribner, 1925.

Rosen, Christine. *Preaching Eugenics: Religious Leaders and the American Eugenics Movement*. New York: Oxford, 2004.

Rosenberg, Alfred. *The Myth of the Twentieth Century: An Evaluation of the Spiritual-Intellectual Confrontations of Our Age*, at aryanism.net.

Rosenberg, Charles E. "Charles Benedict Davenport and the Beginning of Human Genetics." *Bulletin of the History of Medicine*, 1961.

———. *No Other Gods: On Science and American Social Thought*. Baltimore: Johns Hopkins University Press, 1997.

Ross, Dorothy. *The Origins of American Social Science*. Cambridge, UK: Cambridge University Press, 1991.

Ross, Edward A. "The Causes of Race Superiority." *Annals of the American Academy of Political and Social Science*, July 1901.

———. *The Old World in the New: The Significance of Past and Present Immigration to the American People*. New York: Century, 1914.

———. *Seventy Years of It*. New York: Appleton-Century, 1936.

———. *Social Control*. New York: Macmillan, 1901.

Russell, Bertrand. *Marriage and Morals*. Garden City, NY: Star, 1929.

Ryback, Timothy W. *Hitler's Private Library: The Books That Shaped His Life*. New York: Knopf, 2008.

Rydell, Robert W. *World of Fairs*. Chicago: University of Chicago Press, 1993.

Sachar, Howard. *A History of the Jews in America*. New York: Knopf, 1992.

Sadler, William S. *Long Heads and Round Heads, or, What's the Matter with Germany?* Chicago: McClurg, 1918.

Salter, J. T., ed. *Public Men In and Out of Office*. Chapel Hill: University of North Carolina Press, 1946.

Samuels, Ernest. *Henry Adams*. Cambridge, MA: Harvard University Press, 1989.

———. *Henry Adams: The Major Phase*. Cambridge, MA: Harvard University Press, 1964.

Samuels, Ernest, ed. *Selected Letters of Henry Adams*. Cambridge, MA: Harvard University Press, 1992.

Sanger, Margaret. *Margaret Sanger: An Autobiography*. Elmsford, NY: Maxwell Reprint, 1970, originally published 1938.

———. *The Pivot of Civilization*. New York: Brentano's, 1922.

———. *Woman and the New Race*. New York: Brentano's, 1920.

Sapora, Allen V. H. "The Contributions of Joseph Lee to the Modern Recreation Movement and Related Social Movements in the United States." PhD diss., University of Michigan, 1952.

Saretzky, Gary D. "Carl Campbell Brigham, the Native Intelligence Hypothesis, and the Scholastic Aptitude Test." Princeton, NJ: Educational Testing Service, 1982.

———. "The Sponsor of Carl Campbell Brigham's 'A Study of American Intelligence,' Charles A. Gould." Princeton: Educational Testing Service, 1982.

Saveth, Edward N. *American Historians and European Immigrants: 1875–1925*. New York: Russell & Russell, 1965.

Schneiderman, Harry, ed. *The American Jewish Year Book*, Vol. 41. Philadelphia: Jewish Publication Society of America, 1939.

Schrag, Peter. *Not Fit for Our Society: Immigration and Nativism in America*. Berkeley: University of California Press, 2010.

Schriftgiesser, Karl. *The Gentleman from Massachusetts: Henry Cabot Lodge*. Atlantic Monthly/Little, Brown, 1944.

Schuck, Peter H. *Diversity in America: Keeping Government at a Safe Distance*. Cambridge, MA: Belknap/Harvard University Press, 2003.

Scribner, Charles. *In the Web of Ideas: The Education of a Publisher*. Scribner: New York, 1993.

Second International Congress of Eugenics, Scientific Papers. *Eugenics, Genetics and the Family*, Vol. 1. Baltimore: Williams & Wilkins, 1923.

Second International Congress of Eugenics, Scientific Papers. *Eugenics in Race and State*, Vol. 2. Baltimore: Williams and Wilkins, 1923.

Selden, Steven. *Inheriting Shame: The Story of Eugenics and Racism in America*. New York: Teachers College Press, 1999.

Shapiro, Adam R. *Trying Biology: The Scopes Trial, Textbooks, and the Antievolution Movement in American Schools*. Chicago: University of Chicago Press, 2013.

Shuman, Bernard. *A History of the Sioux City Jewish Community, 1869–1969*. Sioux City, IA: Jewish Federation, 1969.

Simon, Linda. *Genuine Reality: A Life of William James*. New York: Harcourt Brace, 1998.

Singley, Carol J., ed. *A Historical Guide to Edith Wharton*. New York: Oxford University Press, 2003.

Smith, Charles H., and George Beccaloni, eds. *Natural Selection and Beyond: The Intellectual Legacy of Alfred Russel Wallace*. Oxford, UK: Oxford University Press, 2008.

Smith, J. David, and Michael C. Wehmeyer. *Good Blood, Bad Blood: Science, Nature, and the Myth of the Kallikaks*. Washington, DC: American Association on Intellectual and Developmental Disabilities, 2012.

Solomon, Barbara Miller. *Ancestors and Immigrants: A Changing New England Tradition*. Chicago: University of Chicago Press, 1956.

Sorin, Gerald. *A Time for Building: The Third Migration, 1880–1920*. Baltimore: Johns Hopkins University Press, 1992.

Spiro, Jonathan Peter. *Defending the Master Race: Conservation, Eugenics, and the Legacy of Madison Grant*. Burlington: University of Vermont Press, 2009.

Stark, Gary D. *Entrepreneurs of Ideology: Neoconservative Publishers in Germany, 1890–1933*. Chapel Hill: University of North Carolina Press, 1981.

Steel, Ronald. *Walter Lippmann and the American Century*. Boston: Little, Brown, 1980.

Stern, Alexandra Minna. *Eugenic Nation: Faults and Frontiers of Better Breeding in Modern America*. Berkeley: University of California Press, 2005.

Steward, Julian H. "Alfred Louis Kroeber," in *Biographical Memoirs*, National Academy of Sciences, 1962.

Stewart, Barbara McDonald. *United States Government Policy on Refugees from Nazism, 1933–1940*. New York: Garland, 1982.

Stocking, George W., Jr. *Race, Culture, and Evolution: Essays in the History of Anthropology*. New York: Free Press, 1968.

Stoddard, Lothrop. *Into the Darkness: An Uncensored Report from Inside the Third Reich at War*. Newport Beach, CA: Noontide Press, 2000.

———. *Racial Realities in Europe*. London: Scribner, 1923.

———. *Re-Forging America*. New York: Scribner, 1927.

———. *The Revolt Against Civilization*. New York: Scribner, 1922.

———. *The Rising Tide of Color Against White World-Supremacy*. New York: Scribner, 1920.

Stokes, W. E. D. *The Right to Be Well Born: or, Horse Breeding in Its Relation to Eugenics*. New York: C. J. O'Brien, 1917.

Straight, Leonard A. *Samuel G. Smith: Pastor, Teacher, Friend*. St. Paul, MN: Baker Printing, 1916.

Straus, Oscar S. *Under Four Administrations*. Boston: Houghton Mifflin, 1922.

Suggs, George G., Jr. *Colorado's War on Militant Unionism: James H. Peabody and the Western Federation of Miners*. Detroit: Wayne State University Press, 1972.

Sullivan, Mark. *Our Times: 1900–1925*. Vol. 1: *The Turn of the Century*. New York: Scribner, 1936.

Takaki, Ronald. *Strangers from a Different Shore: A History of Asian Americans*. Boston: Little, Brown, 1989.

Tchen, John Kuo Wei, and Dylan Yeats, eds. *Yellow Peril! An Archive of Anti-Asian Fear*. New York: Verso, 2014.

Tebbel, John. *George Horace Lorimer and the* Saturday Evening Post. Garden City, NY: Doubleday, 1948.

Terman, Lewis M. "The Intelligence Quotient of Francis Galton in Childhood." *American Journal of Psychology*, April 1917.

Terman, Lewis M., ed. *Genetic Studies of Genius*. Vol. 2: *The Early Mental Traits of Three Hundred Geniuses*. See Cox, Catherine Morris.

Thernstrom, Stephan. *The Other Bostonians: Poverty and Progress in the American Metropolis, 1880–1970*. Cambridge, MA: Harvard University Press, 1973.

Thomas, David Hurst. *Skull Wars: Kennewick Man, Archaeology, and the Battle for Native American Identity*. New York: Basic, 2000.

Thomas, Evan. *The War Lovers: Roosevelt, Lodge, Hearst, and the Rush to Empire, 1898*. New York: Back Bay, 2011.

Tichenor, Daniel J. *Dividing Lines: The Politics of Immigration Control in America*. Princeton, NJ: Princeton University Press, 2002.

Trefil, James, and Margaret Hindle Hazen. *Good Seeing: A Century of Science at the Carnegie Institution of Washington, 1902–2002*. Washington, DC: Joseph Henry, n.d.

Trials of War Criminals Before the Nuernberg Military Tribunals. Washington, DC: Government Printing Office, 1949.

Turnbull, Andrew, ed. *The Letters of F. Scott Fitzgerald*. New York: Scribner, 1963.

Urofsky, Melvin I. *Louis D. Brandeis*. New York: Pantheon, 2009.

Voigts, Eckart, Barbara Schaff, and Monika Pietrzak-Franger, eds. *Reflecting on Darwin*. London: Routledge, 2016.

Vorzimmer, Peter J. "Darwin and Mendel: The Historical Connection." *Isis*, Spring 1968.

Walker, Francis A. "Immigration." *Yale Review*, August 1892.

———. "Immigration and Degradation," in Walker, *Discussions in Economics and Statistics*. Vol. 2. New York: Henry Holt, 1899.

Wallace, Max. *The American Axis: Henry Ford, Charles Lindbergh, and the Rise of the Third Reich*. New York: St. Martin's, 2003.

Wallace, Mike. *Greater Gotham: A History of New York City from 1898 to 1919*. New York: Oxford University Press, 2017.

Wang, Peter H. *Legislating Normalcy: The Immigration Act of 1924*. San Francisco: R and E Research, 1975.

Ward, Robert DeCourcy. "The Immigration Problem Today." *Journal of Heredity*, September–October 1920.

———. "National Eugenics in Relation to Immigration." *North American Review*, July 1910.

Weindling, Paul Julian. *Nazi Medicine and the Nuremberg Trials: From Medical War Crimes to Informed Consent*. Basingstoke, UK: Palgrave Macmillan, 2004.

Weiner, Mark. *Americans Without Law: The Racial Boundaries of Citizenship*. New York: New York University Press, 2006.

Weinland, Thomas P. "A History of the IQ in America." PhD diss., Columbia University, 1970.

Wells, H. G. *Anticipations*. London: Chapman and Hall, 1902.

———. *The Future in America: A Search after Realities*. London: Chapman and Hall, 1906.

Werth, Barry. *Banquet at Delmonico's: Great Minds, the Gilded Age, and the Triumph of Evolution in America*. New York: Random House, 2009.

Whitman, James Q. *Hitler's American Model: The United States and the Making of Nazi Race Law*. Princeton, NJ: Princeton University Press, 2017.

Whitney, Leon F. *The Case for Sterilization*. New York: Frederick A. Stokes, 1934.

Wiggam, Albert Edward. *The New Decalogue of Science*. Indianapolis: Bobbs-Merrill, 1923.

Williams, Vernon J., Jr. *Rethinking Race: Franz Boas and His Contemporaries*. Lexington: University Press of Kentucky, 1966.

Wilson, Woodrow. *A History of the American People*. New York: Harper & Bros., 1903.

Winfield, Ann Gibson. *Eugenics and Education in America: Institutionalized Racism and the Implications of History, Ideology, and Memory*. New York: Peter Lang, 2007.

Wister, Owen. *Philosophy 4: A Story of Harvard University*. New York: Macmillan, 1903.

———. *Theodore Roosevelt: The Story of a Friendship, 1880–1919*. New York: Macmillan, 1930.

Witkowski, Jan A., and John R. Inglis, eds. *Davenport's Dream: 21st Century Reflections on Heredity and Eugenics*. Cold Spring Harbor, NY: Cold Spring Harbor Laboratory Press, 2008.

Woodcock, George, and Ivan Avakumonic. *The Anarchist Prince*. New York: Schocken, 1971.

Woodhull, Victoria Claflin. *The Human Body, the Temple of God*. London: n.p., 1890.

———. *Selected Writings of Victoria Woodhull: Suffrage, Free Love, and Eugenics*. Edited by Cari M. Carpenter. Lincoln: University of Nebraska Press, 2010.

Woods, Robert A., ed. *Americans in Process: A Settlement Study*. Boston: Houghton Mifflin, 1903.

Wyman, David S. *Paper Walls: America and the Refugee Crisis, 1938–1941*. Amherst: University of Massachusetts Press, 1968.

Yearbook of the Brooklyn Institute of Arts and Sciences, 1898–1899. Brooklyn: BIAS, 1899.

Yerkes, Robert M. *Psychological Examining in the United States Army*. Washington, DC: National Academy of Sciences, 1921.

Yoakum, Clarence S., and Robert M. Yerkes. *Army Mental Tests*. New York: Henry Holt, 1920.

Zeidel, Robert F. *Immigrants, Progressives, and Exclusion Politics: The Dillingham Commission, 1900–1927*. DeKalb: Northern Illinois University Press, 2004.

Zenderland, Leila. *Measuring Minds: Henry Herbert Goddard and the Origins of American Intelligence Testing*. Cambridge, UK: Cambridge University Press, 1998.

Zolberg, Aristide R. *A Nation by Design: Immigration Policy in the Fashioning of America*. Cambridge, MA: Harvard University Press, 2006.

CONGRESSIONAL HEARINGS

These are the principal hearings consulted. Others are cited in the Notes.

House of Representatives, Committee on Immigration and Naturalization:

Hearings Relative to the Dillingham Bill, 1912.

Biological Aspects of Immigration, 1920.

Proposed Restriction of Immigration, 1920.

Temporary Suspension of Immigration, 1920.

Emergency Immigration Legislation, 1921.

Analysis of the Metal and Dross in the Modern American Melting Pot, 1922.

Restriction of Immigration, 1923–1924.

Europe as an Emigrant-Exporting Continent and the United States as an Immigrant-Receiving Nation, 1924.
Eugenical Aspects of Deportation, 1928.

Senate, Committee on Immigration

Emergency Immigration Legislation, 1921.
Selective Immigration Legislation, 1924.

Image Credits

14. INTERFOTO/Alamy Stock Photo
15. The Bookwork Collection/Alamy Stock Photo
17. Department of Rare Books and Special Collections, Princeton University Library
20. American Philosophical Society Library
21. Bundesarchiv (Federal Archives of Germany)

Index